The CAR Book

1996 Edition

The Definitive Buyer's Guide to Car Safety, Fuel Economy, Maintenance, and Much More

by Jack Gillis

with
Scott Beatty
and
Karen Fierst

foreword by
Clarence Ditlow
Center for Auto Safety

HarperPerennial
A Division of HarperCollinsPublishers

Acknowledgments

As is the case each year, many talented individuals have contributed to this *sixteenth* edition of *The Car Book*. This year a new name appears as co-author—Scott Beatty. Under his direction, the staff collected, analyzed, and tabulated many thousands of bits of information about today's new vehicles. Because of his incredible project management skills and organizational ability, this amazingly complex project was carried out with grace and competence under extreme deadline pressure. Amy Burch, the other half of the leadership team, assembled the best designed and most seamlessly produced *Car Book* to date. As always, calm and cool under pressure, Amy developed the expertise necessary to deliver, for the first time, an extraordinarily complex cover and page design completely on disk. And she did so singlehandedly! As has been the case for 11 years, the experience and institutional knowledge of *Car Book* veteran Karen Fierst were key elements in this successful effort.

Scott and Amy were able to accomplish great feats due, in particular, to the tremendous assistance of Ashley Cheng, who jumped in with both feet the day he arrived. In addition, Kaz Hickok contributed terrific proofing and copy editing skills, and the gold dust twins, Marshall Einhorn and Ben Becker, were the best summer interns money could buy! Underlying this effort was the excellent foundation provided by last year's co-author, Jay Einhorn, who left our ranks to become a Graduate Fellow at MIT.

This year's edition would not have been possible without essential contributions from many other talented individuals including: Clarence Ditlow and the staff of the Center for AutoSafety; John Noettl, president of Vehicle Support Systems, and his staff; legal expert Phil Nowicki; Carolyn Gorman of the Insurance Information Institute; Susan Cole, color maven; and Amy Shock, who kept everything else in the office going. Very special thanks go to my friend, fellow entrepreneur and terrific literary agent, Stuart Krichevsky.

As always, the most important factor in being able to bring this information to the American car buyer for sixteen years is the encouragement, support, and love from my brilliant and beautiful wife, Marilyn Mohrman–Gillis.

-J.G.

As Always,

for Marilyn &
Katie, John, Brian, and Brennan

THE CAR BOOK *(1996 edition)*. Copyright© 1995, 1994, 1993, 1992, 1991, 1989, 1988, 1987, 1986, 1985, 1984, 1983, 1982, 1981 by Jack Gillis. All rights reserved. Printed in the United States of America. No part of this book may be used or reproduced in any manner whatsoever without written permission except in the case of brief quotations embodied in critical articles and reviews. For information, address HarperCollins Publishers, Inc., 10 East 53rd Street, New York, NY 10022.

HarperCollins books may be purchased for educational, business, or sales promotional use. For information, please write: Special Markets Department, HarperCollins Publishers, Inc., 10 East 53rd Street, New York, NY 10022.

ISSN: 0893-1208

ISBN: 0-06-273282-X
96 97 98 CW 5 4 3

Cover design © Gillis and Associates.
Photo credits: Acura, Chrysler Corporation, Ford Motor Company General Motors Corp., Pontiac Division, Mercedes-Benz of North America, Inc., Toyota Motor Sales, USA, Inc.

Back Cover Photo of Jack Gillis: Donna Cantor-MacLean

Contents

Foreword

by Clarence M. Ditlow, Executive Director, Center for Auto Safety

The 1996 Car Book covers an auto industry filled with inconsistencies. On the one hand, Chrysler touts its minivan as the safe family vehicle but refuses to recall them for defective tail gate latches, even after 42 people were killed when the tail gate popped open in crashes. Volvo, known for safety leadership, refuses to recall over 250,000 1990-93 cars for airbags that go off when the ignition is turned on because a key sensor under the seat gets flooded. General Motors (GM) says it cares but not enough to recall its 1973-87 pickups with side saddle gas tanks which have been involved in fire crashes causing over 1,300 deaths. Ford is where Quality is Job #1 except when it comes to peeling paint. Consumers were stuck with a $2 billion bill to repaint Ford's 1985-92 vehicles which lacked a key primer layer.

The more things change; the more they stay the same. If car companies can get away with it, they will. Chrysler and GM have been caught and fined for selling recycled lemons in California and New York—i.e., they buy back an admitted lemon from one consumer and resell it to another consumer without fixing it and informing the second owner. Car companies talk about the need to protect the environment, but they continually fight stringent fuel economy standards needed to reduce global warming. Car companies are also fighting to block New York and other states from adopting California's stringent emission standards that require auto companies start making electric cars by 1998. And, the car companies are challenging state laws that would require new cars be labeled as to how protective their bumpers are in low speed impacts that cost hundreds of dollars to repair. All the companies oppose laws that would require them to notify consumers of secret warranties.

The worst example of an auto company stepping back in time to when cars were "unsafe at any speed" is GM in its refusal to recall its 1973-87 GM pickups which have killed 20 times as many people in fire crashes as the infamous Ford Pinto. These GM pickups with side saddle gas tanks represent the worst vehicle fire hazard in history. Tragically, many victims of GM's pickup are people in other cars or even motorcycle riders who have the misfortune of striking a GM pickup at speeds as low as 20-mph. When NHTSA asked GM to recall the pickups, GM refused even though a recall would cost less than $100 per truck. A GM Vice President in 1984 called a $23 safety shield for the pickups "a probable easy fix" but GM refused to install it. Such callous disregard for human life will cost GM motor's sales. As one consumer wrote the Center for Auto Safety (CAS), "I don't have a GM pickup but it sure makes me wonder what defects GM is covering up in my car."

Major safety improvements come because the government requires them, not because the auto companies volunteer them. Today, the most wanted feature in a new car is the airbag which reduces deaths by at least 29% in frontal crashes. Yet the auto industry fought lifesaving airbags for 20 years. The Department of Transportation issued a new head injury standard for 1999-2003 that will reduce annual deaths from head injuries by 1,200 and save nearly a billion dollars in injury costs by requiring padding in the vehicle interior. But, in 1954, researchers for GM concluded that 75% of hazards causing head injuries in frontal collisions "could be effectively and readily reduced in hazard by the installation of proper padding material." It took a mandatory safety standard to get the auto industry to do what it knew how to do 41 years ago.

The Car Book is needed now more than ever as safety differences between vehicles get harder to detect. Everyone can tell whether there are airbags in cars, but you can't tell whether a car has good side impact protection, crash tests or 5-mph bumpers just by looking at the car or asking the dealer. Who would have thought that the luxurious 1996 Lexus ES300 does not have 5-mph bumpers or meet the dynamic side impact standard? CAS is working to get such vital information for consumers and make it public.

By highlighting both good and bad examples of auto companies and telling it like it is when it comes to car safety and quality, The Car Book helps consumers make informed choices in the marketplace. As more and more consumers use The Car Book to buy safer and more reliable cars from companies who are the most consumer conscious, the car companies themselves will change or lose sales. When you use The Car Book to buy a 1996 car, you are not only improving your personal safety— you are also changing an industry.

This is the 16th year we have been bringing you the information you need to make one of the most difficult of purchasing decisions. And there is good news—cars are getting safer and quality is getting better! If you make a smart 1996 choice, there is no reason why your new car won't last at least 100,000 miles. By keeping your cars longer, you're not only saving money, you're helping to protect the environment, too.

We're even seeing signs that dealers are getting smarter and treating us better in the show room. And most of this change is due to you. By taking the time to use the information and tips in *The Car Book*, you are telling the marketplace, loud and clear, that you want value for your hard earned dollars, and you won't buy unless you get it.

Along with some dramatic new designs and fancy convenience features, car companies are again selling safety—a concept that a few years ago sent chills through corporate board rooms. But car makers have finally realized something we've been telling them for years—consumers *do* care about safety. And now that they have caught on, nearly every auto ad mentions some aspect of safety. As a result, it's more important than ever to be able to sift through these advertising claims to find what is *truly* the safest and most economical new car. To make this task easier, we've completely updated this year's book—our sixteenth edition! *The Car Book* gives you more information than ever before about the current models.

Your continued use of the information in *The Car Book* dramatically influences the way car companies build and sell their cars. One

result is that they have been forced to make safety improvements which have actually reduced the number of motor vehicle injuries. In fact, in the last twenty-five years, even though the number of vehicles on the road has more than doubled, the fatality rate has dropped by an astonishing 66 percent! Now, however, with increased speed limits we may see that decline slow down. Buying for safety is one way to protect you and your loved ones.

And the new technologies work! Most of us have heard about incredible accidents where the *driver* simply walked away—all because of a simple bag that

inflated to cushion the impact. But what about the *passengers* in those cars? Still, there are too many vehicles in which the maker has chosen to only offer the life-saving protection of airbags to the driver—a sobering thought the next time you drive with a friend or loved one.

Clearly, car makers are listening more carefully to consumers. Our buying habits have the ability to continue to change the practices of one of the nation's most powerful industries—*so don't buy cars without dual airbags*. And make sure you tell the auto dealers why you're not buying.

How does today's consumer buy safety? Many consumers mistak-

Missing Safety: Minivans

Minivans, pickups, and sport utility vehicles are the fastest growing groups of vehicle types. Minivans are convenient because so few station wagons are large enough to hold growing families. If you are interested in one of these vehicles, be warned: They do not have to meet many of the safety standards applied to passenger cars. Even though thousands of Americans buy these vehicles for family and non-commercial use, the National Highway Traffic Safety Administration has been slow to require safety improvements.

Beginning in 1995, minivans, pickups and sport utility vehicles were finally required to provide roofs strong enough to support the vehicle's weight if it rolls over and contain reinforcement beams in the doors to protect occupants in side crashes. In fact, by 1999, these vehicles must meet the same side impact standards as passenger cars. However, these vehicles are not yet required to have bumpers that meet any kind of strength requirements. Most importantly, these vehicles are not yet required to provide any automatic crash protection, in the form of either automatic belts or airbags. Automatic crash protection requirements are currently being phased in, but will not become standard until 1998.

Because of their popularity with car buyers, we've included minivans in *The Car Book*. We also compile *The Truck, Van and 4x4 Book*, which provides hundreds of facts about these popular vehicles, including sport utility vehicles.

enly believe that handling and performance are the key elements in the safety of a car. While an extremely unresponsive car could cause an accident, most new cars meet basic handling requirements. In fact, many people actually feel uncomfortable driving high performance cars because the highly responsive steering, acceleration, and suspension systems can be difficult to get used to. But the main reason handling is overrated as a safety measure is that automobile collisions are, by nature, accidents. Once they've begun, they are beyond human capacity to prevent, no matter how well your car handles. So the key to protecting yourself is to purchase a car that offers a high degree of crash protection.

As our concern for safety has influenced car makers' attitudes, so have our demands for quality; the result—U.S. cars in the '90s continue to be better built than those of the '80s. And, because we're demanding that companies stand behind their products, we're seeing better warranties, too. Since *The Car Book* began comparing warranties in 1986, a number of car makers have told us that they've been forced to improve their warranties now that consumers can tell the difference.

Choosing among 1996 models will not be easy, but *The Car Book* will help separate peaches from lemons.

Consumers are learning that they can get better performing and safer cars by buying the ones with good safety records, low maintenance costs, long warranties, and insurance discounts. Use "The Buying Guide" to compare cars, and read the chapters to learn more about each model. This year "The Buying Guide" is loaded with new and important information. You'll find everything from crash test results to an ease-of-parking rating.

"The Safety Chapter" rates crash safety, describes your options for protection, and is where you'll find the detailed crash test results, tips on avoiding unsafe child seats, and a review of safety belt and child seat laws.

"The Fuel Economy Chapter" uncovers the money-saving gas misers and offers advice on some products to avoid.

"The Maintenance Chapter" allows you to compare those inevitable repair costs *before* you buy.

"The Warranty Chapter" offers a critical comparison of the new warranties and lets you know the best and worst before you get into trouble down the road. If you do have trouble, we'll let you know which companies offer roadside assistance and we'll tip you off to secret warranties.

"The Insurance Chapter" will help you save money on an expense that is often forgotten in the showroom.

Because most of us can't tell one tire from another, we've included "The Tire Chapter" to help you select the best.

"The Complaint Chapter" provides a road map to resolving inevitable problems quickly and efficiently. We provide consumers with their only access to the hundreds of thousands of car complaints on file with the U.S. Government. Thanks to the efforts of the Center for Auto Safety, we continue to include this otherwise unavailable information—and it's all new and updated for 1996.

Review "The Showroom Strategy Chapter" for tips on getting the best price—for many of us one of the hardest and most distasteful aspects of car buying.

Finally, our "Ratings Chapter" provides a detailed review of each of the 1996 cars. These pages provide, at a glance, an overview of all the criteria you need to make a good choice. Here, you'll be able to quickly assess key features and see how the car you're interested in stacks up against its competition so you can make sure your selection is the best car for you. Car prices have more than doubled since 1980, so we've also included the percent of *dealer* mark-up to help you negotiate the very best price.

The information in *The Car Book* is based on data collected and developed by our staff, private automobile engineering firms, the U.S. Department of Transportation, and the Center for Auto Safety. With all of this data in hand, you'll find some great choices for 1996. *The Car Book* will guide you through the trade-offs, claims, promises, facts, and myths to the car that will best meet your needs.

—Jack Gillis

Questions, Comments

If you have any suggestions, questions or comments, you may e-mail us at JAGillis@aol.com

BUYING GUIDE

The Buying Guide provides an overall comparison of the 1996 cars in terms of safety, fuel economy, maintenance, insurance costs, warranty, complaint ratings, and other key items. The cars are arranged by size class based on weight.

Based on these comparisons, we have developed this year's Car Book Best Bets—the 1996 vehicles that rated tops when all of these categories were considered. In general, there are five key steps to buying a car.

1 Narrow your choice down to a particular class of car–sports, station wagon, minivan, sedan, large luxury, or economy car. These are general classifications and some cars may fit into more than one category. In most cases, *The Car Book* presents the vehicles by size class.

2 Determine what features are really important to you. Most buyers consider safety on the top of their list, which is why "The Safety Chapter" is right up front in *The Car Book*. Airbags, power options, ABS, and the number of passengers, as well as "hidden" elements such as maintenance and insurance costs, should be considered at this stage in your selection process.

3 Find 3 or 4 cars that meet the needs you outlined above *and* your pocketbook. It's important not to narrow your choice down to one car because then you lose all your bargaining power in the showroom. In fact, because cars today are more similar than dissimilar, it's not hard to keep three or four choices in mind. On the car rating pages in the back of the book, we suggest some competitive choices for your consideration. For example, if you are interested in the Honda Accord, you should also consider the Toyota Camry and Ford Taurus.

4 Make sure you take a good, long test drive. The biggest car buying mistake most of us make is to overlook those nagging problems that seem to surface only after we've brought the car home. Spend at least an hour driving the car. This includes time on the highway, parking, taking the car in and out of your driveway or garage, sitting in the back seat, and using the trunk or storage area. Whatever you do, *don't talk price until you're ready to buy!*

5 This is the stage most of us dread–negotiating the price. While price negotiation is a car buying tradition, a few car makers and dealers are trying to break tradition by offering so called "no-haggle pricing." Since they're still in the minority, and because it's almost impossible to establish true competition between dealers as individuals, we offer a new means to avoid negotiating altogether by using the non-profit CarBargains pricing service.

Now that you have a quick guide to the steps necessary in making a good choice, use the tables that follow to quickly review the new cars and the pages in the back for a detailed critique of each model. See "The Showroom Strategy Chapter" for more details on getting the best price.

The "Buying Guide" will allow you to quickly compare the 1996 models.

To fully understand these summary charts, it is important to read the appropriate section of the book. You will note that here and throughout the book, some of the charts contain empty boxes. This indicates that data were unavailable at the time of printing.

Here's how to understand what's included in "The Buying Guide."

Page Reference: The page in the back of the book where you'll find all the details for this car.

Overall Rating: This is the "bottom line." It shows how well this car stacks up on a scale of 1 to 10 when compared to all others on the market. The overall rating considers safety, maintenance, fuel economy, warranty, insurance costs and complaints. Due to the importance of crash tests, cars with no results as of our publication date cannot be given an overall rating. More recent results may be available from the Auto Safety Hotline at 1-800-424-9393 (see page 75).

Car Book Crash Test Rating: This indicates how well the car performed in the U.S. Government's 35-mph frontal crash test program. We have analyzed and compared all of the crash test results to date and have given them a rating from *very good* to *very poor*. These ratings allow you to compare the test results of one car with another. A car with a poor rating may have done well according to government injury ratings, but still be among the worst performers of cars being offered in 1996.

Airbags: Hidden in the steering wheel hub and the passenger side of the dashboard, airbags inflate instantly in frontal crashes to prevent the occupant from violently hitting the dashboard, windshield, or steering wheel. An asterisk indicates that this feature is optional, whereas driver or dual (on both driver and passenger sides) indicates that airbags are standard.

Side Impact Protection: By 1997, all passenger cars will have to provide a minimum level of protection in a side impact crash. A *strong* rating indicates the car maker has certified to the government that this car currently offers that level of protection. A *weak* rating means the manufacturer has not certified that level of protection to the government.

Fuel Economy: This is the EPA-rated fuel economy for city and highway driving measured in miles per gallon. A single model may have a number of fuel economy ratings because of different engine and transmission options. We have included the figure for what is expected to be the most popular model.

Best Bets for 1996

Based on information in the *Buying Guide*, this list shows the highest-rated cars in each of the size categories. Ratings are based on expected performance in six important categories (crash tests, fuel economy, repair costs, warranties, insurance costs, and complaints), with the heaviest emphasis on crash test performance.

Subcompact
Saturn SC (10)
Nissan Sentra (9)
Ford Escort (5)

Compact
Subaru Legacy (10)
Chrysler Sebring (9)
Volkswagen Golf/Jetta (8)
Ford Contour (8)
Mercury Mystique (8)

Minivan
Ford Windstar (10)
Oldsmobile Silhouette (7)

Intermediate
Saab 9000 (10)
Volkswagen Passat (10)
Volvo 850 (9)
Saab 900 (9)

Large
Audi A6/S6 (10)
Lexus ES300 (10)
Chevrolet Lumina (10)
Infiniti J30 (9)
Lexus GS300 (9)
Chevrolet Monte Carlo (9)
Mercury Cougar (9)

Repair Rating: This rating is based on nine typical repairs after the warranty expires and the cost of following the manufacturer's preventive maintenance schedule during the warranty period.

Warranty Rating: This is an overall assessment of the car's warranty when compared to all other warranties. The rating considers the important features of each warranty, with emphasis on the length of the basic and powertrain warranties.

Complaint Index: This rating is based on the number of complaints about that car on file at the U.S. Department of Transportation. The complaint index will give you a general idea of experiences others have had with models which are essentially unchanged for this model year. An empty box means that the car is entirely new for 1996 or that we had insufficient data to calculate a rating.

Insurance Cost: Many automobile insurance companies use ratings based on the car's accident and occupant injury history to determine whether or not the insurance premium of a car should be *discounted* or *surcharged*. (Your insurance company may or may not participate in a rating program.) If the car is likely to receive neither, we label it *regular*.

Parking Index: This rating of *very easy* to *very hard* is an indicator of how much difficulty you will typically have parking. If you regularly parallel park, or find yourself maneuvering in and out of tight spaces, this can be an important factor in your choice of a car. This rating is based on the car's wheelbase, length, and turning circle.

Typical Price: This price range will give you a general idea of the "sticker," or asking price of a car. It is based on the lowest to highest retail price of the various models, and it does not include options or the discount that you should be able to negotiate using a service such as CarBargains (see pg. 90).

 ## Typical Operating Costs

Buying a 1996 luxury car rather than an economy model will cost considerably more, in both up-front and operating costs. According to Runzheimer International, maintaining a 1996 Mercedes 320S will cost $19,832 annually, while a Geo Metro will cost only $6,464—a $13,368 annual cost difference. The higher cost of the Mercedes is due not only to higher initial cost, but also to higher fuel, maintenance, tire replacement, insurance, and finance costs. Also, higher-priced cars often decrease in value faster.

The table below shows the operating costs for fifteen popular cars. The costs used for this comparison include operating expenses (fuel, oil, maintenance, and tires) and ownership expenses (insurance, depreciation, financing, taxes, and licensing), and were based on keeping the car for three years and driving 20,000 miles per year.

Vehicle	Annual Costs*		
	Operating	Ownership	Total
Mercedes-Benz 320S	$2,580	$17,252	$19,832
Cadillac DeVille	$2,780	$11,351	$14,131
Lincoln Town Car Exec.	$2,360	$11,332	$13,692
Olds Aurora	$2.400	$10,644	$13,044
Buick Riviera	$2,280	$9,232	$11,512
Chevrolet Impala	$2,680	$7,886	$10,566
Buick LeSabre Limited	$2,180	$8,038	$10,218
Nissan Maxima GXE	$2,220	$6,992	$9,212
Dodge Intrepid	$2,250	$6,538	$8.788
Ford Taurus	$2,090	$6,614	$8,704
Chevrolet Lumina	$2,140	$6,126	$8,266
Ford Contour	$1,900	$6,140	$8,040
Toyota Camry DX	$1,970	$6,064	$8,034
Honda Accord DX	$2,030	$5,027	$7,057
Plymouth Neon	$1,640	$5,275	$6,915
Geo Metro	$1,450	$5,014	$6,464

Source: Runzheimer International, Rochester, Wisconsin.
*Costs are based on four-door models, with automatic transmission, power steering, power disc brakes, air conditioning, tinted glass, AM-FM stereo, body side molding, cruise control, left-hand remote control mirror, rear window defogger, pulse windshield wipers, ABS, dual air bags and tilt-steering.

Car	See Pg.	Overall Rating* Poor ⇔ Good	Crash Test	Airbags	Side Impact	Fuel Economy	Repair Rating
Subcompact							
Dodge/Plym. Neon	129		No Test	Dual	Weak	28/38	Good
Eagle Summit	130		Good	Dual	Weak	26/33	Poor
Ford Aspire	135		Average	Dual	Weak	34/42	Average
Ford Escort	138		Average	Dual	Weak	25/31	Good
Geo Metro	144		Good	Dual	Strong	44/49	Poor
Honda Civic	147		No Test	Dual	Strong	33/38	Poor
Honda del Sol	148		No Test	Dual	Weak	28/35	Poor
Hyundai Accent	151		No Test	Dual	Strong	27/35	Very Good
Kia Sephia	158		No Test	Dual	Strong	29/34	Good
Mazda Miata	168		No Test	Dual	Strong	23/29	Poor
Mazda MX-3	171		No Test	Dual	Weak	30/37	Average
Mazda Protege	173		No Test	Dual	Strong	32/39	Average
Mercury Tracer	180		Average	Dual	Weak	23/29	Good
Mitsubishi Mirage	185		Good	Dual	Weak	32/39	Very Poor
Nissan Sentra	190		Good	Dual	Strong	30/40	Good
Saturn SC	207		Very Good	Dual	Weak	25/35	Good
Saturn SL/SW	208		No Test	Dual	Strong	25/35	Good
Subaru Impreza	209		No Test	Dual	Strong	25/31	Very Good
Suzuki Esteem	212		No Test	Dual	Strong	31/37	Poor
Suzuki Swift	213		Good	Dual	Strong	39/43	Poor
Toyota Paseo	218		No Test	Dual	Strong	30/35	Poor
Toyota Tercel	220		Average	Dual	Strong	30/39	Poor
Compact							
Acura Integra	98		Average	Dual	Weak	24/31	Very Poor
BMW 3-Series	102		Good	Dual	Strong	20/29	Very Poor
Buick Skylark	109		No Test	Dual	Weak	22/32	Good
Chevy Beretta	115		Very Good	Driver	Weak	25/37	Good
Chevy Cavalier	118		Average	Dual	Weak	26/37	Good
Chrysler Sebring	125		Very Good	Dual	Strong	22/31	Average
Eagle Summit Wgn	131		No Test	Dual	Weak	24/29	Poor
Eagle Talon	132		Good	Dual	Strong	22/32	Average
Ford Contour	136		Good	Dual	Strong	23/32	Good
Ford Probe	140		Very Good	Dual	Weak	26/33	Poor
Geo Prizm	145		Good	Dual	Weak	31/35	Poor

*Due to the importance of crash tests, cars with no crash test results as of publication date cannot be given an overall rating.

Warranty	Complaint Rating	Insurance Rating	Parking Index	Typical Price $	Overall Rating* Poor ⇔ Good	See Pg.	Car
							Subcompact
Very Poor		Regular	Easy	$9-13,000		129	Dodge/Plym. Neon
Very Poor	Very Poor	Surcharge	Very Easy	$10-13,500		130	Eagle Summit
Very Poor	Poor	Regular	Very Easy	$8-9,500		135	Ford Aspire
Very Poor	Good	Surcharge	Very Easy	$10-13,000		138	Ford Escort
Very Poor		Surcharge	Very Easy	$8-10,000		144	Geo Metro
Very Poor		Regular	Very Easy	$10-16,000		147	Honda Civic
Very Poor		Regular	Very Easy	$15-20,000		148	Honda del Sol
Poor		Surcharge	Very Easy	$8-9,500		151	Hyundai Accent
Average	Very Poor	Regular	Very Easy	$9-11,500[1]		158	Kia Sephia
Poor	Very Good	Regular	Very Easy	$18-19,000		168	Mazda Miata
Poor	Average	Surcharge	Very Easy	$14-15,000[1]		171	Mazda MX-3
Poor		Regular	Very Easy	$12-15,000		173	Mazda Protege
Very Poor	Good	Surcharge	Very Easy	$11-12,000		180	Mercury Tracer
Average	Average	Surcharge	Very Easy	$10-14,000		185	Mitsubishi Mirage
Poor		Surcharge	Very Easy	$11-15,000		190	Nissan Sentra
Poor	Very Good	Surcharge	Easy	$12-14,000		207	Saturn SC
Poor		Regular	Easy	$10-13,000		208	Saturn SL/SW
Poor	Good	Regular	Very Easy	$13-18,000		209	Subaru Impreza
Very Poor		Regular	Very Easy	$11-14,500		212	Suzuki Esteem
Very Poor		Surcharge	Very Easy	$8-10,000		213	Suzuki Swift
Very Poor	Very Good	Surcharge	Very Easy	$13-14,000		218	Toyota Paseo
Very Poor		Surcharge	Very Easy	$10-13,000		220	Toyota Tercel
							Compact
Average	Very Poor	Surcharge	Easy	$16-21,000[1]		98	Acura Integra
Good	Average	Surcharge	Easy	$25-32,000[1]		102	BMW 3-Series
Very Poor	Good	Discount	Easy	$15-17,500		109	Buick Skylark
Very Poor	Very Good	Surcharge	Easy	$13-16,500		115	Chevy Beretta
Very Poor		Regular	Easy	$10-17,500		118	Chevy Cavalier
Very Poor		Regular	Average	$14-20,000		125	Chrysler Sebring
Very Poor		Surcharge	Very Easy	$14-16,500		131	Eagle Summit Wgn
Very Poor		Surcharge	Easy	$15-20,000		132	Eagle Talon
Very Poor		Regular	Easy	$14-16,000		136	Ford Contour
Very Poor	Poor	Surcharge	Easy	$14-16,500		140	Ford Probe
Very Poor	Average	Surcharge	Very Easy	$12-13,000		145	Geo Prizm

[1]Based on 1995 prices. [2]Coupe only. [3]Sedan/Wagon only.

Car	See Pg.	Overall Rating* Poor ⇔ Good	Crash Test	Airbags	Side Impact	Fuel Economy	Repair Rating
Honda Prelude	150		Very Good	Dual	Weak	22/26	Poor
Hyundai Elantra	152		No Test	Dual	Weak	22/29	Very Good
Mazda 626	166		Good	Dual	Strong	26/34	Poor
Mazda MX-6	172		Very Good	Dual	Weak	26/34	Poor
Mercury Mystique	178		Good	Dual	Strong	23/32	Good
Mitsubishi Eclipse	183		Good	Dual	Strong	23/31	Average
Mitsubishi Galant	184		No Test	Dual	Strong	23/30	Very Poor
Olds Achieva	193		No Test	Dual	Weak	23/33	Good
Pontiac Grand Am	201		No Test	Dual	Weak	23/33	Good
Pontiac Sunfire	203		Average	Dual	Weak	25/37	Good
Subaru Legacy	210		Very Good	Dual	Strong	24/33	Good
Toyota Celica	216		No Test	Dual	Strong	29/34	Good
Toyota Corolla	217		Good	Dual	Weak	31/35	Poor
VW Golf/Jetta	221		Average	Dual	Strong	22/28	Good
Intermediate							
Audi A4	100		No Test	Dual	Strong	18/28	Average
Buick Century	103		Good	Driver	Weak	24/31	Good
Buick Regal	106		Average	Dual	Strong	20/29	Average
Chevy Camaro	116		Very Good	Dual	Strong[2]	19/30	Good
Chrysler Cirrus	122		No Test	Dual	Strong	20/28	Average
Chrysler Concorde	123		Very Good	Dual	Strong	19/27	Very Good
Dodge Intrepid	128		Very Good	Dual	Strong	19/27	Very Good
Eagle Vision	133		Very Good	Dual	Strong	19/27	Very Good
Ford Mustang	139		Good	Dual	Weak	20/30	Average
Ford Taurus	141		No Test	Dual	Strong	20/29	Very Good
Honda Accord	146		Average	Dual	Strong	25/32	Poor
Hyundai Sonata	153		Average	Dual	Strong	22/28	Very Good
Infiniti G20	154		No Test	Dual	Weak	24/32	Poor
Mazda Millenia	169		Very Good	Dual	Strong	20/28	Poor
Merc.-Benz C-Class	174		Good	Dual	Strong	23/29	Very Poor
Mercury Sable	179		No Test	Dual	Strong	20/29	Very Good
Nissan 240SX	186		Average	Dual	Strong	21/26	Good
Nissan Altima	187		Average	Dual	Weak	24/30	Good
Nissan Maxima	188		Average	Dual	Strong	21/28	Average

*Due to the importance of crash tests, cars with no crash test results as of publication date cannot be given an overall rating.

Warranty	Complaint Rating	Insurance Rating	Parking Index	Typical Price $	Overall Rating* Poor ⇔ Good	See Pg.	Car
Very Poor	Very Good	Surcharge	Easy	$19-26,000		150	Honda Prelude
Poor		Regular	Very Easy	$10-14,500		152	Hyundai Elantra
Poor	Poor	Surcharge	Easy	$15-23,000		166	Mazda 626
Poor	Poor	Surcharge	Easy	$18-19,000		172	Mazda MX-6
Very Poor		Regular	Easy	$14-16,000		178	Mercury Mystique
Average		Surcharge	Easy	$15-24,000		183	Mitsubishi Eclipse
Average	Very Poor	Regular	Easy	$15-23,000		184	Mitsubishi Galant
Poor	Very Good	Regular	Easy	$13-16,500		193	Olds Achieva
Very Poor	Good	Regular	Easy	$13-15,500		201	Pontiac Grand Am
Very Poor		Regular	Average	$11-18,000		203	Pontiac Sunfire
Poor		Discount	Easy	$17-23,000		210	Subaru Legacy
Very Poor	Very Good	Surcharge	Average	$17-24,000		216	Toyota Celica
Very Poor	Good	Surcharge	Very Easy	$13-15,000		217	Toyota Corolla
Very Good	Very Poor	Regular	Very Easy	$13-21,000		221	VW Golf/Jetta
Intermediate							
Very Good		Regular	Easy	$26-27,000		100	Audi A4
Very Poor	Good	Discount	Average	$16-19,000		103	Buick Century
Very Poor	Average	Discount	Average	$19-21,500		106	Buick Regal
Very Poor	Very Poor	Surcharge	Hard	$15-21,500		116	Chevy Camaro
Very Poor		Regular	Average	$14-17,500		122	Chrysler Cirrus
	Very Poor	Discount	Average	$19-20,000		123	Chrysler Concorde
Very Poor	Very Poor	Regular	Average	$18-22,000		128	Dodge Intrepid
Very Poor	Very Poor	Discount	Average	$19-24,000		133	Eagle Vision
Very Poor	Poor	Surcharge	Average	$15-25,000		139	Ford Mustang
Very Poor		Regular	Average	$19-22,000		141	Ford Taurus
Very Poor	Poor	Regular	Easy	$15-25,000		146	Honda Accord
Poor		Surcharge	Easy	$14-18,000		153	Hyundai Sonata
Very Good	Very Good	Regular	Easy	$24-28,000		154	Infiniti G20
Poor		Regular	Average	$26-32,000		169	Mazda Millenia
Average		Discount	Easy	$31-50,000		174	Merc.-Benz C-Class
Very Poor		Regular	Average	$19-22,000		179	Mercury Sable
Poor		Surcharge	Very Easy	$18-22,000		186	Nissan 240SX
Poor	Average	Regular	Average	$15-21,000		187	Nissan Altima
Poor		Regular	Easy	$21-26,000		188	Nissan Maxima

[1]Based on 1995 prices. [2]Coupe only. [3]Sedan/Wagon only.

Car	See Pg.	Overall Rating* Poor ⇔ Good	Crash Test	Airbags	Side Impact	Fuel Economy	Repair Rating
Olds Ciera	195		Good	Driver	Weak	24/31	Good
Olds Cut. Supreme	196		Average	Dual	Strong	20/29	Average
Pontiac Firebird	200		Very Good	Dual	Strong[2]	19/30	Good
Pontiac Grand Prix	202		Average	Dual	Strong	20/29	Average
Saab 900	205		Good	Dual	Strong	19/27	Good
Saab 9000	206		Good	Dual	Strong	20/28	Average
Toyota Avalon	214		Very Good	Dual	Strong	20/29	Poor
Toyota Camry	215		Very Good[4]	Dual	Strong[3]	23/31	Very Poor
Volkswagen Passat	222		Good	Dual	Strong	20/27	Good
Volvo 850	223		Good	Dual	Strong	20/29	Poor
Large							
Acura TL	99		No Test	Dual	Strong	20/25	Very Poor
Audi A6/S6	101		Very Good	Dual	Strong	19/25	Average
Buick LeSabre	104		Good	Dual	Strong	19/30	Average
Buick Park Avenue	105		No Test	Dual	Weak	19/29	Average
Buick Riviera	107		No Test	Dual	Strong	19/29	Average
Buick Roadmaster	108		Poor	Dual	Strong	17/26	Good
Cadillac DeVille	110		Good	Dual	Strong	17/26	Average
Cadillac Eldorado	111		No Test	Dual	Strong	17/26	Average
Cadillac Fleetwood	112		No Test	Dual	Strong	17/26	Good
Cadillac Seville	113		Good	Dual	Strong	17/26	Average
Chevy Caprice/Impala	117		Poor	Dual	Strong	18/26	Good
Chevy Lumina	119		Good	Dual	Strong	20/29	Good
Chevy Monte Carlo	121		Very Good	Dual	Strong	19/29	Good
Chrys. LHS/NY'er	124		Good	Dual	Strong	18/26	Good
Ford Crown Victoria	137		Very Good	Dual	Strong	17/26	Good
Ford Thunderbird	142		Very Good	Dual	Strong	19/26	Average
Infiniti J30	155		Good	Dual	Weak	18/23	Average
Infiniti Q45	156		No Test	Dual	Weak	17/22	Poor
Lexus ES300	159		Good	Dual	Strong	20/29	Poor
Lexus GS300	160		Average	Dual	Strong	18/24	Average
Lexus LS400	161		No Test	Dual	Strong	19/26	Poor
Lexus SC300/400	162		No Test	Dual	Strong	18/24	Poor
Lincoln Continental	163		No Test	Dual	Strong	17/25	Average
Lincoln Mark VIII	164		No Test	Dual	Strong	18/26	Average

*Due to the importance of crash tests, cars with no crash test results as of publication date cannot be given an overall rating.

Warranty	Complaint Rating	Insurance Rating	Parking Index	Typical Price $	Overall Rating* Poor ⇔ Good	See Pg.	Car
Poor	Very Good	Discount	Average	$14-17,500		195	Olds Ciera
Poor		Discount	Average	$17-21,000		196	Olds Cut. Supreme
Very Poor	Very Poor	Surcharge	Average	$15-21,500		200	Pontiac Firebird
Very Poor	Good	Discount	Average	$17-21,000		202	Pontiac Grand Prix
Good	Very Poor	Regular	Easy	$23-24,000		205	Saab 900
Good	Poor	Discount	Easy	$29-30,000		206	Saab 9000
Very Poor		Regular	Average	$23-27,500		214	Toyota Avalon
Very Poor	Average	Surcharge	Easy	$16-22,500		215	Toyota Camry
Very Good	Average	Surcharge	Average	$18-20,000		222	Volkswagen Passat
Very Good	Very Poor	Discount	Easy	$26-34,000		223	Volvo 850
Large							
Average		Regular	Average	$28-35,500		99	Acura TL
Very Good		Regular	Easy	$32-34,000		101	Audi A6/S6
Very Poor	Average	Discount	Hard	$21-25,000		104	Buick LeSabre
Very Poor	Good	Discount	Hard	$28-33,000		105	Buick Park Avenue
Very Poor		Discount	Hard	$29-30,000		107	Buick Riviera
Very Poor	Very Poor	Discount	Hard	$25-27,500		108	Buick Roadmaster
Average	Poor	Discount	Hard	$36-40,500		110	Cadillac DeVille
Average	Poor	Discount	Hard	$40-43,000		111	Cadillac Eldorado
Average	Very Poor	Discount	Very Hard	$36-37,000		112	Cadillac Fleetwood
Average	Very Poor	Discount	Hard	$43-47,500		113	Cadillac Seville
Very Poor	Average	Discount	Hard	$20-24,500		117	Chevy Caprice/Impala
Very Poor		Discount	Average	$16-18,000		119	Chevy Lumina
Very Poor		Regular	Hard	$17-19,500		121	Chevy Monte Carlo
Very Poor	Very Poor	Discount	Hard	$27-30,000		124	Chrys. LHS/NY'er
Very Poor	Poor	Discount	Hard	$21-22,500		137	Ford Crown Victoria
Very Poor	Poor	Discount	Average	$17-18,000		142	Ford Thunderbird
Very Good	Average	Regular	Average	$40-42,000		155	Infiniti J30
Very Good	Average	Discount	Average	$53-57,000		156	Infiniti Q45
Very Good	Very Good	Discount	Average	$32-33,000		159	Lexus ES300
Very Good		Regular	Average	$45-46,000		160	Lexus GS300
Very Good		Discount	Easy	$52-53,000		161	Lexus LS400
Very Good	Good	Regular	Easy	$43-52,500		162	Lexus SC300/400
Average		Discount	Hard	$41-42,000		163	Lincoln Continental
Average	Average	Discount	Average	$39-40,000		164	Lincoln Mark VIII

¹Based on 1995 prices. ²Coupe only. ³Sedan/Wagon only. ⁴Data given for 2 dr., 4 dr. overall is 1, crash test is good. **15**

Car	See Pg.	Overall Rating* Poor ⇔ Good	Crash Test	Airbags	Side Impact	Fuel Economy	Repair Rating
Lincoln Town Car	165		No Test	Dual	Strong	17/25	Good
Mazda 929	167		No Test	Dual	Weak	19/24	Poor
Merc.-Benz E-Class	175		No Test	Dual	Strong	28/35	Very Poor
Mercury Cougar	176		Very Good	Dual	Strong	19/26	Average
Merc. Grand Marquis	177		Very Good	Dual	Strong	17/25	Good
Mitsubishi Diamante	182		Good	Dual	Weak	18/24	Very Poor
Olds 88	191		Good	Dual	Weak	18/27	Good
Olds 98	192		No Test	Dual	Weak	19/29	Average
Olds Aurora	194		Average	Dual	Weak	17/26	Good
Pontiac Bonneville	199		Good	Dual	Weak	19/30	Good
Subaru SVX	211		No Test	Dual	Strong	17/24	Good
Volvo 900 Series	224		No Test	Dual	Strong	18/26	Poor
Minivans							
Chevy Astro	114		No Test	Dual	Weak	16/21	Good
Chevy Lumina Mnvn	120		Good	Driver	Weak	19/26	Very Good
Chrys. Town and Cntry	126		No Test	Dual	Strong	17/24	Very Good
Dodge Caravan	127		No Test	Dual	Strong	20/26	Very Good
Ford Aerostar	134		Average	Driver	Weak	18/24	Very Good
Ford Windstar	143		Very Good	Dual	Strong	17/23	Good
Honda Odyssey	149		Good	Dual	Strong	20/24	Poor
Isuzu Oasis	157		No Test	Dual	Weak	20/24	Poor
Mazda MPV	170		No Test	Dual	Weak	16/22	Poor
Mercury Villager	181		No Test	Dual	Weak	17/23	Good
Nissan Quest	189		No Test	Dual	Weak	17/23	Good
Olds Silhouette	197		Good	Driver	Weak	19/26	Very Good
Plymouth Voyager	198		No Test	Dual	Strong	20/26	Very Good
Pontiac Trans Sport	204		Good	Driver	Weak	19/26	Very Good
Toyota Previa	219		Average	Dual	Strong	18/22	Poor

*Due to the importance of crash tests, cars with no crash test results as of publication date cannot be given an overall rating.

Warranty	Complaint Rating	Insurance Rating	Parking Index	Typical Price $	Overall Rating* Poor ⇔ Good	See Pg.	Car
Average	Good	Discount	Very Hard	$37-42,000		165	Lincoln Town Car
Poor	Poor	Discount	Average	$35-36,000[1]		167	Mazda 929
Average		Regular	Average	$41-79,000		175	Merc.-Benz E-Class
Very Poor	Good	Discount	Average	$17-18,000		176	Mercury Cougar
Very Poor	Poor	Discount	Hard	$21-23,000		177	Merc. Grand Marquis
Average	Average	Regular	Average	$35-36,000[1]		182	Mitsubishi Diamante
Poor	Good	Discount	Hard	$20-26,000		191	Olds 88
Poor	Very Good	Discount	Hard	$28-29,000		192	Olds 98
Good		Regular	Hard	$34-35,000		194	Olds Aurora
Very Poor	Good	Discount	Hard	$21-26,500		199	Pontiac Bonneville
Poor	Very Poor	Regular	Easy	$24-34,000		211	Subaru SVX
Very Good	Average	Discount	Very Easy	$34-35,000		224	Volvo 900 Series
Minivans							
Very Poor	Good	Discount	Hard	$18-19,000		114	Chevy Astro
Very Poor	Poor	Discount	Hard	$19-20,000		120	Chevy Lumina Mnvn
Very Poor		Regular	Hard	$24-29,500		126	Chrys. Town and Cntry
Very Poor		Regular	Average	$16-24,000		127	Dodge Caravan
Very Poor	Average	Discount	Hard	$17-23,500		134	Ford Aerostar
Very Poor		Regular	Hard	$18-24,500		143	Ford Windstar
Very Poor		Regular	Average	$22-25,000		149	Honda Odyssey
Good		Regular	Average	$25-28,000		157	Isuzu Oasis
Poor	Poor	Regular	Easy	$21-28,000		170	Mazda MPV
Very Poor	Poor	Discount	Average	$19-26,500		181	Mercury Villager
Poor	Very Poor	Discount	Hard	$21-26,000		189	Nissan Quest
Poor	Average	Discount	Hard	$21-23,000		197	Olds Silhouette
Very Poor		Regular	Average	$16-19,500		198	Plymouth Voyager
Very Poor	Average	Discount	Hard	$18-19,000		204	Pontiac Trans Sport
Very Poor	Good	Discount	Average	$24-32,000		219	Toyota Previa

[1]Based on 1995 prices. [2]Coupe only. [3]Sedan/Wagon only.

Corporate Twins

"Corporate twin" is a term for similar cars sold under different names. In many cases, the cars are identical, such as the Dodge and Plymouth Neon. Sometimes the difference is in body style and luxury items, as with the Ford Thunderbird and Mercury Cougar. Generally, twins have the same mechanics, engine, drive train, size, weight, and internal workings. In addition to corporate twins, there are what we call "Asian cousins." These are Asian imports marketed under a U.S. name. In most cases, the main difference is the name plate and price; sometimes you will find differences in style.

Twins

Chrysler
Chrysler LHS
Chrysler New Yorker

Dodge Caravan
Plymouth Voyager

Chrysler Town & Country
Dodge Grand Caravan
Plymouth Grand Voyager

Chrysler Cirrus
Dodge Stratus
Plymouth Breeze

Chrysler Concorde
Dodge Intrepid
Eagle Vision

Chrysler Sebring
Dodge Avenger

Dodge Neon
Plymouth Neon

Volkswagen
VW Golf
VW Jetta

Toyota
Lexus ES 300
Toyota Camry

Nissan
Infiniti I30
Nissan Maxima

Ford

Ford Crown Victoria
Lincoln Town Car
Mercury Grand Marquis

Ford Taurus
Mercury Sable

Ford Contour
Mercury Mystique

Ford Thunderbird
Lincoln Mark VIII
Mercury Cougar

Ford Escort
Mercury Tracer

General Motors

Buick Century
Oldsmobile Ciera

Buick Roadmaster
Chevrolet Caprice

Buick Park Avenue
Oldsmobile Ninety Eight

Buick Riviera
Oldsmobile Aurora

Chevrolet Astro
GMC Safari

Chevrolet Cavalier
Pontiac Sunfire

Chevrolet Camaro
Pontiac Firebird

Buick LeSabre
Oldsmobile Eight Eight
Pontiac Bonneville

Buick Skylark
Oldsmobile Achieva
Pontiac Grand Am

Buick Regal
Olds Cutlass Supreme
Pontiac Grand Prix

Chevy Lumina Minivan
Oldsmobile Silhouette
Pontiac Trans Sport

Chevrolet Lumina
Chevrolet Monte Carlo

Chevrolet Beretta
Chevrolet Corsica

Asian Cousins

Chry. Sebring/Dodge Avenger-*Mitsubishi Galant*
Eagle Summit-*Mitsubishi Mirage*
Eagle Talon-*Mitsubishi Eclipse*
Ford Probe-*Mazda MX-6*
Geo Metro-*Suzuki Swift*
Geo Prizm-*Toyota Corolla*
Honda Odyssey-*Isuzu Oasis*
Mercury Villager-*Nissan Quest*

SAFETY

For most of us, safety is one of the most important factors in choosing a new car, yet it is also one of the most difficult items to evaluate. To give the greatest possible occupant protection, a car should offer a wide variety of safety features including dual airbags and 4-wheel anti-lock brakes (ABS). While these features are becoming more common, they are not yet on all models.

Another key factor in occupant protection is how well the car performs in a crash test. In order for you to use the U. S. Department of Transportation crash tests to evaluate your new car choices, we have analyzed and presented the results in this chapter. The crash tests measure how well each vehicle protects the driver and front-seat passenger in a frontal crash.

Also described in this chapter are current options and safety features available in this year's models. In addition, we've included a state-by-state list of the safety belt laws and a detailed discussion of an important, and too often overlooked, safety feature—the child safety seat.

Crash Test Program: In 1979, the U.S. Department of Transportation began a crash test program to compare the occupant protection of cars. These crash tests show signifi-

cant differences in the abilities of various automobiles to protect belted occupants in frontal crashes.

In the test, an automobile is sent into a concrete barrier at 35-mph, causing an impact which is similar to that of two identical cars crashing head on at 35-mph. The car contains electronically monitored dummies in the driver and passenger seats. These electronic data are analyzed to measure the impact of such a collision on a human being.

The government releases this data in an incomplete and confusing array of numbers that are difficult to understand and use in comparing cars.

We have analyzed the data and presented the results using *The Car Book Crash Test Index.* This Index provides an overall means of comparing the results. The following tables allow you to compare the crash test performances of today's cars.

It is best to compare the results within weight class, such as compacts to compacts. Do not compare cars with differing weights. For example, a subcompact that is rated "Good" may not be as safe as a large car with the same rating.

The results evaluate performance in frontal crashes only, which account for about 50 percent of auto-related deaths and serious injuries. Even though the tested car may have airbags, the dummies are also belted.

We rate the crash test results of each car relative to all of the cars ever crash tested. This method of rating gives you a better idea of the true top performers among the '96 models and identifies those cars which have substantial room to improve their occupant protection.

The Car Book wants to stimulate competition and that's what this new rating program is intended to do. You, the buyer, now know which are the truly best performers. Manufacturers who have chosen to build better performing cars will likely be rewarded with your decision to purchase their models.

1996 cars missing from this list have not been tested at the time of printing or may not have been selected by the government for testing.

Crash Tests: How the Cars are Rated

A car's ability to protect you in a crash depends on its ability to absorb the force of impact rather than transfer it to you, the occupant. This is a function of the car's size, weight and, most importantly, design. The crash tests measure how much of the crash force is transferred to the head, chest, and thighs of the occupants in a 35-mph crash into a barrier.

The cars are listed here by weight class, then alphabetically by manufacturer. The first column provides *The Car Book's* overall Crash Test Index. This Index is a number which describes all the forces measured by the test. Lower index numbers are better. The Index is best used to compare cars within the same size and weight class.

The second column provides an overall rating of *Very Good*, *Good*, *Average*, *Poor*, or *Very Poor*. These results reflect the car's performance in relation to all other models ever tested. This exclusive *Car Book Crash Test Rating* lets you compare, at a glance, the overall performance of the cars you'll find in the showroom this year.

The next two columns indicate the likelihood of each occupant sustaining a life-threatening injury, based on the dummies' head and chest scores. Lower percentages mean a lower likelihood of being seriously injured. This information is taken directly from government analysis of the crash test results.

The last two columns indicate how the dummies' legs fared. Legs labeled *Poor* did not meet the government's standards. Those that did meet the standards are rated *Average*, *Good*, and *Very Good*, reflecting performance relative to all other cars ever tested. The leg injury ratings are not weighted as heavily as head and chest results in determining overall performance.

Results on the following pages indicate how this year's cars can be expected to perform in the tests. They are included here only when the automobile design has not changed enough to dramatically alter results. Cars that were tested with less crash protection than is standard on the 1996 model are noted. It is expected that with more crash protection, the current version of these models should produce similar or better results. "Corporate twins" that are structurally the same, such as the Dodge Caravan and Plymouth Voyager, can be expected to perform similarly.

Crash test results may vary due to differences in the way cars are manufactured, in how models are equipped, and in test conditions. There is no absolute guarantee that a car which passed the test will adequately protect you in an accident. Keep in mind that some two-door models may not perform exactly like their four-door counterparts.

Crash Test Performance: The Best

Here is a list of the best crash test performers among the 1996 cars for which crash test information is available. Lower Crash Test Index numbers indicate better performance. See the following tables for more results.

Subcompact
Geo Metro 4 dr. (3080)
Suzuki Swift 4 dr. (3080)
Mitsubishi Mirage 4 dr. (3224)
Eagle Summit 4 dr. (3224)

Compact
Chrysler Sebring (1760)
Dodge Avenger (1760)
Honda Prelude (1959)
Ford Probe (2026)
Mazda MX-6 (2026)

Large
Ford Thunderbird (1632)
Mercury Cougar (1632)
Ford Crown Victoria (2116)
Mercury Grand Marquis (2116)
Chevrolet Lumina (2173)

Minivans
Ford Windstar (1911)
Honda Odyssey (2889)
Chevy Lumina Minivan (3263)
Oldsmobile Silhouette (3263)
Pontiac Trans Sport (3263)

Intermediate
Chevrolet Camaro (1705)
Pontiac Firebird (1705)
Mazda Millenia (2085)
Audi A6/S6 (2143)

Chrysler Concorde (2323)
Dodge Intrepid (2323)
Eagle Vision (2323)

Crash Test Performance

	Injury Index	Car Book Rating	Likelihood of Life Threatening Injury		Leg Injury Rating	
			Driver	Passngr	Driver	Passngr
Subcompact						
Eagle Summit (Mirage) 4dr.[1]	3224	Good	23%	12%	Moderate	Vry. Gd.
Ford Aspire 4dr.	3473	Average	16%	19%	Moderate	Moderate
Ford Escort 4dr.	3687	Average	20%	21%	Good	Moderate
Geo Metro 4dr.	3080	Good	15%	16%	Moderate	Good
Mazda Protégé 4dr.	---	---	---	29%	Good	Moderate
Merc.Tracer (Escort) 4dr.	3687	Average	19%	20%	Good	Moderate
Mitsubishi Mirage 4dr.[1]	3224	Good	23%	12%	Moderate	Vry. Gd.
Nissan Sentra 4 dr.	2842	Good	16%	16%	Vry. Gd.	Good
Suzuki Swift (Metro) 4dr.	3080	Good	15%	16%	Moderate	Good
Toyota Tercel 4dr.	3705	Average	24%	17%	Good	Moderate
Compact						
Acura Integra 4dr.	3543	Average	16%	21%	Moderate	Good
BMW 325i 4dr.	3366	Good	19%	17%	Moderate	Good
Chevrolet Beretta 2dr.[2]	1865	*Vry. Gd.*	7%	12%	Good	Vry. Gd.
Chevrolet Cavalier 4dr.	3841	Average	22%	21%	Moderate	Good
Chevrolet Corsica 4dr.	5470	**Poor**	23%	44%	Moderate	Good
Chrys. Sebring (Avenger) 2dr.	1760	*Vry. Gd.*	9%	6%	Moderate	Moderate
Dodge Avenger 2dr.	1760	*Vry. Gd.*	9%	6%	Moderate	Moderate
Dodge Stealth 2 dr.[1]	3241	Good	10%	22%	Moderate	Moderate

HOW TO READ THE CHARTS:

| 1234 | **Injury Index**
The overall numerical injury rating for front seat occupants in a frontal crash. *Lower numbers mean better performance.*

| Very Good | **Car Book Rating**
How the car compares among all government test results to date. The range includes very good, good, average, poor and very poor.

| 00% | **Likelihood of Life Threatening Injury**
The chance of life threatening injury to the driver and passenger in a frontal 35 mph crash. *Lower percentages indicate better performance.*

| Good | **Leg Injury Rating**
Injury rating for driver and passenger legs in a frontal crash, when compared to all government test results to date.

Crash Test Performance	Injury Index	Car Book Rating	Likelihood of Life Threatening Injury		Leg Injury Rating	
			Driver	Passngr	Driver	Passngr
Eagle Talon (Eclipse) 2dr.	3013	Good	18%	13%	Moderate	Moderate
Ford Contour 4dr.	2940	Good	10%	20%	Good	Moderate
Ford Probe 2dr.	2026	*Vry. Gd.*	5%	12%	Moderate	Moderate
Geo Prizm (Corolla) 4dr.	2846	Good	16%	13%	Moderate	Good
Honda Prelude 2dr.[1]	1959	*Vry. Gd.*	12%	9%	Good	Vry. Gd.
Mazda 626 4dr.	2728	Good	17%	9%	Moderate	Moderate
Mazda MX-6 (Probe) 2dr.	2026	*Vry. Gd.*	5%	12%	Moderate	Moderate
Merc. Mystique (Contour) 4dr.	2940	Good	10%	20%	Good	Moderate
Mitsubishi 3000GT (Stealth)[1]	3241	Good	10%	22%	Moderate	Moderate
Mitsubishi Eclipse 2dr.	3013	Good	18%	13%	Moderate	Moderate
Mitsubishi Galant 4dr.	---	---	---	16%	Moderate	Good
Nissan 240SX 2dr.	3669	Average	28%	15%	Vry. Gd.	Vry. Gd.
Pont. Sunfire (Cavalier) 4dr.	3841	Average	22%	21%	Moderate	Good
Saturn SC (SL2) 2dr.	2523	*Vry. Gd.*	13%	13%	Good	Good
Subaru Legacy 4dr.	2526	*Vry. Gd.*	11%	15%	Good	Vry. Gd.
Toyota Corolla 4dr.	2846	Good	16%	13%	Moderate	Good
VW Golf/Jetta (Jetta III) 4dr.	3940	Average	22%	22%	Moderate	Moderate
Intermediate						
Audi A6/S6 4dr.	2143	*Vry. Gd.*	11%	10%	Moderate	Good
Buick Century 4dr.[2]	2992	Good	13%	19%	Good	Vry. Gd.
Buick Regal (Gr. Prix) 2dr.	3481	Average	15%	22%	Moderate	Moderate
Chevrolet Camaro 2dr.	1705	*Vry. Gd.*	8%	9%	Good	Vry. Gd.
Chrys. Cirrus (Stratus) 4dr.	---	---	30.%	---	Moderate	Moderate
Chrys. Concorde (Intrepid) 4dr.[3]	2323	*Vry. Gd.*	9%	12%	Moderate	Moderate

HOW TO READ THE CHARTS:

| 1234 | **Injury Index**

The overall numerical injury rating for front seat occupants in a frontal crash. *Lower numbers mean better performance.*

| Very Good | **Car Book Rating**

How the car compares among all government test results to date. The range includes very good, good, average, poor and very poor.

| 00% | **Likelihood of Life Threatening Injury**

The chance of life threatening injury to the driver and passenger in a frontal 35 mph crash. *Lower percentages indicate better performance.*

| Good | **Leg Injury Rating**

Injury rating for driver and passenger legs in a frontal crash, when compared to all government test results to date.

Crash Test Performance	Injury Index	Car Book Rating	Likelihood of Life Threatening Injury		Leg Injury Rating	
			Driver	Passngr	Driver	Passngr
Dodge Intrepid 4dr.[3]	2323	*Vry. Gd.*	9%	12%	Moderate	Moderate
Dodge Stratus 4dr.	---	---	30%	---	Moderate	Moderate
Eagle Vision (Intrepid) 4dr.[3]	2323	*Vry. Gd.*	9%	12%	Moderate	Moderate
Ford Mustang 2dr.	2758	Good	12%	15%	Moderate	Moderate
Honda Accord 4dr.	3832	Average	18%	26%	Moderate	Vry. Gd.
Hyundai Sonata 4dr.	4034	Average	25%	20%	Moderate	Good
Lexus ES300 (Camry) 4dr.	3398	Good	16%	22%	Vry. Gd.	Good
Mazda Millenia 4dr.	2085	*Vry. Gd.*	11%	8%	Moderate	Moderate
Merc.-Benz C-Class 4dr.	3420	Good	18%	19%	Moderate	Good
Nissan Altima 4dr.	3444	Average	18%	21%	Good	Good
Nissan Maxima	3741	Average	18%	25%	Good	Good
Olds Ciera (Century) 4dr.[2]	2992	Good	13%	19%	Good	Vry. Gd.
Olds Cut. Supr. (Gr. Prix) 2dr.	3481	Average	15%	22%	Moderate	Moderate
Plym. Breeze (Stratus) 4dr.	---	---	30%	---	Moderate	Moderate
Pont. Firebird (Camaro) 2dr.	1705	*Vry. Gd.*	8%	9%	Good	Vry. Gd.
Pontiac Grand Prix 2dr.	3481	Average	15%	22%	Moderate	Moderate
Saab 900 4 dr,	2868	Good	15%	15%	Moderate	Good
Saab 9000 4dr.[1]	2736	Good	12%	17%	Good	Vry. Gd.
Toyota Avalon	2196	*Vry. Gd.*	13%	11%	Vry. Gd.	Good
Toyota Camry 2dr.	2314	*Vry. Gd.*	14%	10%	Vry. Gd.	Vry. Gd.
Toyota Camry 4dr.	3398	Good	16%	22%	Vry. Gd.	Good
Volkswagen Passat 4dr.	3232	Good	19%	18%	Vry. Gd.	Good
Volvo 850 4dr.	2939	Good	10%	20%	Moderate	Good
Large						
Buick LeSabre (B'ville Sse) 4dr.	3334	Good	10%	24%	Moderate	Moderate
Buick Roadmaster (Caprice) 4dr.	4982	**Poor**	19%	40%	Moderate	Good
Cadillac DeVille 4dr.	3188	Good	17%	17%	Good	Good
Cadillac Seville 4dr.[1]	3031	Good	13%	19%	Good	Good
Chevy Caprice/Impala 4dr.	4982	**Poor**	19%	40%	Moderate	Good
Chevrolet Lumina 4dr.	2173	*Vry. Gd.*	9%	13%	Good	Good
Chevrolet Monte Carlo 2dr.	3049	Good	16%	17%	Good	Good

Crash Test Performance	Injury Index	Car Book Rating	Likelihood of Life Threatening Injury		Leg Injury Rating	
			Driver	Passngr	Driver	Passngr
Chrys. LHS/New Yorker 4dr.	3107	Good	20%	13%	Good	Good
Ford Crown Victoria 4dr.	2116	*Vry. Gd.*	13%	8%	Good	Good
Ford Thunderbird 2dr.	1632	*Vry. Gd.*	8%	7%	Moderate	Good
Infiniti J30 4dr.	3361	Good	18%	17%	Moderate	Moderate
Lexus GS300 4dr.	4025	Average	23%	23%	Good	Moderate
Lincoln Town Car 4dr.	---	---	9%	---	Moderate	Good
Merc. Cougar (T-bird) 2dr.	1632	*Vry. Gd.*	8%	7%	Moderate	Good
Merc. Gr. Marq. (Cr. Vic.) 4dr.	2116	*Vry. Gd.*	13%	8%	Good	Good
Mitsubishi Diamante 4dr.[1]	3043	Good	16%	17%	Moderate	Vry. Gd.
Olds 88 (Bonneville Sse) 4dr.	3334	Good	10%	24%	Moderate	Moderate
Oldsmobile Aurora 4dr.	4380	Average	23%	26%	Moderate	Moderate
Pontiac Bonneville 4dr.	3334	Good	10%	24%	Moderate	Moderate
Minivan						
Chevy Lumina (Tr. Sport)	3263	Good	10%	23%	Moderate	Moderate
Ford Aerostar	3544	Average	15%	23%	Moderate	Good
Ford Windstar	1911	*Vry. Gd.*	10%	8%	Good	Good
Honda Odyssey	2889	Good	16%	15%	Moderate	Vry. Gd.
Olds Silhouette (Tr. Sport)	3263	Good	10%	23%	Moderate	Moderate
Pontiac Trans Sport	3263	Good	10%	23%	Moderate	Moderate
Toyota Previa	3858	Average	20%	23%	Moderate	Good

HOW TO READ THE CHARTS:

| 1234 | **Injury Index**

The overall numerical injury rating for front seat occupants in a frontal crash. *Lower numbers mean better performance.*

| Very Good | **Car Book Rating**

How the car compares among all government test results to date. The range includes very good, good, average, poor and very poor.

| 00% | **Likelihood of Life Threatening Injury**

The chance of life threatening injury to the driver and passenger in a frontal 35 mph crash. *Lower percentages indicate better performance.*

| Good | **Leg Injury Rating**

Injury rating for driver and passenger legs in a frontal crash, when compared to all government test results to date.

Parentheses indicate actual model tested.

[1] Vehicle tested with fewer airbags than now available. Similar or better results should occur with 1996 airbag offering.

[2] Vehicle tested with manual belts and now has automatic belts which may not perform as well.

[3] Car Book/*Center for Auto Safety* test results.

Automatic Crash Protection

The concept of automatic protection is not new—automatic fire sprinklers in public buildings, automatic release of oxygen masks in airplanes, purification of drinking water, and pasteurization of milk are all commonly accepted forms of automatic safety protection. Ironically, of all the products we buy, the one most likely to kill us has only recently been equipped with automatic safety protection. As consumer advocates are ready to point out, we encorporate better technology in safely transporting electronic equipment, eggs, and china than we do in packaging humans in automobiles.

Over twenty years ago, in cooperation with the federal government, the automobile industry developed two basic forms of automatic crash protection: airbags and automatic safety belts. These devices will not prevent all deaths, but they will cut in half your chances of being killed or seriously injured in a car accident.

The idea behind automatic crash protection is to protect people from what is called the "second collision" when the occupant comes forward and collides with the interior of his or her own car. Because the "second collision" occurs within milliseconds, and because so many people do not use seat belts, providing automatic rather than manual protection dramatically improves the chances of escaping injury.

Federal law now requires all new cars to be equipped with some form of automatic crash protection that will protect the driver and front seat passenger in a 30-mph collision into a fixed barrier. To meet the standard, auto makers may use airbags or automatic seat belts.

Automatic Belts: Automatic safety belts are supposed to offer protection with little or no effort. As their name implies, they move automatically into place when you enter the car and are released automatically when you leave.

There are two main types of automatic belts—those with an automatic lap and shoulder belt connected to the door, and motorized versions which move out of the way when you open and close the door.

The easiest automatic belt systems to use are the motorized belts where the shoulder belt moves forward, out of your way, when you open the door. When you close the door, the belt moves back, secure over your chest. Unfortunately, these belts only do half the job automatically. You must manually attach a separate lap belt, in this so-called automatic system, which is easy to forget. Forgetting to use the manual lap belt can cause severe injury in an accident.

Non-motorized belts are generally attached to the door. When the door is opened, the attached belt also pulls away to let you in. The General Motors system is a complicated and intimidating web of belts. The problem with all door-mounted belts is that if the door pops open in an accident, you lose the protection of the belt.

Cars with automatic belts often have extra padding under the dash to protect the occupant's knees and lower body. Generally, automatic belts are less expensive than airbags. Airbags, however, offer better protection in a high-speed frontal collision.

Airbags: Hidden in the steering wheel hub and the right side of the dashboard, airbags provide unobtrusive and effective protection in frontal crashes. When needed, they inflate instantly to cushion the driver, and in some cars, the front seat passenger. By spreading crash forces over the head and chest, airbags protect the body from violent contact with the hard surfaces of the car. Cars with airbags also provide manual seat belts to protect occupants in nonfrontal crashes. However,

TIP

A Note for Pregnant Women:

The American College of Obstetricians and Gyne cologists strongly urges pregnant women to always wear a safety belt, including on the ride to the hospital to deliver the baby! In a car crash, the most serious risk to an unborn baby is that the mother may be injured. Obstetricians recommend that the lap and shoulder belts be used, with the lap belt as low as possible on the hips, under the baby. When packing your things for the hospital, make sure you include an infant car safety seat to bring your baby home. As the American Academy of Pediatrics says, "Make the first ride a safe ride!"

airbags offer protection in frontal crashes even if the safety belt is not fastened.

General Motors installed airbags in over 10,000 cars from 1974 to 1976. These cars traveled over 600 million miles, and the death and injury rate of the occupants was 50 percent lower than the rate for non-airbag cars. Studies of the operation of the airbags reported no cases of failure to deploy or malfunction of the inflator. This reliability rate (99.995 percent) is far higher than that of such safety features as brakes, tires, steering, and lights, which show failure rates of up to 10 percent.

Consumers with questions about airbags often find that dealers do not know the facts about these safety devices. The following answers to typical airbag questions are prepared by the Insurance Institute for Highway Safety.

Is the gas that inflates airbags dangerous? Nitrogen, which makes up 79.8 percent of the air we breathe, is the gas that inflates the bags. A solid chemical, sodium azide, generates this nitrogen gas. Sodium azide does not present a safety hazard in normal driving, in crashes, or in disposal. In fact, occupants of the car will never even come in contact with the sodium azide.

Will airbags inflate by mistake? Airbags will inflate only in frontal impacts equivalent to hitting a solid wall at about 10-mph or higher. They will not inflate when you go over bumps or potholes or when you hit something at low speed. Even slamming on your brakes will not cause the airbags to inflate unless you hit something.

In the unlikely event of an inadvertent airbag deployment, you would not lose control of the car. Airbags are designed to inflate and deflate in fractions of a second. GM tested driver reaction by inflating airbags without warning at speeds of up to 45-mph. GM reported that "without exception, the drivers retained control of the automobile."

Will airbag systems last very long? Airbags are reliable and require no maintenance. Only one part moves, the device that senses the impact, so there is nothing to wear out. They work throughout the life of the car although some manufacturers suggest inspections at anywhere from two to ten years.

In a study of 228 cars in which airbags were deployed, 40 had traveled more than 40,000 miles. One car had traveled almost 115,000 miles at the time of the crash. In every case, the airbags worked as designed.

Will airbags protect children? Studies of actual crashes indicate that children are protected by airbags. However, most cars do not offer airbags on the passenger side, where children often sit. In addition, rear-facing child safety seats should *not* be used in the front seat of a car with a passenger airbag.

Will airbags protect occupants without seat belts? Airbags are designed to protect unbelted front-seat occupant in 30-mph frontal crashes into a wall. Equipping cars with airbags reduced the average injury severity in serious frontal crashes by 64 percent, even though over 80 percent of the occupants were unbelted. The best protection, however, is provided by a combination of airbags and lap and shoulder safety belts. With airbags and seat belts, you'll be protected in the event of side impact and rollover crashes, as well as in frontal crashes.

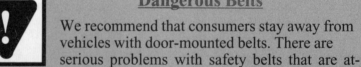

Dangerous Belts

We recommend that consumers stay away from vehicles with door-mounted belts. There are serious problems with safety belts that are attached to the door. If the door opens while driving or during a crash, the belt will not prevent you from flying out of the car or crashing into the dashboard or steering wheel. The following vehicles have door-mounted belts in 1996:

Buick Century   Kia Sephia
Chevrolet Beretta   Oldsmobile Ciera
Chevrolet Corsica   Pontiac Grand Prix

Airbag Stories

The following are true stories about people whose lives have been saved by airbags. Note how long ago these events happened. Tragically, only recently have car makers decided to make them widely available.

Mahopac, NY—*September 1974 and January 1977:* In this case a young woman was involved in two airbag crashes. In September 1974, traveling at 31-mph, she struck a car that was pulling out from an intersection. Her only injuries were some minor bruises. In January 1977, her car was damaged beyond repair when it skidded off an icy road and smashed into a tree at 20 miles per hour. Her seat belts were unfastened in both crashes. "I know it seems foolish, particularly after the first accident, for me not to use seat belts, but the fact is they make me uncomfortable," she said afterward. The beauty of airbags is that, unlike seat belts, they are not subject to the driver's negligence or carelessness.

Irwinton, GA—*July 1985:* A local pulpwood worker, taking a shortcut home on a quiet two-lane road southwest of Irwinton, missed a sharp right turn and plowed into a solid dirt embankment at over 50-mph. After the accident the driver, who had no idea his used 1974 Oldsmobile had airbags, walked away with only minor injuries.

The first people at the accident scene didn't know what to make of the airbags. A deputy sheriff first thought the bags were clothing and that there was a body in the car. The next day, when the driver came back to see the wreck, he said, "I hope I can buy another car with bags." Back then, he couldn't.

Milwaukee, WI—*April 1986:* On rural highway I75 near Milwaukee, Wisconsin, state trooper John Leitner clocked a motorcyclist hurtling by him at 99-mph. Quickly climbing into his cruiser, he took off in pursuit at speeds up to 115-mph. Suddenly, the cruiser skidded and slammed into an embankment at 35-mph.

"I saw the crash coming," Leitner recalls, "so I threw up my arms to protect my face. The next thing I felt was the soft silver bag in my face. It happened so fast that I didn't even remember that my cruiser had an airbag." Leitner climbed out of the car with only a few minor cuts and bruises. His boss reported that Leitner's wife doesn't want him on patrol again unless he has another airbag-equipped cruiser.

Northern VA—*Sept. 1988:* Denise Brodie was driving her 1988 Chrysler LeBaron convertible on Route 3 when an oncoming 1985 Ford Country Squire station wagon suddenly crossed over the median and struck her head-on at a closing speed of over 70-mph. The crash was so violent that her 2,600 lb. car was driven backward by the massive 4,000 lb. Ford. Miraculously Ms. Brodie suffered only moderate injuries. The driver of the Ford, who was wearing a lap and shoulder belt, died. National Highway Traffic Safety Administration investigators credited the airbag with providing the cushion of safety that saved Mrs. Brodie's life.

Boise, ID—*June 1989:* This case was reported to consumer advocate Ralph Nader by CBS television's Kathleen Sullivan. Her parents had just been in a serious car accident near Boise, Idaho. They survived because they were riding in a 1989 Lincoln Continental with dual airbags that inflated and protected them from serious harm. Ms. Sullivan thanked Mr. Nader for working so hard and long to get airbags in cars like the one that saved her parents. Now that the auto industry's 20-year war against automatic crash protection is over, airbags are saving the families of people far less well-known than Ms. Sullivan.

1996 Cars WITHOUT Dual Airbags

The following manufacturers have chosen NOT to put dual airbags in these 1996 models.

Buick Century	Ford Aerostar
Chevrolet Beretta	Oldsmobile Ciera
Chevrolet Corsica	Oldsmobile Silhouette
Chevy Lumina Minivan	Pontiac Trans Sport

Anti-Lock Brakes

After airbags, one of the best safety features available is an anti-lock braking system (ABS). ABS shortens stopping distance on dry, wet, and even icy roads by preventing wheel lock-up and keeps you from skidding out of control when you "slam" on the brakes.

The ABS works by sensing the speed of each wheel. If one or more of the wheels begins to lock up or skid, it releases that wheel's brakes, allowing the wheel to roll normally again, thus stopping the skid. When the wheel stops skidding, the hydraulic pressure is re-applied instantly. This cycle can be repeated several times per second, keeping each wheel at its optimum braking performance even while your foot keeps pushing on the brake pedal. Although ABS is typically connected to all four wheels, in some light trucks and vans it is connected to only the rear wheels.

The ABS is only active when it senses that the wheels are about to lock up. When an ABS is active, you may notice that the brake pedal pulsates slightly. This pulsation is normal, and it indicates that the brakes are being released and reapplied. *Don't pump your brakes*—the ABS is doing it for you. If there is a failure in the ABS, the vehicle reverts to its conventional braking system and a warning light indicates that the ABS needs repair.

Note: Using tires other than the ones originally on the vehicle may affect the anti-lock braking system. If you are planning to change the size of the tires on your vehicle, first consult your owner's manual.

1996 models offer either standard or optional ABS. Unfortunately, you won't find it on the Ford Aerostar or the Mitsubishi Mirage.

Don't Buy Add-On ABS Brakes

Adding "so-called" ABS brakes to your car can be dangerous. These products use a variety of deceptive names that incorporate the letters ABS, such as ABS-Trax (Automotive Breakthrough Science—the company's name) and Brake-Guard ABS (Advanced Braking System). These add-on systems "have virtually no effect on stopping distances, vehicle stability or control," according to government tests. You should *not* purchase or install these systems. Only *electronic* ABS systems are capable of preventing wheel skid in panic braking situations. Currently, true electronic anti-lock brakes are only available as factory installed systems.

What Happens in a Collision

A car crash typically involves two collisions. First, the car hits another object and second, the occupant collides with the inside of the car. Injuries result from this *second collision*. The key to surviving an auto accident is protecting yourself from the second collision. Always wearing your safety belt is the most important defense while having an airbag is a very close second. The whole purpose of the airbag is to protect you in this second collision.

Upon impact, in a typical 35-mph crash, the car begins to crush and slow down. Within 1/10 of a second, the car comes to a stop, but the person keeps moving forward at 35-mph. 1/50 of a second after the car has stopped, the unbelted person slams into the dashboard or windshield.

According to government reports prepared before the widespread use of belts and airbags, these were the major causes of injury in the *second collision:*

Steering wheel	27%
Instrument panel	11%
Side (doors)	10%
Windshield	5%
Front roof pillar	4%
Glove box area	3%
Roof edges	3%
Roof	2%

Safety Belts

About 60 percent of occupants killed or injured in auto crashes would have been saved from serious harm had they been wearing safety belts. Yet many Americans do not use these life-saving devices.

Safety belts are particularly important in minivans, 4x4s and pickups because there is a greater chance of being killed or seriously injured in a rollover accident. The simple precaution of wearing your belt greatly improves your odds of survival.

Why don't people wear their belts? Sometimes they simply don't know the facts. Once you know the facts, you should be willing to buckle up.

While most safety advocates welcome the passage of safety belt usage laws, the ones passed to date are weak and generally unenforced. In addition, most of the laws are based on "secondary" enforcement—meaning that you cannot be stopped for failing to wear your belt. If you are stopped for another reason and the officer notices you don't have your belt on by the time he or she reaches the vehicle, you may be fined. In states with "primary" enforcement, you can be stopped for not wearing a safety belt. Yet, in many cases the fines are less than a parking ticket. In Arkansas, however, you can get a $10 credit toward a primary violation if you are wearing a seat belt and in Wyoming, a $5 credit.

Another unusual feature of these laws is that most of them allow drivers to avoid buckling up if they have a doctor's permission. This loophole was inserted to appease those who were not really in favor of the law. However, many doctors are wondering if they will be held responsible for the injuries of unbuckled patients. In fact, the State of New York Medical Society cautions doctors never to give medical dispensation from the law because "no medical condition has yet been found to warrant a medical exemption for seat belt use."

Even though most state laws are weak, they have heightened awareness and raised the level of usage. Belt use in states that have passed a safety belt law tends to rise sharply after the law is enacted. However, after the law has been on the books a few months, safety belt use drops.

The tables on the following pages describe the current safety belt laws. In some cases, the driver is responsible for all or some of the passengers as noted; otherwise, occupants are responsible for themselves. All states are listed, even those that do not yet have safety belt laws. We hope that the blanks following Maine and New Hampshire will soon be filled with new laws.

Safety Belt Myths and Facts

Myth: *"I don't want to be trapped by a seat belt. It's better to be thrown free in an accident."*

Fact: The chance of being killed is 25 times greater if you're ejected. A safety belt will keep you from plunging through the windshield, smashing into trees, rocks, or other cars, scraping along the ground, or getting run over by your own or another's vehicle. If you are wearing your belt, you're far more likely to be conscious after an accident to free yourself and other passengers.

Myth: *"Pregnant women should not wear safety belts."*

Fact: According to the American Medical Association, "Both the pregnant mother and the fetus are safer, provided the lap belt is worn as low on the pelvis as possible."

Myth: *"I don't need it. In case of an accident, I can brace myself with my hands."*

Fact: At 35 mph, the impact of a crash on you and your passengers is brutal. There's no way your arms and legs can brace you against that kind of collision; the speed and force are just too great. The force of impact at only 10 mph is roughly equivalent to the force of catching a 200-pound bag of cement dropped from a first floor window.

	Law Applies To:	Driver Fined For:	Enforcement	Max. Fine 1st Offense
Alabama	Front seat only	Self only	Secondary	$25
Alaska*	All occupants	0 to 15 year olds	Secondary	$15
Arizona	Front seat only	5 to 16 year olds	Secondary	$10
Arkansas	Front seat only	Self only	Secondary	$25[1]
California*	All occupants	4 to 16 year olds	Primary	$20
Colorado	Front seat only	4 to 16 year olds	Secondary	$15
Connecticut	Front seat only	4 to 16 year olds	Primary	$15
Delaware	Front seat only	All occupants	Secondary	$20
Dist. of Columbia	Front seat only	Self only	Secondary	$15
Florida	Front seat only	0 to 15 year olds	Secondary	$27
Georgia	All occupants	4 to 18 year olds	Secondary[2]	$15[2]
Hawaii	Front seat only	4 to 15 year olds	Primary	$20
Idaho	Front seat only	Self only	Secondary	$5
Illinois	Front seat only	6 to 16 year olds	Secondary	$25
Indiana	Front seat only	Self only	Secondary	$25
Iowa	Front seat only	Self only	Primary	$10
Kansas	Front seat only	Self only	Secondary	$10
Kentucky*	All occupants	Over 40 inches	Secondary	$25
Louisiana	Front seat only	Self only	Primary	$25[1]
Maine	No law			
Maryland	Front seat only	0 to 15 year olds	Secondary	$25
Massachusetts*	All occupants	12 to 16 year olds	Secondary	$25
Michigan	All occupants	4 to 16 year olds	Secondary	$25
Minnesota	All occupants	4 to 11 year olds[3]	Secondary	$25
Mississippi	Front seat only	Self only	Secondary	$25
Missouri	Front seat only	4 to 16 year olds	Secondary	$10

* In these states driver can be held liable in court for *all* passengers.
  See next page for footnotes.

Safety Belt Laws

	Law Applies To:	Driver Fined For:	Enforcement	Max. Fine 1st Offense
Montana*	All occupants	Over 4 years old	Secondary	$20
Nebraska	Front seat	Over 5 years old	Secondary	$25
Nevada*	All occupants	5 to 18 year olds	Secondary	$25
New Hampshire	No law			
New Jersey	Front seat only	5 to 18 year olds	Secondary	$20
New Mexico	Front seat only	Self only	Primary	$25
New York	Front seat[4]	4 to 16 year olds	Primary	$50
North Carolina	Front seat only	6 to 16 year olds	Primary	$25
North Dakota	Front seat	Over 11 years old	Secondary	$20
Ohio	Front seat only	Over 4 years old	Secondary	$25
Oklahoma	Front seat only	Self only	Secondary	$25
Oregon*	All Occupants	0 to 15 year olds	Primary	$95
Pennsylvania	Front seat only	4 to 18 year olds	Secondary	$10
Rhode Island*	All Occupants	Over 12 years old	Secondary	None
South Carolina	All Occupants[5]	6 to 17 year olds	Secondary	$10
South Dakota	Front seat	5 to 18 year olds	Secondary	$20
Tennessee	Front seat only	Over 4 years old	Secondary	$10
Texas	Front seat only	4 to 15 year olds	Primary	$50
Utah	Front seat only	2 to 18 year olds	Secondary	$10
Vermont*	All occupants	Over 13 years old	Secondary	$10
Virginia	Front seat only	4 to 16 year olds	Secondary	$25
Washington*	All occupants	0 to 15 year olds	Secondary	$47
West Virginia	Front seat[6]	All occupants	Secondary	$25
Wisconsin	All occupants[5]	4 to 15 year olds	Secondary	$10
Wyoming	Front seat only	Over 3 years old	Secondary	None[1]

* In these states driver can be held liable in court for *all* passengers.
[1] In Arkansas, reward for buckling up is a $10 reduction in primary violation fine; in Wyoming, a $5 reduction. In Louisiana, 10% reduction in fine for moving violation.
[2] Primary for 14 to 18 year olds; $25 fine if driver is a minor.
[3] Parent driver is responsible for 11 to 15 year olds in front seat.
[4] Driver responsible for 4 to 10 year olds riding in rear seat.
[5] Covers rear seat occupants where shoulder belts are available.
[6] Driver responsible for occupants 0 to 17 years old in rear seat.

Child Safety Seats

How many times have you gone out of your way to prevent your children from being injured, taken care to keep household poisons out of reach, or watched carefully while they swam? Probably quite often. Yet, despite these efforts, many parents let their children sleep, unrestrained in the back of a minivan or roam around in a moving vehicle.

Ironically, of all hazards, the automobile poses the greatest threat to your children's health. After the first weeks of an infant's life, vehicle crashes are the single leading cause of death and serious injury for children. Yet nearly 80 percent of the children who have died in vehicles could have been saved by proper use of child safety seats or safety belts.

Being a safe driver is no excuse for not having everyone in your vehicle buckled up. Quite often crashes or sudden swerves are caused by the recklessness of others. Even at low speeds, a child can be hurled violently against the inside of a vehicle.

At 30-mph, a crash or sudden braking can wrench your child from your arms with a tremendous force. At this speed, even a ten-pound infant would be ripped from your arms with a force of nearly 300 pounds. If you aren't wearing a safety belt, your own body will be an additional hazard to a child in your lap. You will be thrown forward with enough force to crush your child against the dashboard or the back of the front seat.

The best and only reliable way to protect your child in a vehicle is to use a safety seat. In an emergency, if no seat is available and the child can sit upright, buckle up the child in the back seat. But there really is no alternative for an infant.

By using a child safety seat on every ride, you will help to establish the habit of regular safety belt use when your children get older. As a lifelong wearer of safety belts, your child reduces his or her chances of being killed or seriously injured in a crash by 50 percent.

Buying Tips: Most consumers find that seats with an automatic retracting harness and a shield are the easiest to use. Here are some important, additional tips for correct use:

☑ Make sure the seat you buy can be properly installed in your vehicle. You will find that some car seats cannot be properly buckled into certain vehicles.

☑ Determine how many straps or buckles must be fastened to use the seat. The easy-to-use seats require only one, once the seat is buckled into the car.

☑ Make sure the seat is wide enough for growth and bulky winter clothes.

☑ Make sure your child is comfortable. Can your child move his or her arms freely, sleep in the seat, and, if older, see out the window?

Locking Clips

Children are safest if they are restrained in the middle of the back seat of your vehicle. If you put the safety seat somewhere other than the middle, you may need a locking clip. This clip is necessary if the latchplate on the safety belt slides freely along the belt; without it, the safety seat can move or tip over. You should always remove the clip when it is not being used with a safety seat.

Register Your Child Seat

Last year, the U.S. Department of Transportation recalled millions of child safety seats for serious safety defects. Tragically, most parents never heard about these recalls and the majority of these problem seats are still being used. You can do two things to protect your children—first, call the Auto Safety Hotline at 800-424-9393 and find out if your seat has been recalled. If so, they will tell you how to contact the manufacturer for a resolution. Second, make sure you fill out the registration card that must come with all new seats. This will enable the company to contact you should there be a recall. If you currently own a seat, ask the Hotline for the address of your seat's manufacturer and send them your name, address and seat model, asking them to keep it on file for recall notices.

Seat Types

There are six types of child seats: *infant-only, convertible, toddler-only, child/booster, booster* and *built-in*.

Infant-Only Seats: Infant-only seats can be used from birth until your baby reaches a weight of 17-20 pounds. This type of seat must be installed facing the rear in a semi-reclined position. In a collision, the crash forces are spread over the baby's back, the strongest body surface. The seat's harness should come from below the child's shoulders in the rear-facing position.

One benefit of an infant-only seat is that you can easily install and remove the seat with the baby in place. Most infant car seats can also be used as household baby seats. Caution: Some household baby seats look remarkably similar to infant safety seats. These are not crash worthy and should *never* be used as car safety seats.

Convertible Seats: Buying a convertible seat can save you the expense of buying both an infant and a toddler seat. Most convertible seats can be used from birth until the child reaches four years and 40 pounds. When used for an infant, the seat faces rearward in a semi-reclined position. When the child is at least a year old and 20 pounds or more, the frame can be adjusted upright and the seat turned to face forward.

As with any safety seat, it is extremely important that the straps fit snugly over the child's shoulders. A good way to ensure that the straps are adjusted correctly is to buy a seat with an automatically adjusting harness. Like a car safety belt, these models automatically adjust to fit snugly on your child.

Convertible seats come in three basic types:

The *five-point harness* consists of two shoulder and two lap straps that converge at a buckle connected to a crotch strap. These straps are adjustable, allowing for growth and comfort.

The *T-shield* has a small pad joining the shoulder belts. With only one buckle, many parents find this the simplest and easiest-to-use type of convertible seat; but, it will not fit newborns properly.

The *tray shield* is another convenient model, since the safety harness is attached to the shield. As the shield comes down in front of the child, the harness comes over the child's shoulders. The shield is an important part of the restraint system, but like the T-shield, it will not fit small infants.

Toddler-only Seats: These are really booster child seats and they may take the place of convertible seats when a child is between 20 and 30 pounds. Weight and size limits vary greatly among seats.

Child/Booster Seats: Some manufacturers are now making a variety of combination child/booster seats. For example, one model can be converted from a 5-point harness to a high-backed, belt-positioning booster seat. They can be used for children ranging from 20 to 40 pounds, making them a very economical choice.

Booster Seats: Booster seats are used when your child is too big for a convertible seat, but too small to use safety belts. Most car lap/shoulder belts do not adequately fit children with a seating height less than 28". Booster seats can be used for children over 30 pounds and come in three types:

Belt-positioning booster seats raise the child for a better fit with the car's safety belts. If your child is under 3 years old, do not use belt-positioning booster seats because your child may be able to unbuckle him or herself.

The *removable-shield booster seat* can be used with a lap/shoulder belt with the shield removed, or with a lap belt with the shield on. This seat can be adapted to different cars and seating positions, making it a good choice.

The *shield-type booster seat* has a small plastic shield with no straps and can be used only with lap belts. Typically, the safety belt fastens in front of the shield, anchoring it to the car. Most safety experts recommend using these seats until a child is 4 years old and 40 pounds.

Built-in: Chrysler, Ford, GM, and Volvo offer the option of a fold-out toddler seat on some of their models. These seats are only for children older than one and can come as either a five-point harness or a booster with 3-point belt; however, the 3-point booster is not recommended for children under 3 years old. This built-in seat is an excellent feature because it is always in the car and does not pose the problem of comfortability that often occurs with separate child seats.

Name of Seat	Price	Harness Type/Comments
Infant Safety Seats		
Century 565	$40-50	3-pt.; tilt-indicator
Century 590	$60-65	3-pt.; tilt indicator; separate base stays in car; can be used in second car without base
Cosco Arriva	$40-80	3-pt.; detachable base, can use without base, correct recline indicator
Cosco Dream Ride	$60	3-pt.; to 17-20 lbs. (depending on mfg date); use flat as carbed side facing; use as car seat rear facing
Cosco TLC	$25-35	3-pt.
Evenflo Dyn-O-Mite	$25-35	3-pt.; shoulder belt can wrap around back of seat to provide added support
Evenflo Joy Ride	$25-45	3-pt.; shoulder belt wraps around front of seat
Evenflo On My Way	$35-65	3-pt.; detachable base, can use without base
Evenflo Travel Tandem	$35-65	3-pt.; separate base stays in car; can be used in second car without base
Gerry Guard with Glide	$50-70	3-pt.; use as glider in house; must be converted to in-car position
Gerry Secure Ride	$40-50	3-pt.; tilt-indicator
Kolcraft Infant Rider	$60-70	3-pt.; to 18 lbs. only
Kolcraft Rock 'N Ride	$30-50	3-pt.; up to 18 lbs; no harness height adjustment; separate base stays in car; can be used in second car without base
Convertible Safety Seats		
Babyhood Baby Sitter	$90	5-pt.
Century 1000 STE	$50-75	5-pt.; adjustable crotch strap positions
Century 2000 STE	$60-85	T-shield; adjustable crotch strap positions
Century 3000 STE	$70-85	Tray shield; adjustable crotch strap positions
Century 5000 STE	$90-100	Tray shield; adjustable crotch strap positions
Century Smart Move	$120-130	5-pt.; tray shield; adjustable shield grows with child
Cosco Touriva 5-pt.	$50-80	5-pt.
Cosco Touriva Overhead	$60-100	Tray-shield; adjustable shield in luxury model
Cosco Touriva Soft Shield	$70-100	T-shield
Evenflo Champion	$50-70	Tray shield; optional tether available

Based on data collected by the American Academy of Pediatrics.

Name of Seat	Price	Harness Type/Comments
Convertible Safety Seats cont'd.		
Evenflo Scout	$40-60	T-shield/5-pt.; optional tether available
Evenflo Trooper	$40-70	5-pt or Tray shield, optional tether available
Evenflo Ultra I, Premier	$60-110	Tray shield; adjustable shield
Evenflo Ultra V, Premier	$65-110	5-pt.; optional tether available
Gerry Guard SecureLock	$80-90	Tray shield/Automatic/harness adjustment
Gerry Pro-Tech	$70	5-pt.; automatic harness adjustment
Kolcraft Auto-Mate	$50-70	5-pt.; requires 2-handed operation
Kolcraft Traveler 700	$80-90	Tray shield; requires 2-handed operation
Safeline Sit 'N Stroll	$150-170	5-pt.; converts to stroller
Toddler-Only Vests and Built-In Seats		
Chrysler Built-In Seat	$100-200	5-pt. (20-40 lbs.); built in option in Minivans; one converts; to belt-positioning booster (40 lbs.); in sedan, adjust to fit child (20-65 lbs.)
E-Z-On Vest	$60	4-pt. (25+ lbs.); tether strap must be installed in vehicle
Ford Built-In	$225	5-pt. (20-60 lbs.); in minivan
GM Built-In	$125-225	5-pt. (20-40 lbs., Booster 40-60 lbs.); manual harness adjustment
Little Cargo Travel Vest	$40-50	5-pt.; (25-40 lbs.); simplified strap-buckle system;auto lap belt attached through padded stress plate
Booster		

Name of Seat	Price	Belt Position/Comments
Century Breverra	$60-70	Belt through base when used with shield; belt positioning booster seat with lap/shoulder belt
Cosco Explorer	$25-30	Wrap-around/seat has high back to support child's neck and head.
Fisher-Price T-Shield	$45-50	Wrap-around /Belt positioning booster for hip/shoulder belt (30-60 lbs.); shield with crotch post for lap belt (40-60 lbs.)
Gerry Double Guard	$50-55	Wrap-around/Belt through base with shield for lap belt; belt positioning booster for lap shoulder use; internal lap strap
Kolcraft Tot Rider II	$30-40	Wrap-around/Belt positioning booster seat with lap/shoulder belt; shield with crotch post for lap belt

Based on data collected by the American Academy of Pediatrics.

Tips for Using Your Child Safety Seat

The incorrect use of child safety seats has reached epidemic proportions. Problems fall into two categories: incorrect installation of the seat and incorrect use of the seat's straps to secure the child. Over 75 percent of seats in a national survey were incorrectly installed. In the vast majority of these, the car's safety belt was improperly routed through the seat.

The incorrect use of a child safety seat can deny a child life-saving protection and may even contribute to further injury. In addition to following your seat's installation instructions, here are some important usage tips:

☑ The safest place for the seat is the center of the back seat.

☑ Use a locking clip when needed. Check the instructions that come with your seat and those in your car owner's manual.

☑ Keep your child rear-facing for at least a year.

☑ Never place a rear-facing child seat in a seat protected by an airbag.

☑ Regularly check the seat's safety harness and the car's seat belt for a tight, secure fit because the straps will stretch on impact.

☑ Don't leave sharp or heavy objects or groceries loose in the car. Anything loose can be deadly in a crash.

☑ In the winter, dress your baby in a legged suit to allow proper attachment of the harness. If necessary, drape an extra blanket over the seat after your baby is buckled.

☑ Be sure all doors are locked.

☑ Do not give your child lollipops or ice cream on a stick while riding. A bump or swerve could jam the stick into his or her throat.

Buckled Up = Better Behavior: Medical researchers have concluded that belted children are better behaved. When not buckled up, children squirm, stand up, complain, fight, and pull at the steering wheel. When buckled into safety seats, however, they displayed 95 percent fewer incidents of bad behavior.

Children behave better when buckled up because they feel secure. In addition, being in a seat can be more fun because most safety seats are high enough to allow children to see out the window. Also, children are less likely to feel carsick and more likely to fall asleep in a car seat.

Make the car seat your child's own special place, so he or she will enjoy being in it. Pick out some special soft toys or books that can be used only in the car seat to make using the seat a positive experience.

Set a good example for your child by using your own safety belt every time you get in the car.

Safety Belts for Kids: Normally, children under 40 pounds should always be in a child safety seat. If no seat is available, use a safety belt if the child is able to sit up unsupported.

When your child outgrows the safety seat, he or she should always use the car's safety belt. The belt should be snug and as low on the hips as possible. If the shoulder belt crosses the face or neck, it is best to use a belt-positioning booster; otherwise, place the shoulder strap behind the child's back. Never use pillows or cushions to boost your child. In an accident, they may let the child slide under the lap belt or allow the child's head to strike the car's interior.

Never put a belt around yourself with a child in your lap. In an accident or sudden stop, both your weight and the child's would be forced into the belt, with the child absorbing a much greater share of the crash force. The pressure could push the belt deep into the child's body, causing severe injury or death.

Strapping two children into one belt can also be very dangerous—it makes proper fit impossible.

Rear-facing Child Safety Seats

Never use a rear-facing child safety seat in a seating position that has an airbag. To deploy fast enough to protect adult occupants, an airbag inflates with enough force to potentially cause serious head and chest injuries to a child in a rear-facing safety seat. And remember, airbags do not take the place of child safety seats.

Child Restraint Laws

Every state now requires children to be in safety seats or buckled up when riding in automobiles. The following table provides an overview of the requirements and penalties in each state. Note that most states use the child's age to define the law, although some states have height or weight requirements as well. Also, in most states, the laws are not limited to children riding with their parents, but require that any driver with child passengers makes sure those children are buckled up.

	Law Applies To:	Children Covered Through:	Max. Fine 1st Offense	Safety Belt OK:
Alabama	All drivers	5 yrs.	$10	4-5 yrs.
Alaska	All drivers	15 yrs.	$50	4-15 yrs.
Arizona	All drivers	4 yrs. or 40 lbs.	$50	No
Arkansas	All drivers	4 yrs. or 40 lbs.	$25	4 yrs.
California	All drivers	15 yrs.	$100	4-15 yrs.
Colorado	All drivers	15 yrs.	$50	4-15 yrs., over 40 lbs.
Connecticut	All drivers	3 yrs. or 40 lbs.	$90	40 lbs.+
Delaware	All drivers	15 yrs..	$29	4-15 yrs.
Dist. of Columbia	All drivers	15 yrs.	$55	3-15 yrs.
Florida	All drivers	5 yrs.	$155	4-5 yrs.
Georgia	All drivers	4 yrs.	$25	3-4 yrs.
Hawaii	All drivers	3 yrs.	$100	3 yrs. only
Idaho	All drivers	3 yrs. or 40 lbs.	$52	No
Illinois	All drivers	5 yrs.	$25	4-5 yrs.
Indiana	All drivers	4 yrs.	$500	3-4 yrs.
Iowa	All drivers	5 yrs.	$10	3-5 yrs.
Kansas	All drivers	13 yrs.	$20	4-13 yrs.
Kentucky	All drivers	Under 40 inches	$50	No
Louisiana	Resident drivers	4 yrs.	$50	3-4 yrs. in rear
Maine	All drivers	18 yrs.	$55	4-18 yrs.
Maryland	All drivers	9 yrs.	$25	4-9 yrs., over 40 lbs.
Massachusetts	All drivers	11 yrs.	$25	All ages
Michigan	All drivers	3 yrs.	$10	1-3 yrs. in rear
Minnesota	All drivers	3 yrs.	$50	No
Mississippi	All drivers	3 yrs.	$25	No

Child Restraint Laws

	Law Applies To:	Children Covered Through:	Max. Fine 1st Offense	Safety Belt OK:
Missouri	All drivers	3 yrs.	$25	All ages in rear
Montana	Resident Parent/Guardian[1]	3 yrs. or 40 lbs.	$25	2-3 yrs.
Nebraska	Resident drivers	4 yrs.	$25	4 yrs., over 40 lbs.
Nevada	All drivers	4 yrs. or 40 lbs.	$100	No
New Hampshire	All drivers	11 yrs.	$43	4-11 yrs.
New Jersey	All drivers	4 yrs.	$25	11/2-4 yrs. in rear
New Mexico	All drivers	10 yrs.	$25	1-4 yrs. in rear[2]
New York	All drivers	15 yrs.[3]	$100	4-10 yrs. in rear
North Carolina	All drivers	11 yrs.	$25	4-11 yrs.
North Dakota	All drivers	10 yrs.	$20	3-10 yrs.
Ohio	All drivers	3 yrs. or 40 lbs.	$100	No
Oklahoma	Resident drivers	5 yrs.	$25	4-5 yrs.
Oregon	All drivers	15 yrs.	$95	4-15 yrs.
Pennsylvania	All drivers	3 yrs.	$25	No
Rhode Island	All drivers	12 yrs.	$30	3-12 yrs.
South Carolina	All drivers	5 yrs.	$25	1-5 yrs. in rear[4]
South Dakota	All drivers	4 yrs.	$20	2-4 yrs.
Tennessee	All drivers	12 yrs.	$10	4-12 yrs.
Texas	All drivers	3 yrs.	$50	2-3 yrs.
Utah	All drivers	7 yrs.	$20	2-7 yrs.
Vermont	All drivers	12 yrs.	$25	5-12 yrs.
Virginia	Parent/Guardian	3 yrs.	$50	No
Washington	All drivers	9 yrs.	$47	3-9 yrs.
West Virginia	All drivers	8 yrs.	$20	3-8 yrs.
Wisconsin	All drivers	7 yrs.	$75	4-7 yrs.
Wyoming	Parent/Guardian[1]	2 yrs.[5]	$25	1-2 yrs.

[1] In own car only.
[2] 5-10 year olds in all seats
[3] 9 year olds in rear
[4] 4-5 year olds in front seat
[5] 3 yrs. if less than 40 lbs.

FUEL ECONOMY

A car's fuel efficiency affects both our environment and our wallets—which is why comparative mileage ratings are an important factor to most consumers. To save money and the environment, the first and most obvious step is to select a car that gets high mileage, so we've included the Environmental Protection Agency's fuel economy ratings for all 1996 vehicles. We also discuss numerous factors that affect your car's fuel efficiency, and caution you against the many products that falsely promise more gas mileage.

Using EPA ratings is an excellent way to incorporate fuel efficiency in selecting a new car. By comparing these ratings, even among cars of the same size, you'll find that fuel efficiency varies greatly. One compact car might get 36 miles per gallon (mpg) while another gets only 22 mpg. If you drive 15,000 miles a year and you pay $1.20 per gallon for fuel, the 36 mpg car will save you $319 a year over the "gas guzzler."

Octane Ratings: Once you've purchased your car, you'll be faced with choosing the right gasoline. Oil companies spend millions of dollars trying to get you to buy so-called higher performance or high octane fuels. Because high octane fuel can add considerably to your gas bill, it is important that you know what you're buying.

The octane rating of a gasoline is *not* a measure of power or quality. It is simply a measure of the gas's resistance to engine knock, which is the pinging sound you hear when the air and fuel mixture in your engine ignites prematurely during acceleration.

The octane rating appears on a yellow label on the fuel pump. Octane ratings vary with different types of gas (premium or regular), in different parts of the country (higher altitudes require lower octane ratings), and even between brands (Texaco's gasolines may have a different rating than Exxon's).

Determining the Right Octane Rating for Your Car: Using a lower-rated gasoline saves money. Most cars are designed to run on a posted octane rating of 87. The following procedure can help you select the lowest octane level for your car.

1 Have your engine tuned to exact factory specifications by a competent mechanic, and make sure it is in good working condition.

2 When the gas in your tank is very low, fill it up with your usual gasoline. After driving 10 to 15 miles, find a safe place to come to a complete stop and then accelerate rapidly. If your engine knocks during acceleration, switch to a higher octane rating. If there is no knocking sound, wait until your tank is very low and fill up with a lower rated gasoline. Repeat the test. When you determine the level of octane that causes your engine to knock during the test, use gasoline with the next highest rating.

Note: Your engine may knock when accelerating a heavily loaded car uphill or when the humidity is low. This is normal and does not call for a higher-octane gasoline.

Factors Affecting Fuel Economy

Fuel economy is affected by a number of factors that you can consider before you buy.

Transmission: Manual transmissions are generally more fuel-efficient than automatic transmissions. In fact, a four-speed manual transmission can add up to 6.5 miles per gallon over a three-speed automatic. However, the incorrect use of a manual transmission wastes gas, so choose a transmission that matches your preference. Many transmissions now feature an overdrive gear, which can improve a vehicle's fuel economy by as much as 9 percent for an automatic transmission and 3 percent for a manual transmission.

Engine: The size of your car's engine greatly affects your fuel economy. The smaller your engine, the better your fuel efficiency. A 10-percent increase in the size of an engine can increase fuel consumption by 6 percent.

Cruise Control: Cruise control can save fuel because driving at a constant speed uses less fuel than changing speeds frequently.

Air Conditioning: Auto air conditioners add weight and require additional horsepower to operate. They can cost up to 3 miles per gallon in city driving. At highway speeds, however, an air conditioner has about the same effect on fuel economy as the air resistance created by opening the windows.

Trim Package: Upgrading a car's trim, installing soundproofing, and adding undercoating can increase the weight of a typical car by 150 pounds. For each 10 percent increase in weight, fuel economy drops 4 percent.

Power Options: Power steering, brakes, seats, windows, and roofs reduce your mileage by adding weight. Power steering alone can cause a 1-percent drop in fuel economy.

Here are some tips for after you buy:

Tune-Up: If you have a 2 to 3 mpg drop over several fill-ups that is not due to a change of driving pattern or vehicle load, first check tire pressure, then consider a tune-up. A properly tuned engine is a fuel saver.

Tire Inflation: For maximum fuel efficiency, tires should be inflated to the top of the pressure range stamped on the sidewall. Check tire pressure when the tires are cold—before you've driven a long distance.

Short Trips: Short trips can be expensive because they usually involve a "cold" vehicle. For the first mile or two, a cold vehicle gets 30- to 40-percent of the mileage it gets when fully warm.

Using Oxyfuels

Today's gasoline contains a bewildering array of ingredients touted as octane boosters or pollution fighters. Some urban areas with carbon monoxide pollution problems are requiring the use of oxygen-containing components (called oxyfuels) such as ethanol and MTBE (methyl-tertiary-butylether). The use of these compounds is controversial. Some auto companies recommend their use; others caution against them. Most companies approve the use of gasoline with up to 10-percent ethanol, and all approve the use of MTBE up to 15-percent. Many companies recommend against using gasoline with methanol, alleging that it will cause poorer driveability, deterioration of fuel system parts, and reduced fuel economy. These companies may not cover the cost of warranty repairs if these additives are used, so check your owner's manual and warranty to determine what additives are covered. Also check the gas pump, as many states now require the pump to display the percentage of methanol and ethanol in the gasoline.

Products That Don't Work

Hundreds of products on the market claim to improve fuel economy. Not only are most of these products ineffective, some may even damage your engine.

Sometimes the name or promotional material associated with these products implies they were endorsed by the federal government. In fact, no government agency endorses *any* gas saving products. Many of the products, however, *have* been tested by the U. S. EPA.

Of the hundreds of so-called gas saving devices on the market, only five tested by the EPA have been shown to *slightly* improve your fuel economy without increasing harmful emissions. Even these, however, offer limited savings because of their cost. They are the Pass Master Vehicle Air Conditioner P.A.S.S. Kit, Idalert, Morse Constant Speed Accessory Drive, Autotherm, and Kamei Spoilers. We don't recommend these products because the increase in fuel economy is not worth the investment in the product.

Do NOT Buy These Devices

Purported gas-saving devices come in many forms. Listed below are the types of products on the market. Under each category are the names of devices actually reviewed or tested by the EPA for which there was *no evidence of any improvement in fuel economy.*

AIR BLEED DEVICES
ADAKS Vacuum Breaker
Air Bleed
Air-Jet Air Bleed
Aquablast Wyman Valve Air Bleed
Auto Miser
Ball-Matic Air Bleed
Berg Air Bleed
Brisko PCV
Cyclone - Z
Econo Needle Air Bleed
Econo-Jet Air Bleed Idle Screws
Fuel Max
Gas Saving Device
Grancor Air Computer
Hot Tip
Landrum Mini-Carb
Landrum Retrofit Air Bleed
Mini Turbocharger Air Bleed*
Monocar HC Control Air Bleed
Peterman Air Bleed*
Pollution Master Air Bleed
Ram-Jet
Turbo-Dyne G.R. Valve

DRIVING HABIT MODIFIERS
Fuel Conservation Device
Gastell

FUEL LINE DEVICES
Fuel Xpander

Gas Meiser I
Greer Fuel Preheater
Jacona Fuel System
Malpassi Filter King
Moleculetor
Optimizer
Petro-Mizer
Polarion-X
Russell Fuelmiser
Super-Mag Fuel Extender
Wickliff Polarizer

FUELS AND FUEL ADDITIVES
Bycosin*
EI-5 Fuel Additive*
Fuelon Power Gasoline Fuel Additive
Johnson Fuel Additive*
NRG #1 Fuel Additive
QEI 400 Fuel Additive*
Rolfite Upgrade Fuel Additive
Sta-Power Fuel Additive
Stargas Fuel Additive
SYNeRGy-1
Technol G Fuel Additive
ULX-15/ULX-15D
Vareb 10 Fuel Additive*
XRG #1 Fuel Additive

IGNITION DEVICES
Autosaver
Baur Condenser*
BIAP Electronic Ignition Unit

Fuel Economizer
Magna Flash Ignition Ctrl. Sys.
Paser Magnum/Paser 500/ Paser 500 HEI
Special Formula Ignition Advance Springs*

INTERNAL ENGINE MODIFICATIONS
ACDS Auto. Cyl. Deactivation Sys.
Dresser Economizer*
MSU Cylinder Deactivation*

LIQUID INJECTION
Goodman Engine Sys. Model 1800*
Waag-Injection System*

MIXTURE ENHANCERS
Basko Enginecoat
Dresser Economizer
Electro-Dyne Superchoke*
Energy Gas Saver*
Environmental Fuel Saver*
Filtron Urethane Foam Filter*
Gas Saving and Emission Control Improvement Device
Glynn-50*
Hydro-Catalyst Pre-Combustion System
Lamkin Fuel Metering Device

Petromizer System
Sav-A-Mile
Smith Power and Deceleration Governor Spritzer*
Turbo-Carb
Turbocarb

OILS AND OIL ADDITIVES
Analube Synthetic Lubricant
Tephguard*

VAPOR BLEED DEVICES
Atomized Vapor Injector
Econo-Mist Vacuum Vapor Injection System
Frantz Vapor Injection System*
Hydro-Vac
Mark II Vapor Injection System*
Platinum Gasaver
POWER FUeL
Scatpac Vacuum Vapor Induction System
Turbo Vapor Injection System*
V-70 Vapor Injector

MISCELLANEOUS
Brake-Ez*
Dynamix
Fuel Maximiser
Gyroscopic Wheel Cover
Kat's Engine Heater
Lee Exhaust and Fuel Gasification EGR*
Mesco Moisture Extraction Sys.
P.S.C.U. 01 Device
Treis Emulsifier

* For copies of reports on these products, write Test and Evaluation Branch, U.S. EPA, 2565 Plymouth Rd., Ann Arbor, MI 48105. For the other products, contact the National Technical Information Service, Springfield, VA 22161. (703-487-4650).

Fuel Economy Ratings

Every year the Department of Energy publishes the results of the Environmental Protection Agency's fuel economy tests in a comparative guide. In the past, millions of these booklets have been distributed to consumers who are eager to purchase fuel-efficient automobiles. However, the government has recently limited the availability of the guide. Because the success of the EPA program depends on consumers' ability to compare the fuel economy ratings easily, we have reprinted the EPA mileage figures for this year's cars.

The mileage estimates below and on the next few pages are the EPA city and highway figures.

A Note about the Ratings: When the EPA figures were first released, they were best used to compare fuel efficiency among vehicles—not to predict expected mileage. Because of changes in how the EPA presents the mileage ratings, these figures should better predict your expected mileage. When buying a car, however, it's still best to use the EPA mileage estimates on a relative basis: if one car is rated at 20 mpg and another at 25, the 25 mpg car will nearly always perform better than the 20 mpg car.

1996 Fuel Economy Winners and Losers

The Misers	MPG City /Highway	Annual Fuel Cost[1]
Geo Metro (1.0L/3/M5)*	44/49	$391
Honda Civic HB HX (1.6L/4/M5)*	39/45	$439
Geo Metro (1.3L/4/M5)*	39/43	$439
Suzuki Swift (1.3L/4/M5)*	39/43	$439
Honda Civic HX (1.6L/4/AV)*	35/39	$486
Ford Aspire (1.3L/4/M5)	34/42	$486
Toyota Tercel (1.5L/4/M4)	34/40	$500
Honda del Sol (1.6L/4/M5)	34/39	$500
Honda Civic (1.6L/4/M5)	33/38	$515
Mitsubishi Mirage (1.5L/4/M5)	32/39	$515
Mazda Protege (1.5L/4/M5)	32/39	$515
Eagle Summit (1.5L/4/M5)	32/39	$515

The Guzzlers		
Lamborghini DB132/Diablo (5.7L/12/M5)	9/14	$1841
Rolls Royce Silver Spur Limo (6.8L/8/L4)	11/15	$1557
Rolls Royce Bentley Limo (6.8L/8/L4)	11/15	$1557
Rolls Royce Bentley Azure (6.8L/8/L4)	11/15	$1557
Rolls Royce Bentley Continental (6.8L/8/L4)	11/15	$1557
Rolls Royce Turbo R/Turbo RL (6.8L/8/L4)	11/16	$1557
Jaguar XJ12 (6.0L/12/L4)	12/16	$1446
Rolls Royce Bentley Brookland/LWB (6.8L/8/L4)	12/17	$1446
Rolls Royce Silver Spur/Silver Dawn (6.8L/8/L4)	12/17	$1446
Mercedes-Benz S600 (6.0L/12/A5)	13/19	$1351
Porsche 911 Turbo (3.6L/12/M6)	13/19	$1351

Based on 1996 EPA figures. (Engine size/number of cylinders/transmission type)

[1] Based on driving 15,000 miles per year.

* These models have "shift indicator" lights.

1996 EPA Figures

The following pages contain the EPA mileage ratings and the average annual fuel cost for most of the cars and many popular trucks sold in the United States. We have arranged the list in alphabetical order. After the car name, we have listed the engine size in liters, the number of cylinders, and some other iden-

tifiers: A = automatic transmission; L = lockup transmission; M = manual transmission. (G) after the engine description means that buyers will have to pay a "Gas Guzzler" tax.

The table includes the EPA city (first) and highway (second) fuel economy ratings. The city numbers will most closely resemble

your expected mileage for everyday driving. The third column presents your average annual fuel cost. Reviewing this number will give you a better idea of how differences in fuel economy can affect your pocketbook. The amount is based on driving 15,000 miles per year.

Car (eng./trans.)	City	Hwy	Cost	Car (eng./trans.)	City	Hwy	Cost
Acura Integra (1.8L/4/L4)	24	31	$ 666	**Buick Riviera** (3.8L/6/L4)	19	29	$ 783
Acura Integra (1.8L/4/M5)	25	31	$ 723	**Buick Roadmaster** (5.7L/8/L4)	17	26	$ 900
Acura Integra (1.8L/4/M5)	25	31	$ 643	**Buick Roadmaster Wgn** (5.7L/8/L4)	17	26	$ 900
Acura NSX (3.0L/6/L4)	18	24	$1012	**Buick Skylark Skylark** (2.4L/4/L4)	22	32	$ 693
Acura NSX (3.0L/6/M5)	18	24	$1012	**Buick Skylark Skylark** (3.1L/6/L4)	21	29	$ 751
Acura SLX (3.2L/6/L4)	14	18	$1125	**Cadillac DeVille** (4.6L/8/L4)	17	26	$1012
Acura SLX (3.2L/6/M5)	15	18	$1125	**Cadillac Eldorado** (4.6L/8/L4)	17	26	$1012
Acura TL (2.5L/5/L4)	20	25	$ 921	**Cadillac Fleetwood** (5.7L/8/L4)	17	26	$ 900
Acura TL (3.2L/6/L4)	19	24	$ 964	**Cadillac Seville** (4.6L/8/L4)	17	26	$1012
Audi A4 (2.8L/6/L5)	18	28	$ 921	**Chevy Astro** (4.3L/6/L4)	16	20	$1001
Audi A4 (2.8L/6/M5)	19	27	$ 921	**Chevy Astro** (4.3L/6/L4)	16	21	$1001
Audi A4 Quatro (2.8L/6/L5)	18	27	$ 964	**Chevy Astro** (4.3L/6/L4)	15	19	$1058
Audi A4 Quatro (2.8L/6/M5)	19	27	$ 964	**Chevy Astro** (4.3L/6/L4)	17	22	$ 947
Audi A6 (2.8L/6/L4)	19	25	$ 964	**Chevy Beretta** (2.2L/4/L3)	24	31	$ 666
Audi A6 Quatro (2.8L/6/L4)	19	24	$ 964	**Chevy Beretta** (2.2L/4/M5)	25	37	$ 621
Audi A6 Quattro Wgn (2.8L/6/L4)	19	24	$ 964	**Chevy Beretta** (3.1L/6/L4)	21	29	$ 751
Audi A6 Wgn (2.8L/6/L4)	19	25	$ 964	**Chevy Camaro** (3.8L/6/L4)	19	29	$ 819
Audi Cabriolet (2.8L/6/L4)	19	24	$ 964	**Chevy Camaro** (3.8L/6/M5)	19	30	$ 783
BMW 328i (2.8L/6/L4)	20	27	$ 921	**Chevy Camaro** (5.7L/8/L4)	17	25	$ 900
BMW 328i (2.8L/6/M5)	20	29	$ 881	**Chevy Camaro** (5.7L/8/M6)	16	27	$ 900
BMW 328i Conv. (2.8L/6/L4)	20	27	$ 921	**Chevy Caprice** (4.3L/8/L4)	18	26	$ 857
BMW 328i Conv. (2.8L/6/M5)	20	29	$ 881	**Chevy Caprice** (5.7L/8/L4)	17	26	$ 900
BMW 750il (5.4L/12/L5) (G)	15	20	$1191	**Chevy Caprice Wgn** (5.7L/8/L4)	17	26	$ 900
BMW 850ci (5.4L/12/L5) (G)	14	20	$1266	**Chevy Cavalier** (2.2L/4/L3)	24	31	$ 666
Buick Century (2.2L/4/L3)	24	31	$ 666	**Chevy Cavalier** (2.2L/4/L4)	25	34	$ 643
Buick Century (3.1L/6/L4)	20	29	$ 783	**Chevy Cavalier** (2.2L/4/M5)	25	37	$ 621
Buick Century Wgn (3.1L/6/L4)	20	29	$ 783	**Chevy Cavalier** (2.4L/4/L4)	22	32	$ 693
Buick LeSabre (3.8L/6/L4)	19	30	$ 783	**Chevy Cavalier** (2.4L/4/M5)	23	33	$ 693
Buick Park Avenue (3.8L/6/L4)	18	27	$ 964	**Chevy Corsica** (2.2L/4/L3)	24	31	$ 666
Buick Park Avenue (3.8L/6/L4)	19	29	$ 783	**Chevy Corsica** (3.1L/6/L4)	21	29	$ 751
Buick Regal (3.1L/6/L4)	20	29	$ 783	**Chevy Corvette** (5.7L/8/L4)	17	25	$ 900
Buick Regal (3.8L/6/L4)	19	30	$ 783	**Chevy Corvette** (5.7L/8/M6)	16	27	$1012
Buick Riviera (3.8L/6/L4)	18	27	$ 964	**Chevy Lumina** (3.1L/6/L4)	20	29	$ 783

Car (eng./trans.)	City	Hwy	Cost
Chevy Lumina (3.4L/6/L4)	17	26	$ 900
Chevy Lumina MV 2wd (3.4L/5/L4)	19	26	$ 857
Chry. Cirrus (2.4L/4/L4)	20	29	$ 751
Chry. Cirrus (2.5L/6/L4)	20	28	$ 783
Chry. Concorde (3.3L/6/L4)	19	27	$ 819
Chry. Concorde (3.5L/6/L4)	18	26	$ 900
Chry. LHS/New Yorker (3.5L/6/L4)	18	26	$ 900
Chry. Sebring (2.0L/4/L4)	21	30	$ 751
Chry. Sebring (2.0L/4/M5)	22	31	$ 720
Chry. Sebring (2.5L/6/L4)	20	27	$ 819
Chry. Sebring Conv. (2.4L/4/L4)	20	29	$ 751
Chry. Sebring Conv. (2.5L/6/L4)	20	28	$ 783
Chry. T&C (3.3L/6/L4)	17	24	$ 900
Chry. T&C (3.8L/6/L4)	16	22	$1001
Chry. T&C (3.8L/6/L4)	17	24	$ 900
Dodge Avenger (2.0L/4/L4)	21	30	$ 751
Dodge Avenger (2.0L/4/M5)	22	32	$ 720
Dodge Avenger (2.5L/6/L4)	20	27	$ 819
Dodge Caravan 2wd (2.4L/4/L3)	20	26	$ 819
Dodge Caravan 2wd (3.0L/6/L3)	19	25	$ 857
Dodge Caravan 2wd (3.3L/6/L4)	18	24	$ 900
Dodge Caravan 2wd (3.8L/6/L4)	17	24	$ 900
Dodge Caravan 4wd (3.8L/6/L4)	16	22	$1001
Dodge Intrepid (3.3L/6/L4)	19	27	$ 819
Dodge Intrepid (3.5L/6/L4)	18	26	$ 857
Dodge Intrepid (3.5L/6/L4)	17	26	$ 900
Dodge/Plym. Neon (2.0L/4/L3)	25	33	$ 643
Dodge/Plym. Neon (2.0L/4/L3)	25	33	$ 643
Dodge/Plym. Neon (2.0L/4/M5)	28	38	$ 562
Dodge/Plym. Neon (2.0L/4/M5)	28	38	$ 562
Dodge Stealth (3.0L/6/L4)	18	23	$ 900
Dodge Stealth (3.0L/6/L4)	18	24	$1012
Dodge Stealth (3.0L/6/M5)	19	24	$ 857
Dodge Stealth (3.0L/6/M5)	19	25	$ 964
Dodge Stealth (3.0L/6/M6)	18	24	$1012
Dodge Stratus (2.0L/4/M5)	25	36	$ 621
Dodge Stratus (2.4L/4/L4)	20	29	$ 751
Dodge Stratus (2.5L/6/L4)	20	28	$ 783
Dodge Viper (8.0L/10/M6) (G)	13	21	$1266
Eagle Summit (1.5L/4/A3)	28	32	$ 599
Eagle Summit (1.5L/4/M5)	32	39	$ 515
Eagle Summit (1.8L/4/L4)	26	33	$ 621
Eagle Summit (1.8L/4/M5)	26	33	$ 621

Car (eng./trans.)	City	Hwy	Cost
Eagle Summit Wgn (1.8L/4/L4)	23	29	$ 720
Eagle Summit Wgn (1.8L/4/M5)	24	29	$ 693
Eagle Summit Wgn (2.4L/4/L4)	18	23	$ 900
Eagle Summit Wgn (2.4L/4/L4)	20	26	$ 819
Eagle Summit Wgn (2.4L/4/M5)	22	27	$ 751
Eagle Summit Wgn (2.4L/4/M5)	20	24	$ 819
Eagle Talon (2.0L/4/L4)	20	27	$ 881
Eagle Talon (2.0L/4/L4)	19	25	$ 964
Eagle Talon (2.0L/4/L4)	20	30	$ 751
Eagle Talon (2.0L/4/M5)	21	28	$ 844
Eagle Talon (2.0L/4/M5)	22	32	$ 693
Eagle Talon (2.0L/4/M5)	23	31	$ 780
Eagle Vision (3.3L/6/L4)	19	27	$ 819
Eagle Vision (3.5L/6/L4)	18	26	$ 900
Eagle Vision (3.5L/6/L4)	17	26	$ 900
Ford Aerostar (3.0L/6/L4)	18	24	$ 900
Ford Aerostar (4.0L/6/L4)	15	20	$1058
Ford Aerostar (4.0L/6/L4)	17	23	$ 947
Ford Aspire (1.3L/4/L3)	29	34	$ 581
Ford Aspire (1.3L/4/M5)	34	42	$ 486
Ford Contour (2.0L/4/L4)	23	32	$ 693
Ford Contour (2.0L/4/M5)	24	34	$ 643
Ford Contour (2.5L/6/L4)	21	30	$ 751
Ford Contour (2.5L/6/M5)	21	31	$ 751
Ford Crown Victoria (4.6L/8/L4)	17	23	$ 947
Ford Crown Victoria (4.6L/8/L4)	17	25	$ 900
Ford Crown Victoria (4.6L/8/L4)	17	26	$ 533
Ford Escort (1.8L/4/L4)	23	29	$ 720
Ford Escort (1.8L/4/M5)	25	31	$ 666
Ford Escort (1.9L/4/M5)	31	38	$ 529
Ford Escort Wgn (1.9L/4/M5)	31	38	$ 529
Ford Mustang (3.8L/6/L4)	20	30	$ 783
Ford Mustang (3.8L/6/M5)	20	30	$ 751
Ford Mustang (4.6L/8/L4)	17	24	$ 900
Ford Mustang (4.6L/8/M5)	18	26	$ 964
Ford Mustang (4.6L/8/M5)	18	27	$ 857
Ford Probe (2.0L/4/L4)	23	31	$ 693
Ford Probe (2.0L/4/M5)	26	33	$ 621
Ford Probe (2.5L/6/L4)	20	26	$ 921
Ford Probe (2.5L/6/M5)	21	27	$ 881
Ford Taurus (3.0L/6/L4)	20	29	$ 783
Ford Taurus (3.0L/6/L4)	20	29	$ 783
Ford Taurus Wgn (3.0L/6/L4)	19	27	$ 819

Car (eng./trans.)	City	Hwy	Cost
Ford Taurus Wgn (3.0L/6/L4)	19	28	$ 819
Ford Thunderbird (3.8L/6/L4)	19	26	$ 857
Ford Thunderbird (4.6L/8/L4)	17	25	$ 900
Ford Windstar Fwd Van (3.0L/6/L4)	17	25	$ 900
Ford Windstar Fwd Van (3.8L/6/L4)	17	23	$ 900
Ford Windstar Fwd Wgn (3.0L/6/L4)	17	25	$ 900
Ford Windstar Fwd Wgn (3.8L/6/L4)	17	23	$ 900
GMC Safari 2wd Cargo (4.3L/6/L4)	17	22	$ 947
GMC Safari 2wd Pass. (4.3L/6/L4)	16	20	$1001
GMC Safari AWD Cargo (4.3L/6/L4)	16	21	$1001
GMC Safari AWD Pass. (4.3L/6/L4)	15	19	$1058
Geo Metro (1.0L/3/M5)	44	49	$ 391
Geo Metro (1.3L/4/A3)	30	34	$ 562
Geo Metro (1.3L/4/M5)	39	43	$ 439
Geo Prizm (1.6L/4/L3)	26	30	$ 666
Geo Prizm (1.6L/4/M5)	31	35	$ 562
Geo Prizm (1.8L/4/L4)	27	34	$ 599
Geo Prizm (1.8L/4/M5)	29	34	$ 581
Honda Accord (2.2L/4/L4)	23	31	$ 693
Honda Accord (2.2L/4/L4)	23	29	$ 720
Honda Accord (2.2L/4/M5)	25	32	$ 643
Honda Accord (2.2L/4/M5)	25	31	$ 666
Honda Accord (2.7L/6/L4)	19	25	$ 857
Honda Accord Wgn (2.2L/4/L4)	21	27	$ 783
Honda Accord Wgn (2.2L/4/L4)	23	29	$ 720
Honda Accord Wgn (2.2L/4/M5)	23	28	$ 720
Honda Civic (1.6L/4/L4)	28	35	$ 581
Honda Civic (1.6L/4/L4)	29	36	$ 562
Honda Civic (1.6L/4/M5)	30	36	$ 562
Honda Civic (1.6L/4/M5)	33	38	$ 515
Honda Civic HX (1.6L/4/AV)	35	39	$ 486
Honda Civic HX (1.6L/4/M5)	39	45	$ 439
Honda del Sol (1.6L/4/L4)	28	35	$ 581
Honda del Sol (1.6L/4/L4)	29	36	$ 562
Honda del Sol (1.6L/4/M5)	30	36	$ 562
Honda del Sol (1.6L/4/M5)	34	39	$ 500
Honda del Sol (1.6L/4/M5)	26	30	$ 723
Honda Odyssey (2.2L/4/L4)	20	24	$ 819
Honda Prelude (2.2L/4/L4)	22	27	$ 751
Honda Prelude (2.2L/4/M5)	24	29	$ 693
Honda Prelude (2.2L/4/M5)	22	26	$ 881
Honda Prelude (2.3L/4/L4)	21	26	$ 881
Honda Prelude (2.3L/4/M5)	22	27	$ 844

Car (eng./trans.)	City	Hwy	Cost
Hyundai Accent (1.5L/4/L4)	27	36	$ 599
Hyundai Accent (1.5L/4/L4)	26	34	$ 621
Hyundai Accent (1.5L/4/M5)	28	37	$ 562
Hyundai Accent (1.5L/4/M5)	27	35	$ 599
Hyundai Accent Sporty (1.5L/4/L4)	25	33	$ 643
Hyundai Accent Sporty (1.5L/4/M5)	27	35	$ 599
Hyundai Sonata (2.0L/4/L4)	21	29	$ 751
Hyundai Sonata (2.0L/4/M5)	22	28	$ 751
Infiniti G20 (2.0L/4/L4)	22	28	$ 720
Infiniti G20 (2.0L/4/M5)	24	32	$ 666
Infiniti I30 (3.0L/6/L4)	21	28	$ 881
Infiniti I30 (3.0L/6/M5)	21	26	$ 881
Infiniti J30 (3.0L/6/L4)	18	23	$1012
Infiniti Q45 (4.5L/8/L4)	17	22	$1065
Isuzu Oasis (2.2L/4/L4)	20	24	$ 819
Jaguar Vanden Plas (4.0L/6/L4)	17	23	$1065
Jaguar XJ12 (6.0L/12/L4) (G)	12	16	$1446
Jaguar XJ6 (4.0L/6/L4)	17	23	$1065
Kia Sephia (1.6L/4/L4)	24	31	$ 666
Kia Sephia (1.6L/4/M5)	28	34	$ 599
Kia Sephia (1.8L/4/L4)	21	28	$ 751
Kia Sephia (1.8L/4/M5)	25	30	$ 666
Lamb. DB132/Diablo (5.7L/12/M5) (G)	9	14	$1841
Lexus ES300 (3.0L/6/L4)	20	29	$ 783
Lexus GS300 (3.0L/6/L5)	18	24	$1012
Lexus LS400 (4.0L/8/L4)	19	26	$ 921
Lexus SC300/400 (3.0L/6/L4)	18	24	$1012
Lexus SC300/400 (3.0L/6/M5)	19	24	$ 964
Lexus SC300/400 (4.0L/8/L4)	18	23	$1012
Lincoln Continental (4.6L/8/L4)	17	25	$1012
Lincoln Mark VIII (4.6L/8/L4)	18	26	$ 964
Lincoln Town Car (4.6L/8/L4)	17	25	$ 900
Mazda 626 (2.0L/4/L4)	23	31	$ 693
Mazda 626 (2.0L/4/M5)	26	34	$ 621
Mazda 626 (2.5L/6/L4)	20	26	$ 921
Mazda 626 (2.5L/6/M5)	21	26	$ 881
Mazda Miata (1.8L/4/L4)	22	28	$ 751
Mazda Miata (1.8L/4/M5)	23	29	$ 720
Mazda Millenia (2.3L/6/L4)	20	28	$ 921
Mazda Millenia (2.5L/6/L4)	20	27	$ 921
Mazda MPV (3.0L/6/L4)	16	22	$1001
Mazda MPV (3.0L/6/L4)	15	19	$1125
Mazda MX-3 (1.6L/4/L4)	26	34	$ 621

Car (eng./trans.)	City	Hwy	Cost	Car (eng./trans.)	City	Hwy	Cost
Mazda MX-3 (1.6L/4/M5)	30	37	$ 545	Mitsu. 3000GT (3.0L/6/L4)	18	24	$1012
Mazda MX-3 (1.8L/6/L4)	20	27	$ 783	Mitsu. 3000GT (3.0L/6/L4)	19	24	$ 964
Mazda MX-3 (1.8L/6/M5)	23	29	$ 720	Mitsu. 3000GT (3.0L/6/M5)	19	25	$ 964
Mazda MX-6 (2.0L/4/L4)	23	31	$ 693	Mitsu. 3000GT (3.0L/6/M6)	17	25	$1012
Mazda MX-6 (2.0L/4/M5)	26	34	$ 621	Mitsu. 3000GT (3.0L/6/M6)	18	24	$1012
Mazda MX-6 (2.5L/6/L4)	20	26	$ 921	Mitsu. Diamante (3.0L/6/L4)	18	24	$1012
Mazda MX-6 (2.5L/6/M5)	21	26	$ 881	Mitsu. Diamante (3.0L/6/L4)	18	25	$ 964
Mazda Protege (1.5L/4/L4)	27	35	$ 599	Mitsu. Eclipse (2.0L/4/L4)	20	30	$ 751
Mazda Protege (1.5L/4/M5)	32	39	$ 515	Mitsu. Eclipse (2.0L/4/L4)	19	25	$ 964
Mazda Protege (1.8L/4/L4)	23	30	$ 720	Mitsu. Eclipse (2.0L/4/L4)	20	27	$ 881
Mazda Protege (1.8L/4/M5)	26	33	$ 643	Mitsu. Eclipse (2.0L/4/M5)	23	31	$ 780
Merc-Bz C-Class C220 (2.2L/4/A4)	23	29	$ 780	Mitsu. Eclipse (2.0L/4/M5)	22	32	$ 693
Merc-Bz C-Class C280 (2.8L/6/A4)	19	26	$ 921	Mitsu. Eclipse (2.0L/4/M5)	21	28	$ 844
Merc-Bz C-Class C36 Amg (3.6L/6/A4)	18	22	$1065	Mitsu. Eclipse Conv. (2.0L/4/L4)	20	26	$ 921
Merc-Bz E-Class E300 Dies. (3.0L/6/A4)	28	35	$ 581	Mitsu. Eclipse Conv. (2.0L/4/M5)	23	31	$ 780
Merc-Bz E-Class E320 (3.2L/6/A4)	19	26	$ 921	Mitsu. Eclipse Conv. (2.4L/4/L4)	20	28	$ 783
Merc-Bz S-Class (3.2L/6/A5)	17	24	$1012	Mitsu. Eclipse Conv. (2.4L/4/M5)	22	29	$ 720
Merc-Bz S-Class (5.0L/8/A5) (G)	16	23	$1065	Mitsu. Galant (2.4L/4/L4)	22	28	$ 751
Merc-Bz S-Class (6.0L/12/A5) (G)	14	20	$1266	Mitsu. Galant (2.4L/4/M5)	23	30	$ 693
Merc-Bz S-Class S320 (3.2L/6/A5)	17	24	$1012	Mitsu. Mirage (1.5L/4/A3)	28	32	$ 599
Merc-Bz S-Class S320 (3.2L/6/A5)	17	24	$1012	Mitsu. Mirage (1.5L/4/M5)	32	39	$ 515
Merc-Bz S-Class S420 (4.2L/8/A5) (G)	15	22	$1126	Mitsu. Mirage (1.8L/4/L4)	26	33	$ 621
Merc-Bz S-Class S500 (5.0L/8/A5) (G)	15	21	$1191	Mitsu. Mirage (1.8L/4/M5)	26	33	$ 621
Merc-Bz S-Class S500 Cpe (5.0L/8/A5) (G)	15	22	$1126	Nissan 240SX (2.4L/4/L4)	21	26	$ 881
Merc-Bz S-Class S600 (6.0L/12/A5) (G)	13	19	$1351	Nissan 240SX (2.4L/4/M5)	22	28	$ 844
Merc-Bz S-Class S600 Cpe (6.0L/12/A5) (G)	13	20	$1351	Nissan 300ZX (3.0L/6/L4)	18	24	$1012
Merc. Cougar (3.8L/6/L4)	19	26	$ 857	Nissan 300ZX (3.0L/6/L4)	18	23	$1012
Merc. Cougar (4.6L/8/L4)	17	25	$ 900	Nissan 300ZX (3.0L/6/L4)	18	23	$1012
Merc. Grand Marquis (4.6L/8/L4)	17	25	$ 900	Nissan 300ZX (3.0L/6/M5)	18	24	$1012
Merc. Mystique (2.0L/4/L4)	23	32	$ 693	Nissan 300ZX (3.0L/6/M5)	19	24	$ 964
Merc. Mystique (2.0L/4/M5)	24	34	$ 643	Nissan 300ZX (3.0L/6/M5)	19	24	$ 964
Merc. Mystique (2.5L/6/L4)	21	30	$ 751	Nissan Altima (2.4L/4/L4)	21	29	$ 751
Merc. Mystique (2.5L/6/M5)	21	31	$ 751	Nissan Altima (2.4L/4/M5)	24	30	$ 693
Merc. Sable (3.0L/6/L4)	20	29	$ 783	Nissan Maxima (3.0L/6/L4)	21	28	$ 881
Merc. Sable (3.0L/6/L4)	20	29	$ 783	Nissan Maxima (3.0L/6/M5)	22	27	$ 844
Merc. Sable Wgn (3.0L/6/L4)	19	28	$ 819	Nissan Quest (3.0L/6/L4)	17	23	$ 900
Merc. Sable Wgn (3.0L/6/L4)	19	27	$ 819	Nissan Sentra (1.6L/4/L4)	28	37	$ 581
Merc. Tracer (1.8L/4/L4)	23	29	$ 720	Nissan Sentra (1.6L/4/M5)	30	40	$ 545
Merc. Tracer (1.8L/4/M5)	25	31	$ 666	Nissan Sentra (2.0L/4/L4)	23	30	$ 693
Merc. Tracer (1.9L/4/M5)	31	38	$ 529	Nissan Sentra (2.0L/4/M5)	23	31	$ 693
Merc. Tracer Wgn (1.9L/4/M5)	31	38	$ 529	Olds 88 (3.8L/6/L4)	18	27	$ 964
Merc. Villager Fwd Van (3.0L/6/L4)	17	23	$ 900	Olds 88 (3.8L/6/L4)	19	30	$ 783
Merc. Villager Fwd Wgn (3.0L/6/L4)	17	23	$ 900	Olds 98 (3.8L/6/L4)	19	29	$ 783

Car (eng./trans.)	City	Hwy	Cost	Car (eng./trans.)	City	Hwy	Cost
Olds Achieva (2.4L/4/L4)	22	32	$ 693	Saturn SC (1.9L/4/L4)	27	37	$ 581
Olds Achieva (2.4L/4/M5)	23	33	$ 693	Saturn SC (1.9L/4/M5)	29	40	$ 545
Olds Achieva (3.1L/6/L4)	21	29	$ 751	Saturn SC (1.9L/4/M5)	25	35	$ 621
Olds Aurora (4.0L/8/L4)	17	26	$1012	Saturn SC (1.9L/4/L4)	24	34	$ 643
Olds Ciera SL (2.2L/4/L3)	24	31	$ 666	Saturn SL (1.9L/4/L4)	24	34	$ 643
Olds Ciera SL (3.1L/6/L4)	20	29	$ 783	Saturn SL (1.9L/4/L4)	27	36	$ 599
Olds Ciera SL Wgn (3.1L/6/L4)	20	29	$ 783	Saturn SL (1.9L/4/M5)	25	35	$ 621
Olds Cutlass Supreme (3.1L/6/L4)	20	29	$ 783	Saturn SL (1.9L/4/M5)	29	40	$ 545
Olds Cutlass Supreme (3.4L/6/L4)	17	26	$ 900	Saturn SW (1.9L/4/L4)	24	34	$ 643
Olds Silhouette 2wd (3.4L/5/L4)	19	26	$ 857	Saturn SW (1.9L/4/L4)	27	36	$ 599
Plym. Breeze (2.0L/4/M5)	25	36	$ 621	Saturn SW (1.9L/4/M5)	28	38	$ 562
Plym. Voyager 2wd (2.4L/4/L3)	20	26	$ 819	Saturn SW (1.9L/4/M5)	25	35	$ 621
Plym. Voyager 2wd (3.0L/6/L3)	19	25	$ 857	Sub. Impreza (1.8L/4/L4)	24	30	$ 693
Plym. Voyager 2wd (3.3L/6/L4)	18	24	$ 900	Sub. Impreza (1.8L/4/M5)	25	31	$ 666
Plym. Voyager 4wd (3.8L/6/L4)	16	22	$1001	Sub. Impreza AWD (1.8L/4/M5)	23	29	$ 720
Pontiac Bonneville (3.8L/6/L4)	17	26	$1012	Sub. Impreza AWD (2.2L/4/L4)	22	29	$ 720
Pontiac Bonneville (3.8L/6/L4)	19	30	$ 783	Sub. Impreza AWD (2.2L/4/M5)	22	29	$ 751
Pontiac Firebird (3.8L/6/L4)	19	29	$ 819	Sub. Impreza Wgn AWD (2.2L/4/L4)	22	29	$ 720
Pontiac Firebird (3.8L/6/M5)	19	30	$ 783	Sub. Impreza Wgn AWD (2.2L/4/M5)	22	29	$ 751
Pontiac Firebird (5.7L/8/L4)	17	25	$ 900	Sub. Legacy (2.2L/4/L4)	23	32	$ 666
Pontiac Firebird (5.7L/8/M6)	16	26	$ 900	Sub. Legacy (2.2L/4/M5)	24	33	$ 666
Pontiac Grand Am (2.4L/4/L4)	22	32	$ 693	Sub. Legacy AWD (2.2L/4/L4)	22	29	$ 720
Pontiac Grand Am (2.4L/4/M5)	23	33	$ 693	Sub. Legacy AWD (2.2L/4/M5)	22	29	$ 751
Pontiac Grand Am (3.1L/6/L4)	21	29	$ 751	Sub. Legacy AWD (2.5L/4/L4)	20	26	$ 819
Pontiac Grand Prix (3.1L/6/L4)	20	29	$ 783	Sub. Legacy Wgn (2.2L/4/L4)	23	32	$ 666
Pontiac Grand Prix (3.4L/6/L4)	17	26	$ 900	Sub. Legacy Wgn AWD (2.2L/4/L4)	22	29	$ 720
Pontiac Sunfire (2.2L/4/L3)	24	31	$ 666	Sub. Legacy Wgn AWD (2.2L/4/M5)	22	29	$ 751
Pontiac Sunfire (2.2L/4/L4)	25	34	$ 643	Sub. Legacy Wgn AWD (2.5L/4/L4)	20	26	$ 819
Pontiac Sunfire (2.2L/4/M5)	25	37	$ 621	Sub. SVX AWD (3.3L/6/L4)	17	24	$1012
Pontiac Sunfire (2.4L/4/L4)	22	32	$ 693	Suzuki Esteem (1.6L/4/L4)	27	34	$ 599
Pontiac Sunfire (2.4L/4/M5)	23	33	$ 693	Suzuki Esteem (1.6L/4/M5)	31	37	$ 545
Pontiac Tr. Sport 2wd (3.4L/5/L4)	19	26	$ 857	Suzuki Swift (1.3L/4/A3)	30	34	$ 562
Porsche 911 Carrera 4/2 (3.6L/6/A4)	17	24	$1012	Suzuki Swift (1.3L/4/M5)	39	43	$ 439
Porsche 911 Carrera 4/2 (3.6L/6/M6)	17	25	$1012	Toyota Avalon (3.0L/6/L4)	20	29	$ 783
Porsche 911 Carrera 4/2 (3.6L/6/M6) (G)	16	23	$1126	Toyota Camry (2.2L/4/L4)	21	27	$ 783
Porsche 911 Turbo (3.6L/6/M6) (G)	13	19	$1351	Toyota Camry (2.2L/4/M5)	23	31	$ 693
RR Bent. Azure (6.8L/8/L4) (G)	11	16	$1557	Toyota Camry (3.0L/6/L4)	20	29	$ 783
RR Bent. Bent. Limo. (6.8L/8/L4) (G)	11	15	$1557	Toyota Camry Wgn (2.2L/4/L4)	21	27	$ 783
RR Bent. Brooklands (6.8L/8/L4) (G)	12	17	$1446	Toyota Camry Wgn (3.0L/6/L4)	20	28	$ 783
RR Bent. Cont. R (6.8L/8/L4) (G)	11	16	$1557	Toyota Celica (1.8L/4/L4)	27	34	$ 599
RR Bent. Sil. Spur (6.8L/8/L4) (G)	12	17	$1446	Toyota Celica (1.8L/4/M5)	29	34	$ 581
RR Bent. Sil. Spur Limo. (6.8L/8/L4) (G)	11	15	$1557	Toyota Celica (2.2L/4/L4)	22	29	$ 751
RR Bent. Turbo R (6.8L/8/L4) (G)	11	16	$1557	Toyota Celica (2.2L/4/M5)	22	29	$ 720

Car (eng./trans.)	City	Hwy	Cost
Toyota Celica Conv. (2.2L/4/L4)	21	28	$ 751
Toyota Celica Conv. (2.2L/4/M5)	22	29	$ 720
Toyota Corolla (1.6L/4/L3)	26	30	$ 643
Toyota Corolla (1.6L/4/M5)	31	35	$ 562
Toyota Corolla (1.8L/4/L4)	27	34	$ 599
Toyota Corolla (1.8L/4/M5)	29	34	$ 581
Toyota Corolla Wgn (1.8L/4/L4)	27	34	$ 599
Toyota Corolla Wgn (1.8L/4/M5)	29	34	$ 581
Toyota Paseo (1.5L/4/L4)	28	34	$ 599
Toyota Paseo (1.5L/4/M5)	30	35	$ 562
Toyota Previa (2.4L/4/L4)	18	22	$ 947
Toyota Previa AWD (2.4L/4/L4)	17	20	$1001
Toyota Supra (3.0L/6/L4)	18	24	$ 964
Toyota Supra (3.0L/6/M5)	18	23	$1012
Toyota Tercel (1.5L/4/L3)	31	35	$ 545
Toyota Tercel (1.5L/4/L4)	30	39	$ 529
Toyota Tercel (1.5L/4/M4)	34	40	$ 500
Toyota Tercel (1.5L/4/M5)	31	39	$ 529
VW Cabrio (2.0L/4/L4)	22	28	$ 751
VW Cabrio (2.0L/4/M5)	23	30	$ 693
VW Golf/Jetta (2.0L/4/L4)	22	28	$ 751

Car (eng./trans.)	City	Hwy	Cost
VW Golf/Jetta (2.0L/4/M5)	23	30	$ 693
VW Golf/Jetta GTI VR6 (2.8L/6/M5)	19	26	$ 857
VW Golf/Jetta Jetta (2.0L/4/L4)	22	28	$ 751
VW Golf/Jetta Jetta (2.0L/4/M5)	23	30	$ 693
VW Golf/Jetta Jetta GLX (2.8L/6/L4)	18	24	$ 857
VW Golf/Jetta Jetta GLX (2.8L/6/M5)	19	26	$ 857
VW Passat (2.0L/4/L4)	20	27	$ 783
VW Passat (2.0L/4/M5)	21	29	$ 751
VW Passat (2.8L/6/L4)	18	25	$ 900
VW Passat (2.8L/6/M5)	19	26	$ 857
VW Passat Wgn (2.8L/6/L4)	18	25	$ 900
VW Passat Wgn (2.8L/6/M5)	19	26	$ 857
Volvo 850 (2.3L/5/L4)	19	26	$ 921
Volvo 850 (2.4L/5/L4)	20	29	$ 881
Volvo 850 (2.4L/5/M5)	20	29	$ 881
Volvo 850 Wgn (2.3L/5/L4)	19	26	$ 921
Volvo 850 Wgn (2.4L/5/L4)	20	29	$ 881
Volvo 850 Wgn (2.4L/5/M5)	20	29	$ 881
Volvo 960 (2.9L/6/L4)	18	26	$ 964
Volvo 960 Wgn (2.5L/6/L4)	18	23	$1012
Volvo 960 Wgn (2.9L/6/L4)	18	26	$ 964

MAINTENANCE

After you buy a car, maintenance costs will be a significant portion of your operating expenses. This chapter allows you to consider and compare some of these costs *before* deciding which car to purchase. These costs include preventive maintenance servicing—such as changing the oil and filters—as well as the cost of repairs after your warranty expires. On the following pages, we compared the costs of preventive maintenance and nine likely repairs for the 1996 models. Since the cost of a repair also depends on the shop and the mechanic, this chapter includes tips for finding a good shop and for communicating effectively with a mechanic.

Preventive maintenance is the periodic servicing, specified by the manufacturer, that keeps your car running properly. For example, regularly changing the oil and oil filter. Every owner's manual specifies a schedule of recommended servicing for at least the first 50,000 miles, and the tables on the following pages estimate the cost of following this preventive maintenance schedule.

If for some reason you do not have an owner's manual with the preventive maintenance schedule, contact the manufacturer to obtain one.

Note: Some dealers and repair shops create their own maintenance schedules which call for more frequent (and thus more expensive) servicing than the manufacturer's recommendations. If the servicing recommended by your dealer or repair shop doesn't match what the car maker recommends, make sure you understand and agree to the extra items.

The tables also list the costs for nine repairs that typically occur during the first 100,000 miles. There is no precise way to predict exactly when a repair will be needed. But if you keep a car for 75,000 to 100,000 miles, it is likely that you will experience most of these repairs at least once. The last column provides a relative indication of how expensive these nine repairs are for many cars. Repair cost is rated as *Very Good* if the total for nine repairs is in the bottom fifth of all the cars

rated, and *Very Poor* if the total is in the top fifth.

Most repair shops use "flat-rate manuals" to estimate repair costs. These manuals list the approximate time required for repairing many items. Each automobile manufacturer publishes its own manual and there are several independent manuals as well. For many repairs, the time varies from one manual to another. Some repair shops even use different manuals for different repairs. To determine a repair bill, a shop multiplies the time listed in its manual by its hourly labor rate and then adds the cost of parts.

Our cost estimates are based on flat-rate manual repair times multiplied by a nationwide average labor rate of $45 per hour. All estimates also include the cost of replaced parts and related adjustments.

Prices in the following tables may not predict the exact costs of these repairs. For example, the labor rate for your area may be more or less than the national average. However, the prices will provide you with a relative comparison of maintenance costs for various automobiles.

	PM Costs to 50,000 Miles	Water Pump	Alternator	Front Brake Pads	Starter	Fuel Injection	Fuel Pump	Struts	Lower Ball Joints	CVJ or Univ. Joint	Relative Maint. Cost
Subcompact											
Dodge/Plymouth Neon	698	188	304	126	208	120	254	189	216	313	Vry. Gd.
Eagle Summit	727	207	622	103	400	188	350	416	320	485	Vry. Pr.
Ford Aspire	656	307	942	79	495	302	392	318	363	416	Vry. Pr.
Ford Escort	656	209	343	110	273	132	167	287	306	333	Good
Geo Metro	782	236	534	383	400	269	477	332	327	343	Vry. Pr.
Honda Civic	880	215	303	112	308	113	276	295	198	531	Ave.
Honda del Sol	880	182	303	112	530	113	510	295	198	531	Poor
Hyundai Accent	353	158	362	309	280	87	334	263	112	190	Good
Kia Sephia	700	228	418	106	233	240	430	234	99	327	Ave.
Mazda Miata	784	106	253	99	254	274	400	331	488	315	Poor
Mazda MX-3	784	242	285	83	276	296	354	411	245	281	Ave.
Mazda Protégé	784	220	243	109	218	286	401	272	236	340	Ave.
Mercury Tracer	656	209	343	110	273	132	167	287	306	333	Good
Mitsubishi Mirage	1038	207	622	103	400	188	350	416	320	485	Vry. Pr.
Nissan Sentra	719	188	403	99	345	185	125	253	251	276	Good
Saturn SC	875	113	218	83	164	124	242	207	272	195	Vry. Gd.
Saturn SL/SW	875	122	227	84	147	122	232	219	275	307	Vry. Gd.
Subaru Impreza	584	202	407	92	400	120	250	367	107	297	Good
Suzuki Esteem	782	236	872	113	382	255	439	410	393	383	Vry. Pr.
Suzuki Swift	782	236	534	383	400	269	477	332	327	343	Vry. Pr.
Toyota Paseo	934	140	496	127	245	196	315	366	286	425	Poor
Toyota Tercel	934	140	465	122	340	206	315	379	191	425	Poor
Compact											
Acura Integra	1088	237	381	112	360	152	281	369	238	325	Poor
BMW 3-Series	1111	175	406	128	275	222	257	426	310	605	Poor
Buick Skylark	703	147	228	102	296	235	199	394	251	260	Good
Chevy Beretta/Corsica	698	165	211	102	287	198	211	432	252	267	Good
Chevrolet Cavalier	698	177	219	102	299	194	208	443	252	267	Good
Chrysler Sebring	682	380	306	118	200	182	302	215	598	433	Poor
Eagle Summit Wagon	693	231	580	162	355	186	400	332	306	350	Vry. Pr.
Average (all cars)	724	206	380	122	335	197	296	294	292	259	

Maintenance Costs

	PM Costs to 50,000 Miles	Water Pump	Alternator	Front Brake Pads	Starter	Fuel Injection	Fuel Pump	Struts	Lower Ball Joints	CVJ or Univ. Joint	Relative Maint. Cost
Compact (cont.)											
Eagle Talon	698	225	205	96	210	172	273	258	560	449	Ave.
Ford Contour	656	215	413	123	373	131	205	279	488	218	Ave.
Ford Probe	720	248	646	151	1041	315	241	402	611	516	Vry. Pr.
Geo Prizm	848	167	467	94	456	175	322	321	144	316	Ave.
Honda Prelude	882	211	371	112	230	113	495	335	264	569	Poor
Hyundai Elantra	353	125	310	64	270	80	190	276	128	175	Vry. Gd.
Mazda 626	784	110	287	94	220	332	281	429	528	406	Poor
Mazda MX-6	784	110	287	94	220	332	281	429	528	406	Poor
Mercury Mystique	667	215	413	123	373	131	205	279	488	218	Ave.
Mitsubishi Eclipse	698	225	205	96	210	172	273	258	560	449	Ave.
Mitsubishi Galant	992	380	306	118	200	182	302	215	598	433	Poor
Oldsmobile Achieva	703	147	228	102	296	235	199	394	251	260	Good
Pontiac Grand Am	703	147	228	102	296	235	199	394	251	260	Good
Pontiac Sunfire	703	177	219	102	299	194	208	443	252	267	Good
Subaru Legacy	566	202	407	110	400	138	250	375	107	297	Ave.
Toyota Celica	917	199	380	92	361	213	357	347	187	544	Vry. Gd.
Toyota Corolla	848	167	467	94	456	175	322	321	144	316	Ave.
Volkswagen Golf/Jetta	389	252	598	85	326	141	341	315	155	262	Ave.
Intermediate											
Audi A4	0	179	646	248	561	184	249	876	564	364	Vry. Pr.
Buick Century	709	147	191	91	291	203	277	271	173	189	Vry. Gd.
Buick Regal	709	132	241	115	304	204	246	604	170	491	Poor
Chevrolet Camaro	709	289	211	121	305	161	499	402	194	87	Good
Chrysler Cirrus	682	380	306	118	200	182	302	215	598	433	Poor
Chrysler Concorde	682	81	181	125	195	95	229	247	334	253	Vry. Gd.
Dodge Intrepid	682	81	181	125	195	95	229	247	334	253	Vry. Gd.
Eagle Vision	682	81	181	125	195	95	229	247	334	253	Vry. Gd.
Ford Mustang	720	197	400	167	323	165	198	496	400	41	Ave.
Ford Taurus	640	163	388	125	278	149	199	330	178	262	Good
Honda Accord	882	228	405	112	325	113	370	295	264	302	Ave.
Average (all cars)	724	206	380	122	335	197	296	294	292	259	

	PM Costs to 50,000 Miles	Water Pump	Alternator	Front Brake Pads	Starter	Fuel Injection	Fuel Pump	Struts	Lower Ball Joints	CVJ or Univ. Joint	Relative Maint. Cost
Intermediate (cont.)											
Hyundai Sonata	353	187	387	63	270	102	190	280	133	278	Vry. Gd.
Infiniti G20	1173	187	285	105	263	135	171	320	327	572	Ave.
Mazda Millenia	783	245	705	110	268	314	480	414	220	492	Vry. Pr.
Mercedes-Benz C-Class	989	564	653	117	728	160	296	415	191	433	Vry. Pr.
Mercury Sable	640	163	388	125	278	149	199	330	178	262	Good
Nissan 200SX	703	188	423	103	293	148	125	242	249	347	Good
Nissan Altima	698	155	329	103	236	187	188	293	445	361	Ave.
Nissan Maxima	726	226	397	103	349	232	297	260	159	258	Ave.
Oldsmobile Ciera	709	147	191	91	291	203	277	271	173	189	Vry. Gd.
Olds Cutlass Supreme	709	132	241	115	304	204	246	604	170	491	Poor
Pontiac Grand Prix	709	132	241	115	304	204	246	604	170	491	Poor
Saab 900	623	195	765	127	305	140	335	212	176	200	Ave.
Saab 9000	672	195	535	117	285	215	300	510	138	350	Poor
Toyota Avalon	917	235	562	122	265	249	306	421	249	398	Poor
Toyota Camry	917	235	517	122	372	248	306	379	259	396	Vry. Pr.
Volkswagen Passat	400	252	496	106	484	133	326	433	155	156	Poor
Volvo 850	1092	233	557	110	361	114	277	300	118	344	Ave.
Large											
Acura TL	1087	405	1143	127	844	118	436	433	385	376	Vry. Pr.
Audi A6/S6	0	278	574	129	532	206	249	407	564	628	Vry. Pr.
Buick LeSabre	715	212	224	124	297	168	258	385	459	192	Ave.
Buick Park Avenue	715	198	227	125	278	145	266	374	466	322	Ave.
Buick Riviera	715	213	274	119	304	152	507	302	351	189	Ave.
Buick Roadmaster	715	186	304	153	305	168	264	87	158	95	Vry. Gd.
Cadillac DeVille	0	240	285	118	458	201	252	1131	401	189	Vry. Pr.
Cadillac Eldorado	0	158	388	118	435	169	241	1090	401	198	Vry. Pr.
Cadillac Fleetwood	0	281	265	125	226	174	288	374	466	322	Poor
Cadillac Seville	0	155	366	118	504	157	241	1131	378	207	Vry. Pr.
Chevy Caprice/Impala	715	186	304	153	305	168	264	87	158	95	Vry. Gd.
Chevrolet Lumina	715	135	241	115	304	215	243	211	170	179	Vry. Gd.
Average (all cars)	724	206	380	122	335	197	296	294	292	259	

	PM Costs to 50,000 Miles	Water Pump	Alternator	Front Brake Pads	Starter	Fuel Injection	Fuel Pump	Struts	Lower Ball Joints	CVJ or Univ. Joint	Relative Maint. Cost
Large (cont.)											
Chevrolet Monte Carlo	715	135	241	115	304	215	243	211	170	179	Vry. Gd.
Chrys. LHS/New Yorker	698	207	186	125	195	122	229	247	334	253	Vry. Gd.
Ford Crown Victoria	720	173	371	134	345	214	288	155	364	41	Good
Ford Thunderbird	720	139	508	189	357	165	343	279	407	46	Ave.
Infiniti J30	709	242	321	118	253	307	342	730	349	131	Poor
Infiniti Q45	709	320	417	109	347	315	355	437	391	153	Vry. Pr.
Lexus ES300	709	235	517	122	372	248	306	379	259	396	Vry. Pr.
Lexus GS300	709	246	615	118	385	297	368	193	187	280	Poor
Lexus LS400	709	330	670	154	728	314	409	199	254	255	Vry. Pr.
Lexus SC300/400	709	139	675	118	347	310	324	296	835	220	Vry. Pr.
Lincoln Continental	709	288	398	180	289	174	202	717	340	195	Poor
Lincoln Mark VIII	709	139	508	189	357	165	343	279	407	46	Ave.
Lincoln Town Car	709	173	371	134	345	214	288	155	364	41	Good
Mazda 929	784	287	302	115	239	297	580	606	429	112	Vry. Pr.
Mercedes-Benz E-Class	1191	584	1225	151	800	221	286	362	217	262	Vry. Pr.
Mercury Cougar	720	139	508	189	357	165	343	279	407	46	Ave.
Mercury Grand Marquis	720	173	371	134	345	214	288	155	364	41	Good
Mitsubishi Diamante	1061	282	379	118	268	212	464	439	830	516	Vry. Pr.
Oldsmobile 88	703	212	224	124	297	168	258	385	459	192	Ave.
Oldsmobile 98	723	198	227	125	278	145	266	374	466	322	Ave.
Oldsmobile Aurora	723	213	274	119	304	152	225	302	351	189	Good
Pontiac Bonneville	703	212	224	124	297	168	258	385	459	192	Ave.
Subaru SVX	584	240	407	125	405	138	343	409	143	275	Ave.
Volvo 900 Series	1092	189	557	110	422	113	277	300	118	344	Ave.
Minivans											
Chevrolet Astro	660	192	210	80	256	567	219	150	190	87	Good
Chevy Lumina Minivan	660	128	226	109	346	163	235	260	114	232	Vry. Gd.
Chrys. Town and Cntry.	608	150	315	125	188	238	313	195	128	293	Good
Dodge Caravan	608	150	315	125	255	118	249	260	255	313	Good
Ford Aerostar	587	226	388	127	309	171	241	124	180	186	Good
Average (all cars)	724	206	380	122	335	197	296	294	292	259	

	PM Costs to 50,000 Miles	Water Pump	Alternator	Front Brake Pads	Starter	Fuel Injection	Fuel Pump	Struts	Lower Ball Joints	CVJ or Univ. Joint	Relative Maint. Cost
Minivans (cont.)											
Ford Windstar	587	283	414	145	274	197	253	314	192	362	Ave.
Honda Odyssey	880	237	375	112	432	113	445	127	270	335	Ave.
Isuzu Oasis	880	237	375	112	432	113	445	127	270	335	Ave.
Mazda MPV	826	190	248	92	355	304	174	339	610	427	Poor
Mercury Villager	613	187	401	150	280	254	323	241	149	190	Good
Nissan Quest	613	187	401	150	280	254	323	241	149	190	Good
Oldsmobile Silhouette	660	128	226	109	346	163	235	260	114	232	Vry. Gd.
Plymouth Voyager	608	150	315	125	255	118	249	260	255	313	Good
Pontiac Trans Sport	660	128	226	109	346	163	235	260	114	232	Vry. Gd.
Toyota Previa	788	133	370	108	313	226	356	421	178	399	Poor
Average (all cars)	724	206	380	122	335	197	296	294	292	259	

Service Contracts

Each year nearly 50 percent of new car buyers buy "service contracts." Ranging from $400 to $1500 in price, a service contract is one of the most expensive options you can buy. In fact, service contracts are a major profit source for many dealers.

A service contract is not a warranty. It is more like an insurance plan that, in theory, covers repairs that are not covered by your warranty or that occur after the warranty runs out.

Service contracts are generally a very poor value. The companies who sell contracts are very sure that, on average, your repairs will cost considerably less than what you pay for the contract—if not, they wouldn't be in business.

One alternative to buying a service contract is to deposit the cost of the contract into a savings account. If the car needs a major repair, not covered by your warranty, chances are good that the money in your account will cover the cost. Most likely, you'll be building up your down payment for your next car!

If you believe that you really need a service contract, contact an insurance company, such as GEICO. You can save up to 50-percent by buying from an insurance company.

Here are some important questions to ask before buying a service contract:

How reputable is the company responsible for the contract? If the company offering the contract goes out of business, you will be out of luck. Recently, a number of independent service contract companies have gone under, so be very careful about who you buy from. Check with your Better Business Bureau or office of consumer affairs if you are not sure of a company's reputation. Service contracts from car and insurance companies are more likely to remain in effect than those from independent companies.

Exactly what does the contract cover and for how long? Service contracts vary considerably—different items are covered and different time limits are offered. This is true even among service contracts offered by the same company. For example, Ford's plans range from 3 years/50,000 miles maximum coverage to 6 years/100,000 miles maximum coverage, with other options for only powertrain coverage.

If you plan to resell your car in a few years, you won't want to purchase a long-running service contract. Some service contracts automatically cancel when you resell the car, while others require a hefty transfer fee before extending privileges to the new owner.

Some automakers offer a "menu" format which lets you pick the items you want covered in your service contract. Find out if the contract pays for preventive maintenance, towing, and rental car expenses. If not written into the contract, assume they are not covered.

Finally, think twice before purchasing travel services offered in the contract. Such amenities are offered by auto clubs, and you should compare prices before adding them into your contract cost.

How will the repair bills be paid? It is best to have the service contractor pay bills directly. Some contracts require you to pay the repair bill, and reimburse you later.

Where can the car be serviced? Can you take the car to any mechanic if you have trouble on the road? What if you move?

What other costs can be expected? Most service contracts will have a deductible expense. Compare deductibles on various plans. Also, some companies charge the deductible for each individual repair while other companies charge per visit, regardless of the number of repairs made.

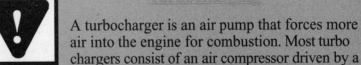

Turbocharging

A turbocharger is an air pump that forces more air into the engine for combustion. Most turbo chargers consist of an air compressor driven by a small turbine wheel that is powered by the engine's exhaust. The turbine takes advantage of energy otherwise lost and forces increased efficiency from the engine. Turbochargers are often used to increase the power and sometimes the fuel efficiency of small engines. Engines equipped with turbochargers are more expensive than standard engines. The extra power may not be necessary when you consider the added expense and the fact that turbocharging adds to the complexity of the engine.

55

Tips for Dealing with a Mechanic

Call around. Don't choose a shop simply because it's nearby. Calling a few shops may turn up estimates cheaper by half.

Don't necessarily go for the lowest price. A good rule is to eliminate the highest and lowest estimates; the mechanic with the highest estimate is probably charging too much, and the lowest may be cutting too many corners.

Check the shop's reputation. Call your local consumer affairs agency and the Better Business Bureau. They don't have records on every shop, but if their reports on a shop aren't favorable, you can disqualify it.

Look for certification. Mechanics can be certified by the National Institute for Automotive Service Excellence, an industry-wide yardstick for competence. Certification is offered in eight areas of repair and shops with certified mechanics are allowed to advertise this fact. However, make sure the mechanic working on your car is certified for the repair.

Take a look around. A well-kept shop reflects pride in workmanship. A skilled and efficient mechanic would probably not work in a messy shop.

Don't sign a blank check. The service order you sign should have specific instructions or describe your vehicle's symptoms. Signing a vague work order could make you liable to pay for work you didn't want. Be sure you are called for approval before the shop does extra work.

Show interest. Ask about the repair. A mechanic may become more helpful just knowing that you're interested. But don't act like an expert if you don't really understand what's wrong. Demonstrating your ignorance, on the other hand, may set you up to be taken by a dishonest mechanic, so strike a balance.

Express your satisfaction. If you're happy with the work, compliment the mechanic and ask for him or her the next time you come in. You'll get to know each other and the mechanic will get to know your vehicle.

Develop a "sider." If you know a mechanic, ask about work on the side—evenings or weekends. The labor will be cheaper.

Test drive, then pay! Before you pay for a major repair, you should take the car for a test drive. The few extra minutes you spend checking out the repair could save you a trip back to the mechanic. If you find that the problem still exists, there will be no question that the repair wasn't properly completed. It is much more difficult to prove the repair wasn't properly made after you've left the shop.

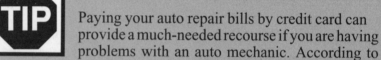

Repair Protection By Credit Card

Paying your auto repair bills by credit card can provide a much-needed recourse if you are having problems with an auto mechanic. According to federal law, you have the right to withhold payment for sloppy or incorrect repairs. Of course, you may withhold no more than the amount of the repair in dispute.

In order to use this right, you must first try to work out the problem with the mechanic. Also, unless the credit card company owns the repair shop (this might be the case with gasoline credit cards used at gas stations), two other conditions must be met. First, the repair shop must be in your home state (or within 100 miles of your current address), and second, the cost of repairs must be over $50. Until the problem is settled or resolved in court, the credit card company cannot charge you interest or penalties on the amount in dispute.

If you decide to take action, send a letter to the credit card company and a copy to the repair shop, explaining the details of the problem and what you want as settlement. Send the letter by certified mail with a return receipt requested.

Sometimes the credit card company or repair shop will attempt to put a "bad mark" on your credit record if you use this tactic. Legally, you can't be reported as delinquent if you've given the credit card company notice of your dispute, but a creditor can report that you are disputing your bill, which goes in your record. However, you have the right to challenge any incorrect information and add your side of the story to your file.

For more information, write to the Federal Trade Commission, Credit Practices Division, 601 Pennsylvania Avenue, NW, Washington, DC 20580.

WARRANTIES

Along with your new car comes a warranty, which is a promise from the manufacturer that the car will perform as it should. Most of us never read the warranty—until it is too late. In fact, because warranties are often difficult to read and understand, most of us don't really know what our warranties offer. This chapter will help you understand what to look for in a new car warranty, tip you off to secret warranties, and provide you with the best and worst among the 1996 warranties.

There are two types of warranties: one provided by the manufacturer and one implied by law.

Manufacturers' warranties are either "full" or "limited." The best warranty you can get is a full warranty because, by law, it must cover all aspects of the product's performance. Any other guarantee is called a limited warranty, which is what most car manufacturers offer. Limited warranties must be clearly marked as such, and you must be told exactly what is covered.

Warranties implied by law are warranties of merchantability and fitness. The "warranty of merchantability" ensures that your new car will be fit for the purpose for which it is used—that means safe, efficient, and trouble-free transportation. The "warranty of fitness" guarantees that if the dealer says a car can be used for a specific purpose, it will perform that purpose.

Any claims made by the salesperson are also considered warranties. They are called expressed warranties and you should have them put in writing if you consider them to be important. If the car does not live up to promises made to you in the showroom, you may have a case against the seller.

The manufacturer can restrict the amount of time the limited warranty is in effect. And in most states, the manufacturer can also limit the time that the warranty implied by law is in effect.

Through the warranty, the manufacturer is promising that the way the car was made and the materials used are free from defects, provided that the car is used in a normal fashion for a certain period after you buy it. This period of time is usually measured in both months and miles— whichever comes first is the limit.

While the warranty is in effect, the manufacturer will perform, at no charge to the owner, repairs that are necessary because of defects in materials or in the way the car was manufactured.

The warranty does not cover parts that have to be replaced because of normal wear, such as filters, fuses, light bulbs, wiper blades, clutch linings, brake pads, or the addition of oil, fluids, coolants, and lubricants. Tires, batteries, and the emission control system are covered by separate warranties. Options, such as a stereo system, should have their own warranties as well. Service should be provided through the dealer. A separate rust (corrosion) warranty is also included.

The costs for the required maintenance listed in the owner's manual are not covered by the warranty. Problems resulting from misuse, negligence, changes you make in the car, accidents, or lack of required maintenance are also not covered.

Any implied warranties, including the warranties of merchantability and fitness, are limited to 12 months or 12,000 miles. Also, the manufacturer is not responsible for other problems caused by repairs, such as the loss of time or use of your car, or any expenses they might cause.

In addition to the rights granted to you in the warranty, you may have other rights under your state laws.

To keep your warranty in effect, you must operate and maintain your car according to the instructions in your owner's manual. Remember, it is important to keep a record of all maintenance performed on your car.

To have your car repaired under the warranty, take it to an authorized dealer or service center. The work should be done in a reasonable amount of time during normal business hours.

Be careful not to confuse your warranty with a service contract. The *service contract* must be purchased separately; and, the warranty is yours at no extra cost when you buy the car. (See page 55 for more on service contracts.)

Corrosion Warranty: All manufacturers warrant against corrosion. The typical corrosion warranty lasts for six years or 100,000 miles, whichever comes first.

Some dealers offer extra rust protection at an additional cost. Before you purchase this option, compare the extra protection offered to the corrosion warranty already included in the price of the car—it probably already provides sufficient protection against rust. (See page 93 for more important information on rust-proofing.)

Emission System Warranty: The emission system is warranted by federal law. Any repairs required during the first two years or 24,000 miles will be paid for by the manufacturer if an original engine part fails because of a defect in materials or workmanship, and the failure causes your car to exceed federal emissions standards. Major components, such as an onboard computer emissions control unit, are covered for eight years or 80,000 miles.

Using leaded fuel in a car designed for unleaded fuel will void your emission system warranty and may prevent the car from passing your state's inspection. Because an increasing number of states are requiring an emissions test before a car can pass inspection, you may have to pay to fix the system if you used the wrong type of fuel. Repairs to emission systems are usually very expensive.

Dealer Options & Your Warranty

Make sure that "dealer-added" options will not void your warranty. For example, some consumers who have purchased cruise control as an option to be installed by the dealer have found that their warranty is void when they take the car in for engine repairs. Also, some manufacturers warn that dealer-supplied rustproofing will void your corrosion warranty. If you are in doubt, contact the manufacturer before you authorize the installation of dealer-supplied options. If the manufacturer says that adding the option will not void your warranty, get it in writing.

Getting Warranty Service

Ford dealers are finally offering better warranty service to their customers! Now, most Ford dealers will perform warranty work on all Ford vehicles, regardless of where the vehicle was purchased. Previously, only the selling dealer was required to perform repairs under warranty. Individual Ford dealers can still set their own policy, however, so it is best to call and ask before taking your vehicle in for warranty service. GM, Japanese and European car dealers also provide this service to their customers, and Chrysler "recommends" that dealers follow this policy.

If dealers report a number of complaints about a certain part and the manufacturer determines that the problem is due to faulty design or assembly, the manufacturer may permit dealers to repair the problem at no charge to the customer even though the warranty is expired. In the past, this practice was often reserved for customers who made a big fuss. The availability of the free repair was never publicized, which is why we call these *secret* warranties.

Manufacturers deny the existence of secret warranties. They call these free repairs "policy adjustments" or "goodwill service." Whatever they are called, most consumers never hear about them.

Many secret warranties are disclosed in service bulletins that the manufacturers send to dealers. These bulletins outline free repair or reimbursement programs, as well as other problems and their possible causes and solutions.

Because of problems with secret warranties in the past, three companies are now required to make many of their bulletins available to the public. *Ford* was required to disclose both bulletins and goodwill adjustments under an FTC Consent Order through 1988. Now Ford's toll-free "defect line," 800-241-3673, provides information only on goodwill adjustments. *General Motors* bulletins from the past three years (which may cover models made earlier) and indexes to the bulletins are available at GM dealers. You may also call 800-551-4123 to obtain a form to order them directly from GM. The indexes are free, but there is a charge for the bulletins. *Volkswagen* is also

required to make this information available to consumers. You can order an index of all service bulletins, which includes information on obtaining the actual bulletins, by calling 800-544-8021.

Service bulletins from other manufacturers may be on file at the National Highway Traffic Safety Administration. For copies of the bulletins on file, send a letter with the make, model and year of the car, and the year you believe the service bulletin was issued, to the NHTSA's Technical Reference Library, Room 5108, NHTSA, Washington, DC 20590. If you write to the government, ask for "service bulletins" rather than "secret warranties."

If you find that a secret warranty is in effect and repairs are being made at no charge after the warranty has expired, contact the Center for Auto Safety, 2001 S Street, NW, Washington, DC 20009. They will publish the information so others can benefit.

Disclosure Laws: Spurred by the proliferation of secret warranties and the failure of the FTC to take action, California, Connecticut, Virginia, and Wisconsin have passed legislation that requires consumers to be notified of secret warranties on their cars. Several other states have introduced similar warranty bills.

Typically, the laws require the following: Direct notice to consumers within a specified time after the adoption of a warranty adjustment policy; notice of the disclosure law to new car buyers; reimbursement, within a number of years after payment, to owners who paid for covered repairs before they learned of the ex-

tended warranty service; and dealers must inform consumers who complain about a covered defect that it is eligible for repair under warranty.

New York's bill has another requirement—the establishment of a toll-free number for consumer questions. Consumer groups, such as CAS, support this requirement, but it has met opposition from Ford, GM, Toyota, and other auto manufacturers.

If you live in a state with a secret warranty law already in effect, write your state attorney general's office (in care of your state capitol) for information. To encourage passage of such a bill, contact your state representative (in care of your state capitol).

A Secret Warranty: Here is an example of a secret warranty uncovered by the Center for Auto Safety. Ford is liable for up to $1 billion for bad paint—mainly on blue, silver and grey 1985-92 F-Series trucks. Ford set up an "Owners Dialogue Program" in 1993 to report peeling F-Series pickups, Broncos, and Mustangs for free, but abandoned the program when it became too costly. CAS is also aware of paint problems on the Aerostar, Bronco, Bronco II, Econoline, Escort, EXP, LTD, Mustang, Probe, Ranger, Sable, Taurus, Tempo, Thunderbird, and Tracer. If your Ford has had problems with the paint peeling, voice your complaint to CAS, the Federal Trade Commission, or your local attorney general's office or state representative.

If you believe you may be covered, first contact a dealer. If they are not willing to help, write to the manufacturer of your vehicle.

Comparing Warranties

Warranties are difficult to compare because they contain lots of fine print and confusing language. The following table will help you understand this year's new car warranties. Because the table does not contain all the details about each warranty, you should review the actual warranty to make sure you understand its fine points. Remember, you have the right to inspect a warranty before you buy≡it's the law.

The table provides information on five areas covered by a typical warranty:

The **Basic Warranty** covers most parts of the car against manufacturer's defects. The tires, batteries, and items you may add to the car are covered under separate warranties. The table describes coverage in terms of months and miles; for example, 36/36,000 means the warranty is good for 36 months or 36,000 miles, whichever comes first. This is the most important part of your warranty.

The **Powertrain Warranty** usually lasts longer than the basic warranty. Because each manufacturer's definition of the powertrain is different, it is important to find out exactly what your warranty will cover. Powertrain coverage should include parts of the engine, transmission, and drivetrain. The warranty on some luxury cars will often cover some additional systems such as steering, suspension, and electrical systems.

The **Corrosion Warranty** usually applies only to actual holes due to rust. Read this section carefully, because many corrosion warranties *do not* apply to what the manufacturer may describe as cosmetic rust or bad paint.

The **Roadside Assistance** column indicates whether or not the warranty includes a program for helping with problems on the road. Typically, these programs cover such things as lock outs, jump starts, flat tires, running out of gas and towing. Most of these are offered for the length of the basic warranty. Some have special limitations or added features, which we have pointed out. Because each one is different, check yours out carefully.

The last column contains the **Warranty Rating Index,** which provides an overall assessment of this year's warranties. The higher the Index number, the better the warranty. The Index number incorporates the important features of each warranty. In developing the Index, we gave the most weight to the basic and powertrain components of the warranties. The corrosion warranty was weighted somewhat less, and the roadside assistance features received the least weight. We also considered special features such as whether you had to bring the car in for corrosion inspections, or if rental cars were offered when warranty repairs were being done.

After evaluating all the features of the new warranties, here are this year's best and worst ratings.

1996 Warranties: The Best and The Worst

The Best		The Worst	
Audi	1591	Suzuki	670
Infiniti	1518	Honda	834
Volkswagen	1440	Ford	942
Volvo	1411	Mercury	942

The higher the index number, the better the warranty. See the following table for complete details.

Manufacturer	Basic Warranty	Powertrain Warranty	Corrosion Warranty	Roadside Assistance	Index	Warranty Rating
Acura	48/50,000	48/50,000	60/unlimited	48/50,000	1163	Average
Audi	36/50,000[1]	36/50,000	120/unlimited	36/50,000[2]	1591	Very Good
BMW	48/50,000	48/50,000	72/unlimited[3]	48/50,000[2]	1254	Good
Buick	36/36,000	36/36,000	72/100,000	36/36,000	956	Very Poor
Cadillac	48/50,000	48/50,000	72/100,000	Lifetime[4,5]	1190	Average
Chevrolet/Geo	36/36,000	36/36,000	72/100,000	36/36,000	956	Very Poor
Chrysler	36/36,000	36/36,000	84/100,000	36/36,000	980	Very Poor
Dodge	36/36,000	36/36,000	84/100,000	36/36,000	980	Very Poor
Eagle	36/36,000	36/36,000	84/100,000	36/36,000	980	Very Poor
Ford	36/36,000	36/36,000	60/unlimited	36/36,000	942	Very Poor
Honda	36/36,000	36/36,000	60/unlimited	None	834	Very Poor
Hyundai	36/36,000	60/60,000	60/100,000	36/36,000[6]	1022	Poor
Infiniti	48/60,000	72/70,000	84/unlimited	48/unlimited	1518	Very Good
Isuzu	36/50,000	60/60,000	72/100,000	60/60,000	1228	Good
Jeep	36/36,000	36/36,000	84/100,000	36/36,000	980	Very Poor
Kia	36/36,000	60/60,000	60/100,000	36/36,000[2]	1126	Average
Land Rover	36/42,000	36/42,000	72/unlimited	36/42,000	1059	Poor
Lexus	48/50,000	72/72,000	72/unlimited	48/50,000	1367	Very Good
Lincoln	48/50,000[7]	48/50,000	60/unlimited	48/50,000	1163	Average
Mazda	36/50,000	36/50,000	60/unlimited	36/50,000	1061	Poor
Mercedes-Benz	48/50,000	48/50,000	48/50,000	Lifetime	1179	Average
Mercury	36/36,000	36/36,000	60/unlimited	36/36,000	942	Very Poor
Mitsubishi	36/36,000	60/60,000	84/100,000	36/36,000	1124	Average
Nissan	36/36,000	60/60,000	60/unlimited	36/36,000[6]	1032	Poor
Oldsmobile	36/36,000	36/36,000	72/100,000	36/36,000[2]	1006	Poor

Manufacturer	Basic Warranty	Powertrain Warranty	Corrosion Warranty	Roadside Assistance	Index	Warranty Rating
Olds Aurora	48/50,000	48/50,000	72/100,000	48/50,000[2]	1227	Good
Plymouth	36/36,000	36/36,000	84/100,000	36/36,000	980	Very Poor
Pontiac	36/36,000	36/36,000	72/100,000	36/36,000	956	Very Poor
Saab	48/50,000	48/50,000	72/unlimited	48/50,000[2]	1279	Good
Saturn	36/36,000	36/36,000	72/unlimited	36/36,000[2]	1058	Poor
Subaru	36/36,000	60/60,000	60/unlimited	36/36,000[8]	1014	Poor
Suzuki[9]	36/36,000	36/36,000	36/unlimited	None	670	Very Poor
Toyota	36/36,000	60/60,000	60/unlimited	Optional	978	Very Poor
Volkswagen	24/24,000[10]	120/100,000	72/unlimited	24/24,000[2]	1440	Very Good
Volvo	48/50,000	48/50,000	96/unlimited	48/50,000[2]	1411	Very Good

[1] Includes all service, repairs and parts to 36/50,000.
[2] Covers trip interuption expenses.
[3] Inspection required every 2 years.
[4] <48/50,000=Free; >48/50,000=Small Charge.
[5] Covers trip interuption expenses up to 12/12,000.
[6] Limited roadside services.
[7] The basic warranty also includes car rental payments of a maximum of $30/day for 5 days (if car kept overnight for servicing).
[8] SVX only.
[9] Suzuki Soft Tops have a 24/24,000 Basic Warranty on the soft top itself.
[10] Includes all service, repairs and parts to 24/24,000.

INSURANCE

Insurance is a big part of ownership expenses, yet it's often forgotten in the showroom. As you shop, remember that the car's design and accident history may affect your insurance rates. Some cars cost less to insure because experience has shown that they are damaged less, less expensive to fix after a collision, or stolen less.

This chapter provides you with the information you need to make a wise insurance purchase. We discuss the different types of insurance, offer special tips on reducing this cost, and include information on occupant injury, theft, and bumper ratings—all factors that can affect your insurance.

More and more consumers are saving hundreds of dollars by shopping around for insurance. In order to be a good comparison shopper, you need to know a few things about automobile insurance. First, there are six basic types of coverage:

Collision Insurance: This pays for the damage to your car after an accident.

Comprehensive Physical Damage Insurance: This pays for damages when your car is stolen or damaged by fire, floods, or other perils.

Property Damage Liability: This pays claims and defense costs if your car damages someone else's property.

Medical Payments Insurance: This pays for your car's occupants' medical expenses resulting from an accident.

Bodily Injury Liability: This provides money to pay claims against you and to pay for the cost of your legal defense if your car injures or kills someone.

Uninsured Motorists Protection: This pays for injuries caused by an uninsured or a hit-and-run driver.

A number of factors determine what these coverages will cost you. A car's design can affect both the chances and severity of an accident. A car with a well-designed bumper may escape damage altogether in a low-speed crash. Some cars are easier to repair than others or may have less expensive parts. Cars with four doors tend to be damaged less than cars with two doors.

The reason one car may get a discount on insurance while another receives a surcharge also depends upon the way it is traditionally driven. Sports cars, for example, are usually surcharged due, in part, to the typical driving habits of their owners. Four-door sedans and station wagons generally merit discounts.

Insurance companies use this and other information to determine whether to offer a *discount* on insurance premiums for a particular car, or whether to levy a *surcharge*.

Not all companies offer discounts or surcharges, and many cars receive neither. Some companies offer a discount or impose a surcharge on collision premiums only. Others apply discounts and surcharges on both collision and comprehensive coverage. Discounts and surcharges usually range from 10 to 30 percent. Allstate offers discounts of up to 35 percent on certain cars. Remember that one company may offer a discount on a particular car while another may not.

Check with your insurance agent to find out whether your company has a rating program. *The Ratings* pages at the end of the book indicate the expected insurance rates for each of the 1996 models.

No-Fault Insurance

One of the major expenses of vehicular accidents has been the cost of determining who is "at fault." Often, both parties hire lawyers and wait for court decisions, which can take a long time. Another problem with this system is that some victims receive considerably less than others for equivalent losses.

To resolve this, many states have instituted "no-fault" vehicle insurance. The concept is that each person's losses are covered by his or her personal insurance protection, regardless of who is at fault. Lawsuits are permitted only under certain conditions.

While the idea is the same from state to state, the details of the no-fault laws vary. These variations include the amounts paid in similar situations, conditions of the right to sue, and the inclusion or exclusion of property damage.

The concept of no-fault means that your insurance company pays for your losses regardless of who is responsible and that lawsuits are restricted by the severity of the injuries. Ironically, some no-fault states still permit lawsuits to determine who is at fault. Although the laws in each state may vary, here is a list of states with and without no-fault laws.

No-Fault States

Colorado	Massachusetts	New York
Florida	Michigan	North Dakota
Hawaii	Minnesota	Pennsylvania*
Kansas	New Jersey*	Utah
Kentucky*		

States Without No-Fault

Alabama	Louisiana	Oregon
Alaska	Maine	Rhode Island
Arizona	Maryland	South Carolina
Arkansas	Mississippi	South Dakota
California	Missouri	Tennessee
Connecticut	Montana	Texas
Delaware	Nebraska	Vermont
District of Columbia	Nevada	Virginia
Georgia	New Hampshire	Washington
Idaho	New Mexico	West Virginia
Illinois	North Carolina	Wisconsin
Indiana	Ohio	Wyoming
Iowa	Oklahoma	

*NJ, KY, PA have a policy option for choosing no-fault.

Insurance Industry Statistics

TIP

The insurance industry regularly publishes information about the accident history of cars currently on the road. The most reliable source of this rating information is the Highway Loss Data Institute (HLDI). These ratings, which range from very good to very poor, are based on the frequency of medical claims under personal injury protection coverages. A few companies will charge you more to insure a car rated poor than for one rated good.

A car's accident history may not match its crash test performance. Such discrepancies arise because the accident history includes driver performance. A sports car, for example, may have good crash test results but a poor accident history because its owners tend to drive relatively recklessly.

If you want more information about the injury history, bumper performance, and theft rating of today's cars, write to HLDI, 1005 North Glebe Road, Arlington, VA 22201.

Reducing Insurance Costs

After you have shopped around and found the best deal by comparing the costs of different coverages, consider these other factors that will affect your final insurance bill.

Your Annual Mileage: The more you drive, the more your vehicle will be "exposed" to a potential accident. The insurance cost for a car rarely used will be less than the cost for a frequently used car.

Where You Drive: If you regularly drive and park in the city, you will most likely pay more than if you drive in rural areas.

Youthful Drivers: Usually the highest premiums are paid by male drivers under the age of 25. Whether or not the under-25-year-old male is married also affects insurance rates. (Married males pay less.) As the driver gets older, rates are lowered.

In addition to shopping around, take advantage of certain discounts to reduce your insurance costs. Most insurance companies offer discounts of 5 to 30 percent on various parts of your insurance bill. The availability of discounts varies among companies and often depends on where you live. Many consumers do not benefit from these discounts simply because they don't ask about them.

To determine whether you are getting all the discounts that you're entitled to, ask your insurance company for a complete list of the discounts that it offers.

Here are some of the most common insurance discounts:

Driver Education/Defensive Driving Courses: Many insurance companies offer (and in some cases mandate) discounts to young people who have successfully completed a state-approved driver education course. Typically, this can mean a $40 reduction in the cost of coverage. Also, a discount of 5-15 percent is available in some states to those who complete a defensive driving course.

Good Student Discounts: Many insurance companies offer discounts of up to 25 percent on insurance to full-time high school or college students who are in the upper 20 percent of their class, on the dean's list, or have a B or better average.

Good Driver Discounts: Many companies offer discounts to drivers with an accident and violation-free record.

Mature Driver Credit: Drivers ages 50 and older may qualify for up to a 10 percent discount, or a lower price bracket.

Sole Female Driver: Some companies offer discounts of 10 percent for females, ages 30 to 64, who are the only driver in a household, citing favorable claims experience.

Non-Drinkers and Non-Smokers: A limited number of companies offer incentives ranging from 10-25 percent to those who abstain.

Farmer Discounts: Many companies offer farmers either a discount of 10-30 percent or a lower price bracket.

Car Pooling: Commuters sharing driving may qualify for discounts of 5-25 percent or a lower price bracket.

Insuring Driving Children: Children away at school don't drive the family car very often, so it's usually less expensive to insure them on the parents' policy rather than separately. If you do insure them separately, discounts of 10-40 percent or a lower price bracket are available.

Desirable Cars: Premiums are usually much higher for cars with high collision rates or that are the favorite target of thieves.

Passive Restraints/Anti-Lock Brake Credit: Many companies offer discounts (from 10 to 30 percent) for automatic belts and air bags. Some large companies are now offering a 5 percent discount to owners of vehicles with anti-lock brakes.

Anti-Theft Device Credits: Discounts of 5 to 15 percent are offered in some states for cars equipped with a hood lock and an alarm or a disabling device (active or passive) that prevents the car from being started.

Multi-Car Discount: Consumers insuring more than one car in the household with the same insurer can save up to 20 percent.

Account Credit: Some companies offer discounts of up to 10 percent for insuring your home and auto with the same company.

Long-Term Policy Renewal: Although not available in all states, some companies offer price breaks of 5-20 percent to customers who renew a long-term policy.

First Accident Allowance: Some insurers offer a "first accident allowance," which guarantees that if a customer achieves five accident-free years, his or her rates won't go up after the first at-fault accident.

Deductibles: Opting for the largest reasonable deductible is the obvious first step in reducing premiums. Increasing your deductible to $500 from $200 could cut your collision premium about 20 percent. Raising the deductible to $1,000 from $200 could lower your premium about 45 percent. Discounts may vary by company.

Collision Coverage: The older the car, the less the need for collision insurance. Consider dropping collision insurance entirely on an older car. Regardless of how much coverage you carry, the insurance company will only pay up to the car's "book value." For example, if your car requires $1,000 in repairs, but its "book value" is only $500, the insurance company is required to pay only $500.

Uninsured Motorist Coverage/Optional Coverage: The necessity of both of these policies depends upon the extent of your health insurance coverage. In states where they are not required, consumers with applicable health insurance may not want uninsured motorist coverage. Also, those with substantial health insurance coverage may not want an optional medical payment policy.

Rental Cars: If you regularly rent cars, special coverage on your personal auto insurance can cover you while renting for far less than rental agencies offer.

Tip: Expensive fender bender repairs can add up for both you and your insurance company. To reduce repairs, look for a car with bumpers that can withstand a 5-mph impact without damage. See page 68 for more information on bumpers.

Beep, Beep

As car instrument panels become more and more sophisticated, there is growing confusion about the location of horn buttons. There are no regulations requiring a standard location so manufacturers put them in various places around the steering wheel. On your test drive, make sure the horn button is easy to locate and use. When renting a car or driving an unfamiliar car, also be sure you know where the horn button is located. Proper use of a car horn can avoid serious accidents. Because of this, the Center for Auto Safety has been urging the government to standardize horn location since 1980. If you have experienced a problem due to a non-standard horn location, we urge you to contact the National Highway Traffic Safety Administration, Rulemaking Division, 400 7th St., SW, Washington, DC 20590 and the Center for Auto Safety, 2001 S Street, NW, Suite 410, Washington, DC 20009.

The risk of your vehicle being stolen is an important factor in the cost of your insurance. In fact, each year over 1.5 million vehicles are stolen. As a result, the market is flooded with expensive devices designed to prevent theft. Before you spend a lot of money on anti-theft devices, consider this: Of the vehicles stolen, nearly 80 percent were unlocked and 40 percent actually had the keys in the ignition. Most of these thefts are by amateurs. While the most important way to protect your vehicle is to keep it locked and remove the keys, this precaution will not protect you from the pros. If you live or travel in an area susceptible to auto thefts, or have a high-priced vehicle, here are some steps you can take to prevent theft.

Inexpensive Prevention:

☑ Replace door lock buttons with tapered tips. They make it difficult to hook the lock with a wire hanger. (But it will also keep you from breaking into your own vehicle!)

☑ Buy an alarm sticker (even if you don't have an alarm) for one of your windows.

☑ Buy an electric etching tool (about $15) and write your driver's license number in the lower corners of the windows and on unpainted metal items where it can be seen. Many police departments offer this service at no charge. They provide a sticker and enter the number into their records. The purpose of these identifying marks is to deter the professional thief who is planning to take the vehicle apart and sell the components. Since the parts can be traced, your vehicle becomes less attractive.

☑ Remove the distributor wire. This is a rather inconvenient, but effective, means of rendering your vehicle inoperable. If you are parking in a particularly suspect place, or leaving your vehicle for a long time, you may want to try this. On the top of the distributor, there is a short wire running to the coil. Removing the wire makes it impossible to start the vehicle.

A recently popular anti-theft device is a long rod that locks the steering wheel into place. It costs about $50 and requires a separate key to remove. Beware, however, that thieves now use a spray can of freon to freeze the lock, making it brittle enough to be smashed open with a hammer.

More Serious Measures:

☑ Cutting off the fuel to the engine will keep someone from driving very far with your vehicle. For around $125, you can have a fuel cutoff device installed that enables you to open or close the gasoline line to the engine. One drawback is that the thief will be able to drive a few blocks before running out of gas. If your vehicle is missing, you'll have to check your neighborhood first!

☑ Another way to deter a pro is to install a second ignition switch

for about $150. To start your vehicle, you activate a hidden switch. The device is wired in such a complicated manner that a thief could spend hours trying to figure it out. Time is the thief's worst enemy, and the longer it takes to start your vehicle, the more likely the thief is to give up.

☑ The most common anti-theft devices on the market are alarms. These cost from $100 to $500 installed. Their complexity ranges from simply sounding your horn when someone opens your door to setting off elaborate sirens when someone merely approaches the vehicle. Alarms usually require a device such as a key or remote control to turn them on or off. Some people buy the switch, mount it on their vehicle, and hope that its presence will intimidate the thief.

The Highway Loss Data Institute regularly compiles statistics on motor vehicle thefts. In rating cars, they consider the frequency of theft and the loss resulting from the theft. The result is an index based on "relative average loss payments per insured vehicle year." The list below includes the most and least stolen cars among the 1996 models.

Auto Theft

Most Stolen		Least Stolen	
Mercedes SL Class Conv.	1517	Buick LeSabre	16
Mercedes S Class LWB	1437	Eagle Summit Wgn.	19
Mercedes S Class Wgn.	777	Buick Regal 4dr.	21
Lexus GS300	754	Ford Escort Wgn.	24
Nissan 300ZX	676	Mercury Tracer Wgn.	27
BMW 5-Series	581	Olds. Achieva 4dr.	28
Chev. Corvette Conv.	520	Buick Skylark 2dr.	29
Infiniti Q45	492	Ford Escort 4dr.	30
BMW 3-Series 2dr.	480	Buick Regal 2dr.	30

Bumpers

The main purpose of the bumper is to protect your car in low-speed collisions. Despite this intention, most of us have been victims of a $200 to $400 repair bill resulting from a seemingly minor impact. Because most bumpers offered little or no damage protection in low-speed crashes, the federal government *used* to require that auto makers equip cars with bumpers capable of withstanding up to 5-mph crashes with no damage. Unfortunately, this is no longer the case.

In the early eighties, under pressure from car companies, the government rolled back the requirement that bumpers protect cars in collisions up to 5-mph. Now, car companies only build bumpers to protect cars in 2.5-mph collisions—about the speed at which we walk. This rollback has cost consumers millions of dollars in increased insurance premiums and repair costs. While the rollback satisfied car companies, most car owners were unhappy.

To let consumers know that today's bumpers offer widely varying amounts of protection in 5-mph collisions, each year the Insurance Institute for Highway Safety tests bumpers to see how well they prevent damage. Thankfully, some automobile manufacturers are betting that consumers still want better bumpers on at least some of their models. For example, in a 5-mph front test, the Ford Contour withstood $1056 worth of damage while the Ford Windstar withstood only $30 worth of damage.

These results are rather startling when you consider that the sole purpose of a bumper is to protect a car from damage in low-speed collisions. Only about one-third of the cars tested to date have bumpers which actually prevented damage in front and rear 5-mph collisions. As the Institute's figures show, there is no correlation between the price of the car and how well the bumper worked.

Unfortunately, we can't simply look at a bumper and determine how good it will be at doing its job—protecting a car from inevitable bumps. The solution to this problem is quite simple—simply require car makers to tell the consumer the highest speed at which their car could be crashed with no damage to the car. Three states—California, Hawaii, and New York—have passed laws requiring car companies to disclose in the showroom, in various formats, the expected performance of the bumper on the car. These laws are currently being challenged by the car companies and we won't see them implemented for some time.

Following are the results of the IIHS bumper crash tests, listed from the best to the worst performers. We have included some of the cars which we believe will have similar bumpers in 1996. *Note:* If the bumpers have changed at all since the time it was tested, the result could be drastically different. This should, however, give you a good basis for comparison. When available, additional information is on each car's page.

Bumper Bashing - Some Damage Repair Costs in 5-mph Crash Tests

Car (Year)	Front Crash	Rear Crash	Total Cost
Best			
Saab 900 S (1994)	$0	$0	$0
Ford Windstar GL (1995)	$0	$30	$30
Buick Century (1991)	$154	$0	$154
Nissan Quest (1994)	$172	$0	$172
Chevy Corsica (1991)	$161	$41	$202
Worst			
Mazda MPV (1994)	$787	$1597	$2384
Mazda 626 (1993)	$801	$1041	$1842
Pont. TransSport SE (1994)	$1336	$346	$1682
Toyota Previa LE (1994)	$661	$962	$1623
Chevy Lumina Minvan (1994)	$809	$438	$1247

TIRES

For most of us, buying tires has become an infrequent task. The reason—most cars now come with radial tires, which last much longer than the bias and bias-belted tires of the past. However, when we do get around to buying tires, making an informed purchase is not easy. The tire has to perform more functions simultaneously than any other part of the car (steering, bearing the load, cushioning the ride, and stopping). And not only is the tire the hardest-working item on the car, but there are nearly 1,800 tire lines to choose from. With only a few major tire manufacturers selling all those tires, the difference in many tires may only be the brand name.

Because it is so difficult to compare tires, it is easy to understand why many consumers mistakenly use price and brand name to determine quality. The difficulty in comparing one tire to another is compounded by the advertising terminology that is used to describe tires. One company's definition of "first line" or "premium" may be entirely different from another's. But there is help. The U.S. government now requires tires to be rated according to their safety and expected mileage.

A little-known system grades tires on their *treadwear*, *traction*, and *heat resistance*. The grades are printed on the sidewall and are also attached to the tire on a paper label. In addition, every dealer can provide you with the grades of the tires he or she sells.

Treadwear: The treadwear grade gives you an idea of the mileage you can expect from a tire. It is shown in numbers—300, 310, 320, 330, and so forth. A tire graded 400 should give you 33 percent more mileage than one graded 300. In order to *estimate* the expected actual mileage, multiply the treadwear grade by 200. Under average conditions a tire graded 300 should last 60,000 miles. Because individual driving habits vary considerably, it is best to use the treadwear as a *relative* basis of comparison rather than an absolute predictor of mileage. Also remember that tire wear is affected by regional differences in the level of abrasive material used in road surfaces.

Traction: Traction grades of A, B, and C describe the tire's ability to stop on wet surfaces. Tires graded A will stop on a wet road in a shorter distance than tires graded B or C. Tires rated C have poor traction. If you drive frequently on wet roads, buy a tire with a higher traction grade.

Heat Resistance: Heat resistance is also graded A, B, and C. This grading is important because hot-running tires can result in blowouts or tread separation. An A rating means the tire will run cooler than one rated B or C, and it is less likely to fail if driven over long distances at highway speeds. In addition, tires that run cooler tend to be more fuel efficient. If you do a lot of high speed driving, a high heat resistance grade is best.

The tables at the end of this section give you a list of the highest rated tires on the market. For a complete listing of all the tires on the market, you can call the Auto Safety Hotline toll free, at 800-424-9393 or 800-424-9153 (TTY). (In Washington, DC, the number is 202-366-7800.)

Tire Pricing: Getting the Best Value

There are few consumer products on the market today as price competitive as tires. While this situation provides a buyer's market, it does require some price shopping.

The price of a tire is based on its size, and tires come in as many as nine sizes. For example, the list price of the same Goodyear Arriva tire can range from $74.20 to $134.35, depending on its size. Some manufacturers do not provide list prices, leaving the appropriate markup to the individual retailer. Even when list prices are provided, dealers rarely use them. Instead, they offer tires at what is called an "everyday low price," which can range from 10 to 25 percent below list.

The following tips can help you get the best buy.

1 Check to see which manufacturer makes the least expensive "off brand." Only twelve major manufacturers produce the over 1,800 types of tires sold in the U.S. So you can save money and still get high quality.

2 Remember, generally the wider the tire, the higher the price.

3 Don't forget to inquire about balancing and mounting costs when comparing tire prices. In some stores, the extra charges for balancing, mounting and valve stems can add up to more than $25. Other stores may offer them as a customer service at little or no cost. That good buy in the newspaper may turn into a poor value when coupled with these extra costs. Also, compare warranties; they do vary from company to company.

4 Never pay list price for a tire. A good rule of thumb is to pay at least 30 to 40 percent off the suggested list price.

5 Use the treadwear grade the same way you would the "unit price" in a supermarket. It is the best way to ensure that you are getting the best tire value. The tire with the lowest cost per grade point is the best value.

For example, if tire A costs $100 and has a treadwear grade of 300, and tire B costs $80 and has a treadwear grade of 200:

Tire A:
$100 ÷ 300 = $.33 per point

Tire B:
$80 ÷ 200 = $.40 per point

Since 33 cents is less than 40 cents, tire A is the better buy even though its initial cost is more.

New Tire Registration

You may be missing out on free or low-cost replacement tires or, worse, driving on potentially hazardous ones, if you don't fill out the tire registration form when you buy tires. The law once required all tire sellers to submit buyers' names automatically to the manufacturer, so the company could contact them if the tires were ever recalled. While this is still mandatory for tire dealers and distributors owned by tire manufacturers, it is not required of independent tire dealers. A recent government study found that 70 percent of independent tire dealers had not registered a single tire purchase. Ask for the tire registration card when you buy tires, and remember to fill it out and send it in. This information will allow the company to notify you if the tire is ever recalled.

Do Tires Effect Fuel Economy?

Yes, a tire's rolling resistance effects its fuel economy. In the past, fuel efficiency (low rolling resistance) was traded off with traction. Tires with good traction had lower fuel economy. Michelin has introduced a new rubber compound that doesn't sacrifice traction for fuel economy. In order to give consumers better information and to encourage the widespread use of this new compound, we have asked that the government change its heat resistance grade to a fuel efficiency rating.

Brand Name	Model	Description	Grades			Expected Mileage		
			Trac.	Heat	Tred.	High	Medium	Low
Dunlop	Elite 65	15 & 16	A	B	540	162,000	108,000	81,000
Falken	FK315	All	A	B	540	162,000	108,000	81,000
Kelly	Aqua Tour	All	A	B	540	162,000	108,000	81,000
Ohtsu	HS311	All	A	B	540	162,000	108,000	81,000
Toyo	800+ 75	All	A	B	540	162,000	108,000	81,000
Toyo	800+ 70	15	A	B	540	162,000	108,000	81,000
Vogue	CBR VII 65/70/75 S	14 & 15	A	B	540	162,000	108,000	81,000
Centennial	Interceptor	15 & 16	A	B	520	156,000	104,000	78,000
Co-Op	Golden Mark 65/70	All	A	B	520	156,000	104,000	78,000
Cooper	Grand Classic STE SR	All	A	B	520	156,000	104,000	78,000
Cordovan	Grand Prix ST	All	A	B	520	156,000	104,000	78,000
Dean	Touring Edition	All	A	B	520	156,000	104,000	78,000
Dunlop	Elite 65	14'	A	B	520	156,000	104,000	78,000
Falls	Mark VII	All	A	B	520	156,000	104,000	78,000
Hallmark	Ultimate Touring	All	A	B	520	156,000	104,000	78,000
Lee	STL Trak	All	A	B	520	156,000	104,000	78,000
Michelin	XH4	14 & 15	A	B	520	156,000	104,000	78,000
Monarch	Ultra Touring GT	All	A	B	520	156,000	104,000	78,000
Multi-Mile	Grand Am ST	All	A	B	520	156,000	104,000	78,000
Remington	Touring	15 & 16	A	B	520	156,000	104,000	78,000
Sigma	Supreme ST	All	A	B	520	156,000	104,000	78,000
Star	Centurion Touring	All	A	B	520	156,000	104,000	78,000
Toyo	800+ 75	14	A	B	520	156,000	104,000	78,000
Toyo	800+ 70	175/70R14	B	B	520	156,000	104,000	78,000
Toyo	800+ 70	All	B	B	520	156,000	104,000	78,000
Pirelli	P300 60/65/80	All	A	A	500	150,000	100,000	75,000
Atlas	Pinnacle TE 70	13	A	B	500	150,000	100,000	75,000
Atlas	Pinnacle TE 70/75	14 & 15	A	B	500	150,000	100,000	75,000
Centennial	Interceptor	14	A	B	500	150,000	100,000	75,000
Dayton	Touring 70	All	A	B	500	150,000	100,000	75,000
Dayton	Touring 70/75S	All	A	B	500	150,000	100,000	75,000
Duralon	IV Plus	All	A	B	500	150,000	100,000	75,000
Duralon	Touring Plus IV	All	A	B	500	150,000	100,000	75,000
Gillette	Kodiak LE	All	A	B	500	150,000	100,000	75,000
Peerless	Permasteel LE	All	A	B	500	150,000	100,000	75,000
Remington	Touring	14	A	B	500	150,000	100,000	75,000
Sumitomo	SC890 75	15	A	B	500	150,000	100,000	75,000
Toyo	800+ 75	235/75RL15	A	B	500	150,000	100,000	75,000
Co-Op	Golden Mark 75	All	A	B	480	144,000	96,000	72,000
Cordovan	Grand Prix STE	All	A	B	480	144,000	96,000	72,000
Douglas	Premium WTE	All	A	B	480	144,000	96,000	72,000
Douglas	Premium Touring	All	A	B	480	144,000	96,000	72,000
Dunlop	Elite 65	13	A	B	480	144,000	96,000	72,000
Hallmark	Prestige PWR4	All	A	B	480	144,000	96,000	72,000
Kelly	Navigator 800S	All	A	B	480	144,000	96,000	72,000
Lee	GT VI Trak	All	A	B	480	144,000	96,000	72,000
Michelin	XH4	13	A	B	480	144,000	96,000	72,000
Monarch	Ultra Trak	All	A	B	480	144,000	96,000	72,000
Multi-Mile	Grand Am STE	All	A	B	480	144,000	96,000	72,000
Republic	Weather King	All	A	B	480	144,000	96,000	72,000
Sigma	Supreme STE	All	A	B	480	144,000	96,000	72,000
Star	Imperial	All	A	B	480	144,000	96,000	72,000
Vanderbilt	Turbo Tech Tour G/T	All	A	B	480	144,000	96,000	72,000
Vogue	Premium	All	A	B	480	144,000	96,000	72,000

Brand Name	Model	Description	Grades			Expected Mileage		
			Trac.	Heat	Tred.	High	Medium	Low
Winston	Signature Premium	All	A	B	480	144,000	96,000	72,000
Cordovan	Grand Prix STE	XL	A	C	480	144,000	96,000	72,000
Hallmark	Prestige PWR4	235/75R15	A	C	480	144,000	96,000	72,000
Kelly	Navigator 800S	235/75R15	A	C	480	144,000	96,000	72,000
Lee	GT VI Trak	235/75R15	A	C	480	144,000	96,000	72,000
Monarch	Ultra Trak	235/75R15	A	C	480	144,000	96,000	72,000
Multi-Mile	Grand Am STE	XL	A	C	480	144,000	96,000	72,000
Republic	Weather King XL	P235/75R15	A	C	480	144,000	96,000	72,000
Sigma	Supreme STE	XL	A	C	480	144,000	96,000	72,000
Star	Imperial	235/75R15	A	C	480	144,000	96,000	72,000
Big-O	Legacy 65	P205/65R15	A	B	460	138,000	92,000	69,000
Big-O	Legacy 70/75	15	A	B	460	138,000	92,000	69,000
Brigadier	Touring 65	P205/65R15	A	B	460	138,000	92,000	69,000
Brigadier	Touring 70/75	15	A	B	460	138,000	92,000	69,000
Centennial	Interceptor	13	A	B	460	138,000	92,000	69,000
Continental	CT24	15	A	B	460	138,000	92,000	69,000
General	Ameri Tech 4 75	15	A	B	460	138,000	92,000	69,000
General	Ameri Tech ST	P215,P225/75R15	A	B	460	138,000	92,000	69,000
General	Ameri Tech ST 70	15	A	B	460	138,000	92,000	69,000
General	GS	All	A	B	460	138,000	92,000	69,000
Kumho	782	All	A	B	460	138,000	92,000	69,000
Pirelli	P300 70/75	70/75	A	B	460	138,000	92,000	69,000
Remington	Touring	13	A	B	460	138,000	92,000	69,000
Reynolds	Touring 70/75	15	A	B	460	138,000	92,000	69,000
Reynolds	Touring 65	P205/65R15	A	B	460	138,000	92,000	69,000
Sonic	Sentinel 65	P205/65R15	A	B	460	138,000	92,000	69,000
Sonic	Sentinel 70/75	15	A	B	460	138,000	92,000	69,000
Touring	65	P205/65R15	A	B	460	138,000	92,000	69,000
Touring	70/75	15	A	B	460	138,000	92,000	69,000
Toyo	800+ 70	13	A	B	460	138,000	92,000	69,000
Toyo	800+ 80	All	A	B	460	138,000	92,000	69,000
Vogue	CBR VII 60 V	16	A	A	440	132,000	88,000	66,000
Atlas	Pinnacle TE 80	13	A	B	440	132,000	88,000	66,000
Big-O	Legacy 70/75	14	A	B	440	132,000	88,000	66,000
Brigadier	Touring 70/75	14	A	B	440	132,000	88,000	66,000
Continental	CS24	14	A	B	440	132,000	88,000	66,000
Delta	Supreme 70/75	15	A	B	440	132,000	88,000	66,000
General	Ameri Tech ST 70	14	A	B	440	132,000	88,000	66,000
General	Ameri Tech 4 75	14	A	B	440	132,000	88,000	66,000
General	Ameri Tech 4 70	P205/70R14	A	B	440	132,000	88,000	66,000
Hercules	Mega TR	15	A	B	440	132,000	88,000	66,000
Medalist	Precept 70/75	15	A	B	440	132,000	88,000	66,000
Montgomery Ward	Yokohama	14 & 15	A	B	440	132,000	88,000	66,000
National	XT6000 70/75	15	A	B	440	132,000	88,000	66,000
Republic	Land Rover	All	A	B	440	132,000	88,000	66,000
Reynolds	Touring 70/75	14	A	B	440	132,000	88,000	66,000
Sears	RD Handler + 60-70	All	A	B	440	132,000	88,000	66,000
Sonic	Sentinel 70/75	14	A	B	440	132,000	88,000	66,000
Sumitomo	SC890 75	14	A	B	440	132,000	88,000	66,000
Touring	70/75	14	A	B	440	132,000	88,000	66,000
Cooper	Discover STE	All	B	B	440	132,000	88,000	66,000
Falls	Courser STD	All	B	B	440	132,000	88,000	66,000
Starfire	Bronco CTD	All	B	B	440	132,000	88,000	66,000

COMPLAINTS

Americans spend billions of dollars on motor vehicle repairs every year. While many of those repairs are satisfactory, there are times when getting your vehicle fixed can be a very difficult process. In fact, vehicle defects and repairs are the number one cause of consumer complaints in the U.S., according to the Federal Trade Commission.

This chapter is designed to help you resolve your complaint, whether it's for a new vehicle still under warranty or for one you've had for years. In addition, we offer a guide to arbitration, the names and addresses of consumer groups, federal agencies and the manufacturers themselves. Finally, we tell you how to take the important step of registering your complaint with the U.S. Department of Transportation.

No matter what your complaint, keep accurate records. Copies of the following items are indispensable in helping to resolve your problems:

☑ your service invoices

☑ bills you have paid

☑ letters you have written to the manufacturer or the repair facility owner

☑ written repair estimates from your independent mechanic.

Resolving Complaints: If you are having trouble, here are some basic steps to help you resolve your problem.

First, return your vehicle to the repair facility that did the work. Bring a written list of the problems and make sure that you keep a copy of the list. Give the repair facility a reasonable opportunity to examine your vehicle and attempt to fix it. Speak directly to the service manager (not to the service writer who wrote up your repair order), and ask him or her to test drive the vehicle with you so that you can point out the problem.

If that doesn't resolve the problem, take the vehicle to a diagnostic center for an independent examination. This may cost $45 to $60. Get a written statement defining the problem and outlining how it may be fixed. Give your repair shop a copy. If your vehicle is under warranty, do not allow any warranty repair by an independent mechanic; you may not be reimbursed by the manufacturer.

If your repair shop does not respond to the independent assessment, present your problem to a mediation panel. These panels hear both sides of the story and try to come to a resolution.

If the problem is with a new vehicle dealer, or if you feel that the manufacturer is responsible, you may be able to use one of the manufacturer's mediation programs discussed on page 76.

If the problem is solely with an independent dealer, a local Better Business Bureau (BBB) may be able to mediate your complaint. It may also offer an arbitration hearing. In any case, the BBB should enter your complaint into its files on that establishment.

When contacting any mediation program, determine how long the process takes, who makes the final decision, whether you are bound by that decision, and whether the program handles all problems or only warranty complaints.

If there are no mediation programs in your area, contact private consumer groups, local government agencies, or your local "action line" newspaper columnist, newspaper editor, or radio or TV broadcaster. A phone call or letter from them may persuade a repair facility to take action. Send a copy of your letter to the repair shop.

One of your last resorts is to bring a law suit against the dealer, manufacturer, or repair facility in small claims court. The fee for filing such an action is usually small, and you generally act as your own attorney, saving attorney's fees. There is a monetary limit on the amount you can claim, which varies from state to state. Your local consumer affairs office, state attorney general's office, or the clerk of the court can tell you how to file such a suit.

Finally, talk with an attorney. It's best to select an attorney who is familiar with handling automotive problems. If you don't know of one, call the lawyer referral service listed in the telephone directory (or see box) and ask for the names of attorneys who deal with automobile problems. If you can't afford an attorney, contact the Legal Aid Society.

Warranty Complaints: If your vehicle is under warranty or you are having problems with a factory-authorized dealership, here are some special guidelines:

Have the warranty available to show the dealer. Make sure you call the problem to the dealer's attention before the end of the warranty period.

If you are still unsatisfied after giving the dealer a reasonable opportunity to fix your vehicle, contact the manufacturer's representative (also called the zone representative) in your area. This person can authorize the dealer to make repairs or take other steps to resolve the dispute. Your dealer will have your zone representative's name and telephone number. Explain the problem and ask for a meeting and a personal inspection of your vehicle.

If you can't get satisfaction from the zone representative, call or write the manufacturer's owner relations department. Your owner's manual contains this phone number and address. In each case, as you move up the chain, indicate the steps you have already taken.

Your next option is to present your problem to a complaint-handling panel or to the arbitration program in which the manufacturer of your vehicle participates.

See page 76 for additional information.

If you complain of a problem during the warranty period, you have a right to have the problem fixed even after the warranty runs out. If your warranty has not been honored, you may be able to "revoke acceptance," which means that you return the vehicle to the dealer. If you are successful, you may be entitled to a replacement vehicle, or to a full refund of the purchase price and reimbursement of legal fees under the Magnuson-Moss Warranty Act. Or, if you are covered by one of the state Lemon Laws (see page 83), you may be able to return the vehicle and receive a refund or replacement from the manufacturer.

Legal Aid

If you need legal assistance with your repair problem, the Center for Auto Safety has a list of lawyers who specialize in helping consumers with auto repair problems. For the names of some attorneys in your area, send a stamped, self-addressed envelope to: Center for Auto Safety, 2001 S Street, NW, Washington, DC 20009-1160.

In addition, the Center has published *The Lemon Book*, a detailed, 368-page guide to resolving automobile complaints. The book is available for $15.95 directly from the Center.

Attorneys Take Note: For information on litigation assistance provided by the Center for Auto Safety, including The Lemon Law Litigation Manual, please contact the Center for Auto Safety at the above address.

One of the most valuable but often unused services of the government is the Auto Safety Hotline. By calling the Hotline to report safety problems, your particular concern or problem will become part of the National Highway Traffic Safety Administration's (NHTSA) complaint database. This complaint program is extraordinarily important to government decision makers who often take action based on this information. In addition, it provides consumer groups, like the Center for Auto Safety, with the evidence they need to force the government to act. Unless government engineers or safety advocates have evidence of a wide-scale problem, little can be done to get the manufacturers to correct the defect.

Few government services have the potential to do as much for the consumer as this complaint database, so we encourage you to voice your concerns to the government.

Your letter can be used as the basis of safety defect investigations and recall campaigns. When you file a complaint, be sure to indicate that your name and address can be made public. Without names and addresses, it is more difficult for consumer groups to uncover safety defects.

Hotline Complaints: When you call the Hotline to report a safety problem, you will be mailed a questionnaire asking for information that the agency's technical staff will need to evaluate the problem. This information also gives the government an indication of which vehicles are causing consumers the most problems.

You can also use this questionnaire to report defects in tires and child safety seats. In fact, we strongly encourage you to report problems with child safety seats. Now that they are required by law in all fifty states, we have noticed that numerous design and safety problems have surfaced. If the government knows about these problems, they will be more likely to take action so that modifications are made to these life-saving devices.

After you complete and return the questionnaire, the following things will happen:
1. A copy will go to NHTSA's safety defect investigators.
2. A copy will be sent to the manufacturer of the car or equipment, with a request for help in resolving the problem.
3. You will be notified that your questionnaire has been received.
4. Your problem will be recorded in the complaint database which we use to provide you with complaint ratings.

Hotline Services: Hotline operators can also provide information on recalls. If you want recall information on a particular automobile, simply tell the Hotline operator the make, model, and year of the car, or the type of equipment involved. You will receive any recall information that NHTSA has about that car or item. This information can be very important if you are not sure whether your car has ever been recalled. If you want a printed copy of the recall information, it will be mailed within twenty-four hours at no charge.

If you have other car-related problems, the Hotline operators can refer you to the appropriate federal, state, and local government agencies. If you need information about federal safety standards and regulations, you'll be referred to the appropriate experts.

You may call the Hotline day or night, seven days a week. If you call when no operators are available, a recorded message will ask you to leave your name and address and a description of the information you want. The appropriate materials will be mailed to you.

Complaints and Safety Information

Auto Safety Hotline
800-424-9393
(in Washington, DC: 202-366-0123)
TTY for hearing impaired:
800-424-9153
(in Washington, DC: 202-366-7800)

The toll-free Auto Safety Hotline can provide information on recalls, record information about safety problems, and refer you to the appropriate government experts on other vehicle related problems. You can even have recall information mailed to you within 24 hours of your call at no charge.

Arbitration

An increasingly popular method of resolving automobile repair problems is through arbitration. This procedure requires that both parties present their cases to a mediator or panel that makes a decision based on the merits of the complaint. You can seek repairs, reimbursement of expenses, or a refund or replacement for your car through arbitration.

In theory, arbitration can be an effective means of resolving disputes. It is somewhat informal, relatively speedy, and you do not need a lawyer to present your case. If you resolve your problem through arbitration, you avoid the time and expense of going to court.

Almost all manufacturers now offer some form of arbitration, usually for problems that arise during the warranty period. Some companies run their own and others subscribe to programs run by groups like the Better Business Bureau or the American Automobile Association. Your owner's manual will identify which programs you can use. Also, contact your state attorney general to find out what programs your state offers.

How it works: Upon receiving your complaint, the arbitration program will attempt to mediate a resolution between you and the manufacturer or dealer. If you are not satisfied with the proposed solution, you have the right to have your case heard at an arbitration hearing.

These hearings vary among the programs. In the BBB program, each party presents its case in person to a volunteer arbitrator. The other programs will decide your case based on written submissions from both you and the manufacturer.

If an arbitration program is incorporated into your warranty, you may have to use that program before filing a legal claim. However, you may always go to small claims court instead of using arbitration. Federal law requires that arbitration programs incorporated into a warranty be nonbinding on the consumer. That is, if you do not like the result, you can seek other remedies.

Arbitration programs have different eligibility requirements, so be sure you are eligible for the program you are considering.

Let the Federal Trade Commission, the Center for Auto Safety (their addresses are on pages 80 and 81), and your state attorney general (c/o your state capitol) know of your experience with arbitration. It is particularly important to contact these offices if you have a complaint about how your case was handled.

Ford Dispute Settlement Board: This was one of the first panels established by a manufacturer. Each case is considered by a four-person panel that includes one dealer, who has no vote. In most cases, no oral presentations are given. Only cases under warranty are reviewed. For information, call 800-392-3673.

Chrysler Customer Arbitration Board: No oral presentations are allowed under this program—decisions are based on written submissions by each party. A Chrysler zone representative and dealer are on the panel but cannot vote. The panel will only hear cases under warranty. (In Maryland, Chrysler will sometimes hear cases beyond the warranty.) For information, call 800-992-1997.

Better Business Bureau Arbitration Programs (Auto Line): The BBB always tries to mediate a dispute before recommending arbitration. Less than 10 percent of the disputes it handles actually go to arbitration. Theoretically, each party receives a list of potential arbitrators with a background description of each person and then ranks them according to preference. The arbitrator with the most votes handles the case. But in actual fact, the consumer rarely has a voice in the selection of an arbitrator.

The arbitrators are volunteers from the local community and sometimes are not automobile experts. This can both help and harm your case. As a result, it is important to be well prepared when participating in the BBB program. If you're not, the potential exists for the dealer or manufacturer to appear as the "expert" on automobiles. For more information, contact your local BBB or 800-955-5100.

Automobile Consumer Action Program: AUTOCAP was established by the National Automobile Dealers Association to assist consumers in resolving auto sales or service disputes with dealers and manufacturers. The program is sponsored on a voluntary basis by state and local dealer associations. Currently, most AUTOCAPs do not operate under the FTC guidelines required for warranty cases. Sixty-five percent of the cases that AUTOCAP considers are resolved in preliminary mediation. Of those cases that go to arbitration, 45 percent are resolved in favor of the consumer, 22 percent are a compromise, and 33 percent are in favor of the company. For more information and the name of your local panel, contact: AUTOCAP, 8400 Westpark Drive, McLean, Virginia 22102; 703-821-7144.

Ten Tips for Arbitration: Arbitration is designed to be easier and less intimidating than going to court. However, the process can still be nerve-racking, especially if you've never been through it before. Here are some tips to help make the process as simple and straightforward as possible.

1. Before deciding to go to arbitration, get a written description of how the program works, and make sure you understand the details. If you have any questions, contact the local representatives of the program. Remember, the manufacturer or dealer probably has more experience with this process than you do.

2. Make sure the final decision is nonbinding on you. If the decision is binding, you give up your right to appeal.

3. Determine whether the program allows you to appear at the hearing. If not, make sure your written statement is complete and contains all the appropriate receipts and documentation. If you think of something that you want considered after you have sent in your material, send it and specifically request that the additional information be included.

4. Make sure the program follows the required procedures. If the arbitration program is incorporated into the car's warranty, for example, the panel must make a decision on your case within 40 days of receiving your complaint.

5. Contact the manufacturer's zone manager and request copies of any technical service bulletins that apply to your car. (See "Secret Warranties" on page 59 for a description of technical service bulletins and how to get them.) Service bulletins may help you prove that your car is defective.

6. Well before the hearing, ask the program representative to send you copies of all material submitted by the other party. You may want to respond to this information.

7. Make sure all your documents are in chronological order, and include a brief outline of the events. Submit copies of all material associated with your problem and a copy of your warranty.

8. Even though you may be very angry about the situation, try to present your case in a calm, logical manner.

9. If you are asking for a refund or a replacement for your car in accordance with your state's Lemon Law, do not assume that the arbitrator is completely familiar with the law. Be prepared to explain how it entitles you to your request.

10. In most programs, you have to reject the decision in order to go to court to pursue other action. If you accept the decision, you may limit your rights to pursue further action. You will, however, have additional claims if the manufacturer or dealer does not properly follow through on the decision or if your car breaks down again.

State-Run Arbitration

State-run arbitration programs are often more fair to consumers than national programs. The following states have set up state programs (or guidelines) which are far better than their national counterparts. If you live in one of these areas, contact your attorney general's office for information. Even if your state is not listed below, you can contact your state attorney general's office (in care of your state capitol) for advice on arbitration.

Connecticut	Hawaii	New Hampshire	South Carolina
D. C.	Maine	New Jersey	Texas
Florida	Massachusetts	New York	Vermont
Georgia	Montana	Rhode Island	Washington

Complaint Index

Thanks to the efforts of the Center for Auto Safety, we are able to provide you with the vehicle complaints on file with the National Highway Traffic Safety Administration (NHTSA). Each year, thousands of Americans call the government to register complaints about their vehicles. The government collects this information but has never released it to the public.

The complaint index is the result of our analysis of these complaints. It is based on a ratio of the number of complaints for each vehicle to the sales of that vehicle. In order to predict the expected complaint performance of the 1996 models, we have examined the complaint history of that car's *series*. The term *series* refers to the fact that when a manufacturer introduces a new model, that vehicle remains essentially unchanged for 4-6 years. For example, the Ford Escort was introduced in 1991 and remains essentially the same car for 1996. As such, we have compiled the complaint experience for that series in order to give you some additional information to use in deciding which car to buy. For those vehicles just introduced in 1995 or 1996, we do not yet have enough data to develop a complaint index.

The following table presents the complaint indexes for the best and worst 1996 models. Higher index numbers mean the vehicle generated a greater number of complaints. Lower numbers indicate fewer complaints. After calculating the indexes, we compared the results among all 1996 vehicles.

1996 Complaint Ratings

The Best		The Worst	
Vehicle	Index	Vehicle	Index
Chevy Beretta/Corsica	1122	Saab 900	31777
Olds Achieva	1726	Chrysler Concorde	15738
Honda Prelude	1738	Chry. LHS/New Yorker	15675
Infiniti G20	1893	Mazda RX-7	13077
Saturn SC	1918	Mitsubishi Galant	12710
Toyota Celica	1934	Acura NSX	12474
Mazda Miata	1958	Dodge Intrepid	11712
Olds 98	1958	Chevy Camaro	11421
Lexus ES300	2022	Toyota Supra	11071
Olds Cutlass Ciera	2042	Cadillac Fleetwood	11056
Toyota Paseo	2072	Eagle Vision	10980
Lexus SC300/400	2156	Acura Integra	10799
Buick Skylark	2245	Pontiac Firebird	9149
Subaru Impreza	2533	Dodge Viper	8945
Pontiac Grand Am	2651	Buick Roadmaster	8359
Lincoln Town Car	2688	Eagle Summit	7771
Pontiac Bonneville	2857	Kia Sephia	7746
Toyota Corolla	2886	Subaru SVX	6978
Ford Escort	2932	Volkswagen Golf/Jetta	6752
Olds 88	2963	Nissan Quest	6749
Chevy Astro	2987	Volvo 850	6646
Pontiac Grand Prix	3007	Cadillac Seville	6621
Buick Park Avenue	3027	Mazda 929	6499
Buick Century	3202	Chevy Lumina	6295
Toyota Previa	3254	Ford Crown Victoria	6268
Mercury Tracer	3265	Cadillac Eldorado	6148
Mercury Cougar	3266	Mercury Grand Marquis	6033
Nissan Altima	3310	Ford Aspire	6026

Center for Auto Safety

Every year automobile manufacturers spend millions of dollars making their voices heard in government decision making. For example, General Motors and Ford have large staffs in Detroit and Washington that work solely to influence government activity. But who looks out for the consumer?

For over twenty years, the non-profit Center for Auto Safety (CAS) has told the consumer's story to government agencies, to Congress and to the courts. Its efforts focus on all consumers rather than only those with individual complaints.

The Center for Auto Safety was established in 1970 by Ralph Nader and Consumers Union. As consumer concerns about auto safety issues expanded, so did the work of CAS. It became an independent group in 1972, and the original staff of two has grown to fourteen attorneys and researchers. CAS' activities include:

Initiating Safety Recalls: CAS analyzes over 50,000 consumer complaints each year. By following problems as they develop, CAS requests government investigations and recalls of defective vehicles. CAS was responsible for the Ford Pinto faulty gas tank recall, the Firestone 500 steel-belted radial tire recall, and the record recall of over 3 million Evenflo One Step child seats.

Representing the Consumer in Washington: CAS follows the activities of federal agencies and Congress to ensure that they carry out their responsibilities to the American taxpayer. CAS brings a consumer's point of view to vehicle safety policies and rule-making. Since 1970, CAS has submitted more than 500 petitions and comments on federal safety standards.

One major effort in this area has been the successful fight for adoption of automatic crash protection in passenger cars. These systems are a more effective and less intrusive alternative to crash protection than mandatory safety belt laws or belts that must be buckled in order to start the car.

Three years ago, the Center for Auto Safety uncovered a fire defect that dwarfed the highly publicized flammability of the Ford Pinto. It had to do with the side-saddle gas tanks on full size 1973-87 GM pickups and 1988-90 crew cabs that tend to explode on impact. Over 1,300 people have been killed in fire crashes involving these trucks. After mounting a national campaign to warn consumers to steer clear of these GM fire hazards, the U.S. Department of Transportation granted CAS' petition and conducted one of its biggest defect investigations in history. The result—GM was asked to recall its pickups. GM, sadly, denied this request.

Thanks to a petition originally filed by CAS, NHTSA adopted a new registration system to better enable manufacturer notification to parents with defective child seats. This will enable more parents to find out about potentially hazardous safety seats.

Exposing Secret Warranties: CAS played a prominent role in the disclosure of secret warranties, "policy adjustments," as they are called by manufacturers. These occur when an auto maker agrees to pay for repair of certain defects beyond the warranty period but refuses to notify consumers. (See "Secret Warranties" in the Warranty Chapter.)

Improving Rust Warranties: Rust and corrosion cost American car owners up to $14 billion annually. CAS has been successful in its efforts to get domestic and foreign auto companies to lengthen their all-important corrosion warranties.

Lemon Laws: CAS' work on Lemon Laws aided in the enactment of state laws which make it easier to return a defective new automobile and get money back.

Tire Ratings: After a suspension between 1982-84, consumers have reliable treadwear ratings to help them get the most miles for their dollar. CAS' lawsuit overturned DOT's revocation of this valuable new tire information program.

Initiating Legal Action: When CAS has exhausted other means of obtaining relief for consumer problems, it will initiate legal action. For example, in 1978 when the Department of Energy attempted to raise the price of gasoline 4 cents per gallon without notice or comment, CAS succeeded in stopping this illegal move through a lawsuit, thus saving consumers $2 billion for the six month period that the action was delayed.

A Center for Auto Safety lawsuit against the Environmental Protection Agency, in 1985, forced the EPA to recall polluting cars, rather than let companies promise to make cleaner cars in the future. As part of the settlement, GM (which was responsible for the polluting cars) funded a $7 million methanol bus demonstration program in New York City.

Publications: CAS has many publications on automobiles, motor homes, recreational vehicles, and fuel economy, including a number of free information packets. For each of the packets listed below, or for a complete description of all of the CAS' publications, send a separate stamped, self-addressed, business-sized envelope with 52 cents postage to the address below. Unless otherwise noted, the packets listed cover all known major problems for the models indicated and explain what to do about them. Requests for information should include make, model, and year of vehicle (with VIN number), as well as the type of problem you are experiencing. (Allow 2 to 3 weeks for delivery.)

Audi Defects (1978-92)
Cad. Seville/Eldorado/DeVille/ Fleetwood/Brougham/Allante HT-4100 Defects (1982-87)
Chrys. Paint/Water Leaks (1983-1995)
Chrys. Ultradrive Trans. (1989-95)
Chrys. FWD Cars (1981-95)
Chrys. Trucks/Vans (1981-95)
Chrys. Cirrus/Stratus/Neon (1994-95)
Chrys. LHS/Intrepid/Concorde (1993-95)
Chrys. Minivan (1984-95)
Ford Aerostar (1986-95)
Ford Cr. Vic./Gr. Marquis/ Lincoln Cont./Town Car/ Mark Series (1983-95)
Ford Escort/Lynx/Tracer (1981-95)
Ford F-Series Pickup Truck/Van Defects (1981-95)
Ford Taurus/Sable (1986-95)
Ford Tempo/Topaz (1984-95)
Ford Mustang/Capri/Probe (1979-95)
Ford Paint (1985-95)

GM Compact Cars-Prizm/Metro/ Storm/LeMans/Sprint/Nova (1985-95)
GM Saturn Defects (1991-1995)
GM Auto. Trans.: FWD (1981-93)
GM Auto. Trans.: RWD (1981-92)
GM Beretta/Corsica (1987-95)
GM Cut. Supr./Gr. Prix/Lumina/ Regal (1988-95)
GM Celebrity/6000/Century/Cut. Ciera & Cruiser (1982-95)
GM Camaro/Firebird (1982-95)
GM Citation/Omega/Phoenix/ Skylark (1981-85)
GM Achieva/Calais/Gr. Am/ Skylark/Somerset Regal (1985-95)
GM Buick Roadmaster/Chevrolet Caprice (1981-95)
GM Cavalier/Cimarron/Firenza/ Skyhawk/Sunbird/J2000 (1982-95)
GM LeSabre/Delta 88 & 98/ Bonneville/Electra & Park Ave. (1986-95)
GM Power Steering Failure (1980-88)
GM Large Pickup/Suburban & Blazer/Jimmy Utility Vehicle (1984-95)
GM S-series Truck/Blazer/Jimmy (1982-95)
GM Big Vans/Astro/Safari/APVs (1980-95)
GM Pontiac Fiero (1984-88)

GM Paint (1985-95)
Honda/Acura Defects (1988-95)
Hyundai Defects (1986-95)
Jeep–all models (1984-95)
Lemon Law Fact Sheet and Chart (1995)
Lemon Lawyer Recommendations (1995)
Mazda Car/Truck Defects (1988-95)
Mercedes Defects (1980-95)
Minivan Safety (1995)
Mitsubishi Defects (1983-95)
Nissan Car and Truck Defects (1988-95)
Renault/Eagle/Dodge Defects (1981-95)
Toyota Defects (1988-95)
Volkswagen Defects (1980-95)
Volvo Defects (1980-95)

CAS depends on the public for its support. Annual consumer membership is $15 ($20 for overseas). All contributions to this nonprofit organization are tax-deductible. Annual membership includes a quarterly newsletter called "LEMON TIMES." To join, send a check to:

Center for Auto Safety
2001 S St. NW, Suite 410
Washington, DC 20009-1160

Lemon Aid

The Center for Auto Safety has published *The Lemon Book,* a detailed, 368 page guide to resolving automobile complaints. Co-authored by Ralph Nader and the CAS Executive Director, Clarence Ditlow, this handbook is designed to help car buyers avoid lemons and tells you what to do if you wind up with one. To obtain this valuable book, send $15.95 to the Center for Auto Safety, 2001 S St., NW, Suite 410, Washington, DC 20009-1160. CAS is a non-profit consumer group supported, in part, by the sales of its publications.

Here are the names of additional consumer groups which you may find helpful:

Consumer Action San Francisco

116 New Montgomery St., #233
San Francisco, CA 94105
(415) 777-9635
Focus: General problems of California residents.

Consumers for Auto Reliability and Safety Foundation

1500 W. El Camino Ave, #419
Sacramento, CA 95833-1945
(916) 759-9440
Focus: Auto safety, airbags, and lemon laws.

Consumers Education and Protective Association

6048 Ogontz Avenue
Philadelphia, PA 19141
(215) 424-1441
Focus: Pickets on behalf of members to resolve auto purchase and repair problems.

SafetyBelt Safe, U.S.A.

P.O. Box 553
Altadena, CA 91003
(800) 745-SAFE or
(310) 673-2666
Focus: Provides excellent information and training on child safety seats and safety belt usage.

VIGOR (Victims Group Opposed to Unsafe Restraint Systems)

3286 Avenida Anacapa Street
Carlsbad, CA 92009
(619) 943-0670
Focus: Promotes the replacement of lap-only seat belts in existing vehicles.

Several federal agencies conduct automobile-related programs. Listed below is each agency with a description of the type of work it performs as well as the address and phone number for its headquarters in Washington, DC.

National Highway Traffic Safety Administration

400 7th Street, SW, NOA-40
Washington, DC 20590
(202) 366-9550

NHTSA issues safety and fuel economy standards for new motor vehicles; investigates safety defects and enforces recall of defective vehicles and equipment; conducts research and demonstration programs on vehicle safety, fuel economy, driver safety, and automobile inspection and repair; provides grants for state highway safety programs in areas such as police traffic services, driver education and licensing, emergency medical services, pedestrian safety, and alcohol abuse.

Environmental Protection Agency

401 M Street, SW
Washington, DC 20460
(202) 260-2090

EPA is responsible for the control and abatement of air, noise, and toxic substance pollution. This includes setting and enforcing air and noise emission standards for motor vehicles and measuring fuel economy in new vehicles (EPA Fuel Economy Guide).

Federal Trade Commission

PA Avenue & 6th Street, NW
Washington, DC 20580
(202) 326-2000

FTC regulates advertising and credit practices, marketing abuses, and professional services and ensures that products are properly labeled (as in fuel economy ratings). The commission covers unfair or deceptive trade practices in motor vehicle sales and repairs, as well as in non-safety defects.

Federal Highway Administration

400 7th Street, SW,
Room 3401, HHS1
Washington, DC 20590
(202) 366-1153

FHA develops standards to ensure highways are constructed to reduce occurrence and severity of accidents.

Department of Justice

Consumer Litigation
Civil Division
1331 Pennsylvania Avenue
National Place Bldg., Suite 950N
Washington, DC 20004
(202) 514-6786

The Department of Justice enforces the federal law that requires manufacturers to label new automobiles and forbids removal or alteration of labels before delivery to consumers. Labels must contain the make, model, vehicle identification number, dealer's name, suggested base price, manufacturer option costs, and manufacturer's suggested retail price.

Automobile Manufacturers

Acura Automobile Division
Mr. Richard B. Thomas
Executive V. P. and General Manager
1919 Torrance Blvd.
Torrance, CA 90501-2746
(310) 783-2000/(310) 783-3900 (fax)

BMW of North America, Inc.
Mr. Victor H. Doolan
President
300 Chestnut Ridge Road
Woodcliff Lake, NJ 07675
(201) 307-4000/(201) 307-4003 (fax)

Chrysler Corporation
Mr. Robert Eaton
Chairman and CEO
12000 Chrysler Drive
Highland Park, MI 48288-0001
(313) 956-5741

Ford Motor Company
Mr. Alex Trotman
Chairman, Pres. and CEO
The American Road
Dearborn, MI 48121
(313) 322-3000/(313) 446-9475 (fax)

General Motors Corporation
Mr. John F. Smith, Jr.
CEO and President
3044 W. Grand Blvd.
Detroit, MI 48202
(313) 556-5000/(313) 556-5108 (fax)

American Honda Motor Co.
Mr. K. Amemiya
President
1919 Torrance Blvd.
Torrance, CA 90501-2746
(310) 783-2000/(310) 783-3900 (fax)

Hyundai Motor America
Mr. Y. I. Lee
President and CEO
10550 Talbert Avenue
Fountain Valley, CA 92728
(714) 965-3939/(714) 965-3816 (fax)

American Isuzu Motors Inc.
Mr. Yoshito Mochizuki
President
13181 Crossroads Pkwy., N.
City of Industry, CA 91746
(310) 699-0500/(310) 692-7135 (fax)

Jaguar Cars Inc.
Mr. Michael H. Dale
President N. American Operations
555 MacArthur Blvd.
Mahwah, NJ 07430-2327
(201) 818-8500/(201) 818-9770 (fax)

Kia Motors America, Inc.
Mr. H.R. Park
President and CEO
2 Cromwell
Irvine, CA 92718
(714) 470-7000/(714) 470-2801 (fax)

Land Rover of America
Mr. Charles R. Hughes
President
4390 Parliament Place
Lanham, MD 20706
(301) 731-9040/(301) 731-9054 (fax)

Mazda Motor of America, Inc.
Mr. George Toyama
President
7755 Irvine Center Dr.
Irvine, CA 92718
(714) 727-1990/(714) 727-6529 (fax)

Mercedes-Benz of N.A.
Mr. Michael Bassermann
President and CEO
1 Mercedes Drive
Montvale, NJ 07645-0350
(201) 573-0600/(201) 573-0117 (fax)

Mitsubishi Motor Sales
Mr. Tohei Takeuchi
President and CEO
6400 Katella Ave.
Cypress, CA 90630-0064
(714) 372-6000/(714) 373-1019 (fax)

Nissan Motor Corp. U.S.A.
Mr. Robert Thomas
President and CEO
P.O. Box 191
Gardena, CA 90248-0191
(310) 532-3111/(310) 719-3343 (fax)

Porsche Cars North America, Inc.
Mr. Frederick J. Schwab
President and CEO
P.O. Box 30911
Reno, NV 89520-3911
(702) 348-3000/(702) 348-3770 (fax)

Rolls Royce Motor Cars, Inc.
Mr. Robert R. Wharen
Managing Dir., American Operations
140 E. Ridgewood Ave.
Paramus, NJ 07652
(201) 967-9100/(201) 967-2070 (fax)

Saab Cars USA, Inc.
Mr. James Crumlish
President and CEO
4405-A Saab Drive
Norcross, GA 30091
(404) 279-0100/(404) 279-6499 (fax)

Subaru of America, Inc.
Mr. Yasuo Fujiki
Chairman and CEO
P.O. Box 6000
Cherry Hill, NJ 08034-6000
(609) 488-8500/(609) 488-0485 (fax)

American Suzuki Motor Corp.
Mr. Masao Nagura
President
3251 E. Imperial Hwy.
Brea, CA 92621-6722
(714) 996-7040/(714) 524-2512 (fax)

Toyota Motors Sales, U.S.A., Inc.
Mr. Shinji Sakai
President and CEO
19001 S. Western Avenue
Torrance, CA 90509
(310) 618-4000/(310) 618-7800 (fax)

Volkswagen of America, Inc.
Mr. Clive Warrilow
President
3800 Hamlin Road
Auburn Hills, MI 48326
(810) 340-5000/(810) 340-4643 (fax)

Volvo Cars of North America
Mr. Helge Alten
President and CEO
7 Volvo Drive
Rockleigh, NJ 07647
(201) 767-4710/(201) 784-4535 (fax)

Sometimes, despite our best efforts, we buy a vehicle that just doesn't work right. There may be little problem after little problem, or perhaps one big problem that never seems to be fixed. Because of the bad taste that such vehicles leave in the mouths of consumers who buy them, these vehicles are known as "lemons."

In the past, it's been difficult to obtain a refund or replacement if a vehicle was a lemon. The burden of proof was left to the consumer. Because it is hard to define exactly what constitutes a lemon, many lemon owners were unable to win a case against a manufacturer. However, as of 1993, all states have passed "Lemon Laws." Although there are some important state-to-state variations, all of the laws have similarities: They establish a period of coverage, usually one year from delivery or the written warranty period, whichever is shorter; they may require some form of noncourt arbitration; and most importantly they define a lemon. In most states a lemon is a new car, truck, or van that has been taken back to the shop at least four times for the same repair, or is out of service for a total of 30 days during the covered period.

This time does not mean consecutive days. In some states the total time must be for the same repair; in others, it can be based on different repair problems.

Be sure to keep careful records of your repairs since some states now require only one of the three or four repairs to be within the specified time period.

Specific information about laws in your state can be obtained from your state attorney general's office (c/o your state capitol) or your local consumer protection office. The following table offers a general description of the Lemon Law in your state and what you need to do to set it in motion (*Notification/Trigger*). An **L** indicates that the law covers leased vehicles and we indicate where state-run arbitration programs are available. State-run programs are the best type of arbitration.

Alabama	**Qualification:** 3 unsuccessful repairs or 30 calendar days out of service within shorter of 24 months or 24,000 miles, provided 1 repair attempt or 1 day out of service is within shorter of 1 year or 12,000 miles. **Notification/Trigger:** Certified mail notice to manufacturer, who has 14 calendar days to make final repair.
Alaska	**Qualification:** 3 unsuccessful repairs or 30 business days out of service within shorter of 1 year or warranty. **Notification/Trigger:** Certified mail notice to manufacturer and dealer, or agent within 60 days after expiration of warranty or 1 year. Consumer must demand refund or replacement to be delivered within 60 days after mailing the notice. Final repair attempt within 30 days of receipt of notice.
Arizona	**Qualification:** 4 unsuccessful repairs or 30 calendar days out of service within shorter of 1 year or warranty. **Notification/Trigger:** Written notice to manufacturer and opportunity to repair.
Arkansas	**Qualification:** 3 unsuccessful repairs, or 1 unsuccessful repair of a problem likely to cause death or serious bodily injury within longer of 24 months or 24,000 miles. **Notification/Trigger:** Certified or registered mail notice to manufacturer. Manufacturer has 10 days to notify consumer of repair facility. Facility has 10 days to repair.
California	**Qualification:** 4 unsuccessful repairs or 30 calendar days out of service within shorter of 1 year or 12,000 miles. **Notification/Trigger:** Written notice to manufacturer and delivery of car to repair facility for repair attempt within 30 days. *State has certified guidelines for arbitration.* **L**
Colorado	**Qualification:** 4 unsuccessful repairs or 30 business days out of service within shorter of 1 year or warranty. **Notification/Trigger:** Prior certified mail notice for each defect occurance and opportunity to repair.
Conn.	**Qualification:** 4 unsuccessful repairs or 30 calendar days out of service within shorter of 2 years or 18,000 miles, or 2 repairs of problem likely to cause death or serious bodily injury within shorter of 1 year or warranty. **Notification/Trigger:** Report to manufacturer, agent or dealer. Written

Conn. (cont.)	notice to manufacturer only if required in owner's manual or warranty. *State-run arbitration program is available.* **L**
Delaware	**Qualification:** 4 unsuccessful repairs or 30 calendar days out of service within shorter of 1 year or warranty. **Notification/Trigger:** Written notice to manufacturer and opportunity to repair. **L**
D. C.	**Qualification:** 4 unsuccessful repairs or 30 calendar days out of service or 1 unsuccesful repair of a safety-related defect, within shorter of 2 years or 18,000 miles. **Notification/Trigger:** Report of each defect occurance to manufacturer, agent or dealer. *State-run arbitration program is available.* **L**
Florida	**Qualification:** 3 unsuccessful repairs or 20 calendar days out of service within shorter of 12 months or 12,000 miles. **Notification/Trigger:** Written notice by certified or express mail to manufacturer who has 14 calendar days (10 if vehicle has been out of service 20 cumulative calendar days) for final repair attempt after delivery to designated dealer. *State-run arbitration program is available.* **L**
Georgia*	**Qualification:** 3 unsuccessful repair attempts or 30 calendar days out of service within shorter of 24,000 miles or 24 months, with 1 repair or 15 days out of service within shorter or 1 year or 12,000 miles; or one unsuccessful repair of a serious safety defect in the braking or steering system within shorter of 1 year or 12,000 miles. **Notification/Trigger:** Certified mail notice return receipt requested. Manufacturer has 7 days to notify consumer of repair facility. Facility has 14 days to repair. *State-run arbitration program is available.* **L**
Hawaii	**Qualification:** 3 unsuccessful repairs, or 1 unsuccessful repair of a nonconformity likely to cause death or serious bodily injury, or out of service within shorter of 2 years or 24,000 miles. **Notification/Trigger:** Written notice to manufacturer and opportunity to repair. *State-run arbitration program is available.* **L**
Idaho	**Qualification:** 4 repair attempts or 30 business days out of service within shorter of 12 months or 12,000 miles. **Notification/Trigger:** Written notice to manufacturer or dealer.
Illinois*	**Qualification:** 4 unsuccessful repairs or 30 business days out of service within shorter of 1 year or 12,000 miles. **Notification/Trigger:** Written notice to manufacturer and opportunity to repair.
Indiana	**Qualification:** 4 unsuccessful repairs or 30 business days out of service within the shorter of 18 months or 18,000 miles. **Notification/Trigger:** Written notice to manufacturer only if required in warranty. **L**
Iowa	**Qualification:** 3 unsuccessful repairs, or 1 unsuccessful repair of a nonconformity likely to cause death or serious bodily injury, or 20 calendar days out of service within shorter of 2 years or 24,000 miles. **Notification/Trigger:** Written notice to manufacturer and final opportunity to repair within 10 calendar days of receipt of notice. *State has certified guidelines for arbitration.* **L**
Kansas	**Qualification:** 4 unsuccessful repairs of the same problem or 30 calendar days out of service or 10 total repairs of any problem within shorter of 1 year or warranty. **Notification/Trigger:** Actual notice to manufacturer.
Kentucky	**Qualification:** 4 unsuccessful repairs or 30 calendar days out of service within shorter of 1 year or 12,000 miles. **Notification/Trigger:** Written notice to manufacturer.
Louisiana	**Qualification:** 4 unsuccessful repairs or 30 calendar days out of service within shorter of 1 year or warranty. **Notification/Trigger:** Report to manufacturer or dealer. **L**
Maine	**Qualification:** 3 unsuccessful repairs (when at least 2 times the same agent attempted the repair) or 15 business days out of service within shorter of 2 years or 18,000 miles. **Notification/Trigger:** Written notice to manufacturer or dealer only if required in warranty or owner's manual. Manufacturer has 7 business days after receipt for final repair attempt. *State-run arbitration program is available.* **L**
Maryland	**Qualification:** 4 unsuccessful repairs, 30 calendar days out of service or 1 unsuccessful repair of braking or steering system within shorter of 15 months or 15,000 miles. **Notification/Trigger:** Certified mail notice, return receipt requested to manu. or factory branch and opportunity to repair within 30 calendar days of receipt of notice. **L**
Mass.	**Qualification:** 3 unsuccessful repairs or 15 business days out of service within shorter of 1 year or 15,000 miles. **Notification/Trigger:** Notice to manufacturer or dealer who has 7 business days to attempt a final repair. *State-run arbitration program is available.*

Michigan	**Qualification:** 4 unsuccessful repairs or 30 calendar days out of service within shorter of 1 year or warranty. **Notification/Trigger:** Certified mail notice, return receipt requested, to manufacturer who has 5 business days to repair after delivery.
Minn.	**Qualification:** 4 unsuccessful repairs or 30 business days out of service or 1 unsuccessful repair of total braking or steering loss likely to cause death or serious bodily injury within shorter of 2 years or warranty. **Notification/Trigger:** At least one written notice to manufacturer, agent or dealer and opportunity to repair. **L**
Miss.	**Qualification:** 3 unsuccessful repairs or 15 business days out of service within shorter of 1 year or warranty. **Notification/Trigger:** Written notice to manufacturer who has 10 business days to repair after delivery to designated dealer.
Missouri	**Qualification:** 4 unsuccessful repairs or 30 business days out of service within shorter of 1 year or warranty. **Notification/Trigger:** Written notice to manufacturer who has 10 calendar days to repair after delivery to designated dealer.
Montana	**Qualification:** 4 unsuccessful repairs or 30 business days out of service after notice within shorter of 2 years or 18,000 miles. **Notification/Trigger:** Written notice to manufacturer and opportunity to repair. *State-run arbitration program is available.*
Nebraska	**Qualification:** 4 unsuccessful repairs or 40 calendar days out of service within shorter of 1 year or warranty. **Notification/Trigger:** Certified mail notice to manufacturer and opportunity to repair.
Nevada	**Qualification:** 4 unsuccessful repairs or 30 calendar days out of service within shorter of 1 year or warranty. **Notification/Trigger:** Written notice to manufacturer.
N. H.	**Qualification:** 3 unsuccessful repairs by same dealer or 30 business days out of service within warranty. **Notification/Trigger:** Report to manufacturer, distributor, agent or dealer (on forms provided by manufacturer) and final opportunity to repair before arbitration. *State-run arbitration program is available.* **L**
N. J.	**Qualification:** 3 unsuccessful repairs or 20 calendar days out of service within shorter of 2 years or 18,000 miles. **Notification/Trigger:** Certified mail notice, written notice to manufacturer who has 15 days to repair. *State-run arbitration program is available.* **L**
N. M.	**Qualification:** 4 unsuccessful repairs or 30 business days within shorter of 1 year or warranty. **Notification/Trigger:** Written notice to manufacturer, agent or dealer and opportunity to repair.
N. Y.	**Qualification:** 4 unsuccessful repairs or 30 calendar days out of service within shorter of 2 years or 18,000 miles. **Notification/Trigger:** Certified notice to manufacturer, agent or dealer. *State-run arbitration program is available.* **L**
N. C.	**Qualification:** 4 unsuccessful repairs within the shorter of 24 months, 24,000 miles or warranty or 20 business days out of service during any 12 month period of the warranty. **Notification/Trigger:** Written notice to manufacturer and opportunity to repair within 15 calendar days of receipt only if required in warranty or owner's manual. **L**
N. D.	**Qualification:** 4 unsuccessful repairs or 30 business days out of service within shorter of 1 year or warranty. **Notification/Trigger:** Direct written notice and opportunity to repair to manufacturer. **L**
Ohio	**Qualification:** 3 unsuccessful repairs of same nonconformity, 30 calendar days out of service, 8 total repairs of any problem, or 1 unsuccessful repair of problem likely to cause death or serious bodily injury within shorter of 1 year or 18,000 miles. **Notification/Trigger:** Report to manufacturer, its agent or dealer.
Okla.	**Qualification:** 4 unsuccessful repairs or 45 calendar days out of service within shorter of 1 year or warranty. **Notification/Trigger:** Written notice to manufacturer and opportunity to repair.
Oregon	**Qualification:** 4 unsuccessful repairs or 30 business days out of service within shorter of 1 year or 12,000 miles. **Notification/Trigger:** Direct written notice to manufacturer and opportunity to repair. **L**
Penn.	**Qualification:** 3 unsuccessful repairs or 30 calendar days out of service within shorter of 1 year, 12,000 miles, or warranty. **Notification/Trigger:** Delivery to authorized service and repair facility. If delivery impossible, written notice to manufacturer or its repair facility obligates them to pay for delivery.

R. I.	**Qualification:** 4 unsuccessful repairs or 30 calendar days out of service within shorter of 1 year or 15,000 miles. **Notification/Trigger:** Report to dealer or manufacturer who has 7 days for final repair opportunity. **L**
S. C.	**Qualification:** 3 unsuccessful repairs or 30 calendar days out of service within shorter of 1 year or 12,000 miles. **Notification/Trigger:** Written notice to manufacturer by certified mail and oppportunity to repair only if manufacturer informed consumer of such at time of sale. Manufacturer has 10 days to notify consumer of repair facility. Facility has 10 days to repair. *State-run arbitration program is available.* **L**
S. D.	**Qualification:** 4 unsuccessful repairs, at least 1 of which occurred during the shorter of 1 year or 12,000 miles, or 30 calendar days out of service during the shorter of 24 months or 24,000 miles. **Notification/Trigger:** Certified mail notice to manufacturer and final opportunity to repair. Manufacturer has 7 calendar days to notify consumer of repair facility. Facility has 14 days to repair. If manufacturer has established a state recognized informal dispute settlement procedure, consumer must use program before instituting a cause of action.
Tenn.	**Qualification:** 4 unsuccessful repairs or 30 calendar days out of service within shorter of 1 year or warranty. **Notification/Trigger:** Certified mail notice to manufacturer and final opportunity to repair within 10 calendar days. **L**
Texas	**Qualification:** 4 unsuccessful repairs when 2 occured within shorter of 1 year or 12,000 miles, and other 2 occur within shorter of 1 year or 12,000 miles from date of 2nd repair attempt; or 2 unsuccessful repairs of a serious safety defect when 1 occured within shorter of 1 year or 12,000 miles and other occured within shorter of 1 year or 12,000 miles from date of 1st repair; or 30 calendar days out of service within shorter of 2 years or 24,000 miles and at least 2 attempts were made within shorter of 1 year or 12,000 miles. **Notification/Trigger:** Written notice to manufacturer. *State-run arbitration program is available.* **L**
Utah	**Qualification:** 4 unsuccessful repairs or 30 business days out of service within shorter of 1 year or warranty. **Notification/Trigger:** Report to manufacturer, agent or dealer. **L**
Vermont	**Qualification:** 3 unsuccessful repairs when at least 1st repair was within warranty, or 30 calendar days within warranty **Notification/Trigger:** Written notice to manufacturer (on provided forms) after 3rd repair attempt, or 30 days. Arbitration must be held within 45 days after notice, during which time manufacturer has 1 final repair. *State-run arbitration program is available.* **L**
Virginia	**Qualification:** 3 unsuccessful repairs, or 1 repair attempt of a serious safety defect, or 30 calendar days out of service within 18 months. **Notification/Trigger:** Written notice to manufacturer. If 3 unsuccessful repairs or 30 days already exhausted before notice, manufacturer has 1 more repair attempt not to exceed 15 days.
Wash.	**Qualification:** 4 unsuccessful repairs, 30 calendar days out of service (15 during warranty period), or 2 repairs of serious safety defects, first reported within shorter of the warranty or 24 months or 24,000 miles. One repair attempt and 15 of the 30 days must fall within manufacturer's express warranty of at least 1 year or 12,000 miles. **Notification/Trigger:** Written notice to manufacturer. *State-run arbitration program is available.* **L** *Note: Consumer should receive replacement or refund within 40 calendar days of request.*
W. V.	**Qualification:** 3 unsuccessful repairs or 30 calendar days out of service or 1 unsuccessful repair of problem likely to cause death or serious bodily injury within shorter of 1 year or warranty. **Notification/Trigger:** Prior written notice to manufacturer and at least one opportunity to repair.
Wisc.	**Qualification:** 4 unsuccessful repairs or 30 calendar days out of service within shorter of 1 year or warranty. **Notification/Trigger:** Report to manufacturer or dealer. **L** *Note: Consumer should receive replacement or refund within 30 calendar days after offer to return title.*
Wyoming	**Qualification:** 3 unsuccessful repairs or 30 business days out of service within 1 year. **Notification/Trigger:** Direct written notice to manufacturer and opportunity to repair.

SHOWROOM STRATEGIES

Buying a car means matching wits with a seasoned professional. But if you know what to expect, you'll have a much better chance of getting a really good deal! This chapter offers practical advice on buying a car, tips on getting the best price, information on buying vs. leasing, and tips on avoiding lemons. We'll also take a peek at some options for the future that will increase driving safety.

For most of us, the auto showroom can be an intimidating environment, and for good reason. We're matching wits with seasoned, professional negotiators over a very complex product. Being prepared is the best way to turn a potentially intimidating showroom experience into a profitable one. Here's some advice on handling what you'll find in the showroom.

Beware of silence. Silence is often used to intimidate, so be prepared for long periods of time when the salesperson is "talking with the manager." This tactic is designed to make you want to "just get the negotiation over with." Instead of becoming a victim, do something that indicates you are serious about looking elsewhere. Bring the classified section of the newspaper with you and begin circling other cars or review brochures from other manufacturers. By sending the message that you have other options, you increase your bargaining power and speed the process.

Don't fall in love with a car. Never look too interested in any particular car. Advise family members who go with you against being too enthusiastic about any one car. *Tip:* Beat the dealers at their own game—bring along a friend who tells you that the price is "too much compared to the *other* deal."

Keep your wallet in your pocket. Don't leave a deposit, even if it's refundable. You'll feel pressure to rush your shopping, and you'll have to return and face the salesperson again, perhaps before you are ready.

Shop at the end of the month. Salespeople anxious to meet sales goals are more willing to negotiate a lower price at this time.

Buy last year's model. The majority of new cars are the same as the previous year, with minor cosmetic changes. You can save considerably by buying in early fall when dealers are clearing space for "new" models. The important trade-off you make using this technique is that the car maker may have added air bags or anti-lock brakes to an otherwise unchanged vehicle.

Buying from stock. You can often get a better deal on a car that the dealer has on the lot. However, these cars usually have expensive options you may not want or need. Do not hesitate to ask the dealer to remove an option (and its accompanying charge) or sell you the car without charging for the option. Another advantage of buying from stock is that the longer the car sits there, the more interest the dealer pays on the car, which increases the dealer's incentive to sell.

Ordering a car. Domestic cars can be ordered from the manufacturer. Simply offering a fixed amount over invoice may be attractive because it's a sure sale and the dealership has not invested in the car. All the salesperson has to do is take your order.

If you do order a car, make sure when it arrives that it includes only the options you requested. Don't fall for the trick where the dealer offers you unordered options at a "special price," because it was their mistake. If you didn't order the option, don't pay for it.

Don't trade in. Although it is more work, you can almost always do better by selling your old car yourself than by trading it in. To determine what you'll gain by selling the car yourself, check the NADA "Blue Book" at your credit union or library. The difference between the trade-in price (what the dealer will give you) and the retail price (what you typically can sell it for) is your extra payment for selling the car yourself.

If you do decide to trade your car in at the dealership, *keep the buying and selling separate*. First, negotiate the best price for your new car, then find out how much the dealer will give you for your old car. Keeping the two deals separate ensures that you know what you're paying for your new car and simplifies the entire transaction.

Avoiding Lemons

One way to avoid the sour taste of a lemon after you've bought your car is to protect yourself *before* you sign on the dotted line. These tips will help you avoid problems down the road.

1 **Avoid new models.** Any new car in its very first year of production often turns out to have a lot of defects. Sometimes the manufacturer isn't able to remedy the defects until the second, third, or even fourth year of production. If the manufacturer has not worked out problems by the third model year, the car will likely be a lemon forever.

2 **Avoid the first cars off the line.** Most companies close down their assembly lines every year to make annual style changes. In addition to adding hundreds of dollars to the price of a new car, these changes can introduce new defects. It can take a few months to iron out these bugs. Ask the dealer when the vehicle you are interested in was manufactured, or look on the metal tag found on the inside of the driver-side door frame to find the date of manufacture.

3 **Avoid delicate options.** Delicate options have the highest frequency-of-repair records. Power seats, power windows, power antennas, and special roofs are nice conveniences≡until they break down. Of all the items on the vehicles, they tend to be the most expensive to repair.

4 **Inspect the dealer's checklist.** Request a copy of the dealer's pre-delivery service and adjustment checklist (also called a "make-ready list") at the time your new vehicle is delivered. Write the request directly on the new vehicle order. This request informs the dealer that you are aware of the dealer's responsibility to check your new car for defects.

5 **Examine the car on delivery.** Most of us are very excited when it comes time to take the vehicle home. This is the time where a few minutes of careful inspection can save hours of aggravation later. Carefully look over the body for any damage, check for the spare tire and jack equipment, make sure all electrical items work, and make sure all the hubcaps and body molding are on. You may want to take a short test drive. Finally, make sure you have the owner's manual, warranty forms, and all the legal documents.

One of the most difficult aspects of buying a new car is getting the best price. Most of us are at a disadvantage negotiating because we don't know how much the car actually cost the dealer. The difference between what the dealer paid and the sticker price represents the negotiable amount.

Until recently, the key to getting the best price was finding out the dealer cost. Many shoppers now ask to see the factory invoice, so some dealers promote their cars by offering to sell at only $49 or $99 over invoice. This sounds like a good deal, but these cars often have options you may not want and most invoice prices do not reveal the extra, hidden profit to the dealer.

Now that most savvy consumers know to check the so-called "dealer invoice," the industry has camouflaged this number. Special incentives, rebates, and kickbacks can account for $500 to $2,000 worth of extra profit to a dealer selling a car at "dealer invoice." The non-profit Center for the Study of Services recently discovered that in 37 percent of cases when dealers are forced to bid against each other for the sale, they offered the buyer a price below the "dealer invoice"—an unlikely event if the dealer was actually losing money. The bottom line is that "dealer invoice" doesn't mean anything anymore.

Because the rules have changed, we believe that most consumers are ill-advised to try and negotiate with a dealer. Introducing competition is the best way to get the lowest price on a new car. What this means is that you have to convince 3 or 4 dealers that you are, in fact, prepared to buy a car; that you have decided on the make, model, and features; and that

your decision now rests solely on which dealer will give you the best price. You can try to do this by phone, but often dealers will not give you the best price, or will quote you a price over the phone that they will not honor later. Instead, you should try to do this in person. As anyone knows who has ventured into an auto showroom simply to get the best price, the process can be lengthy and arduous. Nevertheless, if you can convice the dealer that you are serious and are willing to take the time to go to a number of dealers, it will pay off. Otherwise, we suggest you use the CarBargains service listed on the next page.

If you find a big savings at a dealership far from your home, call a local dealer with the price. They may very well match it. If not, pick up the car from the distant dealer, knowing your trip has saved you hundreds of dollars. You can still bring it to your local dealer for warranty work and repairs. Here are some other showroom strategies:

Beware of misleading advertising. New car ads are meant to get you into the showroom. They usually promise low prices, big rebates, high trade-in, and spotless integrity—don't be deceived. Advertised prices are rarely the true selling price. They usually exclude trans-

portation charges, service fees, or document fees. And always look out for the asterisk, both in advertisements and on invoices. It can be a signal that the advertiser has something to hide.

Don't talk price until you're ready to buy. On your first trips to the showroom, simply look over the cars, decide what options you want, and do your test driving.

Shop the corporate twins. Page 18 contains a list of corporate twins—nearly identical cars that carry different name plates. Check the price and options of the twins of the car you like. A higher priced twin may have more options, so it may be a better deal than the lower priced car without the options you want.

Watch out for dealer preparation overcharges. Before paying the dealer to clean your car, make sure that preparation is not included in the basic price. The price sticker will state: "Manufacturer's suggested retail price of this model includes dealer preparation."

If you must negotiate . . . Negotiate from the "invoice" price. Rather than see how much you can get off the sticker price, simply make an offer close to or at the "invoice" price. If the sales person says that your offer is too low to make a profit, ask to see the factory invoice.

The 180 Degree Turn

If you try to negotiate a car purchase, remember that you have the most important weapon in the bargaining process: *the 180-degree turn.* Be prepared to walk away from a deal, even at the risk of losing the "very best deal" your salesperson has ever offered, and you will be in the best position to get a genuine "best deal." Remember: dealerships need you, the buyer, to survive.

Price Shopping Service

Even with the information that we provide you in this chapter of *The Car Book,* most of us will *not* be well prepared to negotiate a good price for the cars we are considering. In fact, as we indicated on the previous page, we don't believe that you can negotiate the best price with *a* dealer. The key to getting the best price is to get the dealers to compete with each other. This page describes a new and easy way to find the best price by actually getting the dealers to compete.

CarBargains is a service of the non-profit Center for the Study of Services, a Washington, DC, consumer group, set up to provide comparative price information for many products and services.

CarBargains will "shop" the dealerships in your area and obtain at least five price quotes for the make and model of the car that you want to buy. The dealers who submit quotes know that they are competing with other area dealerships and have agreed to honor the prices that they submit. It is important to note that CarBargains is not an auto broker or "car buying" service; they have no affiliation with dealers.

Here's how the service works:

1. You provide CarBargains with the make, model, and style of car you wish to buy (Ford Taurus GL, for example) by phone or mail.

2. Within two weeks, CarBargains will send you dealer quote sheets from at least 5 local dealers who have bid against one another to sell you that car. The offer is actually a commitment to a dollar amount above (or below) "factory invoice cost" for that model.

You will also receive a printout with the exact dealer cost for the car and each available option. Included in the information will be the name of the sales manager responsible for honoring the quote.

3. Use the factory invoice cost printout to add up the invoice cost for the base car and the options you want and then determine which dealer offers the best price using the dealer quote sheets. Contact the sales manager of that dealership and arrange to purchase the car.

If a car with the options you want is not available on the dealer's lot, you can have the dealer order the car from the factory or, in some cases, from another dealer at the agreed price.

When you receive your quotes, you will also get some suggestions on low-cost sources of financing and a valuation of your used car (trade-in).

The price for this service may seem expensive, but when you consider the savings that will result by having dealers bid against each other, as well as the time and effort of trying to get these bids yourself, we believe it's a great value. First of all, the dealers know they have a bona fide buyer (you've paid $150 for the service) and they know they are bidding against 5-7 of their competitors.

To obtain CarBargains' competitive price quotes, send a check for $150 to CarBargains, 733 15th St., NW, Suite 820CB, Washington, DC 20005. Include your complete mailing address, phone number (in case of questions), and the exact make, model, and year of the car you want to buy. You should receive your bids within 2-3 weeks. For faster service, call them at 800-475-7283. They will accept Visa or Mastercard on phone orders.

Auto Brokers

While CarBargains is a non-profit organization created to help you find the best price for the car you want to purchase, auto brokers are typically in the business to make money. As such, whatever price you end up paying for the car will include additional profit for the broker. While many brokers are legitimately trying to get their customers the best price, others have developed special relationships with certain dealers and may not do much shopping for you. As a consumer, it is difficult to tell which are which. If you use a broker, make sure the contract to purchase the car is with the dealer, not the broker. In addition, it is best to pay the broker *after* the service is rendered, not before. There have been cases where the auto broker makes certain promises, takes your money, and you never hear from him or her again. If CarBargains is not for you, then we suggest you consider using a buying service associated with your credit union or auto club, which can arrange for the purchase of a car at some fixed price over "dealer invoice."

Depreciation

Over the past 20 years, new vehicle depreciation costs have steadily increased. A recent study conducted by the Runzheimer International management consulting firm shows that depreciation and interest now account for slightly over 50-percent of the costs of owning and operating a vehicle. This number is up from 41 percent in 1976. On the other hand, the relative cost of gasoline has dropped by half, from 35-percent to 17 percent of every dollar spent on the average car. Other costs, including insurance, maintenance, and tires, have remained at relatively steady shares of the automotive dollar.

The high cost of depreciation is largely due to skyrocketing new car prices. While there is no reliable method of predicting retained value, your best bet is to purchase a popular new car. Chances are that it will also be popular as a used car.

1991 Cars with the Best and Worst Resale Value

In general, cars are a very poor investment in terms of value retention. However, the following table indicates which of the 100 top-selling 1991 cars held their value the best and which did not. Most new cars are traded in within four years and are then available on the used car market. The priciest used cars may not necessarily be the highest quality. Supply and demand, as well as appearance, are extremely important factors in determining used car prices.

The Best				The Worst			
Model	1991 Price	1995 Price	Retained Value	Model	1991 Price	1995 Price	Retained Value
Toyota Tercel	$7,798	$7,450	96%	Lincoln Continental	$32,304	$14,300	44%
Honda Civic	$8,745	$7,650	88%	Cadillac Seville	$33,935	$15,775	47%
Mazda Miata	$13,800	$11,800	86%	Pontiac 6000	$18,399	$8,700	47%
Hyundai Sonata	$13,799	$11,800	86%	Ford LTD/Cr. Vic.	$18,863	$9,250	49%
Saturn SL	$7,995	$6,775	85%	Dodge Dynasty	$13,625	$6,875	50%
VW Golf/Jetta	$9,055	$7,625	84%	Ford Taurus	$13,873	$6,875	50%
Honda CRX	$9,145	$7,700	84%	Cad. Fltwd./Dev.	$34,925	$17,725	51%
Mazda 323	$7,484	$6,525	83%	Infiniti Q45	$39,000	$20,025	51%
Honda Accord	$12,545	$10,250	82%	Cad. Brougham	$30,225	$15,750	52%
Nissan Sentra	$9,100	$7,400	81%	Chev. Caprice/Imp.	$16,515	$8,600	52%

Prices based on the *N.A.D.A. Official Used Car Guide*, July 1995.

Leasing vs. Buying

As car prices continue to rise and dealer ads scream out the virtues of leasing, many car buyers are wondering whether they should lease rather than buy. Here is some information to help you make the right decision.

With a lease, you pay a monthly fee for a predetermined length of time in exchange for the use of a car. Usually, however, you pay for maintenance, insurance, and repairs as if the car were your own. There are two types of leases—*closed*- and *open-ended*. Most consumer leases are closed-ended and you simply return the car at the lease's end. Your monthly payment depends on the original cost of the car and what the company thinks the car can sell for after the lease is up. An open-ended lease is riskier because you pay the difference between the car's expected value and its actual resale value when the lease ends. If the lessor underestimated the resale value of your payments, you'll pay a lump sum at the end.

While these terms describe general types of leases, within these categories the details may vary considerably. Some companies combine these concepts with a vehicle purchase option. They guarantee to sell you the car at the end of the lease for a pre-determined amount, called the residual value. If, at the end, the car is worth more than the pre-determined price, you may want to buy it. If it's worth less, simply turn it in.

Generally speaking, leasing costs more than buying outright or financing. In fact, when you lease a car, you have all the head-aches and responsibilities of ownership with none of the benefits. In addition, leased cars are often not covered by the Lemon Laws. However, if the benefit of the lower monthly payments outweighs the overall added costs, consider the following when shopping for a lease:

Know the make and model of the vehicle you want. Tell the agent exactly how you want the car equipped. You don't have to pay for options you don't request. Decide in advance how long you will keep the car.

Find out the price of the options on which the lease is based. Typically, it will be full retail price. The price can be negotiated (albeit with some difficultly)—before you settle on the monthly payment.

Find out how much you are required to pay at delivery. Most leases require at least the first month's payment. Others have a security deposit, registration fees, or other "hidden" costs. When shopping around, make sure price quotes include security deposit and taxes—sales tax, monthly use tax, or gross receipt tax. Ask how the length of the lease affects your monthly cost.

Find out the annual mileage limit. Don't accept a contract with a lower limit than you need. Most standard contracts allow 15,000 to 18,000 miles per year. If you go under the allowance one year, you can go over it the next.

Avoid "capitalized cost reduction" or "equity leases." Here the lessor offers to lower the monthly payment by asking you for more money up front. This defeats the principal benefit of a lease. By paying more initially, you lose the opportunity to use or earn interest on this money. These opportunity costs are based on the interest rate that you would otherwise earn.

Ask about early termination. If you terminate the lease before it is up, what are the financial penalties? Ask the dealer *exactly* what you would owe at the end of each year if you wanted out of the lease. Remember, if your car is stolen, the lease will typically be terminated. While your insurance should cover the value of the car, you still may owe additional amounts per your lease contract.

Avoid maintenance contracts. Getting work done privately is cheaper in the long run—and don't forget, this is a new car with a standard warranty.

Arrange for your own insurance. You can generally find less expensive insurance than the programs offered by the lessor.

Ask how quickly you can expect delivery. If your agent can't deliver in a reasonable time, maybe he or she can't meet the price quoted.

Find out the service charges at the end of the lease. Usually around $100, they can go up to $250.

Retain your option to buy the car at the end of the lease at a predetermined price. The price should equal the residual value; if it is more, then the lessor is trying to make an additional profit. Regardless of how the end-of-lease value is determined, if you want the car make an offer based on the current "Blue Book" value of the car at the end of the lease.

Find out how the lease price was figured. Lease prices are generally based on the manufacturer's suggested retail price, less the pre-determined residual value. The best values are cars with a high expected residual value. To protect themselves, lessors tend to underestimate residual value, but you can do little about this estimate.

Here's what First National Lease Systems' Automotive Lease Guide estimates the residual values for a few 1996 cars will be after four years:

Buick Century Sedan Spec.	36%
Chevrolet Beretta cpe.	37%
Dodge Intrepid	43%
Ford Taurus GL	42%
Honda Accord DX sdn.	47%
Infiniti Q45	36%
Lexus LS400	46%
Lincoln Mark VIII	37%
Mazda Miata	44%
Mercury Tracer sdn.	32%
Olds Ciera Series I	39%
Plymouth Neon sdn.	37%
Toyota Camry DX cpe.	44%

The following table compares the typical costs of leasing vs. buying the same car. Your actual costs will vary slightly, but you can use this format to compare the cars you are considering. Our example assumes that the residual value of a purchased car is 60 percent after two years and 45 percent after four.

Finally, keep in mind that at the end of a lease period you have nothing—but at the end of your finance period you will own a car.

Financing vs. Leasing

	2 Years		4 Years	
	Lease	Finance*	Lease	Finance*
Number of Months	24	24	48	48
Manu. Suggested Price	$15,000	$15,000	$15,000	$15,000
Cash Down Payment		$1,500		$1,500
Monthly Payment	$425	$678	$300	$366
Total Amt. of Pymnts**	$10,200	$16,272	$14,400	$17,568
Less Veh. Value at End	$0	$9,000	$0	$6,750
Actual Cost	$10,200	$8,772	$14,400	$12,318

*Based on an annual percentage rate of 8%

**In a lease, this is the total amount paid for the use of the vehicle. When financing, this is the total amount paid to become the owner.

Don't Buy Rustproofing

For years, we've recommended *against* spending the hundreds of dollars dealers charge for rustproofing. Some manufacturers (GM, Nissan, Saturn, Subaru, Suzuki, Toyota, and Volkswagen) now also recommend against aftermarket rustproofing. General Motors' warranty presents one of the clearest arguments against buying this expensive item: *Some after-manufacture rustproofing may create a potential environment which reduces the corrosion resistance designed and built into your vehicle. Depending upon application technique, some after-manufacture rustproofing could result in damage or failure of some electrical or mechanical systems of your vehicle. Repairs to correct damage or malfunctions caused by after-manufacture rustproofing are not covered under any of your GM new vehicle warranties.* Other manufacturers who suggest that rustproofing may void your corrosion warranty include Nissan, Saturn, and Volkswagen.

Options: The Future of Safety

Many car manufacturers claim that cars are safe enough today since airbags, anti-lock brakes and traction control are becoming standard features. The fact is there's lots more that can be done. We continue to pay high prices in personal injury and insurance premiums for accidents that could be less serious if manufacturers would market more advanced safety features.

While these features may increase the car costs, those increases would be minor in relation to the dramatic reduction in the risk of injuries in crashes. To get an idea of the future, we talked to safety engineer and inventor, Carl Clark. As one of the inventors of the airbag, Dr. Clark envisions a future where advanced airbag technology is only a small component of added protection to cars.

How long will we have to wait for these innovations? Hopefully not the twenty years we waited for airbags. Unfortunately, car makers are slow to offer us new technology. Following are a few options that will dramatically increase driving safety—if manufacturers choose to offer them.

Radar Brakes: Using radar to detect objects in front of you, a warning sounds for the need to brake. It could perhaps be used to automatically apply the brakes when a driver falls asleep.

Side Airbags: The newest automatic crash protection technology has found its way into a handful of 1996 models, and one day may become the standard. These airbags ignite out of doors and out of the back of the front seat to protect the driver and passenger in crashes from all directions as well as rollovers.

Air Pads: Air pads are double layers of plastic with multiple compartments which look like ordinary trim in the uninflated condition. When the crash sensors for the airbags detect a crash, the air pads inflate out a few inches over all hard surfaces, such as the area over the windshield.

Glass-Plastic Glazing: This adds a layer of thin, strong, transparent plastic on the inside surface of all windows. When the glass breaks, the plastic layer holds the pieces of glass away from the occupants and provides a "safety net" to reduce the chance of ejection. A six year old child hitting a tempered glass window at less than 15-mph can break through it and eject. Glass-plastic glazing would greatly reduced the chance of this happening.

Daytime Running Lights: The government has issued a new rule which allows car makers to offer daytime running lights. In the past, certain state laws prevented their use. Studies conducted in the U.S., Canada, and Scandinavia (where daytime running lights are mandatory) show that keeping your headlights on during the day reduces crashes by seven to 40 percent. The new ruling from NHTSA does not make the lights mandatory, but simply takes away any penalty for their use. GM and Volvo, among others, have begun offering this feature.

Night Vision Enhancement: This device will see through fog, rain, and darkness to provide an image of any obstacles or problems in the road. Infared light cameras project a visible image of what is ahead on a screen located on the car's instrument panel. The system could also detect, through a heat-seeking infrared system, someone lurking in a darkened parking lot.

Navigation Computer: With the use of global-positioning satellites, these on-board computers would eliminate the need for road maps. They could provide instructions on how to get to particular locations, such as hospitals, airports, restaurants and hotels, as well as warn of traffic and construction delays. GM and Volvo have begun experimenting with these systems in their cars. Using much the same technology, Lincoln's RESCU (Remote Emergency Satellite Cellular Unit) will send a distress signal for help to either a tow truck or an ambulance, depending on which signal you send.

Black Box Monitor: This device would detect whether the driver is driving drunk or irresponsibly. By monitoring the car's behavior and noting irregular actions, it will shut the car down.

Intelligent Brakes: These brakes sense and compensate for over- or under-steering.

Crash Recorder: This would record airbag performance in the event of an accident. (Introduced in 1995 Saturns.)

Toyota's Drowsy Driving Warning Sytem: By monitoring the steering and pulse of the driver, this innovation checks the driver to verify alertness. Once it detects drowsiness, the system will warn the driver with lights and sound to wake up. If this doesn't help, the system will shake the seat. And if this doesn't work, the system will automatically stop the car.

RATINGS

This chapter provides an overview of the most important features of the new 1996 cars. In this section of *The Car Book,* you can see on each "car page" all the ingredients you need to make a smart choice. In addition to some descriptive text and a photo, the page contains seven important information boxes:

THE DESCRIPTION

The vast majority of information in *The Car Book* is purely objective—we research and present the facts so that you can make an informed choice among the models that fit your taste and pocketbook. For the second year we are adding, among other new features, some background details. Specifically, for every car we include some general information to help you round out the hard facts. Much of the information in this section is subjective and you may not share our opinion. Nevertheless, like the photo which gives you a general idea of what the car looks like, the description will give you a snapshot of some of the features we think are worth noting and which may not show up in the statistics.

GENERAL INFORMATION

This is additional information you may want to consider when buying a new car.

Where made: Here we tell you where the car was assembled.

Year of Production: We generally recommend against buying a car during its first model year of production. In addition, we believe that the longer a car company makes the same car, the less likely the car is to have manufacturing and design defects. Each year the model is made, the production process is usually improved and there are fewer minor design defects. Therefore, the longer a car has been made, the less likely you are to be plagued with defects. On the other hand, the newer a car is, the more likely it is to have the latest in engineering.

Parking Index: Using the car's length, wheelbase and turning circle, we have calculated how easy it will be to maneuver this car in tight spots. This rating of *very easy* to *very hard* is an indicator of how much difficulty you may have parking. If you regularly parallel park, or find yourself maneuvering in and out of tight spaces, this can be an important factor in your choice.

Bumpers: Here we indicate the damage-resistance of the car's bumpers. *Weak* bumpers meet only the basic government requirements at 2.5-mph. *Strong* bumpers are just as damage-resistant at 5-mph. This information may not be available for some minivans.

Theft Rating: This rating is given by the Insurance Institute for Highway Safety. It predicts the likelihood of the car being stolen or broken into based on its past history. If no information appears, it means that the car is too new to have a rating.

Corporate Twins: Often a car company will make numerous models on the same platform. This is a list of this car's twins.

Drive: This tells if the car comes with front, rear or four wheel drive, or if you have a choice.

PRICES

This box contains sample price information. When available, we list the base and the most luxurious version of the car. The difference is often substantial. Usually the more expensive versions have fancy trim, larger engines and lots of automatic equipment. The least expensive versions usually have manual transmission and few extra features. In addition, some manufacturers try to sell popular options as part of a package. For example, to get air conditioning you may have to buy power steering and deluxe seats.

This information provides an idea of the price range and the expected dealer markup. Be prepared for higher retail prices when you get to the showroom. Manufacturers like to load their cars with factory options, and dealers like to add their own items such as fabric protection and paint sealant. Remember, prices and dealer costs can change during the year. Use these figures for general reference and comparisons, not as a precise indication of exactly how much the car you are interested in will cost. See page 90 for a new buying service designed to ensure that you get the very best price.

RATINGS

These are ratings in nine important categories, as well as an overall comparative rating. We have adopted the Olympic rating system with "10" being the best.

Comparative Rating: This is the "bottom line." Using a combination of all of the ratings, this tells how this car stacks up against the other '96's on a scale of 1 to 10. Due to the importance of crash tests, cars with no crash test results as of our publication date cannot be given an overall rating. More recent results may be available from the Auto Safety Hotline at 1-800-424-9393.

Crash Test Performance: This rating compares the 1996 models against all crash test results to date. We give the best performers a 10 and the worst a 1. Remember to compare crash test results relative to other cars in the same size class. For complete details, see "The Safety Chapter."

Safety Features: This is an evaluation of how much extra safety is built into the car. We give credit for airbags, ABS, side impact protection, belt height adjustors, and built-in child safety seats.

Fuel Economy: Here we compare the EPA mileage ratings of each car. The gas misers get a 10 and the guzzlers get a 1. For more information, see "The Fuel Economy Chapter."

PM Cost: Each manufacturer suggests a preventive maintenance schedule designed to keep the car in good shape and to protect your rights under the warranty. The cost of these schedules varies from car to car—ranging from $0 to $1390 for the first 50,000 miles of driving. Those with the lowest PM costs get a 10 and the highest a 1. See "The Maintenance Chapter" for the actual costs.

Repair Cost: It is virtually impossible to predict exactly what any new car will cost you in repairs. As such, we take nine typical repairs that you are likely to experience *after* your warranty expires and compare those costs among this year's models. Those with the lowest cost get a 10 and the highest a 1. For details, see "The Maintenance Chapter."

Warranty: There are good warranties and not so good warranties. This is an overall assessment of the car's warranty when compared to all 1996 warranties. The rating considers the important features of each warranty, with emphasis on the length of the basic and powertrain warranties. We give the highest rated warranties a 10 and the lowest a 1. See "The Warranty Chapter" for details.

Complaints: This is where you'll find how your car stacks up against hundreds of others on the road, based on the U.S. government complaint data. We can only rate cars which have enough on-the-road complaint history; so, if no information is listed, the car has not been around long enough to have developed a complaint history—good or bad. The least complained about cars get a 10 and the most problematic a 1.

Insurance Cost: Insurance companies have rated most of the cars on the road to determine how they plan to charge for insurance. Here, you'll find whether you can expect a discount or a surcharge for what we expect to be the most popular model. If the car is likely to receive neither, we label it *regular*. Those receiving a discount get a 10, while cars with a surcharge get a 1; any with neither get a 5.

SAFETY

For most of us, safety is a critical consideration in buying a new car. This box will tell you, at a glance, whether or not the car has the safety features you care about.

Crash Test: Here's where we tell you if its crash test was *very good, good, average, poor,* or *very poor*.

Airbag: Here's where you'll find out which occupants benefit from this invaluable safety feature and who is left unprotected.

Anti-lock Brakes: Find out if this model has the two- or four-wheel version of this safety feature, and whether you'll have to pay extra for it. Two-wheel ABS is of marginal value.

Side Crash Protection: By 1997, all cars will have to have increased side impact protection built-in. This year, some companies are offering this extra protection in advance of the law. Find out which companies reported to the government that they were offering this extra protection.

Child Safety Seats: Some manufacturers are offering "built-in" child safety seats which reduces the chances that your child rides unprotected.

Belt Adjustors: This tells if the car maker offers a safety belt height/comfort adjustor. People often don't wear safety belts because they are uncomfortable. In fact, a belt's effectiveness is due, in part, to how well it fits your body. In order to make sure shoulder belts fit properly (squarely across the front of your chest) some manufacturers have installed devices that let you ad-

just the height of the belt. This allows for proper fit among drivers and passengers of various heights. In addition to allowing a safer fit, it helps prevent such problems as the belt scraping across the neck of a shorter driver. Availability is indicated for both front seat occupants, unless otherwise noted.

Occupant Injury: This is the expected injury rating, as presented by the Insurance Institute for Highway Safety, based on actual experience. If the model or style is all new this year, it has no rating. A car may have a good crash test rating, but a poor injury rating. This could be due to the way the car is driven. For example, a sporty car may have a good crash test result, but a poor injury rating. This may be due to the fact that the car is typically driven by young males who are in accidents more frequently than others.

SPECIFICATIONS

Here are the "nuts and bolts." In this box we have listed seven key specifications which enable you to evaluate how best that car meets your particular needs. We provide the information for what we expect to be the most popular model.

Fuel Economy: This is the EPA-rated fuel economy for city and highway driving measured in miles per gallon. Most models have a number of fuel economy ratings because of different engine and transmission options. For more individual ratings, see "The Fuel Economy Chapter."

Driving Range: Given the car's expected fuel economy and gas tank size, this gives an idea of how far you can go on a full tank.

Seating: This figure represents the maximum number of seating positions equipped with safety belts. When more than one number is listed (for example, 5/6/7) it means that different models have different seat configurations.

Length: This is the overall length of the vehicle from bumper to bumper.

Head/Leg Room: This tells how roomy the front seat is.

Interior Space: This tells how roomy the car is. For minivans, see cargo space.

Cargo Space: This gives you the cubic feet available for cargo. For minivans, it is the back of the two front seats to the rear of the vehicle. In cars, it's the trunk space.

COMPETITION

Here we tell you how the car stacks up with what is expected to be its competition. Use this information to compare the overall rating of similar cars and as a stepping-off point to broaden your choice of new car possibilities. This may help you select a more economical or better performing car than the one you were originally considering. We've added page references so you can easily check out the details on the competition. This list is meant as a guideline, not as an all-inclusive list of every possible competitive choice.

The Integra, which is built on the same chassis as the Honda Civic, was all-new in 1994 and carries on unchanged in 1996. It is the least expensive of the cars from the premium Japanese manufacturers - Lexus, Infiniti and Acura - but is one of the most fun to drive. Dual airbags are standard; ABS is optional. A possible alphanumeric name change may occur as early as next year.

The Integra coupes and sedans emphasize sportiness rather than luxury. The standard engine, found on the base RS and mid-level LS models, delivers over 140 horsepower, more than enough power for this fairly light car. The GS-R gets a 170-hp VTEC version of the same engine and doesn't lose a bit in fuel economy. The 5-speed is fun to shift. Handling ranks among the best for small cars. Front seats, driver's controls, and instruments are fine, but the rear seat is cramped, definitely not for adults on long trips.

The Ratings

	POOR	GOOD
COMPARATIVE RATING	■	
CRASH TEST		■
SAFETY FEATURES		■
FUEL ECONOMY		■
PM COST	■	
REPAIR COST	■	
WARRANTY		■
COMPLAINTS	■	
INSURANCE COST	■	

Safety

CRASH TEST	Average
AIRBAGS	Dual
ABS	4-wheel (Optional)
SIDE CRASH PROTECT.	Weak
BELT ADJUSTORS	Std. (sdn. only)
BUILT-IN CHILD SEAT	None
OCCUPANT INJURY	Average

General Information

WHERE MADE	Japan
YEAR OF PRODUCTION	Third
PARKING INDEX	Easy
BUMPERS	Strong
THEFT RATING	Average
TWINS	
DRIVE	Front

Specifications

FUEL ECONOMY (cty/hwy)	24/31	Average
DRIVING RANGE (miles)	356	Short
SEATING	5	
LENGTH (inches)	172.4	Very Short
HEAD/LEG ROOM (in.)	38.6/42.7	Average
INTERIOR SPACE (cu. ft.)	83	Cramped
CARGO SPACE (cu. ft.)	13	Average

Specifications may vary.

Prices**

Model	Retail	Mkup
Integra RS Coupe	15,880	16%
Integra LS Coupe	18,560	16%
Integra LS Sedan	20,360	16%
Integra GS-R Coupe	20,770	16%
Integra GS-R Sedan	21,100	16%

Competition

	POOR	GOOD	Pg.
Acura Integra	■		98
Eagle Talon	■		132
Ford Probe	■		140
Honda Prelude		■	150
Mitsubishi Eclipse		■	183

** 1996 prices not available at press time. Prices based on 1995 data.

The replacement for the Acura Legend has arrived for 1996 and it is officially called the TL (Touring Luxury). Acura has decided to focus the attention on "Acura" and not on the models themselves by adopting an alphanumeric designation. The new TL comes standard with dual airbags, 4-wheel ABS, and side impact protection; traction control is an option.

The TL comes in two models, the 3.2TL or the 2.5TL. Like other luxury models, the 3.2 and 2.5 stand for engine sizes and both engines should provide plenty of power; though you lose gas mileage if you choose the larger engine. There are few options to choose from, so be prepared for a high base price. Comfort and style are what you would expect from a luxury car. The TL should be just as strong a competitor with other luxury models as its predecessor was.

The Ratings

	POOR	GOOD
COMPARATIVE RATING*		
CRASH TEST		
SAFETY FEATURES		
FUEL ECONOMY		
PM COST		
REPAIR COST		
WARRANTY		
COMPLAINTS		
INSURANCE COST		

Safety

CRASH TEST	No government results
AIRBAGS	Dual
ABS	4-wheel
SIDE CRASH PROTECT.	Strong
BELT ADJUSTORS	Standard
BUILT-IN CHILD SEAT	None
OCCUPANT INJURY	

General Information

WHERE MADE	Japan
YEAR OF PRODUCTION	First
PARKING INDEX	Average
BUMPERS	Strong
THEFT RATING	
TWINS	
DRIVE	Front

Specifications

FUEL ECONOMY (cty/hwy)	20/25	Average
DRIVING RANGE (miles)	378	Short
SEATING	5/6	
LENGTH (inches)	191.5	Long
HEAD/LEG ROOM (in.)	39.1/43.7	Vry. Roomy
INTERIOR SPACE (cu. ft.)	95	Average
CARGO SPACE (cu. ft.)	14	Average

Specifications may vary.

Prices

Model	Retail	Mkup
TL 2.5-Liter Base	27,900	15%
TL 2.5-Liter Premium	29,950	15%
TL 3.2-Liter Base	32,950	15%
TL 3.2-Liter Premium	35,500	15%

Competition

	POOR	GOOD	Pg.
Acura TL			**99**
BMW 3-Series			102
Lexus ES300			159
Mazda Millenia			169
Merc.-Benz C-Class			174

*Due to the importance of crash tests, cars with no results as of publication date cannot be given an overall rating.

In with the new, out with the old, is Audi's philosophy as they not only redesign the 90, but rename it also. The A4, the replacement for the 90, brings with it many new changes including a price tag which is $4,000 cheaper. The A4 is, in some ways, a lower priced version of the Audi A6. ABS and dual airbags are standard, and the A4 meets 1997 side impact standards.

The base engine, a 1.8-liter four cylinder will provide ample power, but if you are looking for more power, go for the optional 2.8 liter V6. Like the 90, the A4 is available with either front-wheel drive or all-wheel drive, called Quattro, which improves overall handling and traction on slick roads. With a larger trunk and cabin, the A4 will be better equipped to handle passengers than in previous years. Preventive maintenance costs are minimal, and the warranty is tops. This is a much better vehicle than the 90 it replaces.

The Ratings

	POOR — GOOD
COMPARATIVE RATING*	(no rating)
CRASH TEST	(no rating)
SAFETY FEATURES	Good
FUEL ECONOMY	Average
PM COST	Good
REPAIR COST	Poor
WARRANTY	Good
COMPLAINTS	(no rating)
INSURANCE COST	Average

Safety

CRASH TEST	No government results
AIRBAGS	Dual
ABS	4-wheel
SIDE CRASH PROTECT.	Strong
BELT ADJUSTORS	Standard
BUILT-IN CHILD SEAT	None
OCCUPANT INJURY	

General Information

WHERE MADE	Germany
YEAR OF PRODUCTION	First
PARKING INDEX	Easy
BUMPERS	Strong
THEFT RATING	
TWINS	
DRIVE	Front/All

Specifications

FUEL ECONOMY (cty/hwy)	18/28	Average
DRIVING RANGE (miles)	361	Short
SEATING	5	
LENGTH (inches)	178.0	Short
HEAD/LEG ROOM (in.)	38.1/41.3	Cramped
INTERIOR SPACE (cu. ft.)	88	Cramped
CARGO SPACE (cu. ft.)	14	Average

Specifications may vary.

Prices

Model	Retail	Mkup
A4 4-door	26,500	

Competition

	POOR — GOOD	Pg.
Audi A4	(no rating)	**100**
BMW 3-Series	Average	102
Infiniti J30	Good	155
Merc.-Benz C-Class	Good	174
Volvo 850	Good	223

*Due to the importance of crash tests, cars with no results as of publication date cannot be given an overall rating.

The A6 and S6, which used to be called the 100 and S4 respectively, are slightly larger versions of the Audi A4. The alphanumeric names, which Audi will use exclusively in the future, are meant to clear up confusion; the 6 stands for the mid-level size of the cars, while the A is for Audi (the base model) and the S is for the Sport model. Dual airbags and 4-wheel ABS are standard and, like the A4, the A6 meets the government's 1997 side impact standard.

The 2.8-liter V6 found on the A6, as well as most other Audi's, will deliver ample power; however, the smaller 2.2-liter 5-cylinder turbo on the S6 offers more power. There is plenty of room for four, but five might be a squeeze. You don't have many option choices on the S6; on the other hand, the A6 offers several option packages. Both the sedan and wagon A6 offer all-wheel drive, which will improve handling and poor-weather traction.

The Ratings

	POOR — GOOD
COMPARATIVE RATING	9/10
CRASH TEST	8/10
SAFETY FEATURES	8/10
FUEL ECONOMY	3/10
PM COST	8/10
REPAIR COST	1/10
WARRANTY	10/10
COMPLAINTS	(blank)
INSURANCE COST	5/10

Safety

CRASH TEST	Very Good
AIRBAGS	Dual
ABS	4-wheel
SIDE CRASH PROTECT.	Strong
BELT ADJUSTORS	Standard
BUILT-IN CHILD SEAT	None
OCCUPANT INJURY	

General Information

WHERE MADE	Germany
YEAR OF PRODUCTION	First
PARKING INDEX	Easy
BUMPERS	Strong
THEFT RATING	
TWINS	
DRIVE	Front/All

Specifications

FUEL ECONOMY (cty/hwy)	19/25	Poor
DRIVING RANGE (miles)	443	Long
SEATING	5	
LENGTH (inches)	192.6	Long
HEAD/LEG ROOM (in.)	68.4/42.4	Vry. Roomy
INTERIOR SPACE (cu. ft.)	92	Average
CARGO SPACE (cu. ft.)	17	Large

Specifications may vary.

Prices

Model	Retail	Mkup
A6 4-door	32,300	
A6 Wagon	34,000	

Competition

	POOR — GOOD	Pg.
Audi A6/S6	9/10	**101**
Mazda Millenia	6/10	169
Merc.-Benz C-Class	7/10	174
Saab 9000	8/10	206
Volvo 850	8/10	223

BMW has made only minor changes to its line of 3-Series cars for 1996. You can get either a 318 or 325, in their sedan, coupe and convertible incarnations, or the relatively new (spring of '95) 318 hatchback version. This new hatchback is almost a foot shorter and nearly $5,000 less expensive.

The 1.8-liter powerplant on the 318 is strong enough. The 2.5-liter on the 325 is much more powerful, but less fuel efficient. The optional limited-slip differential will help control the engine's power. Front seats offer excellent comfort on long trips; however, the back seat is a squeeze for adults. Controls are excellent. One negative is the easily-damaged, and expensive-to-repair, front bumper. If you really enjoy driving a responsive car and don't mind spending around $30,000, this BMW is a fine choice. The cheaper hatchback is also a good choice.

The Ratings

	POOR ‖ GOOD
COMPARATIVE RATING	▣
CRASH TEST	▣
SAFETY FEATURES	▣
FUEL ECONOMY	▣
PM COST	▣
REPAIR COST	▣
WARRANTY	▣
COMPLAINTS	▣
INSURANCE COST	▣

Safety

CRASH TEST	Good
AIRBAGS	Dual
ABS	4-wheel
SIDE CRASH PROTECT.	Strong
BELT ADJUSTORS	Standard
BUILT-IN CHILD SEAT	None
OCCUPANT INJURY	Average

General Information

WHERE MADE	Germany
YEAR OF PRODUCTION	Fifth
PARKING INDEX	Easy
BUMPERS	Weak
THEFT RATING	Very Poor
TWINS	
DRIVE	Rear

Specifications

FUEL ECONOMY (cty/hwy)	20/29	Average
DRIVING RANGE (miles)	396	Average
SEATING	4	
LENGTH (inches)	174.5	Short
HEAD/LEG ROOM (in.)	38.1/41.2	Cramped
INTERIOR SPACE (cu. ft.)	86	Cramped
CARGO SPACE (cu. ft.)	10	Small

Specifications may vary.

Prices**

Model	Retail	Mkup
3-Series 318i Sedan	24,975	19%
3-Series 318i Coupe	26,675	19%
3-Series 318i Conv.	31,050	19%
3-Series 325i Sedan	31,450	19%
3-Series 325i Conv.	39,600	19%

Competition

	POOR ‖ GOOD	Pg.
BMW 3-Series	▣	**102**
Mazda Millenia	▣	169
Merc.-Benz C-Class	▣	174
Saab 900	▣	205
Volvo 850	▣	223

** 1996 prices not available at press time. Prices based on 1995 data.

The Ratings

	POOR	GOOD
COMPARATIVE RATING		
CRASH TEST		
SAFETY FEATURES		
FUEL ECONOMY		
PM COST		
REPAIR COST		
WARRANTY		
COMPLAINTS		
INSURANCE COST		

The Century enters its fifteenth year with very few changes. The most notable change is a new and improved optional V6 engine. Your choices consist of sedans and wagons in three trim levels: Special, Custom, and Limited. ABS and a driver's airbag are standard, but all Century models retain GM's wretched, and potentially hazardous, door-mounted seat belts.

Typical of Buicks, the Century offers a comfortable ride as long as the road is smooth. If you are unhappy with the handling, you can't do much about it, as there are no suspension options. The room and comfort inside are OK. The redesigned instrument panel, though not stylish, is functional. The 2.2-liter 4-cylinder engine is inadequate for the wagon. The best powertrain for any Century is the 3.1-liter V6 with automatic overdrive, though you pay for the power with poorer fuel economy in the city.

Safety

CRASH TEST	Good
AIRBAGS	Driver
ABS	4-wheel
SIDE CRASH PROTECT.	Weak
BELT ADJUSTORS	None
BUILT-IN CHILD SEAT	None
OCCUPANT INJURY	Good

General Information

WHERE MADE	U.S./Canada
YEAR OF PRODUCTION	Fifteenth
PARKING INDEX	Average
BUMPERS	Strong
THEFT RATING	Average (Wgn.=Good)
TWINS	Oldsmobile Ciera
DRIVE	Front

Specifications

FUEL ECONOMY (cty/hwy)	24/31	Average
DRIVING RANGE (miles)	446	Long
SEATING	6	
LENGTH (inches)	189.1	Average
HEAD/LEG ROOM (in.)	38.6/42.1	Average
INTERIOR SPACE (cu. ft.)	97	Average
CARGO SPACE (cu. ft.)	16	Average

Specifications may vary.

Prices

Model	Retail	Mkup
Century Special Sedan	16,720	7%
Century Custom Sedan	18,383	7%
Century Limited Sedan	19,406	7%
Century Special Wagon	18,135	7%

Competition

	POOR	GOOD	Pg.
Buick Century			103
Ford Contour			136
Honda Accord			146
Oldsmobile Ciera			195
Toyota Camry			215

There are few changes for the '96 LeSabre, the most notable being the new, more powerful 3.8-liter V6 engine. LeSabre's come in two trim levels: a limited or custom sedan, all with standard safety features like dual airbags and ABS. LeSabre's also meet the 1997 side impact standards.

Like its twin, the Oldsmobile 88, the LeSabre emphasizes a soft ride. However, the cost of the soft ride is mediocre handling. For crisper handling, like that of the Bonneville SSE (another LeSabre twin), without sacrificing ride, order LeSabre's Gran Touring package. Buick offers only one engine with the LeSabre, and it has the same mediocre gas mileage as some of its more powerful cousins, such as the Bonneville, 88 and 98. An anti-theft system is standard, and, like other Buicks, you can't get the transmission out of park without your foot on the brake.

The Ratings

	POOR — GOOD
COMPARATIVE RATING	
CRASH TEST	
SAFETY FEATURES	
FUEL ECONOMY	
PM COST	
REPAIR COST	
WARRANTY	
COMPLAINTS	
INSURANCE COST	

Safety

CRASH TEST	Good
AIRBAGS	Dual
ABS	4-wheel
SIDE CRASH PROTECT.	Strong
BELT ADJUSTORS	Standard
BUILT-IN CHILD SEAT	None
OCCUPANT INJURY	Very Good

General Information

WHERE MADE	U.S.
YEAR OF PRODUCTION	Fifth
PARKING INDEX	Hard
BUMPERS	Strong
THEFT RATING	Very Good
TWINS	Olds 88, Pont. Bonneville
DRIVE	Front

Specifications

FUEL ECONOMY (cty/hwy)	19/30	Average
DRIVING RANGE (miles)	414	Average
SEATING	6	
LENGTH (inches)	200.0	Long
HEAD/LEG ROOM (in.)	38.8/42.5	Average
INTERIOR SPACE (cu. ft.)	109	Vry. Roomy
CARGO SPACE (cu. ft.)	17	Large

Specifications may vary.

Prices

Model	Retail	Mkup
LeSabre Custom	21,380	9%
LeSabre Limited	25,385	9%

Competition

	POOR — GOOD	Pg.
Buick LeSabre		**104**
Eagle Vision		133
Mitsu. Diamante		182
Nissan Maxima		188
Toyota Camry		215

The Park Avenue enters its sixth model year without significant changes. Traction control is now optional, and ABS and dual airbags are standard. For '96, new features include platinum-tipped spark plugs with the first recommended service at 100,000 miles.

Like the Olds 98, the Park Avenue specializes in a soft, smooth ride. However, you pay a price in handling ability. The optional Gran Touring package makes the Park Avenue more enjoyable to drive, with little deterioration in ride. There's plenty of room for five and a big trunk. The optional supercharged V8, standard on the Ultra, gives you a slight boost in power in exchange for slightly lower fuel economy. The Ultra is a waste of money. Get the base model with Gran Touring suspension. If you can't find a Park Avenue equipped this way, take a look at the Chrysler New Yorker or the Mercury Grand Marquis.

The Ratings

	POOR → GOOD
COMPARATIVE RATING *	(no rating)
CRASH TEST	(no rating)
SAFETY FEATURES	Good
FUEL ECONOMY	Below average
PM COST	Above average
REPAIR COST	Above average
WARRANTY	Poor
COMPLAINTS	Above average
INSURANCE COST	Good

Safety

CRASH TEST	No government results
AIRBAGS	Dual
ABS	4-wheel
SIDE CRASH PROTECT.	Weak
BELT ADJUSTORS	Standard
BUILT-IN CHILD SEAT	None
OCCUPANT INJURY	Very Good

General Information

WHERE MADE	U.S.
YEAR OF PRODUCTION	Sixth
PARKING INDEX	Hard
BUMPERS	Strong
THEFT RATING	Very Good
TWINS	Oldsmobile 98
DRIVE	Front

Specifications

FUEL ECONOMY (cty/hwy)	19/29	Average
DRIVING RANGE (miles)	414	Average
SEATING	6	
LENGTH (inches)	205.9	Very Long
HEAD/LEG ROOM (in.)	38.9/42.7	Roomy
INTERIOR SPACE (cu. ft.)	109	Vry. Roomy
CARGO SPACE (cu. ft.)	20	Large

Specifications may vary.

Prices

Model	Retail	Mkup
Park Avenue	28,205	12%
Park Avenue Ultra	32,820	12%

Competition

	POOR → GOOD	Pg.
Buick Park Avenue	(no rating)	**105**
Chrys. LHS/NY'er	Poor	124
Infiniti J30	Good	155
Merc. Gr. Marquis	Average	177
Mitsu. Diamante	Poor	182

*Due to the importance of crash tests, cars with no results as of publication date cannot be given an overall rating.

The Regal has a few notable changes for 1996 such as a more powerful engine and an anti-theft system. The new additions join standard features like dual airbags and side impact protection which meets 1997 standards. 4-wheel ABS is also standard.

You have a choice between two V6 engines and both V6's provide ample power, though you get slightly more power from the 3.8-liter with no loss in fuel economy. Typical of Buicks, the Regal provides low-grade handling with a good ride on smooth roads; the Gran Touring package, which is also standard on Gran Sport, should help improve cornering ability. Room inside is very reasonable, but comfort and cargo space are only average. You can choose between a sedan or a coupe but beware, the Regal has not been restyled in eight years, and it shows.

The Ratings

	POOR → GOOD
COMPARATIVE RATING	▮ (5/10)
CRASH TEST	▮ (5/10)
SAFETY FEATURES	▮ (9/10)
FUEL ECONOMY	▮ (4/10)
PM COST	▮ (7/10)
REPAIR COST	▮ (4/10)
WARRANTY	▮ (2/10)
COMPLAINTS	▮ (6/10)
INSURANCE COST	▮ (10/10)

Safety

CRASH TEST	Average
AIRBAGS	Dual
ABS	4-wheel
SIDE CRASH PROTECT.	Strong
BELT ADJUSTORS	Standard
BUILT-IN CHILD SEAT	None
OCCUPANT INJURY	Very Good

General Information

WHERE MADE	Canada
YEAR OF PRODUCTION	Ninth
PARKING INDEX	Average
BUMPERS	Strong
THEFT RATING	Very Good
TWINS	Cutlass Supr., Gr. Prix
DRIVE	Front

Specifications

FUEL ECONOMY (cty/hwy)	20/29	Average
DRIVING RANGE (miles)	393	Average
SEATING	5	
LENGTH (inches)	193.7	Long
HEAD/LEG ROOM (in.)	38.6/42.4	Average
INTERIOR SPACE (cu. ft.)	111	Vry. Roomy
CARGO SPACE (cu. ft.)	16	Average

Specifications may vary.

Prices

Model	Retail	Mkup
Regal Custom Coupe	19,445	9%
Regal Custom Sedan	19,740	9%
Regal Limited Sedan	21,195	9%
Regal Gran Sport Coupe	21,340	9%
Regal Gran Sport Sedan	21,800	9%

Competition

	POOR → GOOD	Pg.
Buick Regal	▮ (5/10)	**106**
Eagle Vision	▮ (6/10)	133
Honda Accord	▮ (2/10)	146
Mazda 626	▮ (2/10)	166
Toyota Camry	▮ (2/10)	215

Buick Riviera

The Riviera, all-new last year, receives few new additions for 1996. This rejuvenated Riviera is perhaps the most exciting car that Buick offers. New features include platinum-tipped spark plugs and engine coolant that doesn't need to be changed for 100,000 miles. Traction control is optional, and dual airbags and ABS are standard.

At over 17 feet and almost two tons, the Riviera is big. Buick is touting the car's rigidity; with all that weight, it needs to be rigid to maintain a comfortable ride and responsive handling. The standard V6 offers enough power, but the optional 3.8-liter provides more horsepower in exchange for a couple of mpg. The scientifically designed seats are very comfortable. The Riviera beats out many higher priced luxury cars in terms of ride, interior and style.

The Ratings

	POOR → GOOD
COMPARATIVE RATING*	
CRASH TEST	
SAFETY FEATURES	████████ (high)
FUEL ECONOMY	███ (mid)
PM COST	████ (mid)
REPAIR COST	████ (mid)
WARRANTY	█ (low)
COMPLAINTS	
INSURANCE COST	██████████ (high)

Safety

CRASH TEST	No government results
AIRBAGS	Dual
ABS	4-wheel
SIDE CRASH PROTECT.	Strong
BELT ADJUSTORS	Standard
BUILT-IN CHILD SEAT	None
OCCUPANT INJURY	

General Information

WHERE MADE	U.S.
YEAR OF PRODUCTION	Second
PARKING INDEX	Hard
BUMPERS	Strong
THEFT RATING	
TWINS	Oldsmobile Aurora
DRIVE	Front

Specifications

FUEL ECONOMY (cty/hwy)	19/29	Average
DRIVING RANGE (miles)	460	Long
SEATING	5	
LENGTH (inches)	207.2	Very Long
HEAD/LEG ROOM (in.)	38.2/42.6	Average
INTERIOR SPACE (cu. ft.)	99	Roomy
CARGO SPACE (cu. ft.)	17	Large

Specifications may vary.

Prices

Model	Retail	Mkup
Riviera Coupe	29,475	12%

Competition

	POOR → GOOD	Pg.
Buick Riviera		**107**
Chevy Monte Carlo	████████	121
Ford Thunderbird	████	142
Mercury Cougar	█████████	176
Pontiac Grand Prix	█████	202

*Due to the importance of crash tests, cars with no results as of publication date cannot be given an overall rating.

1996 will be the final year of production for these full-size rear-wheel-drive models. Both the Roadmaster, Buick's biggest model, and the Estate Wagon come with few options. On both the sedan and the wagon, you can opt for the plush Limited version. Dual airbags and ABS are standard on all models, and the Roadmaster meets 1997 standards for side impact.

The standard V8 is powerful, which is good because you have no engine choices. Though the standard suspension is a bit firmer than on earlier models, the car still wallows in turns. The optional suspension helps, but to get it, you have to order the 5,000-pound trailer towing package. There is room for six and the trunk is immense. You can save some money by ordering a well-equipped Chevy Caprice instead of a Roadmaster.

The Ratings

	POOR — GOOD
COMPARATIVE RATING	■□□□□□□□□□
CRASH TEST	□□■□□□□□□□
SAFETY FEATURES	□□□□□□□□■□
FUEL ECONOMY	□□□■□□□□□□
PM COST	□□□□□□■□□□
REPAIR COST	□□□□□□□□□■
WARRANTY	■□□□□□□□□□
COMPLAINTS	■□□□□□□□□□
INSURANCE COST	□□□□□□□□□■

Safety

CRASH TEST	Poor
AIRBAGS	Dual
ABS	4-wheel
SIDE CRASH PROTECT.	Strong
BELT ADJUSTORS	None
BUILT-IN CHILD SEAT	None
OCCUPANT INJURY	Very Good

General Information

WHERE MADE	U.S.
YEAR OF PRODUCTION	Sixth
PARKING INDEX	Hard
BUMPERS	Weak (Wgn. rear=strong)
THEFT RATING	Average
TWINS	Chevy Caprice/Impala
DRIVE	Rear

Specifications

FUEL ECONOMY (cty/hwy)	17/26	Poor
DRIVING RANGE (miles)	460	Long
SEATING	6	
LENGTH (inches)	215.8	Very Long
HEAD/LEG ROOM (in.)	39.2/42.1	Average
INTERIOR SPACE (cu. ft.)	170	Vry. Roomy
CARGO SPACE (cu. ft.)	21	Very Large

Specifications may vary.

Prices

Model	Retail	Mkup
Roadmaster	25,560	9%
Roadmaster Limited	27,490	9%
Roadmaster Estate Wagon	27,575	9%

Competition

	POOR — GOOD	Pg.
Buick Roadmaster	■□□□□□□□□□	**108**
Cadillac DeVille	□□□□□□□□■□	110
Chevrolet Caprice	□□□■□□□□□□	117
Chrys. LHS/NY'er	□□■□□□□□□□	124
Ford Crown Victoria	□□□□□■□□□□	137

Both the Skylark sedan and coupe received significant changes inside and out. The exterior has a fresh, new contemporary look while the dash contains new standard dual airbags. This is Buick's smallest model and it is almost identical to its twins, the Oldsmobile Achieva and the Pontiac Grand Am. ABS and traction control are both standard, and GM has finally gotten rid of the dreadful door-mounted safety belts.

Buyers now have a choice of a 2.4-liter 4-cylinder engine which delivers good power or an optional 3.1-liter V6 which delivers slightly more power, but eats considerably more gas. Seating for four adults is average; try to squeeze in five and it becomes very snug. The trunk is of average size. With its new look and improved safety features, the Skylark may finally be able to match its competitors.

The Ratings

	POOR ⟷ GOOD
COMPARATIVE RATING*	(no rating)
CRASH TEST	(no rating)
SAFETY FEATURES	▮ at 7
FUEL ECONOMY	▮ at 6
PM COST	▮ at 6
REPAIR COST	▮ at 7
WARRANTY	▮ at 2
COMPLAINTS	▮ at 7
INSURANCE COST	▮ at 8

Safety

CRASH TEST	No government results
AIRBAGS	Dual
ABS	4-wheel
SIDE CRASH PROTECT.	Weak
BELT ADJUSTORS	Standard
BUILT-IN CHILD SEAT	None
OCCUPANT INJURY	

General Information

WHERE MADE	U.S.
YEAR OF PRODUCTION	Fifth
PARKING INDEX	Easy
BUMPERS	Strong
THEFT RATING	Very Good
TWINS	Achieva, Grand Am
DRIVE	Front

Specifications

FUEL ECONOMY (cty/hwy)	22/32	Average
DRIVING RANGE (miles)	395	Average
SEATING	5	
LENGTH (inches)	189.2	Average
HEAD/LEG ROOM (in.)	37.8/43.1	Average
INTERIOR SPACE (cu. ft.)	103	Roomy
CARGO SPACE (cu. ft.)	13	Average

Specifications may vary.

Prices

Model	Retail	Mkup
Skylark Custom Coupe	15,495	5%
Skylark Custom Sedan	15,495	5%
Skylark Limited Coupe	16,626	5%
Skylark Limited Sedan	16,626	5%
Skylark Gran Sport Coupe	17,701	5%

Competition

	POOR ⟷ GOOD	Pg.
Buick Skylark	(no rating)	109
Chrylser Sebring	▮ at 7	125
Honda Accord	▮ at 2	146
Mazda 626	▮ at 2	166
Toyota Camry	▮ at 1	215

*Due to the importance of crash tests, cars with no results as of publication date cannot be given an overall rating.

The 1996 DeVille is not much different from last year. Only available as a 4-door sedan, the deluxe model is called Concours, a name Chevrolet used on fancier Chevelles and Novas in the seventies. The DeVille comes standard with almost every possible safety feature, including traction control, dual airbags and ABS.

Like most other big GM cars, the DeVille emphasizes a soft, quiet ride and lots of room for six adults; the trunk is large. Speed-sensitive steering and suspension are standard in 1996 and help firm up what used to be a mushy ride. The Northstar that was only offered on the Concours last year is now standard for all DeVilles. Other interesting and attractive features include 100,000 mile spark plugs and daytime running lamps. This car competes very well with other luxury models of its size.

The Ratings

Rating	POOR → GOOD
COMPARATIVE RATING	Good
CRASH TEST	Average-Good
SAFETY FEATURES	Good
FUEL ECONOMY	Poor
PM COST	Good
REPAIR COST	Poor
WARRANTY	Average
COMPLAINTS	Poor-Average
INSURANCE COST	Good

Safety

CRASH TEST	Good
AIRBAGS	Dual
ABS	4-wheel
SIDE CRASH PROTECT.	Strong
BELT ADJUSTORS	Standard
BUILT-IN CHILD SEAT	None
OCCUPANT INJURY	Very Good

General Information

WHERE MADE	U.S.
YEAR OF PRODUCTION	Third
PARKING INDEX	Hard
BUMPERS	Strong
THEFT RATING	Good
TWINS	
DRIVE	Front

Specifications

FUEL ECONOMY (cty/hwy)	17/26	Poor
DRIVING RANGE (miles)	400	Average
SEATING	5/6	
LENGTH (inches)	209.7	Very Long
HEAD/LEG ROOM (in.)	38.5/42.6	Average
INTERIOR SPACE (cu. ft.)	138	Vry. Roomy
CARGO SPACE (cu. ft.)	20	Large

Specifications may vary.

Prices

Model	Retail	Mkup
DeVille	35,995	9%
DeVille Concours	40,495	9%

Competition

	POOR → GOOD	Pg.
Cadillac DeVille	Good	**110**
Cadillac Seville	Average	113
Chrys. LHS/NY'er	Poor	124
Lexus GS300	Good	160
Mitsu. Diamante	Poor	182

The Eldorado and Seville share a chassis, but are marketed to different buyers. The Eldorado is a smaller, 2-door coupe in comparison to the slick, 4-door Seville sedans. You also have the choice of a fancier Touring Coupe. The Eldorado comes standard with 4-wheel ABS and dual airbags.

A strong, but thirsty Northstar V8 comes with the base model Eldorado and the Touring Coupe comes with an even more powerful engine. The Touring Coupe also features a special handling package, but it doesn't improve handling all that much. As in other Cadillacs, fuel economy suffers dramatically in exchange for power and smoothness. The front seat is as comfortable and roomy as you'd expect, but the rear seat is cramped and inaccessible, as on other sports coupes. Driver's controls are fair, and the gauges are good.

The Ratings

	POOR	GOOD
COMPARATIVE RATING*		
CRASH TEST		
SAFETY FEATURES		
FUEL ECONOMY		
PM COST		
REPAIR COST		
WARRANTY		
COMPLAINTS		
INSURANCE COST		

Safety

CRASH TEST	No government results
AIRBAGS	Dual
ABS	4-wheel
SIDE CRASH PROTECT.	Strong
BELT ADJUSTORS	None
BUILT-IN CHILD SEAT	None
OCCUPANT INJURY	Very Good

General Information

WHERE MADE	U.S.
YEAR OF PRODUCTION	Fifth
PARKING INDEX	Hard
BUMPERS	Strong
THEFT RATING	Poor
TWINS	
DRIVE	Front

Specifications

FUEL ECONOMY (cty/hwy)	17/26	Poor
DRIVING RANGE (miles)	400	Average
SEATING	5	
LENGTH (inches)	200.2	Long
HEAD/LEG ROOM (in.)	37.8/42.6	Average
INTERIOR SPACE (cu. ft.)	116	Vry. Roomy
CARGO SPACE (cu. ft.)	15	Average

Specifications may vary.

Prices

Model	Retail	Mkup
Eldorado	39,595	16%
Eldorado Touring Coupe	42,995	16%

Competition

	POOR	GOOD	Pg.
Cadillac Eldorado			111
Ford Thunderbird			142
Infiniti J30			155
Mercury Cougar			176
Volvo 850			223

*Due to the importance of crash tests, cars with no results as of publication date cannot be given an overall rating.

Cadillac Fleetwood

The Fleetwood, a plusher version of the Buick Roadmaster and Chevrolet Caprice, is the biggest car you can buy, and it changes little for 1996. This is your last year to buy this living room on wheels; it is slated to be discontinued in '97. The standard Fleetwood is well-equipped, but you can add a vinyl roof and leather seats, or upgrade to a plusher Brougham with a lumbar support system and heated seats.

All Fleetwood's have a large, powerful V8 engine. The Fleetwood's handling tends to isolate you from the road. The car plows through turns, and severe bumps can upset the ride. The trailer package, upgraded to a hefty 7,000 pounds, has a heavier-duty suspension, but it doesn't really improve handling. The interior is huge, so you should have no problem seating six comfortably, and the trunk is very large.

The Ratings

	POOR	GOOD
COMPARATIVE RATING *		
CRASH TEST		
SAFETY FEATURES		■
FUEL ECONOMY	■	
PM COST		■
REPAIR COST	■	
WARRANTY	■	
COMPLAINTS	■	
INSURANCE COST		■

Safety

CRASH TEST	No government results
AIRBAGS	Dual
ABS	4-wheel
SIDE CRASH PROTECT.	Strong
BELT ADJUSTORS	None
BUILT-IN CHILD SEAT	None
OCCUPANT INJURY	

General Information

WHERE MADE	U.S.
YEAR OF PRODUCTION	Fourth
PARKING INDEX	Very Hard
BUMPERS	Front=Strong, Rear=Weak
THEFT RATING	
TWINS	
DRIVE	Rear

Specifications

FUEL ECONOMY (cty/hwy)	17/26	Poor
DRIVING RANGE (miles)	460	Long
SEATING	5/6	
LENGTH (inches)	225.0	Very Long
HEAD/LEG ROOM (in.)	38.7/42.5	Average
INTERIOR SPACE (cu. ft.)	125	Vry. Roomy
CARGO SPACE (cu. ft.)	21	Very Large

Specifications may vary.

Prices

Model	Retail	Mkup
Fleetwood	36,995	9%

Competition

	POOR	GOOD	Pg.
Cadillac Fleetwood			**112**
Buick Roadmaster	■		108
Chrys. LHS/NY'er	■		124
Lexus GS300		■	160
Mitsu. Diamante	■		182

*Due to the importance of crash tests, cars with no results as of publication date cannot be given an overall rating.

The Seville and Eldorado have the same chassis, but different styles. The Seville is a contemporary-looking 4-door aimed at BMW and Lexus buyers, while the Eldorado is a 2-door sports coupe. There are two trim levels to choose from, the Seville Luxury Sedan (SLS) or the Seville Touring Sedan (STS). Options are limited, but most everything you'll want, including traction control, dual airbags and ABS, comes standard.

The base Seville now has a smaller version of Cadillac's Northstar V8; the Seville Touring Sedan has even more power. Don't expect good gas mileage with either model. The handling is better in the Touring Sedan, but it isn't great. Room inside is good for four and the trunk is of average size. You can do as well or better, and save around $15,000, by choosing a Bonneville SE with the handling package.

The Ratings

	POOR — GOOD
COMPARATIVE RATING	
CRASH TEST	
SAFETY FEATURES	
FUEL ECONOMY	
PM COST	
REPAIR COST	
WARRANTY	
COMPLAINTS	
INSURANCE COST	

Safety

CRASH TEST	Good
AIRBAGS	Dual
ABS	4-wheel
SIDE CRASH PROTECT.	Strong
BELT ADJUSTORS	Standard
BUILT-IN CHILD SEAT	None
OCCUPANT INJURY	Very Good

General Information

WHERE MADE	U.S.
YEAR OF PRODUCTION	Fifth
PARKING INDEX	Hard
BUMPERS	Strong
THEFT RATING	Average
TWINS	
DRIVE	Front

Specifications

FUEL ECONOMY (cty/hwy)	17/26	Poor
DRIVING RANGE (miles)	400	Average
SEATING	5	
LENGTH (inches)	204.1	Very Long
HEAD/LEG ROOM (in.)	38.0/43.0	Average
INTERIOR SPACE (cu. ft.)	120	Vry. Roomy
CARGO SPACE (cu. ft.)	14	Average

Specifications may vary.

Prices

Model	Retail	Mkup
Seville	42,995	16%
Seville Touring Sedan	47,495	16%

Competition

	POOR — GOOD	Pg.
Cadillac Seville		113
Chrys. LHS/NY'er		124
Infiniti J30		155
Lexus GS300		160
Mitsu. Diamante		182

A completely refurbished interior makes the Astro look and feel more like the more modern GM minivans: the Lumina, Oldsmobile Silhouette and Pontiac Trans Sport. It now has dual airbags, and integrated child safety seats are now optional.

The standard 4.3-liter V6 and automatic overdrive provide ample power, but gas mileage is poor, even for a minivan. Handling is sloppy, although the optional touring suspension will help. Ride is unsettling once you get off the highway. Getting in and out of the front seats is tricky. The seats are reasonably comfortable, but make sure you have enough leg room in the front. You should have plenty of room to haul just about anything as the cargo space is very large. This vehicle is greatly outclassed by its rivals. Make sure you look at the new Chrysler's before purchasing this vehicle.

The Ratings

	POOR — GOOD
COMPARATIVE RATING *	
CRASH TEST	
SAFETY FEATURES	■ (7th)
FUEL ECONOMY	■ (3rd)
PM COST	■ (8th)
REPAIR COST	■ (7th)
WARRANTY	■ (2nd)
COMPLAINTS	■ (7th)
INSURANCE COST	■ (9th)

Safety

CRASH TEST	No government results
AIRBAGS	Dual
ABS	4-wheel
SIDE CRASH PROTECT.	Weak
BELT ADJUSTORS	Standard
BUILT-IN CHILD SEAT	Optional
OCCUPANT INJURY	Average

General Information

WHERE MADE	U.S.
YEAR OF PRODUCTION	Twelfth
PARKING INDEX	Hard
BUMPERS	Strong
THEFT RATING	Good
TWINS	GMC Safari
DRIVE	Rear/All

Specifications

FUEL ECONOMY (cty/hwy)	16/21	Poor
DRIVING RANGE (miles)	486	Very Long
SEATING	5-8	
LENGTH (inches)	189.8	Average
HEAD/LEG ROOM (in.)	39.2/41.6	Average
INTERIOR SPACE (cu. ft.)		
CARGO SPACE (cu. ft.)	152	Very Large

Specifications may vary.

Prices

Model	Retail	Mkup
Astro Passenger Base	19,176	10%
Astro Cargo Base	18,592	10%

Competition

	POOR — GOOD	Pg.
Chevrolet Astro		**114**
Ford Aerostar	■	134
Ford Windstar	■	143
Honda Odyssey	■	149
Toyota Previa	■	219

*Due to the importance of crash tests, cars with no results as of publication date cannot be given an overall rating.

The Beretta (2 doors) and Corsica (4 doors) share the same chassis and most components. The Beretta is more stylish and relatively inexpensive. Chevrolet continues to sell the Beretta and Corsica with only a driver's airbag, and both front seat passengers are stuck with awful door-mounted belts. For these reasons, this otherwise highly rated car is not one of our "Best Bets."

These models are among the first to get standard daytime running lights, a feature that allows drivers of other cars to see yours more easily. The optional 3.1-liter V6 will improve acceleration, but fuel economy will suffer. The base-model Beretta and Corsica are not very exciting, but the Beretta Z26 has a handling package that makes driving more fun, without giving you a stiff ride. Seats are snug for four, and trunk space is just adequate. The dashboard lacks a well-designed look and feel.

The Ratings

	POOR → GOOD
COMPARATIVE RATING	Good
CRASH TEST **	Very Good
SAFETY FEATURES	Poor
FUEL ECONOMY	Above Average
PM COST	Above Average
REPAIR COST	Above Average
WARRANTY	Poor
COMPLAINTS	Good
INSURANCE COST	Poor

Safety

CRASH TEST	Very Good
AIRBAGS	Driver
ABS	4-wheel
SIDE CRASH PROTECT.	Weak
BELT ADJUSTORS	None
BUILT-IN CHILD SEAT	None
OCCUPANT INJURY	Average

General Information

WHERE MADE	U.S.
YEAR OF PRODUCTION	Tenth
PARKING INDEX	Easy
BUMPERS	Strong
THEFT RATING	Average (Cors.=Very Gd.)
TWINS	
DRIVE	Front

Specifications

FUEL ECONOMY (cty/hwy)	25/37	Good
DRIVING RANGE (miles)	441	Long
SEATING	5	
LENGTH (inches)	187.3	Average
HEAD/LEG ROOM (in.)	37.6/43.4	Average
INTERIOR SPACE (cu. ft.)	89	Cramped
CARGO SPACE (cu. ft.)	13	Average

Specifications may vary.

Prices

Model	Retail	Mkup
Beretta Base	13,490	11%
Beretta Z26	16,690	11%
Corsica Base	14,385	11%

Competition

	POOR → GOOD	Pg.
Chevy Beretta/Cors.		115
Chrysler Sebring		125
Ford Contour		136
Mazda MX-6		172
Pontiac Grand Prix		202

** Data given for Beretta. See Safety Chapter for difference in crash test results. Overall rating for Corsica is Very Poor (2).

Chevrolet Camaro

The Camaro enters 1996 with only minor changes. Like its twin, the Pontiac Firebird, the Camaro is a strong performer in the crash tests. The Camaro comes standard with dual airbags and ABS. It also already meets 1997 side impact standards.

Two significant changes for '96 are a new 3.8-liter V6 with more horsepower than last year, and the addition of a new trim level, the RS. The Z28 still has a 5.7-liter V8 that is more powerful and only slightly less economical. The standard manual transmission is more fuel efficient compared to the optional automatic. Enthusiasts will find a firm ride and good handling. The Camaro is roomy for the driver and front seat passenger, but the rear seat is almost too small for young children—but this is not a typical parent's car!

The Ratings

	POOR → GOOD
COMPARATIVE RATING	■ (1)
CRASH TEST	(10) ■
SAFETY FEATURES	(8)
FUEL ECONOMY	(5)
PM COST	(7)
REPAIR COST	(7)
WARRANTY	(2)
COMPLAINTS	(2)
INSURANCE COST	(2)

Safety

CRASH TEST	Very Good
AIRBAGS	Dual
ABS	4-wheel
SIDE CRASH PROTECT.	Strong (cpe. only)
BELT ADJUSTORS	None
BUILT-IN CHILD SEAT	None
OCCUPANT INJURY	Average

General Information

WHERE MADE	Canada
YEAR OF PRODUCTION	Fourth
PARKING INDEX	Hard
BUMPERS	Strong
THEFT RATING	Average
TWINS	Pontiac Firebird
DRIVE	Rear

Specifications

FUEL ECONOMY (cty/hwy)	19/30	Average
DRIVING RANGE (miles)	357	Short
SEATING	4	
LENGTH (inches)	193.2	Long
HEAD/LEG ROOM (in.)	37.2/43.0	Cramped
INTERIOR SPACE (cu. ft.)	82	Vry. Cramped
CARGO SPACE (cu. ft.)	13	Average

Specifications may vary.

Prices

Model	Retail	Mkup
Camaro Coupe	14,990	9%
Camaro Z28 Coupe	19,390	9%
Camaro Convertible	21,270	9%

Competition

	POOR → GOOD	Pg.
Chevrolet Camaro	■ (1)	**116**
Ford Mustang	(2)	139
Mazda MX-6	(4)	172
Nissan 240SX	(3)	186
Pontiac Firebird	(2)	200

Despite modern aerodynamic styling that has put off some buyers, the Caprice enters its 20th year reminding us of the past. The upgraded sedans and wagons are being marketed as the "Caprice Classic," while the Impala SS is now a sportier, more powerful Caprice. The Caprice is the cheapest of GM's full-size rear-wheel-drive cars. ABS and dual airbags are standard, but the Caprice did a poor job of protecting the front-seat passenger in the government crash test.

Like its twins, the Caprice prefers smooth roads, wallows in turns and does not handle severe bumps well, though the optional sport suspension will help. Both engines offer more than enough power, but the 5.7-liter (optional on the Caprice sedan, standard on the Impala and Caprice wagon) gives you even more power with little sacrifice in fuel economy. Overall these are the best of the GM large cars.

The Ratings

	POOR — GOOD
COMPARATIVE RATING	▮ (low-mid)
CRASH TEST	▮ (low-mid)
SAFETY FEATURES	▮ (high)
FUEL ECONOMY	▮ (mid)
PM COST	▮ (mid-high)
REPAIR COST	▮ (high)
WARRANTY	▮ (low)
COMPLAINTS	▮ (mid)
INSURANCE COST	▮ (high)

Safety

CRASH TEST	Poor
AIRBAGS	Dual
ABS	4-wheel
SIDE CRASH PROTECT.	Strong
BELT ADJUSTORS	None
BUILT-IN CHILD SEAT	None
OCCUPANT INJURY	Very Good

General Information

WHERE MADE	U.S.
YEAR OF PRODUCTION	Twentieth
PARKING INDEX	Hard
BUMPERS	Strong
THEFT RATING	Average (Wgn.=Very Gd.)
TWINS	Buick Roadmaster
DRIVE	Rear

Specifications

FUEL ECONOMY (cty/hwy)	18/26	Poor
DRIVING RANGE (miles)	483	Very Long
SEATING	6	
LENGTH (inches)	214.1	Very Long
HEAD/LEG ROOM (in.)	39.2/42.2	Average
INTERIOR SPACE (cu. ft.)	115	Vry. Roomy
CARGO SPACE (cu. ft.)	20	Large

Specifications may vary.

Prices

Model	Retail	Mkup
Caprice Sedan	19,905	9%
Caprice Wagon	22,405	9%
Impala SS	24,405	9%

Competition

	POOR — GOOD	Pg.
Chevy Caprice/Impala	▮ (low-mid)	**117**
Buick Roadmaster	▮ (low)	108
Chrys. LHS/NY'er	▮ (low-mid)	124
Ford Crown Victoria	▮ (mid)	137
Merc. Gr. Marquis	▮ (mid)	177

The Cavalier, all-new last year, receives minor changes in 1996. Its fresh new styling has made this car one of the most popular selling vehicles on the road today. You get your pick of safety features. Daytime running lamps and optional traction control are added to a safety list which already includes standard dual airbags and 4-wheel ABS. Without a doubt, the Cavalier is one of the safest compact cars on the road.

As in '95, you will be unable to buy a Cavalier wagon. However, a convertible joins the up-level LS sedan and the slick Z24 coupe this year. In addition to the standard 2.2-liter, a morepowerful 2.4-liter engine is now optional. Ride is good on smooth roads, but like other compact cars, you will feel the bumps on not-so-smooth roads. The '96 Cavalier will definitely create headaches for its competition.

The Ratings

	POOR ⟶ GOOD
COMPARATIVE RATING	▮ (middle)
CRASH TEST	▮ (middle)
SAFETY FEATURES	▮ (right-center)
FUEL ECONOMY	▮ (right-center)
PM COST	▮ (right-center)
REPAIR COST	▮ (center)
WARRANTY	▮ (poor)
COMPLAINTS	(blank)
INSURANCE COST	▮ (center)

Safety

CRASH TEST	Average
AIRBAGS	Dual
ABS	4-wheel
SIDE CRASH PROTECT.	Weak
BELT ADJUSTORS	Std. (sdn. only)
BUILT-IN CHILD SEAT	None
OCCUPANT INJURY	Average

General Information

WHERE MADE	U.S./Mexico
YEAR OF PRODUCTION	Second
PARKING INDEX	Easy
BUMPERS	Strong
THEFT RATING	
TWINS	Pontiac Sunfire
DRIVE	Front

Specifications

FUEL ECONOMY (cty/hwy)	26/37	Good
DRIVING RANGE (miles)	441	Long
SEATING	5	
LENGTH (inches)	180.3	Short
HEAD/LEG ROOM (in.)	39.0/42.3	Average
INTERIOR SPACE (cu. ft.)	100	Roomy
CARGO SPACE (cu. ft.)	14	Average

Specifications may vary.

Prices

Model	Retail	Mkup
Cavalier Coupe	10,500	6%
Cavalier Sedan	10,700	6%
Cavalier LS Sedan	12,900	8%
Cavalier Z24 Coupe	14,200	9%
Cavalier LS Convertible	17,500	8%

Competition

	POOR ⟶ GOOD	Pg.
Chevrolet Cavalier	▮ (middle)	**118**
Ford Escort	▮ (center-left)	138
Mercury Tracer	▮ (left-center)	180
Saturn SC	▮ (right/good)	207
Toyota Corolla	▮ (right-center)	217

The Lumina, completely redesigned in '95, receives few changes for 1996. A car that was once always grouped with the Monte Carlo is now beginning to have an identity of its own. One of the notable additions for '96 is the new long-life 100,000 mile engine coolant and spark plugs that Chevrolet has added to many of its models. All models meet 1997 government side impact standards and have dual airbags. ABS is optional on the base Lumina, standard on all other trim levels.

The standard 3.1-liter provides adequate power, though the optional 3.4-liter provides even more power with similar gas mileage. If you like a firmer ride, choose the sport suspension which is optional on the Lumina LS. With its redesign in 1995, the Lumina has picked up a lot of ground in the crowded compact/intermediate market.

The Ratings

	POOR — GOOD
COMPARATIVE RATING	■ (far right)
CRASH TEST	■
SAFETY FEATURES	■
FUEL ECONOMY	■
PM COST	■
REPAIR COST	■
WARRANTY	■ (far left)
COMPLAINTS	(blank)
INSURANCE COST	■

Safety

CRASH TEST	Good
AIRBAGS	Dual
ABS	4-wheel (optional)
SIDE CRASH PROTECT.	Strong
BELT ADJUSTORS	Standard
BUILT-IN CHILD SEAT	Optional
OCCUPANT INJURY	Average

General Information

WHERE MADE	Canada
YEAR OF PRODUCTION	Second
PARKING INDEX	Average
BUMPERS	Strong
THEFT RATING	
TWINS	
DRIVE	Front

Specifications

FUEL ECONOMY (cty/hwy)	20/29	Average
DRIVING RANGE (miles)	380	Short
SEATING	6	
LENGTH (inches)	200.9	Long
HEAD/LEG ROOM (in.)	38.4/42.4	Average
INTERIOR SPACE (cu. ft.)	100	Roomy
CARGO SPACE (cu. ft.)	16	Average

Specifications may vary.

Prices

Model	Retail	Mkup
Lumina	16,355	10%
Lumina LS	18,055	10%

Competition

	POOR — GOOD	Pg.
Chevrolet Lumina	■ (right)	119
Dodge Intrepid	■ (middle)	128
Honda Accord	■ (left)	146
Mazda 626	■ (left)	166
Toyota Camry	■ (left)	215

The Lumina Minivan, which is the twin of the Pontiac Trans Sport and Oldsmobile Silhouette, receives very few changes for 1996. A driver's side airbag and 4-wheel ABS are standard, and traction control is optional.

New for 1996 is a more powerful standard engine. The old 3.1-liter is replaced this year with a 3.4-liter V6 which delivers 60 more horsepower than the previous year's engine. This new engine even beats the 3.8-liter V8 that was optional last year. Rear child seats are an excellent option, and you have your choice of one seat or two, but be careful that you don't end up paying for other options that you don't need. Ride is smooth on good roads, but handling is a bit sluggish. Driving position and visibility take some getting used to. Center and rear seats are easy to remove and install, but there isn't as much cargo room as in other minivans.

The Ratings

	POOR — GOOD
COMPARATIVE RATING	▮ (low)
CRASH TEST	▮ (high)
SAFETY FEATURES	▮ (mid)
FUEL ECONOMY	▮ (low-mid)
PM COST	▮ (high)
REPAIR COST	▮ (high)
WARRANTY	▮ (low)
COMPLAINTS	▮ (low)
INSURANCE COST	▮ (high)

Safety

CRASH TEST	Good
AIRBAGS	Driver
ABS	4-wheel
SIDE CRASH PROTECT.	Weak
BELT ADJUSTORS	Standard
BUILT-IN CHILD SEAT	Optional (two)
OCCUPANT INJURY	

General Information

WHERE MADE	U.S.
YEAR OF PRODUCTION	Seventh
PARKING INDEX	Hard
BUMPERS	Weak
THEFT RATING	Average
TWINS	Silhouette, Trans Sport
DRIVE	Front

Specifications

FUEL ECONOMY (cty/hwy)	19/26	Poor
DRIVING RANGE (miles)	420	Average
SEATING	7	
LENGTH (inches)	191.5	Long
HEAD/LEG ROOM (in.)	39.2/40.0	Cramped
INTERIOR SPACE (cu. ft.)		
CARGO SPACE (cu. ft.)	113	Large

Specifications may vary.

Prices

Model	Retail	Mkup
Lumina Minivan	19,890	10%

Competition

	POOR — GOOD	Pg.
Chevy Lumina Mnvn	▮ (low)	**120**
Ford Windstar	▮ (high)	143
Honda Odyssey	▮ (high)	149
Olds Silhouette	▮ (mid-high)	197
Toyota Previa	▮ (low-mid)	219

Chevrolet Monte Carlo

The Monte Carlo, a name that Chevrolet has carried over from the '70's and '80's, receives minor changes in '96. The Monte Carlo is the 2-door version of the Lumina, and like the Lumina it was completely redesigned in 1995. With this redesign, the two cars gained separate identities and are no longer grouped together as they were for many years. All models meet 1997 government side impact standards and have dual airbags, which help make the Monte Carlo one of the best performers in the government's crash test program. It also has standard 4-wheel ABS.

The standard 3.1-liter V6 provides adequate power and gets adequate gas mileage. The more powerful 3.4-liter V6 delivers much more power and slightly lower gas mileage. The Monte Carlo offers many options which can turn it into a near-luxury car.

The Ratings

	POOR	GOOD
COMPARATIVE RATING		(high)
CRASH TEST		(high)
SAFETY FEATURES		(high)
FUEL ECONOMY		(mid)
PM COST		(mid)
REPAIR COST		(high)
WARRANTY		(low)
COMPLAINTS		(high)
INSURANCE COST		(mid)

Safety

CRASH TEST	Very Good
AIRBAGS	Dual
ABS	4-wheel
SIDE CRASH PROTECT.	Strong
BELT ADJUSTORS	None
BUILT-IN CHILD SEAT	None
OCCUPANT INJURY	

General Information

WHERE MADE	Canada
YEAR OF PRODUCTION	Second
PARKING INDEX	Hard
BUMPERS	Strong
THEFT RATING	
TWINS	
DRIVE	Front

Specifications

FUEL ECONOMY (cty/hwy)	19/29	Average
DRIVING RANGE (miles)	396	Average
SEATING	6	
LENGTH (inches)	200.7	Long
HEAD/LEG ROOM (in.)	37.9/42.4	Cramped
INTERIOR SPACE (cu. ft.)	100	Roomy
CARGO SPACE (cu. ft.)	16	Average

Specifications may vary.

Prices

Model	Retail	Mkup
Monte Carlo LS	17,255	11%
Monte Carlo Z34	19,455	11%

Competition

	POOR	GOOD	Pg.
Chevy Monte Carlo		(high)	**121**
Buick Riviera		(high)	107
Ford Thunderbird		(mid)	142
Mercury Cougar		(high)	176
Pontiac Grand Prix		(mid)	202

The Chrysler Cirrus and Dodge Stratus replaced the LeBaron sedan and Dodge Spirit last year. In 1996, Plymouth joins the Cirrus and Stratus by introducing the Breeze. Also new for '96 is the Sebring JT, a convertible which is based on these three cars and not on the Sebring coupe as the name might suggest. Dual airbags and ABS are standard, and the JA cars meet the government's 1997 side impact standard.

Among the many options is speed-sensitive steering and you also get your choice of three engines: 2.0-, 2.4- or 2.5-liter. An excellent option is a built-in child restraint. The cab-forward design increases interior room, similar to their bigger LH cousins. Chrysler has managed to squeeze a lot of interior room into a small-looking exterior. However, the trunk space is still pretty average in comparison. This car competes well in the intermediate car market.

The Ratings

	POOR				GOOD
COMPARATIVE RATING *					
CRASH TEST					
SAFETY FEATURES					■
FUEL ECONOMY		■			
PM COST				■	
REPAIR COST	■				
WARRANTY	■				
COMPLAINTS					
INSURANCE COST			■		

Safety

CRASH TEST	No government results
AIRBAGS	Dual
ABS	4-wheel
SIDE CRASH PROTECT.	Strong
BELT ADJUSTORS	Standard
BUILT-IN CHILD SEAT	Optional
OCCUPANT INJURY	

General Information

WHERE MADE	U.S.
YEAR OF PRODUCTION	Second
PARKING INDEX	Average
BUMPERS	Weak
THEFT RATING	
TWINS	Dodge Stratus, Plym. Breeze
DRIVE	Front

Specifications

FUEL ECONOMY (cty/hwy)	20/28	Average
DRIVING RANGE (miles)	368	Short
SEATING	5	
LENGTH (inches)	186.0	Average
HEAD/LEG ROOM (in.)	38.1/42.3	Average
INTERIOR SPACE (cu. ft.)	96	Average
CARGO SPACE (cu. ft.)	14	Average

Specifications may vary.

Prices

Model	Retail	Mkup
Cirrus	17,560	9%
Stratus	14,460	9%
Stratus ES	16,110	9%

Competition

	POOR			GOOD	Pg.
Chrysler Cirrus					**122**
Honda Accord	■				146
Mazda 626	■				166
Oldsmobile Ciera				■	195
Toyota Camry	■				215

*Due to the importance of crash tests, cars with no results as of publication date cannot be given an overall rating.

The Chrysler Concorde has been a solid car since it was introduced in 1993, so Chrysler has left it virtually unchanged for 1996. The LH cars were pioneers of Chrysler's unique cab-forward design which pushes the wheels to the corners of the vehicle and moves the windshield out over the front wheels. Traction control and a built-in child seat are excellent options. Dual airbags and ABS are standard, and all Concorde's meet 1997 government side impact standards.

The Concorde has a touring suspension which offers a solid ride and standard 16-inch wheels provide better cornering. The cab-forward design results in a surprisingly spacious interior. The standard 3.3-liter V6 provides adequate power; the 3.5-liter V6 pumps out much more power with comparable gas mileage, but requires more expensive, mid-grade fuel. A good, safe choice.

The Ratings

	POOR ... GOOD
COMPARATIVE RATING	Good
CRASH TEST	Good
SAFETY FEATURES	Good
FUEL ECONOMY	Below Average
PM COST	Average
REPAIR COST	Good
WARRANTY	Poor
COMPLAINTS	Poor
INSURANCE COST	Good

Safety

CRASH TEST	Very Good
AIRBAGS	Dual
ABS	4-wheel
SIDE CRASH PROTECT.	Strong
BELT ADJUSTORS	Standard
BUILT-IN CHILD SEAT	Optional
OCCUPANT INJURY	Very Good

General Information

WHERE MADE	Canada
YEAR OF PRODUCTION	Fourth
PARKING INDEX	Average
BUMPERS	Weak
THEFT RATING	Average
TWINS	Dodge Intrepid, Eag. Vision
DRIVE	Front

Specifications

FUEL ECONOMY (cty/hwy)	19/27	Average
DRIVING RANGE (miles)	396	Average
SEATING	5/6	
LENGTH (inches)	201.5	Long
HEAD/LEG ROOM (in.)	38.3/42.4	Average
INTERIOR SPACE (cu. ft.)	102	Roomy
CARGO SPACE (cu. ft.)	19	Large

Specifications may vary.

Prices

Model	Retail	Mkup
Concorde	19,445	9%

Competition

	POOR ... GOOD	Pg.
Chrysler Concorde	Good	123
Buick Regal	Average	106
Infiniti J30	Good	155
Nissan Maxima	Average	188
Toyota Camry	Poor	215

The LHS and New Yorker, longer versions of Chrysler's LH cars, continue to be safe and solid large-car choices. The LHS seats five and competes with luxury sports sedans, while the 6-passenger New Yorker targets the large, upscale domestics from Buick and Lincoln.

Most anything you'll want comes standard on the LHS with the only options being a sunroof and a CD-player. The New Yorker, more stripped down, allows you to add what you need, but you can't get the excellent built-in child seat that is optional on LH sedans. Thanks to the standard touring suspension, the handling is as precise as any other car this size. The 3.5-liter V6 is plenty powerful and should deliver average gas mileage for a large car. The regular LH models offer slightly less room, but also cost a lot less. Be sure to check out the Ford Crown Victoria, the Cadillac Seville, and the Mercury Grand Marquis before deciding on this car.

The Ratings

	POOR → GOOD
COMPARATIVE RATING	Poor-ish
CRASH TEST	Good
SAFETY FEATURES	Very Good
FUEL ECONOMY	Poor
PM COST	Good
REPAIR COST	Good
WARRANTY	Poor
COMPLAINTS	Very Poor
INSURANCE COST	Very Good

Safety

CRASH TEST	Good
AIRBAGS	Dual
ABS	4-wheel
SIDE CRASH PROTECT.	Strong
BELT ADJUSTORS	Standard
BUILT-IN CHILD SEAT	None
OCCUPANT INJURY	Very Good

General Information

WHERE MADE	Canada
YEAR OF PRODUCTION	Third
PARKING INDEX	Hard
BUMPERS	Weak
THEFT RATING	Average
TWINS	
DRIVE	Front

Specifications

FUEL ECONOMY (cty/hwy)	18/26	Poor
DRIVING RANGE (miles)	360	Short
SEATING	5	
LENGTH (inches)	207.4	Very Long
HEAD/LEG ROOM (in.)	28.3/42.4	Vry. Cramped
INTERIOR SPACE (cu. ft.)	108	Roomy
CARGO SPACE (cu. ft.)	18	Large

Specifications may vary.

Prices

Model	Retail	Mkup
LHS	30,255	9%
New Yorker	27,300	9%

Competition

	POOR → GOOD	Pg.
Chrys. LHS/NY'er	Poor	**124**
Cadillac Seville	Good	113
Chevrolet Caprice	Poor-ish	117
Ford Crown Victoria	Good	137
Merc. Gr. Marquis	Good	177

The Chrysler Sebring and its twin, the Dodge Avenger, were brand-new in 1995, replacing the Chrysler LeBaron coupe and Dodge Daytona. This year, Chrysler is hoping to attract Integra, Prelude, and Celica buyers with these cars that they term aggressive, yet practical. Dual airbags are standard, as is ABS, and both meet 1997 government side impact standards.

The standard 2-liter 4-cylinder engine will probably not satisfy the drivers Chrysler is reaching for. However, the 2.5-liter V6 is slightly more peppy. Fuel economy on both engines is competitive. Interior room is greater than that of competitors and rear-seat occupants will most definitely be more comfortable in the Sebring/Avenger. Trunk room, however, is on the skimpy side. The convertible Sebring JT is not the same car as the hard-top Sebring; it is based on the Cirrus.

The Ratings

	POOR	GOOD
COMPARATIVE RATING		▓
CRASH TEST		▓
SAFETY FEATURES		▓
FUEL ECONOMY	▓	
PM COST	▓	
REPAIR COST	▓	
WARRANTY	▓	
COMPLAINTS		
INSURANCE COST	▓	

Safety

CRASH TEST	Very Good
AIRBAGS	Dual
ABS	4-wheel
SIDE CRASH PROTECT.	Strong
BELT ADJUSTORS	Standard
BUILT-IN CHILD SEAT	None
OCCUPANT INJURY	

General Information

WHERE MADE	U.S.
YEAR OF PRODUCTION	Second
PARKING INDEX	Average
BUMPERS	Strong
THEFT RATING	
TWINS	Dodge Avenger, Mit. Galant
DRIVE	Front

Specifications

FUEL ECONOMY (cty/hwy)	22/31	Average
DRIVING RANGE (miles)	398	Average
SEATING	5	
LENGTH (inches)	187.4	Average
HEAD/LEG ROOM (in.)	39.1/43.3	Roomy
INTERIOR SPACE (cu. ft.)	91	Average
CARGO SPACE (cu. ft.)	12	Small

Specifications may vary.

Prices

Model	Retail	Mkup
Sebring LX	16,441	9%
Sebring LXi	20,150	9%
Avenger Base	14,040	8%
Avenger ES	18,121	9%

Competition

	POOR	GOOD	Pg.
Chrysler Sebring		▓	**125**
Acura Integra	▓		98
Honda Prelude	▓		150
Mazda MX-6	▓		172
Pontiac Grand Prix	▓		202

The Town & Country, all-new for 1996, is the luxury version of the new Dodge and Plymouth Grand minivans. This new design is likely to attract many luxury-oriented minivan buyers. For the extra money, you get lots of power equipment and the option of leather upholstery. The Town & Country seats seven, with four in captain's chairs. Dual airbags and ABS are standard.

The Town & Country offers a 3.8-liter V6 to go with the standard automatic overdrive, and gas mileage is among the lowest for minivans. All-wheel drive is optional. You can't get the "sport handling" package that's optional on the Grand Voyager, but if you want a firmer suspension, check out the trailer-towing package. Ride is comfortable on smooth roads. The built-in child restraints are an excellent option, but not available when you order leather seats.

The Ratings

	POOR	GOOD
COMPARATIVE RATING *		
CRASH TEST		
SAFETY FEATURES		■
FUEL ECONOMY	■	
PM COST		■
REPAIR COST		■
WARRANTY	■	
COMPLAINTS		
INSURANCE COST	■	

Safety

CRASH TEST	No government results
AIRBAGS	Dual
ABS	4-wheel
SIDE CRASH PROTECT.	Strong
BELT ADJUSTORS	Standard
BUILT-IN CHILD SEAT	Optional (two)
OCCUPANT INJURY	Very Good

General Information

WHERE MADE	U.S.
YEAR OF PRODUCTION	First
PARKING INDEX	Hard
BUMPERS	Strong
THEFT RATING	
TWINS	Gr. Caravan, Gr. Voyager
DRIVE	Front

Specifications

FUEL ECONOMY (cty/hwy)	17/24	Poor
DRIVING RANGE (miles)	400	Average
SEATING	7	
LENGTH (inches)	199.7	Long
HEAD/LEG ROOM (in.)	39.8/41.2	Average
INTERIOR SPACE (cu. ft.)		
CARGO SPACE (cu. ft.)	167	Very Large

Specifications may vary.

Prices

Model	Retail	Mkup
Town & Country LX (SWB)	23,905	10%
Town & Country (LWB)	23,960	10%
Town & Country LXi	29,420	11%

Competition

	POOR	GOOD	Pg.
Chrys. T & C			**126**
Ford Windstar		■	143
Chevy Lumina Mnvn	■		119
Olds Silhouette		■	197
Toyota Previa	■		219

*Due to the importance of crash tests, cars with no results as of publication date cannot be given an overall rating.

Dodge Caravan

The Caravan, all-new for 1996, will gain much deserved attention of minivan buyers. The new look still maintains much of the original feel, while bringing fresh new styling to a crowded minivan market. For '96, the Caravan comes with standard airbags, 4-wheel ABS and also meets 1997 government side impact standards for passenger cars.

The longer wheelbase and length of the Grand Caravan translates into more cargo room. The 4-cylinder engine is really not adequate - go for one of the three V6 engines to get more power with only a small sacrifice in fuel efficiency. Order the heavy duty suspension or "sport handling group" for improved cornering ability. The built-in child restraints are a great option. With its new design and added features, the Caravan is likely to remain at the top of the sales list for 1996.

The Ratings

	POOR — GOOD
COMPARATIVE RATING *	
CRASH TEST	
SAFETY FEATURES	████ (9)
FUEL ECONOMY	██ (5)
PM COST	██ (8)
REPAIR COST	██ (7)
WARRANTY	█ (2)
COMPLAINTS	
INSURANCE COST	██ (5)

Safety

CRASH TEST	No government results
AIRBAGS	Dual
ABS	4-wheel
SIDE CRASH PROTECT.	Strong
BELT ADJUSTORS	Standard
BUILT-IN CHILD SEAT	Optional (two)
OCCUPANT INJURY	Good (4WD=Vry. Gd.)

General Information

WHERE MADE	U.S./Canada
YEAR OF PRODUCTION	First
PARKING INDEX	Average
BUMPERS	Strong
THEFT RATING	
TWINS	Voyager, T & C
DRIVE	Front

Specifications

FUEL ECONOMY (cty/hwy)	20/26	Average
DRIVING RANGE (miles)	440	Long
SEATING	7	
LENGTH (inches)	186.3	Average
HEAD/LEG ROOM (in.)	39.8/41.2	Average
INTERIOR SPACE (cu. ft.)		
CARGO SPACE (cu. ft.)	172	Very Large

Specifications may vary.

Prices

Model	Retail	Mkup
Caravan Base	16,575	10%
Caravan SE	18,855	10%
Grand Caravan Base	17,825	10%
Grand Caravan SE	19,595	10%
Grand Caravan ES	24,205	11%

Competition

	POOR — GOOD	Pg.
Dodge Caravan		**127**
Chevy Lumina Mnvn	█ (2)	120
Ford Windstar	████ (10)	143
Olds Silhouette	██ (7)	197
Toyota Previa	██ (3)	219

*Due to the importance of crash tests, cars with no results as of publication date cannot be given an overall rating.

The Intrepid, the least expensive member of Chrysler's cab-forward LH triplets, enters its fourth year with minor changes. Notable ones are the freshened front facia and a slightly redesigned side appearance. Though Dodge is Chrysler's performance division, the Eagle offers the sportiest LH with the Vision TSi. While the new Cirrus and Stratus go after the imports, the LH's continue to target domestic car buyers. The Intrepid has been a very strong performer in the government's crash test program. A good option is the well-designed, built-in rear child restraint. ABS is also optional.

The Intrepid's standard "touring" suspension offers an excellent balance between ride and handling. If you want even better handling and don't mind a stiffer ride, try the "performance" suspension on the ED. The standard 3.3-liter V6 performs well; the somewhat noisier 3.5-liter V6 offers more power with similar gas mileage.

The Ratings

	POOR				GOOD
COMPARATIVE RATING			■		
CRASH TEST				■	
SAFETY FEATURES				■	
FUEL ECONOMY		■			
PM COST			■		
REPAIR COST					■
WARRANTY	■				
COMPLAINTS	■				
INSURANCE COST		■			

Safety

CRASH TEST	Very Good
AIRBAGS	Dual
ABS	4-wheel (optional)
SIDE CRASH PROTECT.	Strong
BELT ADJUSTORS	Standard
BUILT-IN CHILD SEAT	Optional
OCCUPANT INJURY	Good

General Information

WHERE MADE	Canada
YEAR OF PRODUCTION	Fourth
PARKING INDEX	Average
BUMPERS	Weak
THEFT RATING	Very Good
TWINS	Chry. Concorde, Eag. Vision
DRIVE	Front

Specifications

FUEL ECONOMY (cty/hwy)	19/27	Average
DRIVING RANGE (miles)	396	Average
SEATING	5	
LENGTH (inches)	201.8	Long
HEAD/LEG ROOM (in.)	38.3/42.4	Average
INTERIOR SPACE (cu. ft.)	102	Roomy
CARGO SPACE (cu. ft.)	19	Large

Specifications may vary.

Prices

Model	Retail	Mkup
Intrepid Base	18,445	9%
Intrepid ES	22,260	9%

Competition

	POOR			GOOD	Pg.
Dodge Intrepid			■		**128**
Honda Accord	■				146
Mazda 626	■				166
Oldsmobile Ciera				■	195
Toyota Camry	■				215

Dodge/Plymouth Neon

The Neon has few changes for 1996. The Neon, the first small car to benefit from Chrysler's cab-forward design, has outstanding interior room for a small car. Dual airbags are standard, but you'll have to pay extra for ABS.

The single-cam version of the 2-liter engine provides adequate power, but the dual-cam version has even more zing. Not only is the cab longer than other cars its size, but it's also taller, resulting in more head room. There is plenty of room for four, although five may be a squeeze. Cargo space is adequate for a car this size. Choose the sedan with add-on options, or get the "sport" coupe package with dual cams and a firmer suspension. A built-in child restraint is an excellent option. More powerful and roomier than its competitors, the Neon is a good choice.

The Ratings

(Scale: POOR to GOOD)

Rating	Value
COMPARATIVE RATING	(blank)
CRASH TEST	(blank)
SAFETY FEATURES	above average
FUEL ECONOMY	above average
PM COST	average
REPAIR COST	good
WARRANTY	poor
COMPLAINTS	(blank)
INSURANCE COST	below average

Safety

CRASH TEST	No government results
AIRBAGS	Dual
ABS	4-wheel (optional)
SIDE CRASH PROTECT.	Weak
BELT ADJUSTORS	Standard
BUILT-IN CHILD SEAT	Optional
OCCUPANT INJURY	

General Information

WHERE MADE	U.S.
YEAR OF PRODUCTION	Second
PARKING INDEX	Easy
BUMPERS	Strong
THEFT RATING	
TWINS	
DRIVE	Front

Specifications

FUEL ECONOMY (cty/hwy)	28/38	Good
DRIVING RANGE (miles)	400	Average
SEATING	5	
LENGTH (inches)	171.8	Very Short
HEAD/LEG ROOM (in.)	39.6/42.5	Roomy
INTERIOR SPACE (cu. ft.)	103	Roomy
CARGO SPACE (cu. ft.)	12	Small

Specifications may vary.

Prices

Model	Retail	Mkup
Neon Coupe Base	9,495	6%
Neon Coupe Highline	11,300	9%
Neon Sedan Base	9,995	6%
Neon Sedan Highline	11,500	9%
Neon Sedan Sport	12,700	

Competition

(Scale: POOR to GOOD)

Model	Rating	Pg.
Dodge/Plym. Neon	(blank)	129
Chevrolet Cavalier	below average	118
Ford Escort	below average	138
Mercury Tracer	poor	180
Toyota Corolla	average	217

There are no notable changes for the Eagle Summit in 1996. You can buy either a coupe or a sedan and each comes in a base trim level or an upgraded ESi. Dual airbags are standard on all models and ABS can only be bought on the fancier ESi sedan.

The coupe comes with a weak 1.5-liter engine. With the 2-door ESi package, you get the same 1.8-liter engine that comes standard with the sedan; the larger engine produces more power, but you'll lose 6 mpg in fuel economy. Handling is about what you'd expect from a car in this size and price range; the touring suspension which comes with the ESi package, on both coupes and sedans, should firm up the ride. Expect high repair costs, especially when compared to its competitors. The redesign in 1993 gave this car a contemporary feel with a fairly roomy interior.

The Ratings

	POOR	GOOD
COMPARATIVE RATING	■	
CRASH TEST		■
SAFETY FEATURES		■
FUEL ECONOMY		■
PM COST		■
REPAIR COST	■	
WARRANTY	■	
COMPLAINTS	■	
INSURANCE COST	■	

Safety

CRASH TEST	Good
AIRBAGS	Dual
ABS	4-wheel (optional)
SIDE CRASH PROTECT.	Weak
BELT ADJUSTORS	Standard
BUILT-IN CHILD SEAT	None
OCCUPANT INJURY	

General Information

WHERE MADE	Japan
YEAR OF PRODUCTION	Fourth
PARKING INDEX	Very Easy
BUMPERS	Strong
THEFT RATING	
TWINS	Mitsubishi Mirage
DRIVE	Front

Specifications

FUEL ECONOMY (cty/hwy)	26/33	Good
DRIVING RANGE (miles)	383	Short
SEATING	5	
LENGTH (inches)	174.0	Short
HEAD/LEG ROOM (in.)	38.4/42.9	Average
INTERIOR SPACE (cu. ft.)	98	Average
CARGO SPACE (cu. ft.)	11	Small

Specifications may vary.

Prices

Model	Retail	Mkup
Summit DL 2-door	10,900	5%
Summit ESi 2-door	11,154	5%
Summit LX 4-door	12,537	6%
Summit ESi 4-door	13,334	6%

Competition

	POOR	GOOD	Pg.
Eagle Summit	■		**130**
Chevrolet Cavalier		■	118
Ford Escort		■	138
Mitsubishi Mirage	■		185
Toyota Corolla		■	217

The Summit Wagon is not the station wagon version of the Summit; rather, it is a combination subcompact wagon and minivan. The Summit Wagon's twins, the Plymouth Colt Vista and the Mitsubishi Expo LRV, disappeared last year, leaving the Summit Wagon to carry on as the unique choice in this half-wagon, half-minivan category. The Summit wagon comes with standard dual airbags, but you'll have to pay extra for ABS.

The DL comes with an adequate 1.8-liter engine; however, you can order the more powerful 2.4-liter engine that comes standard on the LX and all-wheel-drive models, and you won't lose much in the way of fuel economy. Handling is sluggish, and it tends to lean in corners - more than most cars, but less than minivans. The Summit Wagon has more cargo space than smaller wagons, but larger wagons like the Ford Taurus have more room with better handling.

The Ratings

	POOR GOOD
COMPARATIVE RATING *	
CRASH TEST	
SAFETY FEATURES	
FUEL ECONOMY	
PM COST	
REPAIR COST	
WARRANTY	
COMPLAINTS	
INSURANCE COST	

Safety

CRASH TEST	No government results
AIRBAGS	Dual
ABS	4-wheel (optional)
SIDE CRASH PROTECT.	Weak
BELT ADJUSTORS	Standard
BUILT-IN CHILD SEAT	None
OCCUPANT INJURY	

General Information

WHERE MADE	Japan
YEAR OF PRODUCTION	Fifth
PARKING INDEX	Very Easy
BUMPERS	Strong
THEFT RATING	Very Good
TWINS	
DRIVE	Front

Specifications

FUEL ECONOMY (cty/hwy)	24/29	Average
DRIVING RANGE (miles)	377	Short
SEATING	5	
LENGTH (inches)	168.5	Very Short
HEAD/LEG ROOM (in.)	40.0/40.8	Average
INTERIOR SPACE (cu. ft.)	96	Average
CARGO SPACE (cu. ft.)	35	Very Large

Specifications may vary.

Prices

Model	Retail	Mkup
Summit Wagon DL	14,499	8%
Summit Wagon LX	15,737	8%
Summit Wagon AWD	16,374	9%

Competition

	POOR GOOD	Pg.
Eagle Summit Wgn.		**131**
Ford Contour		136
Ford Escort Wgn.		138
Mitsubishi Mirage		185
Toyota Corolla Wgn.		217

*Due to the importance of crash tests, cars with no results as of publication date cannot be given an overall rating.

The Talon, a twin of the Mitsubishi Eclipse, was re-designed last year and receives few changes for 1996. The Talon is available in three trim levels: ESi, TSi and TSi AWD (all-wheel drive). It has standard dual airbags, but you will still have to pay extra for ABS. All Talons meet 1997 government side impact standards.

The base ESi model comes with a 2-liter engine that provides ample power. However, the turbo version found on the up-level TSi is much more powerful and just as efficient. All-wheel drive is an attractive option, but is only available on the more expensive TSi. Space is rather cramped inside, seating only two comfortably. After a successful redesign in '95, competitive pricing and dual airbags make the Talon a strong competitor and a good value in a sports car.

The Ratings

	POOR — GOOD
COMPARATIVE RATING	▓ (2/10)
CRASH TEST	▓ (7/10)
SAFETY FEATURES	▓ (8/10)
FUEL ECONOMY	▓ (6/10)
PM COST	▓ (5/10)
REPAIR COST	▓ (4/10)
WARRANTY	▓ (2/10)
COMPLAINTS	(blank)
INSURANCE COST	▓ (1/10)

Safety

CRASH TEST	Good
AIRBAGS	Dual
ABS	4-wheel (optional)
SIDE CRASH PROTECT.	Strong
BELT ADJUSTORS	Standard
BUILT-IN CHILD SEAT	None
OCCUPANT INJURY	Poor

General Information

WHERE MADE	U.S.
YEAR OF PRODUCTION	Second
PARKING INDEX	Easy
BUMPERS	Strong
THEFT RATING	
TWINS	Mitsubishi Eclipse
DRIVE	Front

Specifications

FUEL ECONOMY (cty/hwy)	22/32	Average
DRIVING RANGE (miles)	413	Average
SEATING	4	
LENGTH (inches)	172.2	Very Short
HEAD/LEG ROOM (in.)	37.9/43.3	Average
INTERIOR SPACE (cu. ft.)	79	Vry. Cramped
CARGO SPACE (cu. ft.)	15	Average

Specifications may vary.

Prices

Model	Retail	Mkup
Talon ESi	14,830	8%
Talon TSi Turbo (FWD)	18,015	8%
Talon TSi Turbo (4WD)	20,271	8%

Competition

	POOR — GOOD	Pg.
Eagle Talon	▓ (2/10)	**132**
Acura Integra	▓ (1/10)	98
Chevrolet Camaro	▓ (1/10)	116
Ford Probe	▓ (1/10)	140
Honda Prelude	▓ (3/10)	150

Like its LH twins, the Eagle Vision is a solid and stylish car. Although you'll have to pay extra for ABS on the base ESi model, dual airbags are standard and all Visions meet 1997 government side impact standards. New for '96 is an electronic, driver-controlled, four-speed shiftable transmission called "AutoStick," a blend of both manual and automatic transmissions.

The base ESi and the up-level TSi are well-equipped, and the "touring" suspension on both Visions provides a nice compromise between ride and handling. The TSi's optional "performance handling" suspension may make the ride a bit too firm, but does improve handling. The ESi's 3.3-liter V6 accelerates well, but the TSi's potent 3.5-liter V6 offers more power with only slightly lower gas mileage. With a cab-forward design that increases interior room, the Vision offers large-car comfort and safety in a mid-sized package.

The Ratings

	POOR	GOOD
COMPARATIVE RATING		
CRASH TEST		
SAFETY FEATURES		
FUEL ECONOMY		
PM COST		
REPAIR COST		
WARRANTY		
COMPLAINTS		
INSURANCE COST		

Safety

CRASH TEST	Very Good
AIRBAGS	Dual
ABS	4-wheel (optional)
SIDE CRASH PROTECT.	Strong
BELT ADJUSTORS	Standard
BUILT-IN CHILD SEAT	Optional
OCCUPANT INJURY	Good

General Information

WHERE MADE	Canada
YEAR OF PRODUCTION	Fourth
PARKING INDEX	Average
BUMPERS	Weak
THEFT RATING	Good
TWINS	Concorde, Intrepid
DRIVE	Front

Specifications

FUEL ECONOMY (cty/hwy)	19/27	Average
DRIVING RANGE (miles)	396	Average
SEATING	5	
LENGTH (inches)	201.6	Long
HEAD/LEG ROOM (in.)	38.3/42.4	Average
INTERIOR SPACE (cu. ft.)	102	Roomy
CARGO SPACE (cu. ft.)	19	Large

Specifications may vary.

Prices

Model	Retail	Mkup
Vision ESi	19,245	9%
Vision TSi	23,835	9%

Competition

	POOR	GOOD	Pg.
Eagle Vision			**133**
Buick LeSabre			104
Nissan Maxima			188
Toyota Camry			215
Volvo 850			223

The Aerostar was scheduled to cease production in 1994, with the introduction of the Windstar, but it has been carried over into 1996 buoyed by continued steady sales. The Aerostar only comes with a driver airbag and rear-wheel ABS—two huge strikes against it.

The passenger van is actually called a wagon, while the cargo van is called a van. The wagon is available in rear-wheel drive regular- and extended-length, or 4WD extended-length. The 3-liter V6, standard on the rear-wheel drive models, is adequate. The 4-liter V6, standard on 4WD models and available on the rear-wheel-drive extended-length model, is slightly more powerful. Handling improves with 4WD, and ride is fairly good. Built-in child restraints are a noteworthy option. Watch out for the brakes, especially on wet roads. The Aerostar drives more like a van than a car, unlike most of its competition.

The Ratings

	POOR — GOOD
COMPARATIVE RATING	
CRASH TEST	
SAFETY FEATURES	
FUEL ECONOMY	
PM COST	
REPAIR COST	
WARRANTY	
COMPLAINTS	
INSURANCE COST	

Safety

CRASH TEST	Average
AIRBAGS	Driver
ABS	2-wheel
SIDE CRASH PROTECT.	Weak
BELT ADJUSTORS	None
BUILT-IN CHILD SEAT	Optional
OCCUPANT INJURY	Average (4WD=Good)

General Information

WHERE MADE	U.S.
YEAR OF PRODUCTION	Twelfth
PARKING INDEX	Hard
BUMPERS	Weak
THEFT RATING	Very Good
TWINS	
DRIVE	Rear/All

Specifications

FUEL ECONOMY (cty/hwy)	18/24	Poor
DRIVING RANGE (miles)	420	Average
SEATING	2/7	
LENGTH (inches)	174.9	Short
HEAD/LEG ROOM (in.)	39.5/41.4	Average
INTERIOR SPACE (cu. ft.)		
CARGO SPACE (cu. ft.)	141	Large

Specifications may vary.

Prices

Model	Retail	Mkup
Aerostar Van Regular (2WD)	17,190	10%
Aerostar Wgn Regular (2WD)	17,820	10%
Aerostar Wgn Extended (2WD)	21,120	11%
Aerostar Wgn Extended (4WD)	23,445	11%

Competition

	POOR — GOOD	Pg.
Ford Aerostar		**134**
Chevy Lumina Mnvn		120
Ford Windstar		143
Honda Odyssey		149
Toyota Previa		219

The Aspire, all-new in 1994, was the replacement for the econobox Festiva, and enters 1996 with only minor changes. The Aspire was partially designed in Japan and is built in South Korea by Kia. Ford has deleted the SE version of the car which, in turn, shortens the options list and keeps the prices down. Dual airbags are standard and ABS is optional.

The 1.3-liter 4-cylinder has as much power as its competition, but don't be fooled, acceleration is anything by quick. Fuel economy is good, but falls behind the Geo Metro. You can choose between manual or automatic transmissions, but with the automatic you will lose even more fuel efficiency. You can choose between a 2-, 4- or even a 5-door hatchback, which makes the Aspire's claim to being a four-seater finally believable, though adults will still be uncomfortable in the back. However, the trunk is surprisingly spacious.

The Ratings

	POOR GOOD
COMPARATIVE RATING	▮ (2nd)
CRASH TEST	▮ (6th)
SAFETY FEATURES	▮ (6th)
FUEL ECONOMY	▮ (10th)
PM COST	▮ (9th)
REPAIR COST	▮ (2nd)
WARRANTY	▮ (3rd)
COMPLAINTS	▮ (3rd)
INSURANCE COST	▮ (6th)

Safety

CRASH TEST	Average
AIRBAGS	Dual
ABS	4-wheel (optional)
SIDE CRASH PROTECT.	Weak
BELT ADJUSTORS	None
BUILT-IN CHILD SEAT	None
OCCUPANT INJURY	

General Information

WHERE MADE	South Korea
YEAR OF PRODUCTION	Third
PARKING INDEX	Very Easy
BUMPERS	Strong
THEFT RATING	
TWINS	
DRIVE	Front

Specifications

FUEL ECONOMY (cty/hwy)	34/42	Very Good
DRIVING RANGE (miles)	370	Short
SEATING	4	
LENGTH (inches)	152.8	Very Short
HEAD/LEG ROOM (in.)	37.8/41.6	Cramped
INTERIOR SPACE (cu. ft.)	82	Vry. Cramped
CARGO SPACE (cu. ft.)	17	Large

Specifications may vary.

Prices

Model	Retail	Mkup
Aspire 3-door	8,790	7%
Aspire 5-door	9,405	7%

Competition

	POOR GOOD	Pg.
Ford Aspire	▮	**135**
Chevrolet Cavalier	▮	118
Eagle Summit	▮	130
Geo Metro	▮	144
Suzuki Swift	▮	213

The Ford Contour, along with its twin the Mercury Mystique, are the American versions of Ford's new "world car," which is called the Mondeo in Europe. The Contour fills the void left by the departure of the Tempo, but will be marketed to a broader audience. It enters 1996 with few changes from its debut last year. Dual airbags are standard, but you'll have to pay extra for ABS.

The base GL is pretty plain. The mid-level LX is somewhat more plush. Both of these get a 2-liter engine that is only adequate. The sportier SE model comes with a much more powerful 2.5-liter V6 that is very quiet and peppy. Ford claims that you won't have to have the engine tuned for the first 100,000 miles. The handling with the SE's tighter sports suspension is outstanding, making it the best car in the lineup, though you'll pay about $1,700 more for it.

The Ratings

	POOR → GOOD
COMPARATIVE RATING	▮ (good side)
CRASH TEST	▮ (good side)
SAFETY FEATURES	▮ (good side)
FUEL ECONOMY	▮ (middle)
PM COST	▮ (good side)
REPAIR COST	▮ (middle)
WARRANTY	▮ (poor side)
COMPLAINTS	(blank)
INSURANCE COST	▮ (poor-middle)

Safety

CRASH TEST	Good
AIRBAGS	Dual
ABS	4-wheel (optional)
SIDE CRASH PROTECT.	Strong
BELT ADJUSTORS	Standard
BUILT-IN CHILD SEAT	None
OCCUPANT INJURY	

General Information

WHERE MADE	U.S./Mexico
YEAR OF PRODUCTION	Second
PARKING INDEX	Easy
BUMPERS	Strong
THEFT RATING	
TWINS	Mercury Mystique
DRIVE	Front

Specifications

FUEL ECONOMY (cty/hwy)	23/32	Average
DRIVING RANGE (miles)	377	Short
SEATING	5	
LENGTH (inches)	183.9	Average
HEAD/LEG ROOM (in.)	39.0/42.4	Average
INTERIOR SPACE (cu. ft.)	89	Cramped
CARGO SPACE (cu. ft.)	14	Average

Specifications may vary.

Prices

Model	Retail	Mkup
Contour GL	13,785	9%
Contour LX	14,470	9%
Contour SE	16,170	9%

Competition

	POOR → GOOD	Pg.
Ford Contour	▮ (good side)	**136**
Buick Regal	▮ (middle)	106
Chevrolet Lumina	▮ (good side)	119
Mazda 626	▮ (poor side)	166
Oldsmobile Ciera	▮ (good side)	195

Ford Crown Victoria

After being freshened up in 1995, the Ford Crown Victoria enters 1996 with only minor changes. The Crown Vic is almost identical to the Mercury Grand Marquis, and both are less expensive versions of the Lincoln Town Car. Dual airbags are standard, but you inexplicably have to pay extra for ABS. The Crown Victoria also meets 1997 government side impact standards.

The 4.6-liter V8 is powerful, but you have an option to choose an upgrade on the same engine which delivers 20 more horses with little decrease in fuel efficiency. The base-level model comes with plenty of equipment, but to get some of the more choice options, you have to move up to the LX. The Crown Victoria's standard suspension isn't as mushy-riding or awkward in cornering as some other big American sedans. Still, it benefits from the performance and handling package. There's plenty of room for six and their luggage.

The Ratings

	POOR → GOOD
COMPARATIVE RATING	▮ (mid)
CRASH TEST	▮ (high)
SAFETY FEATURES	▮ (high)
FUEL ECONOMY	▮ (low)
PM COST	▮ (mid-high)
REPAIR COST	▮ (high)
WARRANTY	▮ (low)
COMPLAINTS	▮ (low)
INSURANCE COST	▮ (highest)

Safety

CRASH TEST	Very Good
AIRBAGS	Dual
ABS	4-wheel (optional)
SIDE CRASH PROTECT.	Strong
BELT ADJUSTORS	Standard
BUILT-IN CHILD SEAT	None
OCCUPANT INJURY	Very Good

General Information

WHERE MADE	Canada
YEAR OF PRODUCTION	Fifth
PARKING INDEX	Hard
BUMPERS	Strong
THEFT RATING	Good
TWINS	Gr. Marquis, Town Car
DRIVE	Rear

Specifications

FUEL ECONOMY (cty/hwy)	17/26	Poor
DRIVING RANGE (miles)	400	Average
SEATING	6	
LENGTH (inches)	212.0	Very Long
HEAD/LEG ROOM (in.)	39.4/42.5	Roomy
INTERIOR SPACE (cu. ft.)	111	Vry. Roomy
CARGO SPACE (cu. ft.)	21	Very Large

Specifications may vary.

Prices

Model	Retail	Mkup
Crown Victoria Base	20,760	7%
Crown Victoria LX	22,585	7%

Competition

	POOR → GOOD	Pg.
Ford Cr. Victoria	▮ (mid)	**137**
Buick Roadmaster	▮ (lowest)	108
Chevy Caprice	▮ (low)	117
Chrysler LHS/NY'er	▮ (low)	124
Oldsmobile 88	▮ (mid)	191

The Ford Escort enters its sixth year with only minor changes. Unfortunately, they did not change the motorized front seat shoulder belts which force you to remember to buckle the separate lap belt. The 3-door comes in base, LX and sporty GT, and the 4-door, 5-door and wagon are all LX's. Dual airbags are standard, but you'll have to pay extra for ABS.

The GT's 1.8-liter engine is quick, and the automatic's overdrive gear helps gas mileage. The standard 1.9-liter on all other trim levels is larger but much less powerful. An excellent option is the built-in child safety seat in the rear. For better ride and handling, get 14-inch or bigger wheels by avoiding the base 3-door. Comfort is good in front, fair in the rear. The wagons have respectable cargo space for a subcompact. The GT with ABS is probably the best choice.

The Ratings

	POOR — GOOD
COMPARATIVE RATING	(below average)
CRASH TEST	(below average)
SAFETY FEATURES	(average)
FUEL ECONOMY	(below average)
PM COST	(above average)
REPAIR COST	(above average)
WARRANTY	(poor)
COMPLAINTS	(above average)
INSURANCE COST	(poor)

Safety

CRASH TEST	Average
AIRBAGS	Dual
ABS	4-wheel (optional)
SIDE CRASH PROTECT.	Weak
BELT ADJUSTORS	None
BUILT-IN CHILD SEAT	Optional
OCCUPANT INJURY	Avg. (2-dr.=Vry Pr)

General Information

WHERE MADE	U.S.
YEAR OF PRODUCTION	Sixth
PARKING INDEX	Very Easy
BUMPERS	Strong
THEFT RATING	Average (4-dr.=Vry Gd)
TWINS	Mercury Tracer
DRIVE	Front

Specifications

FUEL ECONOMY (cty/hwy)	25/31	Average
DRIVING RANGE (miles)	321	Very Short
SEATING	5	
LENGTH (inches)	170.9	Very Short
HEAD/LEG ROOM (in.)	38.4/41.7	Cramped
INTERIOR SPACE (cu. ft.)	91	Average
CARGO SPACE (cu. ft.)	17	Large

Specifications may vary.

Prices

Model	Retail	Mkup
Escort Hatchback Base	10,065	6%
Escort LX Hatchback 3-door	10,910	7%
Escort GT Hatchback	13,205	7%
Escort LX Sedan	11,515	7%
Escort LX Wagon	11,900	7%

Competition

	POOR — GOOD	Pg.
Ford Escort	(below average)	**138**
Chevrolet Cavalier	(below average)	118
Eagle Summit	(poor)	130
Mercury Tracer	(below average)	180
Toyota Corolla	(average)	217

Ford Mustang

The Mustang, totally redesigned in 1994, enters 1996 with only minor changes. Coupes and convertibles are available in base, sporty GT or limited-production Cobra models. All models get dual airbags, but ABS, standard on the other models, will cost extra on base Mustangs.

The Mustang's standard engine, the 3.8-liter V6 which is optional on the Ford Taurus, is ample for most drivers, and comes with 5 more horses this year. New for this year are two 4.6-liter V8 engines. They are smaller than last year's V8 engine, but they deliver the same amount of horsepower with smoother shifts. Fuel economy with all of these engines is average. With steering and suspension improvements, handling should be better than on the older models. Controls and dashboard are more up-to-date. Think of the Mustang as a two-seater, as the rear seat is only for kids.

The Ratings

	POOR				GOOD
COMPARATIVE RATING	■ (1)				
CRASH TEST				(8) ■	
SAFETY FEATURES			(5) ■		
FUEL ECONOMY			(5) ■		
PM COST			(6) ■		
REPAIR COST			(6) ■		
WARRANTY	(2) ■				
COMPLAINTS		(4) ■			
INSURANCE COST	■ (1)				

Safety

CRASH TEST	Good
AIRBAGS	Dual
ABS	4-wheel (optional)
SIDE CRASH PROTECT.	Weak
BELT ADJUSTORS	None
BUILT-IN CHILD SEAT	None
OCCUPANT INJURY	Poor

General Information

WHERE MADE	U.S.
YEAR OF PRODUCTION	Third
PARKING INDEX	Average
BUMPERS	Strong
THEFT RATING	Poor (Conv.=Very Poor)
TWINS	
DRIVE	Rear

Specifications

FUEL ECONOMY (cty/hwy)	20/30	Average
DRIVING RANGE (miles)	370	Short
SEATING	4	
LENGTH (inches)	181.5	Short
HEAD/LEG ROOM (in.)	38.2/42.5	Average
INTERIOR SPACE (cu. ft.)	89	Cramped
CARGO SPACE (cu. ft.)	11	Small

Specifications may vary.

Prices

Model	Retail	Mkup
Mustang Coupe Base	15,180	9%
Mustang GT Coupe	17,610	9%
Mustang Cobra Coupe	24,810	10%
Mustang Convertible Base	21,060	10%
Mustang GT Convertible	23,495	10%

Competition

	POOR			GOOD	Pg.
Ford Mustang	■				139
Chevy Camaro	■				116
Honda Prelude			■		150
Nissan 240SX		■			186
Pontiac Firebird	■				200

Ford Probe

The Ford Probe receives no major changes as it enters 1996. The Probe and its close relative, the Mazda MX-6, were all-new in 1993, when they were given more modern, rounded styling and they received a freshing up last year. Dual airbags are standard, but ABS, standard on the GT, costs extra on the base Probe.

The base model has a 2-liter 4-cylinder engine that is barely powerful enough. If you want more power, the GT, with its 2.5-liter V6, will cost another couple of thousand. One benefit of the GT is a firmer suspension that gives excellent handling. Ride can be uncomfortable and noisy. The 5-speed is much more enjoyable than the primitive-feeling automatic. Like other sporty cars, the Probe is really a 2-seater with a back seat for occasional use only. The Probe received little design attention this year, and the controls in particular could have used a facelift.

The Ratings

	POOR → GOOD
COMPARATIVE RATING	■□□□□□□□□□
CRASH TEST	□□□□□□□□□■
SAFETY FEATURES	□□□□□■□□□□
FUEL ECONOMY	□□□□□□□■□□
PM COST	□□□□□□■□□□
REPAIR COST	■□□□□□□□□□
WARRANTY	□□■□□□□□□□
COMPLAINTS	□□■□□□□□□□
INSURANCE COST	■□□□□□□□□□

Safety

CRASH TEST	Very Good
AIRBAGS	Dual
ABS	4-wheel (optional)
SIDE CRASH PROTECT.	Weak
BELT ADJUSTORS	None
BUILT-IN CHILD SEAT	None
OCCUPANT INJURY	Average

General Information

WHERE MADE	U.S.
YEAR OF PRODUCTION	Fourth
PARKING INDEX	Easy
BUMPERS	Strong
THEFT RATING	Average
TWINS	Mazda MX-6
DRIVE	Front

Specifications

FUEL ECONOMY (cty/hwy)	26/33	Good
DRIVING RANGE (miles)	450	Long
SEATING	4	
LENGTH (inches)	178.7	Short
HEAD/LEG ROOM (in.)	37.8/43.1	Average
INTERIOR SPACE (cu. ft.)	80	Vry. Cramped
CARGO SPACE (cu. ft.)	19	Large

Specifications may vary.

Prices

Model	Retail	Mkup
Probe Base	13,930	9%
Probe GT	16,450	9%

Competition

	POOR → GOOD	Pg.
Ford Probe	■□□□□□□□□□	**140**
Acura Integra	■□□□□□□□□□	98
Eagle Talon	□■□□□□□□□□	132
Honda Prelude	□□□■□□□□□□	150
Mitsubishi Eclipse	□□□□□□■□□□	183

Ford Taurus

The Taurus led the way in revolutionizing car design in the mid-1980's and now it is doing it again as it enters 1996 with a totally new design nearly as radical as its predecessor. The major changes include a longer wheelbase and oval shaped headlights and dash. The Taurus is available in base, GL or LX trim levels and comes standard with dual airbags, but ABS is optional.

A standard 3-liter V6 engine should provide ample power, although you can opt for the same sized engine with more horses. The SHO is due midyear and will come with many features that are optional on the base models as well as a 3.4-liter V8 which will really make the car move. With the longer wheelbase, interior room and rear legroom have increased, making the car even more comfortable. This is a fine choice in the intermediate size class.

The Ratings

	POOR	GOOD
COMPARATIVE RATING *		
CRASH TEST		
SAFETY FEATURES		▮
FUEL ECONOMY		▮
PM COST		▮
REPAIR COST		▮
WARRANTY	▮	
COMPLAINTS		
INSURANCE COST		▮

Safety

CRASH TEST	No government results
AIRBAGS	Dual
ABS	4-wheel (optional)
SIDE CRASH PROTECT.	Strong
BELT ADJUSTORS	Standard
BUILT-IN CHILD SEAT	Optional
OCCUPANT INJURY	Average (Wgn.=Good)

General Information

WHERE MADE	U.S.
YEAR OF PRODUCTION	First
PARKING INDEX	Average
BUMPERS	Strong
THEFT RATING	
TWINS	Mercury Sable
DRIVE	Front

Specifications

FUEL ECONOMY (cty/hwy)	20/29	Average
DRIVING RANGE (miles)	368	Short
SEATING	5/6	
LENGTH (inches)	197.5	Long
HEAD/LEG ROOM (in.)	39.2/42.6	Roomy
INTERIOR SPACE (cu. ft.)	102	Roomy
CARGO SPACE (cu. ft.)	16	Average

Specifications may vary.

Prices

Model	Retail	Mkup
Taurus GL Sedan	18,600	9%
Taurus LX Sedan	20,980	10%
Taurus GL Wagon	19,680	9%
Taurus LX Wagon	22,000	10%

Competition

	POOR	GOOD	Pg.
Ford Taurus			141
Chevrolet Lumina		▮	119
Honda Accord	▮		146
Mazda 626	▮		166
Toyota Camry	▮		215

*Due to the importance of crash tests, cars with no results as of publication date cannot be given an overall rating.

The Thunderbird, which shares a chassis with the Mercury Cougar and the Lincoln Mark VIII, receives a fresh new look for 1996 with redone front and back ends. The only trim level you can get is the base (LX); the high-performance Super Coupe (SC) has been discontinued. Dual airbags are standard, and ABS is optional.

The LX's standard 3.8-liter V6 is OK for this fairly heavy car. If you'd like a lot more performance, you can order the optional modular 4.6-liter V8. The LX is very well-equipped, and the gauges are well-designed. Ride is comfortable, but the LX's handling isn't as crisp as it should be. This is one coupe with enough room for four (five in a pinch) plus luggage. With its freshened look, the Thunderbird is able to compete well with the Monte Carlo and others in its size class.

The Ratings

	POOR	GOOD
COMPARATIVE RATING		
CRASH TEST		
SAFETY FEATURES		
FUEL ECONOMY		
PM COST		
REPAIR COST		
WARRANTY		
COMPLAINTS		
INSURANCE COST		

Safety

CRASH TEST	Very Good
AIRBAGS	Dual
ABS	4-wheel (optional)
SIDE CRASH PROTECT.	Strong
BELT ADJUSTORS	None
BUILT-IN CHILD SEAT	None
OCCUPANT INJURY	Average

General Information

WHERE MADE	U.S.
YEAR OF PRODUCTION	Eighth
PARKING INDEX	Average
BUMPERS	Strong
THEFT RATING	Average
TWINS	Cougar, Mark VIII
DRIVE	Rear

Specifications

FUEL ECONOMY (cty/hwy)	19/26	Poor
DRIVING RANGE (miles)	378	Short
SEATING	5	
LENGTH (inches)	200.3	Long
HEAD/LEG ROOM (in.)	38.1/42.5	Average
INTERIOR SPACE (cu. ft.)	101	Roomy
CARGO SPACE (cu. ft.)	15	Average

Specifications may vary.

Prices

Model	Retail	Mkup
Thunderbird LX Coupe	17,485	9%

Competition

	POOR	GOOD	Pg.
Ford Thunderbird			**142**
Buick Riviera			107
Chevy Monte Carlo			121
Mercury Cougar			176
Pontiac Grand Prix			202

Ford Windstar

Little has changed for 1996 on Ford's latest entry into the minivan market. Unfortunately for Ford, Chrysler is unveiling a new minivan this year and Ford will have its work cut out in order to keep sales up. The Windstar offers optional built-in child restraints; dual airbags and 4-wheel ABS are both standard.

The base GL comes standard with the same 3-liter V6 as is available on the Aerostar and Ranger. A 3.8-liter V6 is optional on the GL and standard on the LX, and it provides much more power. At over 200 inches, the Windstar is the longest minivan you can buy, and it has more interior room than a Grand Caravan, but not quite as much as a Toyota Previa. Most of that room is given to rear seat passengers. With its contemporary styling and decent handling, the Windstar provides a good challenge to the current generation of Chrysler minivans.

The Ratings

	POOR — GOOD
COMPARATIVE RATING	▮ (high)
CRASH TEST	▮ (high)
SAFETY FEATURES	▮ (high)
FUEL ECONOMY	▮ (low)
PM COST	▮ (high)
REPAIR COST	▮ (mid)
WARRANTY	▮ (low)
COMPLAINTS	(blank)
INSURANCE COST	▮ (mid)

Safety

CRASH TEST	Very Good
AIRBAGS	Dual
ABS	4-wheel
SIDE CRASH PROTECT.	Strong
BELT ADJUSTORS	Standard
BUILT-IN CHILD SEAT	Optional
OCCUPANT INJURY	

General Information

WHERE MADE	U.S.
YEAR OF PRODUCTION	Second
PARKING INDEX	Hard
BUMPERS	Strong
THEFT RATING	
TWINS	
DRIVE	Front

Specifications

FUEL ECONOMY (cty/hwy)	17/23	Poor
DRIVING RANGE (miles)	400	Average
SEATING	7	
LENGTH (inches)	201.2	Long
HEAD/LEG ROOM (in.)	39.3/41.8	Average
INTERIOR SPACE (cu. ft.)		
CARGO SPACE (cu. ft.)	144	Large

Specifications may vary.

Prices

Model	Retail	Mkup
Windstar GL Wagon	19,590	10%
Windstar LX Wagon	24,465	11%

Competition

	POOR — GOOD	Pg.
Ford Windstar	▮ (high)	**143**
Chevy Lumina Mnvn	▮ (low)	119
Honda Odyssey	▮ (low)	149
Olds Silhouette	▮ (mid-high)	197
Toyota Previa	▮ (low)	219

This fuel economy champ changes little for 1996. The Metro is built jointly by GM and Suzuki. You can choose between a 3-door coupe or a roomier 4-door sedan. Each model comes in base or LSi trim levels. Daytime running lights and dual airbags are standard; ABS is optional. The Metro also passes 1997 government side impact standards.

3-door Metros get last year's 1-liter 3-cylinder engine, which doesn't have a lot of power. However, the Metro does lead the industry in fuel efficiency. The sedan looks a lot like a Prizm and is more substantive than the hatchbacks, especially with the 4-cylinder engine. However, the sedan's extra 14 inches in length is almost entirely in the trunk; passengers get only fractions of an inch more headroom, and no more legroom. Price is what drives this vehicle and Geo is doing its best to make sure that every dollar counts.

The Ratings

	POOR	GOOD
COMPARATIVE RATING	▨	
CRASH TEST		▨
SAFETY FEATURES	▨	
FUEL ECONOMY		▨
PM COST	▨	
REPAIR COST	▨	
WARRANTY	▨	
COMPLAINTS		
INSURANCE COST	▨	

Safety

CRASH TEST	Good
AIRBAGS	Dual
ABS	4-wheel (optional)
SIDE CRASH PROTECT.	Strong
BELT ADJUSTORS	None
BUILT-IN CHILD SEAT	None
OCCUPANT INJURY	Very Poor

General Information

WHERE MADE	Canada
YEAR OF PRODUCTION	Second
PARKING INDEX	Very Easy
BUMPERS	Strong
THEFT RATING	
TWINS	Suzuki Swift
DRIVE	Front

Specifications

FUEL ECONOMY (cty/hwy)	44/49	Very Good
DRIVING RANGE (miles)	488	Very Long
SEATING	4	
LENGTH (inches)	164.0	Very Short
HEAD/LEG ROOM (in.)	39.3/42.5	Roomy
INTERIOR SPACE (cu. ft.)	89	Cramped
CARGO SPACE (cu. ft.)	10	Small

Specifications may vary.

Prices

Model	Retail	Mkup
Metro Hatchback Coupe Base	8,380	6%
Metro LSi Hatchback Coupe	8,780	7%
Metro Sedan Base	9,330	7%
Metro LSi Sedan	9,730	7%

Competition

	POOR	GOOD	Pg.
Geo Metro	▨		**144**
Chevrolet Cavalier	▨		118
Eagle Summit	▨		130
Ford Escort	▨		138
Mitsubishi Mirage	▨		185

Geo Prizm

The Prizm, which changes little in 1996, is a clone of Toyota's popular Corolla. It is less expensive than the Corolla, but because of Toyota's reputation, the Corolla outsells it by almost 3 to 1. Prizm's come only in sedans, in either base or LSi trim levels. Dual airbags are standard, and ABS is optional on both models.

Prizm is one of the smallest and least expensive cars that will hold four people in comfort with room for luggage. Handling and ride are good. Controls are logical and easy to use. All models come standard with a 1.6-liter 4-cylinder engine, though the LSi offers an optional 1.8-liter 4-cylinder with slightly more power in exchange for slightly lower fuel economy. The addition of daytime running lamps helps make Prizm a good choice if you want something a bit bigger than the average subcompact at a very reasonable price.

The Ratings

	POOR — GOOD
COMPARATIVE RATING	
CRASH TEST	
SAFETY FEATURES	
FUEL ECONOMY	
PM COST	
REPAIR COST	
WARRANTY	
COMPLAINTS	
INSURANCE COST	

Safety

CRASH TEST	Good
AIRBAGS	Dual
ABS	4-wheel (optional)
SIDE CRASH PROTECT.	Weak
BELT ADJUSTORS	Standard
BUILT-IN CHILD SEAT	Optional
OCCUPANT INJURY	Poor

General Information

WHERE MADE	U.S.
YEAR OF PRODUCTION	Fourth
PARKING INDEX	Very Easy
BUMPERS	Strong
THEFT RATING	Very Good
TWINS	Toyota Corolla
DRIVE	Front

Specifications

FUEL ECONOMY (cty/hwy)	31/35	Good
DRIVING RANGE (miles)	422	Average
SEATING	5	
LENGTH (inches)	173.0	Short
HEAD/LEG ROOM (in.)	38.5/41.7	Cramped
INTERIOR SPACE (cu. ft.)	88	Cramped
CARGO SPACE (cu. ft.)	13	Average

Specifications may vary.

Prices

Model	Retail	Mkup
Prizm Base	12,495	
		5%
Prizm LSi	13,145	8%

Competition

	POOR — GOOD	Pg.
Geo Prizm		**145**
Chevrolet Cavalier		118
Eagle Summit		130
Mercury Tracer		180
Toyota Corolla		217

Honda Accord

The Accord receives new front and rear styling for 1996, giving the car a more sophisticated look. It is uncertain how this new front design will perform in government crash tests; keep in mind that it did poorly after a total redesign of the car in 1994. Dual airbags are standard, but ABS is still optional.

Accords come in three body styles including coupes, sedans and wagons, and each with three trim levels: base DX, mid-level LX and up-level EX. The standard 4-cylinder engine is powerful enough, but the VTEC version found on the EX will probably suit you better. Both versions are pretty economical, even with the optional automatic transmission. Performance and handling are comparable to its competitors. The Accord DX lacks some of the comforts of the more expensive models. As with other Hondas, controls and gauges are excellent.

The Ratings

Rating	POOR → GOOD
COMPARATIVE RATING	Poor
CRASH TEST	Average
SAFETY FEATURES	Good
FUEL ECONOMY	Good
PM COST	Poor-Average
REPAIR COST	Average
WARRANTY	Poor
COMPLAINTS	Average-Good
INSURANCE COST	Average

Safety

CRASH TEST	Average
AIRBAGS	Dual
ABS	4-wheel (optional)
SIDE CRASH PROTECT.	Strong
BELT ADJUSTORS	Std. (sdn/wgn only)
BUILT-IN CHILD SEAT	None
OCCUPANT INJURY	Average

General Information

WHERE MADE	U.S./Japan
YEAR OF PRODUCTION	Third
PARKING INDEX	Easy
BUMPERS	Strong
THEFT RATING	Average
TWINS	
DRIVE	Front

Specifications

FUEL ECONOMY (cty/hwy)	25/32	Good
DRIVING RANGE (miles)	476	Very Long
SEATING	5	
LENGTH (inches)	185.6	Average
HEAD/LEG ROOM (in.)	39.4/42.7	Roomy
INTERIOR SPACE (cu. ft.)	95	Average
CARGO SPACE (cu. ft.)	13	Average

Specifications may vary.

Prices

Model	Retail	Mkup
Accord DX Sedan Man.	15,100	13%
Accord DX Sedan Auto	15,900	13%
Accord LX Sedan Man. w/ABS	19,040	13%
Accord LX Sedan Auto. w/ABS	19,840	13%
Accord EX V-6 Sedan Auto.	25,100	13%

Competition

	POOR → GOOD	Pg.
Honda Accord	Poor	146
Chevrolet Lumina	Good	119
Mazda 626	Average	166
Nissan Maxima	Average	188
Toyota Camry	Poor	215

There are many changes to this Honda which are sure to be attention getters. The all-new 1996 Civic has new dynamic styling, a stronger body and a refined suspension. As before, you can buy a coupe with trim levels DX, HX, and EX; a sedan with trim levels DX, LX and EX; or a hatchback with trim levels CX or DX. Dual airbags are standard and ABS is standard on the EX sedan, but remains optional on all other models.

The engines this year are more powerful and produce lower emissions than in years past. The base engine is a 1.6-liter 4-cylinder which delivers 106 horsepower, and you can upgrade to more powerful engines which will deliver 115 or 127 horsepower depending on which one you choose. There is more interior space than last year, which should make the back seat more comfortable. Features and engines differ by model, so shop carefully.

The Ratings

	POOR ... GOOD
COMPARATIVE RATING *	(no rating)
CRASH TEST	(no rating)
SAFETY FEATURES	Good
FUEL ECONOMY	Good
PM COST	Poor
REPAIR COST	Average
WARRANTY	Poor
COMPLAINTS	(no rating)
INSURANCE COST	Average

Safety

CRASH TEST	No government results
AIRBAGS	Dual
ABS	4-wheel (optional)
SIDE CRASH PROTECT.	Strong
BELT ADJUSTORS	Std. (sdn. only)
BUILT-IN CHILD SEAT	None
OCCUPANT INJURY	Average (Cpe.=Vry. Pr.)

General Information

WHERE MADE	U.S./Canada/Japan
YEAR OF PRODUCTION	First
PARKING INDEX	Very Easy
BUMPERS	Strong
THEFT RATING	
TWINS	
DRIVE	Front

Specifications

FUEL ECONOMY (cty/hwy)	33/38	Very Good
DRIVING RANGE (miles)	417	Average
SEATING	5	
LENGTH (inches)	175.1	Short
HEAD/LEG ROOM (in.)	39.8/42.7	Roomy
INTERIOR SPACE (cu. ft.)	85	Cramped
CARGO SPACE (cu. ft.)	12	Small

Specifications may vary.

Prices**

Model	Retail	Mkup
Civic CX Hatchback man.	9,750	9%
Civic Si Hatchback man.	13,540	14%
Civic EX Sedan auto.	16,950	14%
Civic DX Coupe man.	11,590	14%
Civic EX Coupe auto.	15,630	14%

Competition

	POOR ... GOOD	Pg.
Honda Civic	(no rating)	147
Chevrolet Cavalier	Poor-Average	118
Ford Escort	Average	138
Geo Prizm	Poor	145
Toyota Corolla	Average	217

** 1996 prices not available at press time. Prices based on 1995 data.

*Due to the importance of crash tests, cars with no results as of publication date cannot be given an overall rating.

The del Sol does not change much for 1996. In possibly its last year of production, the del Sol receives only a minor facelift, rather than a complete overhaul like the car it's based on—the Civic. Dual airbags are standard and, new for this year, Honda is offering optional ABS.

You can choose 102 HP (S), 120 HP (Si), or 160 HP (VTEC) versions of the same 4-cylinder engine. The 5-speed shifts smoothly; the automatic is acceptable for those who don't like to shift. Gas mileage is particularly good on the del Sol S. Handling is OK on the S, better on the Si, very good on the VTEC. Ride isn't bad. The del Sol has no rear seat. Be sure you have enough room inside before you plunk down your money. The top panel is easily removable, although you'll have even less cargo space after you stow it. Controls are well designed.

The Ratings

	POOR				GOOD
COMPARATIVE RATING *					
CRASH TEST					
SAFETY FEATURES		■			
FUEL ECONOMY				■	
PM COST	■				
REPAIR COST	■				
WARRANTY	■				
COMPLAINTS					
INSURANCE COST			■		

Safety

CRASH TEST	No government results
AIRBAGS	Dual
ABS	4-wheel (optional)
SIDE CRASH PROTECT.	Weak
BELT ADJUSTORS	None
BUILT-IN CHILD SEAT	None
OCCUPANT INJURY	Average

General Information

WHERE MADE	Japan
YEAR OF PRODUCTION	Fourth
PARKING INDEX	Very Easy
BUMPERS	Strong
THEFT RATING	Average
TWINS	
DRIVE	Front

Specifications

FUEL ECONOMY (cty/hwy)	28/35	Good
DRIVING RANGE (miles)	369	Short
SEATING	2	
LENGTH (inches)	157.3	Very Short
HEAD/LEG ROOM (in.)	37.5/40.3	Vry. Cramped
INTERIOR SPACE (cu. ft.)	NOT AVAILABLE	
CARGO SPACE (cu. ft.)	11	Small

Specifications may vary.

Prices**

Model	Retail	Mkup
del Sol S man.	15,160	14%
del Sol auto.	16,140	14%
del Sol Si man.	17,330	14%
del Sol Si auto.	18,080	14%
del Sol VTEC	19,580	14%

Competition

	POOR			GOOD		Pg.
Honda del Sol						**148**
Acura Integra	■					98
Honda Prelude			■			150
Mazda MX-6			■			172
Mitsubishi Eclipse				■		183

** 1996 prices not available at press time. Prices based on 1995 data.

148

*Due to the importance of crash tests, cars with no results as of publication date cannot be given an overall rating.

The Odyssey enters '96 with no major changes. This front-wheel drive vehicle is different than most other minivans in many respects. It is lower than, but not as wide as, other minivans, making it easier to maneuver. The most striking feature about the Odyssey is that it has two sedan-type doors for access to the rear seats, while most minivans have only one sliding door. Dual airbags and ABS are standard. The Odyssey meets 1997 passenger car side impact standards.

Honda is rumored to be introducing a V6 on the Odyssey for next year's model, but for now, it gets the same 2.2-liter 4-cylinder engine found on the Accord. The middle bench seat doesn't come out, and the rear seat, which cleverly folds into the floor of the cargo bay, doesn't quite become flush with the floor, making the loading surface uneven. As a result, cargo space is not quite as generous as the competition.

The Ratings

	POOR ⟶ GOOD
COMPARATIVE RATING	▣
CRASH TEST	▣
SAFETY FEATURES	▣
FUEL ECONOMY	▣
PM COST	▣
REPAIR COST	▣
WARRANTY	▣
COMPLAINTS	
INSURANCE COST	▣

Safety

CRASH TEST	Good
AIRBAGS	Dual
ABS	4-wheel
SIDE CRASH PROTECT.	Strong
BELT ADJUSTORS	Standard
BUILT-IN CHILD SEAT	None
OCCUPANT INJURY	

General Information

WHERE MADE	Japan
YEAR OF PRODUCTION	Second
PARKING INDEX	Average
BUMPERS	Strong
THEFT RATING	
TWINS	Isuzu Oasis
DRIVE	Front

Specifications

FUEL ECONOMY (cty/hwy)	20/24	Average
DRIVING RANGE (miles)	378	Short
SEATING	7	
LENGTH (inches)	187.2	Average
HEAD/LEG ROOM (in.)	40.1/40.7	Average
INTERIOR SPACE (cu. ft.)		
CARGO SPACE (cu. ft.)	103	Large

Specifications may vary.

Prices**

Model	Retail	Mkup
Odyssey LX 7-passenger	23,130	15%
Odyssey LX 6-passenger	23,625	13%
Odyssey EX	25,225	13%

Competition

	POOR ⟶ GOOD	Pg.
Honda Odyssey	▣	149
Chevy Lumina Mnvn	▣	120
Ford Windstar	▣	143
Olds Sihouette	▣	197
Toyota Previa	▣	219

** 1996 prices not available at press time. Prices based on 1995 data.

The Prelude remains essentially unchanged for the 1996 model year. It is a combination sport/luxury coupe, with an emphasis on performance. Dual airbags are standard, and ABS comes on all but the S models.

The Prelude basically comes in three trim levels, each defined by its version of the same 4-cylinder engine; the S has a 135-HP, the Si has a 160-HP, and the VTEC has a peppy 190-HP. All of the engines are adequate, but the VTEC is the most responsive, and it's just as fuel efficient as the others. Ride is firm and acceptable for a sporty coupe. The Prelude's 5-speed is smooth shifting, and the automatic overdrive is excellent. Front seats are comfortable, but rear seat comfort is minimal. Cargo space is also very small. The instrument panel could use some work.

The Ratings

	POOR ··· GOOD
COMPARATIVE RATING	▮ (below average)
CRASH TEST	▮ (very good)
SAFETY FEATURES	▮ (average)
FUEL ECONOMY	▮ (average)
PM COST	▮ (below average)
REPAIR COST	▮ (below average)
WARRANTY	▮ (poor)
COMPLAINTS	▮ (very good)
INSURANCE COST	▮ (poor)

Safety

CRASH TEST	Very Good
AIRBAGS	Dual
ABS	4-wheel (optional)
SIDE CRASH PROTECT.	Weak
BELT ADJUSTORS	None
BUILT-IN CHILD SEAT	None
OCCUPANT INJURY	Average

General Information

WHERE MADE	Japan
YEAR OF PRODUCTION	Fifth
PARKING INDEX	Easy
BUMPERS	Strong
THEFT RATING	Very Poor
TWINS	
DRIVE	Front

Specifications

FUEL ECONOMY (cty/hwy)	22/26	Average
DRIVING RANGE (miles)	366	Short
SEATING	4	
LENGTH (inches)	174.8	Short
HEAD/LEG ROOM (in.)	38.0/44.2	Roomy
INTERIOR SPACE (cu. ft.)	80	Vry. Cramped
CARGO SPACE (cu. ft.)	8	Very Small

Specifications may vary.

Prices**

Model	Retail	Mkup
Prelude S Coupe	19,760	13%
Prelude Si Coupe	22,430	13%
Prelude VTEC Coupe	25,620	13%
Prelude SE Coupe	23,650	13%

Competition

	POOR ··· GOOD	Pg.
Honda Prelude	▮ (below average)	150
Chevrolet Camaro	▮ (poor)	116
Ford Probe	▮ (poor)	140
Mazda MX-6	▮ (below average)	172
Mitsubishi Eclipse	▮ (good)	183

** 1996 prices not available at press time. Prices based on 1995 data.

Hyundai Accent

The Accent receives only minor changes for 1996. The front-wheel drive Accent is much improved over its predecessor, the Hyundai Excel. The Accent brings more contemporary styling along the lines of the Honda Civic, and delivers more interior room and horsepower than the Excel. Most importantly, the Accent comes with dual airbags and ABS is available. The Accent also meets the 1997 side impact standards.

The 1.5-liter 4-cylinder engine that comes on all Accents is adequate for this light car and is fuel efficient. Although front seat occupants will be comfortable, passengers in the rear will feel cramped. The Accent is just as powerful as the new Toyota Tercel, but it's not quite as fuel efficient or as roomy as the Geo Metro and Suzuki Swift. The Accent does not beat the competition in any one category, but it is a good competitor by offering a little bit of everything.

The Ratings

	POOR GOOD
COMPARATIVE RATING *	
CRASH TEST	
SAFETY FEATURES	
FUEL ECONOMY	
PM COST	
REPAIR COST	
WARRANTY	
COMPLAINTS	
INSURANCE COST	

Safety

CRASH TEST	No government results
AIRBAGS	Dual
ABS	4-wheel (optional)
SIDE CRASH PROTECT.	Strong
BELT ADJUSTORS	Standard
BUILT-IN CHILD SEAT	None
OCCUPANT INJURY	

General Information

WHERE MADE	Korea
YEAR OF PRODUCTION	Second
PARKING INDEX	Very Easy
BUMPERS	Strong
THEFT RATING	
TWINS	
DRIVE	Front

Specifications

FUEL ECONOMY (cty/hwy)	27/35	Good
DRIVING RANGE (miles)	357	Short
SEATING	5	
LENGTH (inches)	161.5	Very Short
HEAD/LEG ROOM (in.)	38.7/42.6	Average
INTERIOR SPACE (cu. ft.)	88	Cramped
CARGO SPACE (cu. ft.)	16	Average

Specifications may vary.

Prices

Model	Retail	Mkup
Accent Hatchback Coupe	8,285	10%
Accent Sedan	9,295	10%

Competition

	POOR GOOD	Pg.
Hyundai Accent		151
Chevrolet Cavalier		118
Ford Escort		138
Mitsubishi Mirage		185
Toyota Corolla		217

*Due to the importance of crash tests, cars with no results as of publication date cannot be given an overall rating.

The 1996 Elantra is all-new, but will not make its debut until March. If you wait for the new '96, you will find standard dual airbags which should help improve the abysmal crash test rating it received in '95. Unfortunately, you still have to pay extra for ABS.

The only engine offered will be a 1.8-liter 4 cylinder which should provide enough power to move this compact car. This engine was the optional engine offered last year and will deliver adequate gas mileage. Ride is expected to be OK, typical of many compact cars. The front seats are comfortable, but adults will feel cramped in the back. The trunk space is barely adequate. One of the best things going for this car is its price which is expected to stay low, and preventive maintenance and repair costs are also low, which makes this car a solid choice.

The Ratings

	POOR ⟷ GOOD
COMPARATIVE RATING *	(no rating)
CRASH TEST	(no rating)
SAFETY FEATURES	mid
FUEL ECONOMY	mid
PM COST	good
REPAIR COST	good
WARRANTY	poor
COMPLAINTS	(no rating)
INSURANCE COST	poor-mid

Safety

CRASH TEST	No government results
AIRBAGS	Dual
ABS	4-wheel (optional)
SIDE CRASH PROTECT.	Weak
BELT ADJUSTORS	None
BUILT-IN CHILD SEAT	None
OCCUPANT INJURY	

General Information

WHERE MADE	Korea
YEAR OF PRODUCTION	First
PARKING INDEX	Very Easy
BUMPERS	Strong
THEFT RATING	
TWINS	
DRIVE	Front

Specifications

FUEL ECONOMY (cty/hwy)	22/29	Average
DRIVING RANGE (miles)	343	Very Short
SEATING	5	
LENGTH (inches)	174.0	Short
HEAD/LEG ROOM (in.)	38.6/43.2	Roomy
INTERIOR SPACE (cu. ft.)	90	Cramped
CARGO SPACE (cu. ft.)	12	Small

Specifications may vary.

Prices**

Model	Retail	Mkup
Elantra Base man.	10,199	11%
Elantra Base auto.	11,499	11%
Elantra GLS man.	11,599	13%
Elantra GLS auto.	12,324	13%
Elantra GLS auto. w/ABS	14,402	13%

Competition

	POOR ⟷ GOOD	Pg.
Hyundai Elantra	(no rating)	**152**
Chevrolet Cavalier	mid	118
Ford Escort	mid	138
Geo Prizm	poor-mid	145
Toyota Corolla	good	217

** 1996 prices not available at press time. Prices based on 1995 data.

*Due to the importance of crash tests, cars with no results as of publication date cannot be given an overall rating.

The Sonata, all-new in 1995, receives very few changes for '96. The wheelbase on the Sonata is slightly longer than most other intermediate cars, resulting in a little more legroom inside. One of the best standard features is dual airbags, although you still get motorized belts. ABS will cost extra and is only available on the more expensive GL or GLS models. The Sonata meets the government's 1997 side impact standard.

The base and GL models come with an adequately powered 2-liter engine. The 3-liter that is standard on the GLS and optional on the GL only provides 5 more horsepower, and you'll lose several mpg in fuel economy. The Sonata is environmentally friendly—over 85% of the Sonata is recyclable, and no harmful CFCs were used in the manufacturing process. All of these features make the Sonata a good competitor in the intermediate size class.

The Ratings

(Scale: POOR ← → GOOD)

Rating	
COMPARATIVE RATING	below average
CRASH TEST	below average
SAFETY FEATURES	good
FUEL ECONOMY	below average
PM COST	very good
REPAIR COST	good
WARRANTY	poor
COMPLAINTS	(no rating)
INSURANCE COST	poor

Safety

CRASH TEST	Average
AIRBAGS	Dual
ABS	4-wheel (optional)
SIDE CRASH PROTECT.	Strong
BELT ADJUSTORS	Standard
BUILT-IN CHILD SEAT	None
OCCUPANT INJURY	Very Poor

General Information

WHERE MADE	Korea
YEAR OF PRODUCTION	Second
PARKING INDEX	Easy
BUMPERS	Strong
THEFT RATING	
TWINS	
DRIVE	Front

Specifications

FUEL ECONOMY (cty/hwy)	22/28	Average
DRIVING RANGE (miles)	413	Average
SEATING	5	
LENGTH (inches)	185.0	Average
HEAD/LEG ROOM (in.)	38.5/43.3	Roomy
INTERIOR SPACE (cu. ft.)	101	Roomy
CARGO SPACE (cu. ft.)	13	Average

Specifications may vary.

Prices

Model	Retail	Mkup
Sonata Sedan Man.	13,999	12%
Sonata Sedan Auto.	14,799	12%
Sonata GL Sedan	15,699	12%
Sonata GLS Sedan	17,999	12%

Competition

(Scale: POOR ← → GOOD)

Model	Rating	Pg.
Hyundai Sonata	below average	153
Buick Century	good	103
Honda Accord	poor	146
Oldsmobile Ciera	very good	195
Toyota Camry	poor	215

The G20, Infiniti's least expensive car, is based on the Nissan Sentra's platform. The car has not changed much this year. Dual airbags and ABS are standard.

The G20 is less of a status symbol than other Infiniti's. The 2-liter 4-cylinder engine, which the G20 shares with the Sentra SE-R, is only adequate and works better with the standard manual transmission than the available automatic. The manual provides better fuel economy as well. Handling can be a bit challenging in sudden high-speed maneuvers, but otherwise it's predictable and responsive; the available touring package, sold as the G20t for $3,000 extra, does not include a firmer suspension. The instrument panel is a pleasure to use, but the car is small for four adults. The added features, such as an excellent warranty, make this affordable luxury car a good competitor.

The Ratings

	POOR	GOOD
COMPARATIVE RATING*		
CRASH TEST		
SAFETY FEATURES		
FUEL ECONOMY		
PM COST		
REPAIR COST		
WARRANTY		
COMPLAINTS		
INSURANCE COST		

Safety

CRASH TEST	No government results
AIRBAGS	Dual
ABS	4-wheel
SIDE CRASH PROTECT.	Weak
BELT ADJUSTORS	Standard
BUILT-IN CHILD SEAT	None
OCCUPANT INJURY	Average

General Information

WHERE MADE	Japan
YEAR OF PRODUCTION	Sixth
PARKING INDEX	Easy
BUMPERS	Weak
THEFT RATING	Average
TWINS	
DRIVE	Front

Specifications

FUEL ECONOMY (cty/hwy)	24/32	Average
DRIVING RANGE (miles)	429	Long
SEATING	5	
LENGTH (inches)	174.8	Short
HEAD/LEG ROOM (in.)	38.8/42.0	Average
INTERIOR SPACE (cu. ft.)	89	Cramped
CARGO SPACE (cu. ft.)	14	Average

Specifications may vary.

Prices

Model	Retail	Mkup
G20 Base Man.	23,800	18%
G20 Base Auto.	24,800	18%
G20t w/Touring Package Man.	26,900	18%
G20t w/Touring Package Auto.	27,900	18%

Competition

	POOR	GOOD	Pg.
Infiniti G20			154
Buick LeSabre			104
Honda Accord			146
Subaru Legacy			210
Toyota Camry			215

*Due to the importance of crash tests, cars with no results as of publication date cannot be given an overall rating.

The J30, which some say looks like a Jaguar, does not change much for 1996. The most significant change includes additional color choices. The fluid style of the car is a nice break from the traditional low front/high rear styling that is seen on many large cars today. All models feature dual airbags and ABS.

The 3-liter V6 is more than powerful enough and provides average fuel economy for a car this size. Ride is smooth on most roads, but handling isn't as responsive as the Jaguar styling suggests. The touring package, sold as the J30t, comes with firmer springs, 4-wheel steering, a spoiler on the trunk and a price tag that's $2,000 higher. The J30 focuses on luxurious accommodation for two up-front; adults in the rear seat will not be comfortable. Instruments and controls are very nice, but trunk space is tight.

The Ratings

	POOR ... GOOD
COMPARATIVE RATING	▓ (high)
CRASH TEST	▓ (mid)
SAFETY FEATURES	▓ (mid)
FUEL ECONOMY	▓ (low-mid)
PM COST	▓ (mid)
REPAIR COST	▓ (low)
WARRANTY	▓ (high)
COMPLAINTS	▓ (mid)
INSURANCE COST	▓ (low-mid)

Safety

CRASH TEST	Good
AIRBAGS	Dual
ABS	4-wheel
SIDE CRASH PROTECT.	Weak
BELT ADJUSTORS	Standard
BUILT-IN CHILD SEAT	None
OCCUPANT INJURY	Average

General Information

WHERE MADE	Japan
YEAR OF PRODUCTION	Fourth
PARKING INDEX	Average
BUMPERS	Weak
THEFT RATING	Poor
TWINS	
DRIVE	Rear

Specifications

FUEL ECONOMY (cty/hwy)	18/23	Poor
DRIVING RANGE (miles)	380	Short
SEATING	5	
LENGTH (inches)	191.3	Long
HEAD/LEG ROOM (in.)	37.7/41.3	Vry. Cramped
INTERIOR SPACE (cu. ft.)	87	Cramped
CARGO SPACE (cu. ft.)	10	Small

Specifications may vary.

Prices

Model	Retail	Mkup
J30 Base Auto.	39,920	19%
J30t w/Touring Package Auto	41,920	19%

Competition

	POOR ... GOOD	Pg.
Infiniti J30	▓ (high)	**155**
Chrys. LHS/NY'er	▓ (low)	124
Lexus GS300	▓ (high)	160
Merc.-Benz C-Class	▓ (high)	174
Mitsu. Diamante	▓ (lowest)	182

The Q45 is Infiniti's flagship, the model in which they've invested their future. The Q45's styling was touched up last year, and it is due for a replacement sometime in the near future. For 1996, the most significant changes include the addition of two new exterior colors. As usual, dual airbags and ABS are standard.

The Q45's 4.5-liter, 272-HP V8 with automatic overdrive accelerates rapidly and is quite powerful, but not very fuel efficient. The Q45 comes with just about everything you can imagine, but you can still spend $5,000 more on the Q45a or $3,000 more on the touring package, sold as the Q45t, with a rear stabilizer bar and many luxurious amenities. The most valuable option is the $1,500 traction control package. Handling is excellent. Accommodations in the front seat are generous, though people in back won't be quite as pleased.

The Ratings

	POOR GOOD
COMPARATIVE RATING *	
CRASH TEST	
SAFETY FEATURES	
FUEL ECONOMY	
PM COST	
REPAIR COST	
WARRANTY	
COMPLAINTS	
INSURANCE COST	

Safety

CRASH TEST	No government results
AIRBAGS	Dual
ABS	4-wheel
SIDE CRASH PROTECT.	Weak
BELT ADJUSTORS	Standard
BUILT-IN CHILD SEAT	None
OCCUPANT INJURY	Very Good

General Information

WHERE MADE	Japan
YEAR OF PRODUCTION	Seventh
PARKING INDEX	Average
BUMPERS	Weak
THEFT RATING	Very Poor
TWINS	
DRIVE	Rear

Specifications

FUEL ECONOMY (cty/hwy)	17/22	Poor
DRIVING RANGE (miles)	428	Long
SEATING	6	
LENGTH (inches)	199.8	Long
HEAD/LEG ROOM (in.)	38.2/43.9	Roomy
INTERIOR SPACE (cu. ft.)	95	Average
CARGO SPACE (cu. ft.)	15	Average

Specifications may vary.

Prices

Model	Retail	Mkup
Q45 Base Auto.	53,520	19%
Q45t w/Touring Package Auto.	56,970	19%

Competition

	POOR GOOD	Pg.
Infiniti Q45		**156**
Cadillac DeVille		110
Cadillac Seville		113
Lexus GS300		160
Mitsu. Diamante		182

*Due to the importance of crash tests, cars with no results as of publication date cannot be given an overall rating.

The first minivan entrant for Isuzu is not really Isuzu's creation, but Honda's. Just as Honda sells Isuzu's Rodeo as the Passport, Isuzu now sells Honda's Odyssey as the Oasis. Like the Odyssey, the Oasis is designed to be more like a car than a minivan. With a wide stance and low ground clearance, the Oasis drives much like a car and also has conventional doors instead of a sliding door like the rest of its minivan competition. Dual airbags and ABS are standard.

The power comes from a 2.2-liter 4-cylinder engine which delivers only adequate power, but unfortunately, there are no other engine choices. The middle seat in the Oasis does not come out, and the rear seat cleverly folds into the floor, but not quite flush, making the loading surface uneven. As a result, cargo space is not as generous as the competition.

The Ratings

	POOR	GOOD
COMPARATIVE RATING *		
CRASH TEST		
SAFETY FEATURES		
FUEL ECONOMY		
PM COST		
REPAIR COST		
WARRANTY		
COMPLAINTS		
INSURANCE COST		

Safety

CRASH TEST	No government results
AIRBAGS	Dual
ABS	4-wheel
SIDE CRASH PROTECT.	Weak
BELT ADJUSTORS	Standard
BUILT-IN CHILD SEAT	None
OCCUPANT INJURY	

General Information

WHERE MADE	Japan
YEAR OF PRODUCTION	First
PARKING INDEX	Average
BUMPERS	Strong
THEFT RATING	
TWINS	Honda Odyssey
DRIVE	Front

Specifications

FUEL ECONOMY (cty/hwy)	20/24	Average
DRIVING RANGE (miles)	378	Short
SEATING	7	
LENGTH (inches)	187.2	Average
HEAD/LEG ROOM (in.)	40.1/40.7	Average
INTERIOR SPACE (cu. ft.)		
CARGO SPACE (cu. ft.)	103	Large

Specifications may vary.

Prices

Model	Retail	Mkup
Prices unavailable at press time.		
Expected range: $25-28,000		

Competition

	POOR	GOOD	Pg.
Isuzu Oasis			**157**
Chevy Lumina Mnvn			120
Ford Windstar			143
Honda Odyssey			149
Toyota Previa			219

*Due to the importance of crash tests, cars with no results as of publication date cannot be given an overall rating.

Kia Sephia

Kia, the Korean manufacturer that has been making Festivas for Ford, is the first new manufacturer in the U.S. in several years. The Kia Sephia (it rhymes), their first model, came out mid-1994 and enters 1996 with only minor changes. The Sephia comes standard with dual airbags and optional ABS.

To power this car, Kia has equipped the Sephia with an impressive 1.8-liter 4 cylinder engine which can produce 122 horsepower, enough to move this small car. The Sephia comes in several trim levels: RS, LS, and GS—but unfortunately, only one body style (sedan) is available, unlike the Sephia's competitors. The styling is similar to the old Mazda 323, which should not be too surprising, as Mazda is a part-owner of Kia. Interior space is adequate, with skimpy trunk space. The Sephia could be a major player in the small sedan market, especially with its attractive price tag.

The Ratings

	POOR	GOOD
COMPARATIVE RATING *		
CRASH TEST		
SAFETY FEATURES		▉
FUEL ECONOMY		▉
PM COST		▉
REPAIR COST		▉
WARRANTY	▉	
COMPLAINTS	▉	
INSURANCE COST	▉	

Safety

CRASH TEST	No government results
AIRBAGS	Dual
ABS	2-wheel (optional)
SIDE CRASH PROTECT.	Strong
BELT ADJUSTORS	Standard
BUILT-IN CHILD SEAT	None
OCCUPANT INJURY	

General Information

WHERE MADE	Japan/South Korea
YEAR OF PRODUCTION	Third
PARKING INDEX	Very Easy
BUMPERS	Strong
THEFT RATING	
TWINS	
DRIVE	Front

Specifications

FUEL ECONOMY (cty/hwy)	29/34	Good
DRIVING RANGE (miles)	381	Short
SEATING	5	
LENGTH (inches)	171.7	Very Short
HEAD/LEG ROOM (in.)	38.2/42.9	Average
INTERIOR SPACE (cu. ft.)	93	Average
CARGO SPACE (cu. ft.)	11	Small

Specifications may vary.

Prices **

Model	Retail	Mkup
Sephia RS	8,880	12%
Sephia RS Auto.	9,830	12%
Sephia LS	10,630	13%
Sephia GS	10,780	15%
Sephia GS Auto.	11,530	15%

Competition

	POOR	GOOD	Pg.
Kia Sephia			**158**
Chevrolet Cavalier	▉		118
Eagle Summit	▉		130
Ford Escort	▉		138
Toyota Corolla		▉	217

** 1996 prices not available at press time. Prices based on 1995 data.

*Due to the importance of crash tests, cars with no results as of publication date cannot be given an overall rating.

Lexus ES300

The ES300 enters 1996 having only received one minor adjustment from 1995—two new exterior colors. This entry-level Lexus shares some body parts with the less-fancy Toyota Camry, though you wouldn't necessarily guess that from seeing the two cars next to each other. Dual airbags and ABS are standard.

The ES300 comes with the same 3-liter V6 found on the Avalon and up-level Camrys. Despite the ES300's additional 400 pounds, acceleration is rapid, but gas mileage is poor. The only transmission is a smooth-shifting automatic. Handling is fine, and the ride is firm but pleasant; both are more refined than with the Camry. Accommodations are spacious in front, but less so in the rear. You can get most of the ES300's virtues in the V6 Camry for almost $10,000 less. However, you could spend more and do a lot worse.

The Ratings

	POOR — GOOD
COMPARATIVE RATING	▓ (near good)
CRASH TEST	▓ (mid-high)
SAFETY FEATURES	▓ (mid-high)
FUEL ECONOMY	▓ (mid-low)
PM COST	▓ (mid-high)
REPAIR COST	▓ (poor)
WARRANTY	▓ (good)
COMPLAINTS	▓ (good)
INSURANCE COST	▓ (good)

Safety

CRASH TEST	Good
AIRBAGS	Dual
ABS	4-wheel
SIDE CRASH PROTECT.	Weak
BELT ADJUSTORS	Standard
BUILT-IN CHILD SEAT	None
OCCUPANT INJURY	Good

General Information

WHERE MADE	Japan
YEAR OF PRODUCTION	Fifth
PARKING INDEX	Average
BUMPERS	Weak
THEFT RATING	Poor
TWINS	Toyota Camry
DRIVE	Front

Specifications

FUEL ECONOMY (cty/hwy)	20/29	Average
DRIVING RANGE (miles)	426	Long
SEATING	5	
LENGTH (inches)	187.8	Average
HEAD/LEG ROOM (in.)	37.8/43.5	Average
INTERIOR SPACE (cu. ft.)	92	Average
CARGO SPACE (cu. ft.)	14	Average

Specifications may vary.

Prices

Model	Retail	Mkup
ES300 Base	32,400	22%

Competition

	POOR — GOOD	Pg.
Lexus ES300	▓ (near good)	**159**
BMW 3-Series	▓ (mid-low)	102
Infiniti J30	▓ (good)	155
Saab 9000	▓ (good)	206
Volvo 850	▓ (good)	223

The GS300 has not changed since it was introduced in 1993, though the styling is by no means outdated. Lexus first introduced the GS300 to bridge the nearly $20,000 gap between the entry-level ES300 and the luxurious LS400. It has done this nicely and become a popular luxury car. As can be expected, dual airbags and ABS are standard.

The GS300 is powered by a gas-guzzling 3-liter 6-cylinder engine that will provide more than enough power for any driver. New for 1996 is a redesigned 5-speed automatic transmission that should make driving more enjoyable. The GS300 emphasizes a smooth, silent ride for two front-seat passengers; rear-seat occupants will be cramped. You can find less expensive cars with the GS300's luxurious feel; for example, consider the BMW 3-Series, or save even more money and look at a Bonneville, Volvo 850 or Taurus SHO.

The Ratings

(scale: POOR — GOOD)

COMPARATIVE RATING	Good
CRASH TEST	Below Average
SAFETY FEATURES	Good
FUEL ECONOMY	Poor
PM COST	Above Average
REPAIR COST	Poor
WARRANTY	Good
COMPLAINTS	(none shown)
INSURANCE COST	Below Average

Safety

CRASH TEST	Average
AIRBAGS	Dual
ABS	4-wheel
SIDE CRASH PROTECT.	Strong
BELT ADJUSTORS	Standard
BUILT-IN CHILD SEAT	None
OCCUPANT INJURY	Average

General Information

WHERE MADE	Japan
YEAR OF PRODUCTION	Third
PARKING INDEX	Average
BUMPERS	Weak
THEFT RATING	Very Poor
TWINS	
DRIVE	Rear

Specifications

FUEL ECONOMY (cty/hwy)	18/24	Poor
DRIVING RANGE (miles)	422	Average
SEATING	5	
LENGTH (inches)	194.9	Long
HEAD/LEG ROOM (in.)	38.3/44.0	Roomy
INTERIOR SPACE (cu. ft.)	97	Average
CARGO SPACE (cu. ft.)	13	Average

Specifications may vary.

Prices

Model	Retail	Mkup
GS300 Base	45,700	22%

Competition

(scale: POOR — GOOD)

Model	Rating	Pg.
Lexus GS300	Good	160
Cadillac Seville	Average	113
Infiniti J30	Good	155
Merc.-Benz C-Class	Good	174
Volvo 850	Good	223

The LS400, Lexus's flagship sedan, underwent a major redesign in 1995 and enters 1996 with no major changes. Dual airbags and ABS are standard. It also meets the 1997 government side crash protection standards a year early.

The engine that powers this large car is a 4.0-liter V8 which provides plenty of power, making it one of the quickest luxury cars around. Fuel economy in the city, though certainly not great, is surprising for a car in this size class. With the addition of a longer wheelbase in 1995, a previously smooth ride was made even smoother and the rear seat became even more roomy. Trunk space was also expanded in '95, but is still rather small when compared to other large cars. With all its standard features and its powerful engine, the LS400 is worth the money, though you can probably find what you're looking for in something less expensive.

The Ratings

Rating	POOR → GOOD
COMPARATIVE RATING *	□□□□□□□□□□
CRASH TEST	□□□□□□□□□□
SAFETY FEATURES	□□□□□□■□
FUEL ECONOMY	□□□■□□□
PM COST	□□□□□■□
REPAIR COST	■□□□□□□
WARRANTY	□□□□□□■□
COMPLAINTS	□□□□□□□□
INSURANCE COST	□□□□□□□■

Safety

CRASH TEST	No government results
AIRBAGS	Dual
ABS	4-wheel
SIDE CRASH PROTECT.	Strong
BELT ADJUSTORS	Standard
BUILT-IN CHILD SEAT	None
OCCUPANT INJURY	Very Good

General Information

WHERE MADE	Japan
YEAR OF PRODUCTION	Second
PARKING INDEX	Easy
BUMPERS	Weak
THEFT RATING	
TWINS	
DRIVE	Rear

Specifications

FUEL ECONOMY (cty/hwy)	19/26	Average
DRIVING RANGE (miles)	495	Very Long
SEATING	5	
LENGTH (inches)	196.7	Long
HEAD/LEG ROOM (in.)	38.9/43.7	Vry. Roomy
INTERIOR SPACE (cu. ft.)	102	Roomy
CARGO SPACE (cu. ft.)	14	Average

Specifications may vary.

Prices

Model	Retail	Mkup
LS400 Base	52,900	22%

Competition

	POOR → GOOD	Pg.
Lexus LS400	□□□□□□□□□	**161**
Cadillac DeVille	□□□□□□■□	110
Chrys. LHS/NY'er	□□■□□□□	124
Merc. Gr. Marquis	□□□□■□□	177
Mitsu. Diamante	■□□□□□□□	182

*Due to the importance of crash tests, cars with no results as of publication date cannot be given an overall rating.

Lexus SC300/400

These two luxuriously-equipped coupes differ only in standard engines and luxury appointments; many items standard on the more-expensive SC400 will cost extra on the SC300. Other than subtle front- and rear-end styling updates, both models receive few changes for 1996. A nice new feature is the addition of self-dimming mirrors. All SC models have dual airbags and ABS.

The SC300 shares a powerful 3-liter 6-cylinder engine with the GS300 and Toyota Supra. For $7,500 more, you can step up to the SC400, with the 4-liter V8, from the big Lexus LS400. Be sure to get traction control. Handling is excellent, and ride is comfortably firm. The front seats are close to ideal for people of the right size, but check them out before you buy. Back seat is for kids only, and the trunk is skimpy. The instrument panel and controls are well designed.

The Ratings

	POOR — GOOD
COMPARATIVE RATING *	
CRASH TEST	
SAFETY FEATURES	
FUEL ECONOMY	
PM COST	
REPAIR COST	
WARRANTY	
COMPLAINTS	
INSURANCE COST	

Safety

CRASH TEST	No government results
AIRBAGS	Dual
ABS	4-wheel
SIDE CRASH PROTECT.	Strong
BELT ADJUSTORS	Standard
BUILT-IN CHILD SEAT	None
OCCUPANT INJURY	Very Good

General Information

WHERE MADE	Japan
YEAR OF PRODUCTION	Fifth
PARKING INDEX	Easy
BUMPERS	Weak
THEFT RATING	Very Poor
TWINS	
DRIVE	Rear

Specifications

FUEL ECONOMY (cty/hwy)	18/24	Poor
DRIVING RANGE (miles)	412	Average
SEATING	4	
LENGTH (inches)	191.1	Long
HEAD/LEG ROOM (in.)	38.3/44.1	Roomy
INTERIOR SPACE (cu. ft.)	85	Cramped
CARGO SPACE (cu. ft.)	9	Very Small

Specifications may vary.

Prices

Model	Retail	Mkup
SC300 Base Man.	43,400	22%
SC300 Base Auto.	44,300	25%
SC400 Base	52,400	22%

Competition

	POOR — GOOD	Pg.
Lexus SC300/400		**162**
Infiniti J30		155
Mercury Cougar		176
Saab 9000		206
Volvo 850		223

*Due to the importance of crash tests, cars with no results as of publication date cannot be given an overall rating.

The Continental underwent its first major overhaul since 1988 last year, and enters 1996 with few changes. Dual airbags and ABS are standard.

The most major change in 1995 was the addition of a huge 4.6-liter V8 engine that did a good job of accelerating this two-ton car, and this carries over into '96. No one should complain about the lack of power, and the Continental will finally be able to compete with the Cadillac Seville. Most anything you'll want comes standard, including a computer that stores each driver's seat position, radio stations, and other innovations geared toward convenient luxuries. Heated seats and traction control are among the few options. Also as an option, Lincoln is offering a special 75th anniversary package, but be careful, the price can jump quickly. With a good year behind it, the Continental enters 1996 as a true competitor in the sporty large car market.

The Ratings

	POOR → GOOD
COMPARATIVE RATING*	(no rating)
CRASH TEST	(no rating)
SAFETY FEATURES	●●●●●●●●■●
FUEL ECONOMY	●●■●●●●●●●
PM COST	●●●●●●●■●●
REPAIR COST	●●■●●●●●●●
WARRANTY	●●●■●●●●●●
COMPLAINTS	(no rating)
INSURANCE COST	●●●●●●●●●■

Safety

CRASH TEST	No government results
AIRBAGS	Dual
ABS	4-wheel
SIDE CRASH PROTECT.	Strong
BELT ADJUSTORS	Standard
BUILT-IN CHILD SEAT	None
OCCUPANT INJURY	Good

General Information

WHERE MADE	U.S.
YEAR OF PRODUCTION	Second
PARKING INDEX	Hard
BUMPERS	Strong
THEFT RATING	
TWINS	
DRIVE	Front

Specifications

FUEL ECONOMY (cty/hwy)	17/25	Poor
DRIVING RANGE (miles)	356	Short
SEATING	5/6	
LENGTH (inches)	206.3	Very Long
HEAD/LEG ROOM (in.)	39.0/41.9	Average
INTERIOR SPACE (cu. ft.)	102	Roomy
CARGO SPACE (cu. ft.)	18	Large

Specifications may vary.

Prices

Model	Retail	Mkup
Continental Base	41,800	13%

Competition

	POOR → GOOD	Pg.
Lincoln Continental	(no rating)	**163**
Cadillac Seville	●●●●●●■●●●	113
Chrys. LHS/NY'er	●●■●●●●●●●	124
Lexus GS300	●●●●●●●●■●	160
Mitsu. Diamante	■●●●●●●●●●	182

*Due to the importance of crash tests, cars with no results as of publication date cannot be given an overall rating.

The Mark VIII, which receives few noticeable changes for 1996, is based on the same chassis as the Mercury Cougar and Ford Thunderbird. However, you can pay up to twice as much for the Lincoln nameplate. For all that money, you do get distinctive styling, inside and out. The only noticeable changes for '96 are new exterior colors. Dual airbags and ABS are standard, and traction control is optional.

This heavy (nearly two-ton) car comes in only one well-equipped version, though you can add about $4,000 worth of options to the sticker price, including the new 75th anniversary options package. The modular 4.6-liter V8 engine is smooth and quite powerful. The ride is outstanding on smooth roads. There's room for four, but the rear seat is tight. The Thunderbird SC is a much better buy, if you don't want the Lincoln name and distinctive style.

The Ratings

	POOR → GOOD
COMPARATIVE RATING *	(no rating)
CRASH TEST	(no rating)
SAFETY FEATURES	8
FUEL ECONOMY	3
PM COST	6
REPAIR COST	5
WARRANTY	5
COMPLAINTS	5
INSURANCE COST	9

General Information

WHERE MADE	U.S.
YEAR OF PRODUCTION	Fourth
PARKING INDEX	Average
BUMPERS	Strong
THEFT RATING	Poor
TWINS	Thunderbird, Cougar
DRIVE	Rear

Safety

CRASH TEST	No government results
AIRBAGS	Dual
ABS	4-wheel
SIDE CRASH PROTECT.	Strong
BELT ADJUSTORS	Standard
BUILT-IN CHILD SEAT	None
OCCUPANT INJURY	Very Good

Specifications

FUEL ECONOMY (cty/hwy)	18/26	Poor
DRIVING RANGE (miles)	378	Short
SEATING	5	
LENGTH (inches)	207.3	Very Long
HEAD/LEG ROOM (in.)	38.1/42.6	Average
INTERIOR SPACE (cu. ft.)	97	Average
CARGO SPACE (cu. ft.)	14	Average

Specifications may vary.

Prices

Model	Retail	Mkup
Mark VIII Base	39,650	13%

Competition

	POOR → GOOD	Pg.
Lincoln Mark VIII	(no rating)	**164**
Infiniti J30	8	155
Mercury Cougar	7	176
Saab 9000	8	206
Volvo 850	8	223

*Due to the importance of crash tests, cars with no results as of publication date cannot be given an overall rating.

The Town Car, which shares the Ford Crown Victoria/Mercury Grand Marquis chassis, was freshened-up in 1995, and enters '96 with only minor changes. The base-model Executive is very well-equipped. The Signature Series and Cartier Designer Series have extra finishing touches that may not be worth the higher price. Optional extras include heated outside mirrors with position memory tied into the seat position memory buttons, as well as traction control. Dual airbags and ABS are standard on all models.

Typical of American luxury cars, the Town Car ride is smooth and quiet, and not for speedy corners or sudden maneuvers. The 4.6-liter V8 is smooth, responsive and fairly fuel-efficient for its class, but you can't avoid the digital dashboard. These big cars truly provide room for six and an immense trunk. The Town Car competes well with the Cadillac Fleetwood.

The Ratings

	POOR — GOOD
COMPARATIVE RATING *	(blank)
CRASH TEST	(blank)
SAFETY FEATURES	▮
FUEL ECONOMY	▮
PM COST	▮
REPAIR COST	▮
WARRANTY	▮
COMPLAINTS	▮
INSURANCE COST	▮

Safety

CRASH TEST	No government results
AIRBAGS	Dual
ABS	4-wheel
SIDE CRASH PROTECT.	Strong
BELT ADJUSTORS	Standard
BUILT-IN CHILD SEAT	None
OCCUPANT INJURY	Very Good

General Information

WHERE MADE	U.S.
YEAR OF PRODUCTION	Seventh
PARKING INDEX	Very Hard
BUMPERS	Strong
THEFT RATING	Poor
TWINS	Cr. Victoria, Gr. Marquis
DRIVE	Rear

Specifications

FUEL ECONOMY (cty/hwy)	17/25	Poor
DRIVING RANGE (miles)	400	Average
SEATING	6	
LENGTH (inches)	218.9	Very Long
HEAD/LEG ROOM (in.)	39.1/42.6	Roomy
INTERIOR SPACE (cu. ft.)	116	Vry. Roomy
CARGO SPACE (cu. ft.)	22	Very Large

Specifications may vary.

Prices

Model	Retail	Mkup
Town Car Base	36,910	13%
Town Car Executive	37,300	13%
Town Car Signature	39,350	13%
Town Car Cartier	42,350	14%

Competition

	POOR — GOOD	Pg.
Lincoln Town Car	▮	**165**
Buick Roadmaster	▮	108
Cadillac DeVille	▮	110
Chrysler LHS/NY'er	▮	124
Lexus GS300	▮	160

*Due to the importance of crash tests, cars with no results as of publication date cannot be given an overall rating.

The Mazda 626 receives appearance changes as it enters 1996; most notably, Mazda has redesigned the grill and the hood. Dual airbags are standard, but you'll have to pay extra for ABS. Also new for '96 are door-beams which meet the 1997 side impact standards.

The 626 is aimed directly at the Accord/Taurus/Camry market. With more room up front, slightly better crash test results and a smaller price tag than these, the 626 should hold its own; its sales haven't even come close, however. Like most Japanese mid-sized cars, the base 626 has plenty of standard equipment. The base 2-liter 4-cylinder engine is adequate and reasonably economical. For more power, consider the 2.5-liter V6 available on the LX and ES; this engine, however, requires premium fuel and gets worse mileage. Room, comfort and trunk space are adequate for four.

The Ratings

	POOR — GOOD
COMPARATIVE RATING	■ (2)
CRASH TEST	■ (8)
SAFETY FEATURES	■ (7)
FUEL ECONOMY	■ (6)
PM COST	■ (5)
REPAIR COST	■ (3)
WARRANTY	■ (4)
COMPLAINTS	■ (3)
INSURANCE COST	■ (1)

Safety

CRASH TEST	Good
AIRBAGS	Dual
ABS	4-wheel (optional)
SIDE CRASH PROTECT.	Strong
BELT ADJUSTORS	Standard
BUILT-IN CHILD SEAT	None
OCCUPANT INJURY	Average

General Information

WHERE MADE	U.S.
YEAR OF PRODUCTION	Fourth
PARKING INDEX	Easy
BUMPERS	Strong
THEFT RATING	Good
TWINS	
DRIVE	Front

Specifications

FUEL ECONOMY (cty/hwy)	26/34	Good
DRIVING RANGE (miles)	461	Long
SEATING	5	
LENGTH (inches)	184.4	Average
HEAD/LEG ROOM (in.)	39.2/43.5	Vry. Roomy
INTERIOR SPACE (cu. ft.)	97	Average
CARGO SPACE (cu. ft.)	14	Average

Specifications may vary.

Prices

Model	Retail	Mkup
626 DX	15,495	9%
626 LX	17,695	12%
626 LX 6-liter	19,895	14%
626 ES	22,795	15%

Competition

	POOR — GOOD	Pg.
Mazda 626	■ (2)	**166**
Chrysler Concorde	■ (8)	123
Honda Accord	■ (2)	146
Olds Cut. Supreme	■ (7)	196
Toyota Camry	■ (2)	215

Mazda 929

The 929 enters 1996 with no major changes, although it is expected to be all-new next year. With its amenities and higher price tag, the 929 targets the same market as the Infiniti J30. Dual airbags and ABS are standard.

The 3-liter V6 provides adequate power and acceleration, normal for a car this size. Like the Lincoln Continental and Buick Park Avenue, the 929 emphasizes a smooth ride, and no optional suspensions are available. Real wood trim, leather seats and most anything else you'll want are standard. One intriguing option is a solar-activated ventilation system (about $750) to keep the inside cool when parked in the sun. Four adults will be quite comfortable with fairly decent leg room, though the trunk is surprisingly skimpy. Expect repair costs to be on the expensive side.

The Ratings

	POOR → GOOD
COMPARATIVE RATING *	(no rating)
CRASH TEST	(no rating)
SAFETY FEATURES	good side
FUEL ECONOMY	middle
PM COST	middle
REPAIR COST	poor side
WARRANTY	poor-middle
COMPLAINTS	poor-middle
INSURANCE COST	good

Safety

CRASH TEST	No government results
AIRBAGS	Dual
ABS	4-wheel
SIDE CRASH PROTECT.	Weak
BELT ADJUSTORS	Standard
BUILT-IN CHILD SEAT	None
OCCUPANT INJURY	Average

General Information

WHERE MADE	Japan
YEAR OF PRODUCTION	Fifth
PARKING INDEX	Average
BUMPERS	Strong
THEFT RATING	Very Poor
TWINS	
DRIVE	Rear

Specifications

FUEL ECONOMY (cty/hwy)	19/24	Average
DRIVING RANGE (miles)	407	Average
SEATING	5	
LENGTH (inches)	193.7	Long
HEAD/LEG ROOM (in.)	37.4/43.4	Average
INTERIOR SPACE (cu. ft.)	NOT AVAILABLE	
CARGO SPACE (cu. ft.)	12	Small

Specifications may vary.

Prices **

Model	Retail	Mkup
929 Base	35,795	18%

Competition

	POOR → GOOD	Pg.
Mazda 929	(no rating)	**167**
Cadillac Seville	good side	113
Chrysler LHS/NY'er	poor side	124
Infiniti J30	good	155
Mitsu. Diamante	poor	182

** 1996 prices not available at press time. Prices based on 1995 data.

*Due to the importance of crash tests, cars with no results as of publication date cannot be given an overall rating.

Mazda Miata

The Miata has been around for seven years now, and should continue for several more. It enters 1996 with only minor changes. The models sold now are quite similar to those sold in 1990; however, dual airbags are now standard, and ABS is an expensive option. Also, the Miata meets 1997 side impact standards.

The most notable change to this year's Miata is a more powerful standard engine; the 1.8-liter 4-cylinder receives 5 more horsepower. Brakes are good, even better with ABS. Controls and displays are sensibly designed. Fuel economy is just average and could be much better with only 2,200 pounds to haul. You won't get a soft, quiet ride, a spacious interior, or much of a trunk in a Miata, but you won't be buying it for any of those reasons either. You'll get crisp, responsive handling, a peppy engine, and a car that will turn heads with the top down.

The Ratings

	POOR	GOOD
COMPARATIVE RATING *		
CRASH TEST		
SAFETY FEATURES		
FUEL ECONOMY		
PM COST		
REPAIR COST		
WARRANTY		
COMPLAINTS		
INSURANCE COST		

Safety

CRASH TEST	No government results
AIRBAGS	Dual
ABS	4-wheel (optional)
SIDE CRASH PROTECT.	Strong
BELT ADJUSTORS	None
BUILT-IN CHILD SEAT	None
OCCUPANT INJURY	Average

General Information

WHERE MADE	Japan
YEAR OF PRODUCTION	Seventh
PARKING INDEX	Very Easy
BUMPERS	Weak
THEFT RATING	Average
TWINS	
DRIVE	Rear

Specifications

FUEL ECONOMY (cty/hwy)	23/29	Average
DRIVING RANGE (miles)	318	Very Short
SEATING	2	
LENGTH (inches)	155.4	Very Short
HEAD/LEG ROOM (in.)	37.1/42.7	Cramped
INTERIOR SPACE (cu. ft.)	NOT AVAILABLE	
CARGO SPACE (cu. ft.)	4	Very Small

Specifications may vary.

Prices

Model	Retail	Mkup
Miata MX-5	18,450	

Competition

	POOR	GOOD	Pg.
Mazda Miata			**168**
Acura Integra			98
Honda Prelude			150
Mazda MX-6			172
Mitsubishi Eclipse			183

*Due to the importance of crash tests, cars with no results as of publication date cannot be given an overall rating.

Mazda Millenia

The Millenia, all-new in 1995, enters '96 with no major changes. The Millenia was to have been sold by a new up-market Mazda manufacturer called Amati, similar to Lexus, Infiniti and Acura. The declining yen, however, forced Mazda to hold off introducing a new division and offer the Millenia itself. Billed as a performance luxury sedan, the styling is very subtle. Dual airbags and ABS are standard.

The standard 2.5-liter V6 found on the base model is more than adequate; however, the Millenia S comes with the more powerful and responsive "Miller-cycle," a supercharged version of the same engine. The base engine runs on regular, while the S version requires premium fuel. The Millenia is similar in size and price to its cousin the 929, though the Millenia is front-wheel drive and slightly smaller. The Millenia competes well in the luxury market.

The Ratings

	POOR — GOOD
COMPARATIVE RATING	
CRASH TEST	
SAFETY FEATURES	
FUEL ECONOMY	
PM COST	
REPAIR COST	
WARRANTY	
COMPLAINTS	
INSURANCE COST	

Safety

CRASH TEST	Very Good
AIRBAGS	Dual
ABS	4-wheel
SIDE CRASH PROTECT.	Strong
BELT ADJUSTORS	Standard
BUILT-IN CHILD SEAT	None
OCCUPANT INJURY	

General Information

WHERE MADE	Japan
YEAR OF PRODUCTION	Second
PARKING INDEX	Average
BUMPERS	Strong
THEFT RATING	
TWINS	
DRIVE	Front

Specifications

FUEL ECONOMY (cty/hwy)	20/28	Average
DRIVING RANGE (miles)	396	Average
SEATING	5	
LENGTH (inches)	189.8	Average
HEAD/LEG ROOM (in.)	39.3/43.3	Vry. Roomy
INTERIOR SPACE (cu. ft.)	94	Average
CARGO SPACE (cu. ft.)	13	Average

Specifications may vary.

Prices**

Model	Retail	Mkup
Millenia Base	25,995	12%
Millenia Leather	28,895	16%
Millenia S	31,995	15%

Competition

	POOR — GOOD	Pg.
Mazda Millenia		169
BMW 3-Series		102
Merc.-Benz C-Class		174
Oldsmobile Aurora		194
Volvo 850		223

** 1996 prices not available at press time. Prices based on 1995 data.

The Mazda MPV, or multi-purpose passenger vehicle, which was unchanged for seven years, finally receives an overhaul for 1996. Among the many changes is the addition of a rear door on the driver's side and a freshened look. Also new this year is the addition of standard dual airbags and 4-wheel ABS.

The MPV offers 3 trim levels: DX, LX, and ES, and plenty of options. Among the options are the choice of four captain's chairs or a bench seat which will raise the seating to eight. Fuel economy is poor; it gets even worse with the optional 4-wheel drive, otherwise a fine choice. Brakes, handling and ride are inferior to most minivans. With the new revisions, the MPV moves up competitively in the crowded minivan market, although other models offer much more. Be sure to look at the Ford Aerostar or the Toyota Previa before making any decision.

The Ratings

	POOR GOOD
COMPARATIVE RATING *	
CRASH TEST	
SAFETY FEATURES	
FUEL ECONOMY	
PM COST	
REPAIR COST	
WARRANTY	
COMPLAINTS	
INSURANCE COST	

Safety

CRASH TEST	No government results
AIRBAGS	Dual
ABS	4-wheel
SIDE CRASH PROTECT.	Weak
BELT ADJUSTORS	None
BUILT-IN CHILD SEAT	None
OCCUPANT INJURY	Poor

General Information

WHERE MADE	Japan
YEAR OF PRODUCTION	Eighth
PARKING INDEX	Easy
BUMPERS	Weak
THEFT RATING	Average
TWINS	
DRIVE	Rear/All

Specifications

FUEL ECONOMY (cty/hwy)	16/22	Poor
DRIVING RANGE (miles)	353	Short
SEATING	7	
LENGTH (inches)	183.5	Average
HEAD/LEG ROOM (in.)	40.0/40.4	Average
INTERIOR SPACE (cu. ft.)		
CARGO SPACE (cu. ft.)	38	Very Small

Specifications may vary.

Prices**

Model	Retail	Mkup
MPV L 2WD	21,495	11%
MPV LX 2WD	22,375	11%
MPV LX 4WD	25,770	11%
MPV LXE 2WD	24,765	
		11%

Competition

	POOR GOOD	Pg.
Mazda MPV		**170**
Chevy Lumina Mnvn		120
Ford Aerostar		134
Honda Odyssey		149
Toyota Previa		219

** 1996 prices not available at press time. Prices based on 1995 data.

Mazda MX-3

The MX-3, which competes with small sporty coupes like the Hyundai Scoupe and the Toyota Paseo, does not change much for 1996. Dual airbags are standard and, like last year, you'll have to pay extra for ABS.

The MX-3 is powered by a small 1.6-liter 4-cylinder engine which is still competitive and provides above-average fuel economy. A more powerful 1.8-liter engine was dropped two years ago and would have been a nice option to have had. The MX-3 is a two seater with room for kids and a little luggage. Tall people will be a little cramped in the front seat, so make sure you're comfortable inside. Handling is taut and responsive. Ride and noise are about what you'd expect from a sports car. Fuel economy deteriorates with the optional automatic transmission, but the manual is more fun anyway.

The Ratings

	POOR — GOOD
COMPARATIVE RATING *	
CRASH TEST	
SAFETY FEATURES	
FUEL ECONOMY	
PM COST	
REPAIR COST	
WARRANTY	
COMPLAINTS	
INSURANCE COST	

Safety

CRASH TEST	No government results
AIRBAGS	Dual
ABS	4-wheel (optional)
SIDE CRASH PROTECT.	Weak
BELT ADJUSTORS	None
BUILT-IN CHILD SEAT	None
OCCUPANT INJURY	

General Information

WHERE MADE	Japan
YEAR OF PRODUCTION	Fifth
PARKING INDEX	Very Easy
BUMPERS	Weak
THEFT RATING	Average
TWINS	
DRIVE	Front

Specifications

FUEL ECONOMY (cty/hwy)	30/37	Good
DRIVING RANGE (miles)	436	Long
SEATING	4	
LENGTH (inches)	165.7	Very Short
HEAD/LEG ROOM (in.)	38.2/42.6	Average
INTERIOR SPACE (cu. ft.)	80	Vry. Cramped
CARGO SPACE (cu. ft.)	15	Average

Specifications may vary.

Prices**

Model	Retail	Mkup
MX-3 Base	14,440	10%

Competition

	POOR — GOOD	Pg.
Mazda MX-3		171
Chevrolet Cavalier		118
Ford Escort		138
Mercury Tracer		180
Mitsubishi Mirage		185

** 1996 prices not available at press time. Prices based on 1995 data.

*Due to the importance of crash tests, cars with no results as of publication date cannot be given an overall rating.

The MX-6, which shares a chassis with the Mazda 626 and the Ford Probe, enters 1996 with few changes. Though it approaches the size of the 626, it really only seats two comfortably, like the Probe. Its looks are also much like the Probe's. Dual airbags are standard; ABS is optional.

The base model has a long list of standard features and a 2-liter 4-cylinder engine. The up-level LS comes with a 2.5-liter V6 that is more powerful, though fuel economy suffers in comparison. Avoid the unpleasant, rough-shifting optional automatic transmission that the MX-6 shares with the 626. Driving position and front seat comfort are as good as the best sporty cars. Ride tends to be harsh, and controls could stand some improvement. Mazda is trying to make a luxurious commuter car that's fun on the weekends.

The Ratings

	POOR — GOOD
COMPARATIVE RATING	(middle)
CRASH TEST	(very good)
SAFETY FEATURES	(good side)
FUEL ECONOMY	(good side)
PM COST	(middle)
REPAIR COST	(poor side)
WARRANTY	(poor side)
COMPLAINTS	(poor side)
INSURANCE COST	(poor)

Safety

CRASH TEST	Very Good
AIRBAGS	Dual
ABS	4-wheel (optional)
SIDE CRASH PROTECT.	Weak
BELT ADJUSTORS	None
BUILT-IN CHILD SEAT	None
OCCUPANT INJURY	Average

General Information

WHERE MADE	U.S.
YEAR OF PRODUCTION	Fourth
PARKING INDEX	Easy
BUMPERS	Weak
THEFT RATING	Average
TWINS	Ford Probe
DRIVE	Front

Specifications

FUEL ECONOMY (cty/hwy)	26/34	Good
DRIVING RANGE (miles)	450	Long
SEATING	4	
LENGTH (inches)	181.5	Short
HEAD/LEG ROOM (in.)	38.1/44.0	Roomy
INTERIOR SPACE (cu. ft.)	80	Vry. Cramped
CARGO SPACE (cu. ft.)	12	Small

Specifications may vary.

Prices **

Model	Retail	Mkup
MX-6 Coupe	18,895	12%

Competition

	POOR — GOOD	Pg.
Mazda MX-6	(middle)	**172**
Acura Integra	(poor)	98
Eagle Talon	(poor side)	132
Honda Prelude	(middle-poor)	150
Mitsubishi Eclipse	(good side)	183

** 1996 prices not available at press time. Prices based on 1995 data.

172

Mazda Protégé

The Protégé, which was all new in 1995 and replaced the 323, receives very few changes in 1996. The one truly noticeable difference between the Protégé and the old 323 is that the Protégé is a touch larger, which improves ride and increases interior space. Dual airbags are finally available, and ABS can be found on higher models.

The Protégé comes in only one body style (4-door sedan) with three trim levels designed to meet individual needs. DX and LX models come standard with a 1.5-liter 4-cylinder engine that is relatively weak, although quite fuel efficient. The up-level ES comes with last year's 1.8-liter engine - more powerful, but less efficient. With its redesign in 1995, the Protégé competes nicely with its foreign friends the Chevy Cavalier, Ford Escort, and Toyota Corolla.

The Ratings

	POOR	GOOD
COMPARATIVE RATING *		
CRASH TEST		
SAFETY FEATURES		
FUEL ECONOMY		
PM COST		
REPAIR COST		
WARRANTY		
COMPLAINTS		
INSURANCE COST		

Safety

CRASH TEST	No government results
AIRBAGS	Dual
ABS	4-wheel (optional)
SIDE CRASH PROTECT.	Strong
BELT ADJUSTORS	Standard
BUILT-IN CHILD SEAT	None
OCCUPANT INJURY	Very Poor

General Information

WHERE MADE	Japan
YEAR OF PRODUCTION	Second
PARKING INDEX	Very Easy
BUMPERS	Weak
THEFT RATING	
TWINS	
DRIVE	Front

Specifications

FUEL ECONOMY (cty/hwy)	32/39	Very Good
DRIVING RANGE (miles)	462	Long
SEATING	5	
LENGTH (inches)	174.8	Short
HEAD/LEG ROOM (in.)	39.2/42.2	Average
INTERIOR SPACE (cu. ft.)	95	Average
CARGO SPACE (cu. ft.)	13	Average

Specifications may vary.

Prices

Model	Retail	Mkup
Protege DX	11,695	10%
Protege LX	13,095	11%
Protege ES	14,695	11%

Competition

	POOR	GOOD	Pg.
Mazda Protege			**173**
Chevrolet Cavalier			118
Eagle Summit			130
Ford Escort			138
Toyota Corolla			217

Unchanged for 1996, the C-class is the least expensive Mercedes sold in the U.S., which doesn't necessarily make it affordable; it is in the same price class as the Infiniti J30 and the Lexus ES300. Though its styling resembles the larger S-class sedans, the C-class has replaced the 190E as the smallest Mercedes sedan you can buy. Dual airbags and ABS are standard.

The C stands for the car's platform, while the number tells you which engine the car has. The C-class is available with a 2.2-liter 4-cylinder engine (C220), a 2.8-liter 6-cylinder engine (C280), or a 3.6-liter 6-cylinder engine (C360), which is almost twice as powerful as the 2.2-liter. Steering may not be quite as responsive as with a BMW 3-series, but it should be close. Front seats are firm but comfortable; the trunk is too small for a sedan this size.

The Ratings

	POOR	GOOD
COMPARATIVE RATING		
CRASH TEST		
SAFETY FEATURES		
FUEL ECONOMY		
PM COST		
REPAIR COST		
WARRANTY		
COMPLAINTS		
INSURANCE COST		

Safety

CRASH TEST	Good
AIRBAGS	Dual
ABS	4-wheel
SIDE CRASH PROTECT.	Strong
BELT ADJUSTORS	Standard
BUILT-IN CHILD SEAT	None
OCCUPANT INJURY	

General Information

WHERE MADE	Germany
YEAR OF PRODUCTION	Third
PARKING INDEX	Easy
BUMPERS	Weak
THEFT RATING	
TWINS	
DRIVE	Rear

Specifications

FUEL ECONOMY (cty/hwy)	23/29	Average
DRIVING RANGE (miles)	426	Long
SEATING	5	
LENGTH (inches)	177.4	Short
HEAD/LEG ROOM (in.)	37.2/41.5	Vry. Cramped
INTERIOR SPACE (cu. ft.)	90	Cramped
CARGO SPACE (cu. ft.)	12	Small

Specifications may vary.

Prices

Model	Retail	Mkup
C-Class C220	29,900	
C-Class C280	35,250	
C-Class C360	51,000	

Competition

	POOR	GOOD	Pg.
Merc.-Benz C-Class			174
BMW 3-Series			102
Infiniti J30			155
Saab 9000			206
Volvo 850			223

The E-Class, all-new for '96, makes a sweeping departure from the traditional Mercedes in both look and feel. The new E-Class has oval headlamps and a molded hood which make it look more like a Neon than a Mercedes. Dual airbags and ABS are standard.

With Mercedes' new nomenclature, the E stands for the mid-level size, and the numbers stand for the engine size. Available engines include a 3-liter diesel (E300), a 3.2-liter 6-cylinder (E320), and a 4.2-liter V8 (E420). Only the sedan version is available now, with the wagon arriving sometime in mid-1996, and the convertible waiting until '97 to join the group. When shopping for a Mercedes, prepare for options with four- and five-digit price tags. Front seats are decent—firm, yet relaxing on long drives. Rear seats are nearly as good. Interior space has increased due to the increased length and width of the vehicle.

The Ratings

	POOR	GOOD
COMPARATIVE RATING *		
CRASH TEST		
SAFETY FEATURES		
FUEL ECONOMY		
PM COST		
REPAIR COST		
WARRANTY		
COMPLAINTS		
INSURANCE COST		

Safety

CRASH TEST	No government results
AIRBAGS	Dual
ABS	4-wheel
SIDE CRASH PROTECT.	Strong
BELT ADJUSTORS	Standard
BUILT-IN CHILD SEAT	None
OCCUPANT INJURY	Good

General Information

WHERE MADE	Germany
YEAR OF PRODUCTION	First
PARKING INDEX	Average
BUMPERS	Weak
THEFT RATING	
TWINS	
DRIVE	Rear

Specifications

FUEL ECONOMY (cty/hwy)	28/35	Good
DRIVING RANGE (miles)	533	Very Long
SEATING	5	
LENGTH (inches)	189.4	Average
HEAD/LEG ROOM (in.)	37.6/41.3	Vry. Cramped
INTERIOR SPACE (cu. ft.)	95	Average
CARGO SPACE (cu. ft.)	15	Average

Specifications may vary.

Prices

Model	Retail	Mkup
E-Class E300 Diesel	39,900	
E-Class E320	43,500	
E-Class E420	49,900	

Competition

	POOR	GOOD	Pg.
Merc.-Benz E-Class			175
Cadillac DeVille			110
Chrysler LHS/NY'er			124
Infiniti J30			155
Lexus GS300			160

*Due to the importance of crash tests, cars with no results as of publication date cannot be given an overall rating.

The Cougar XR7 receives fresh new front and rear styling and a few other minor changes for 1996. The Cougar is a twin of the Ford Thunderbird and, in many respects, a less-expensive version of the Lincoln Mark VIII. Dual airbags are standard, but you'll have to pay extra for ABS.

The Cougar comes in one model, the XR7, which has just about everything you need. Engine choices are a 3.8-liter V6 and a 4.6-liter V8 with much more power; both are connected to a very smooth automatic overdrive. The Cougar's long wheelbase leads to a smooth ride and handling is average for a car this large. There are no optional suspensions to give you a more high-performance ride. Inside, there's room for four and plenty of luggage space. If you can live without the extras and the nameplate, the cheaper Thunderbird may be the way to go.

The Ratings

	POOR — GOOD
COMPARATIVE RATING	
CRASH TEST	
SAFETY FEATURES	
FUEL ECONOMY	
PM COST	
REPAIR COST	
WARRANTY	
COMPLAINTS	
INSURANCE COST	

Safety

CRASH TEST	Very Good
AIRBAGS	Dual
ABS	4-wheel (optional)
SIDE CRASH PROTECT.	Strong
BELT ADJUSTORS	None
BUILT-IN CHILD SEAT	None
OCCUPANT INJURY	Average

General Information

WHERE MADE	U.S.
YEAR OF PRODUCTION	Eighth
PARKING INDEX	Average
BUMPERS	Strong
THEFT RATING	Average
TWINS	Thunderbird, Mark VIII
DRIVE	Rear

Specifications

FUEL ECONOMY (cty/hwy)	19/26	Poor
DRIVING RANGE (miles)	378	Short
SEATING	5	
LENGTH (inches)	199.9	Long
HEAD/LEG ROOM (in.)	38.1/42.5	Average
INTERIOR SPACE (cu. ft.)	102	Roomy
CARGO SPACE (cu. ft.)	15	Average

Specifications may vary.

Prices

Model	Retail	Mkup
Cougar Base	17,430	9%

Competition

	POOR — GOOD	Pg.
Mercury Cougar		176
Buick Riviera		107
Chevy Monte Carlo		121
Ford Thunderbird		142
Pontiac Grand Prix		202

Like its twins, the Ford Crown Victoria and the upscale Lincoln Town Car, the Grand Marquis gets very few changes for the 1996 model year. It comes in two versions and the less expensive GS is quite well equipped. No matter which you get, you'll have to pay extra for ABS; dual airbags are standard.

While the Grand Marquis isn't quite as difficult to handle as some other big American sedans, it will benefit from the performance and handling option which includes a firmer suspension and 20 more horsepower. Skip the "electronic group" option, unless you like a digital dashboard. There's plenty of room for six and their luggage. The 4.6-liter V8 is responsive and powerful, but has predictably poor gas mileage for a car this size. If you are looking for a large luxury car to haul both people and a trailer, this is the one for you. The Grand Marquis can tow over 5000 lbs.

The Ratings

	POOR	GOOD
COMPARATIVE RATING		
CRASH TEST		
SAFETY FEATURES		
FUEL ECONOMY		
PM COST		
REPAIR COST		
WARRANTY		
COMPLAINTS		
INSURANCE COST		

Safety

CRASH TEST	Very Good
AIRBAGS	Dual
ABS	4-wheel (optional)
SIDE CRASH PROTECT.	Strong
BELT ADJUSTORS	Standard
BUILT-IN CHILD SEAT	None
OCCUPANT INJURY	Very Good

General Information

WHERE MADE	Canada
YEAR OF PRODUCTION	Fifth
PARKING INDEX	Hard
BUMPERS	Strong
THEFT RATING	Average
TWINS	Cr. Victoria, Town Car
DRIVE	Rear

Specifications

FUEL ECONOMY (cty/hwy)	17/25	Poor
DRIVING RANGE (miles)	400	Average
SEATING	6	
LENGTH (inches)	211.8	Very Long
HEAD/LEG ROOM (in.)	39.4/42.5	Roomy
INTERIOR SPACE (cu. ft.)	109	Vry. Roomy
CARGO SPACE (cu. ft.)	21	Very Large

Specifications may vary.

Prices

Model	Retail	Mkup
Grand Marquis GS	21,870	7%
Grand Marquis LS	23,305	7%

Competition

	POOR	GOOD	Pg.
Merc. Gr. Marquis			**177**
Buick Roadmaster			108
Chevrolet Caprice			117
Chrysler LHS/NY'er			124
Mitsu. Diamante			182

The Mystique, along with its twin, the Ford Contour, were all-new last year and enter 1996 with only minor changes. Styling is contemporary yet conservative. Dual airbags are standard, but you'll have to pay extra for ABS or traction control. The Mystique also passes 1997 side impact standards a year early.

The Mystique is about 6 inches longer than its predecessor, the Topaz, and front seat passengers are the biggest beneficiaries of the extra room. Both the base GS and the up-level LS come standard with a 2-liter engine that is only adequate. A more powerful 2.5-liter V6 with a tighter suspension system is optional. The Mystique's suspension is softer than the Contour's to target buyers who want a more luxurious ride, so you may want the optional suspension. A good choice if you're looking for a small, inexpensive version of a large, plush car.

The Ratings

	POOR → GOOD
COMPARATIVE RATING	(above average)
CRASH TEST	(above average)
SAFETY FEATURES	(above average)
FUEL ECONOMY	(average)
PM COST	(above average)
REPAIR COST	(below average)
WARRANTY	(poor)
COMPLAINTS	(no rating)
INSURANCE COST	(below average)

Safety

CRASH TEST	Good
AIRBAGS	Dual
ABS	4-wheel (optional)
SIDE CRASH PROTECT.	Strong
BELT ADJUSTORS	Standard
BUILT-IN CHILD SEAT	None
OCCUPANT INJURY	

General Information

WHERE MADE	U.S./Mexico
YEAR OF PRODUCTION	Second
PARKING INDEX	Easy
BUMPERS	Strong
THEFT RATING	
TWINS	Ford Contour
DRIVE	Front

Specifications

FUEL ECONOMY (cty/hwy)	23/32	Average
DRIVING RANGE (miles)	377	Short
SEATING	5	
LENGTH (inches)	183.5	Average
HEAD/LEG ROOM (in.)	39.0/42.4	Average
INTERIOR SPACE (cu. ft.)	89	Cramped
CARGO SPACE (cu. ft.)	14	Average

Specifications may vary.

Prices

Model	Retail	Mkup
Mystique GS	14,330	9%
Mystique LS	15,705	9%

Competition

	POOR → GOOD	Pg.
Mercury Mystique	(above average)	**178**
Chevrolet Lumina	(good)	119
Honda Accord	(poor)	146
Mazda 626	(poor)	166
Oldsmobile Ciera	(good)	195

Like its twin, the Ford Taurus, the Sable is all-new for 1996. Leaving its traditional look behind, Mercury presents a radically reengineered car that is likely to be as much of a style trendsetter as its predecessor. The Sable is designed to be the luxury line of the Taurus and it does so by having more standard features. Dual airbags are standard and ABS is optional.

Like its headlights, the interior is also done in an ovoid shape which allows for easy-to-use controls and dash. The standard engine, a 3-liter V6, is quite powerful and delivers decent gas millage. For more power and slightly lower gas mileage, you can choose a more powerful version of the same engine. A stiffer structure should improve handling over the past Sable. There is plenty of room for 4 adults and you can even squeeze in 5 or 6 if needed. The new Sable will provide much competition to the crowded intermediate market.

The Ratings

	POOR			GOOD
COMPARATIVE RATING *				
CRASH TEST				
SAFETY FEATURES			■	
FUEL ECONOMY		■		
PM COST			■	
REPAIR COST			■	
WARRANTY	■			
COMPLAINTS				
INSURANCE COST		■		

Safety

CRASH TEST	No government results
AIRBAGS	Dual
ABS	4-wheel (optional)
SIDE CRASH PROTECT.	Strong
BELT ADJUSTORS	Standard
BUILT-IN CHILD SEAT	None
OCCUPANT INJURY	Avg. (Wgn.=Vry. Gd.)

General Information

WHERE MADE	U.S.
YEAR OF PRODUCTION	First
PARKING INDEX	Average
BUMPERS	Strong
THEFT RATING	
TWINS	Ford Taurus
DRIVE	Front

Specifications

FUEL ECONOMY (cty/hwy)	20/29	Average
DRIVING RANGE (miles)	368	Short
SEATING	5/6	
LENGTH (inches)	199.7	Long
HEAD/LEG ROOM (in.)	39.4/42.6	Roomy
INTERIOR SPACE (cu. ft.)	103	Roomy
CARGO SPACE (cu. ft.)	16	Average

Specifications may vary.

Prices

Model	Retail	Mkup
Sable GS Sedan	18,995	9%
Sable LS Sedan	21,295	9%
Sable GS Wagon	20,015	9%
Sable LS Wagon	22,355	10%

Competition

	POOR		GOOD	Pg.
Mercury Sable				179
Eagle Vision			■	133
Honda Accord	■			146
Mazda 626	■			166
Toyota Camry	■			215

*Due to the importance of crash tests, cars with no results as of publication date cannot be given an overall rating.

The 1996 Mercury Tracer has few noticeable changes from last year's model. Although a Mercury name-plate, Mazda helped design the Tracer and its twin, the Ford Escort, explaining their popularity with import buyers. Dual airbags are standard, but front seat occupants must still cope with annoying motorized shoulder belts and separate lap belts. You'll have to pay extra for ABS. An excellent new option is a built-in child restraint in the rear seat.

Acceleration is quick with the sporty LTS's 1.8-liter engine, but somewhat less than inspiring with the base model's 1.9-liter. If you select the automatic, you get an overdrive gear that helps gas mileage. The Tracer's handling is skittish in high-speed cornering; the LTS's sport suspension may help. Room and comfort are good in front, average in the rear, for a subcompact. The trunk is adequate for a small car.

The Ratings

	POOR → GOOD
COMPARATIVE RATING	▮ (poor side)
CRASH TEST	▮ (middle)
SAFETY FEATURES	▮ (good side)
FUEL ECONOMY	▮ (middle)
PM COST	▮ (good side)
REPAIR COST	▮ (good side)
WARRANTY	▮ (poor side)
COMPLAINTS	▮ (good side)
INSURANCE COST	▮ (poor)

Safety

CRASH TEST	Average
AIRBAGS	Dual
ABS	4-wheel (optional)
SIDE CRASH PROTECT.	Weak
BELT ADJUSTORS	None
BUILT-IN CHILD SEAT	Optional
OCCUPANT INJURY	

General Information

WHERE MADE	U.S./Mexico
YEAR OF PRODUCTION	Sixth
PARKING INDEX	Very Easy
BUMPERS	Strong
THEFT RATING	Very Good
TWINS	Ford Escort
DRIVE	Front

Specifications

FUEL ECONOMY (cty/hwy)	23/29	Average
DRIVING RANGE (miles)	298	Very Short
SEATING	5	
LENGTH (inches)	170.9	Very Short
HEAD/LEG ROOM (in.)	38.4/41.9	Cramped
INTERIOR SPACE (cu. ft.)	91	Average
CARGO SPACE (cu. ft.)	12	Small

Specifications may vary.

Prices

Model	Retail	Mkup
Tracer Base	11,755	9%

Competition

	POOR → GOOD	Pg.
Mercury Tracer	▮ (poor side)	**180**
Chevrolet Cavalier	▮ (middle)	118
Eagle Summit	▮ (poor)	130
Ford Escort	▮ (middle-good)	138
Toyota Corolla	▮ (good side)	217

The Villager minivan, a near-twin of the Nissan Quest, receives fresh styling for 1996, including new nose, tail and side moldings. The interior is also freshened, creating a nicer looking minivan. The Villager is available in three trim levels - base GS, luxury LS, and sport-luxury Nautica. The Villager's resemblance to the Dodge Caravan is no coincidence; Mercury is trying to emulate Chrysler's minivan success. ABS and dual airbags are standard, but the Villager keeps awkward motorized shoulder belts and separate lap belts.

The ride is a bit soft, very much like a regular passenger car's, with standard suspension. Handling is competent, but can be firmed up with the optional handling package. The 3-liter V6, with automatic overdrive, is acceptably responsive. Go for the towing package if you'll be hauling anything at all. The new integrated child seats are excellent options.

The Ratings

	POOR → GOOD
COMPARATIVE RATING *	(no rating)
CRASH TEST	(no rating)
SAFETY FEATURES	Good side
FUEL ECONOMY	Poor-to-average
PM COST	Good side
REPAIR COST	Above average
WARRANTY	Poor side
COMPLAINTS	Below average
INSURANCE COST	Good side

Safety

CRASH TEST	No government results
AIRBAGS	Dual
ABS	4-wheel
SIDE CRASH PROTECT.	Weak
BELT ADJUSTORS	Standard
BUILT-IN CHILD SEAT	Optional
OCCUPANT INJURY	Very Good

General Information

WHERE MADE	U.S.
YEAR OF PRODUCTION	Fourth
PARKING INDEX	Average
BUMPERS	Weak
THEFT RATING	Very Good
TWINS	Nissan Quest
DRIVE	Front

Specifications

FUEL ECONOMY (cty/hwy)	17/23	Poor
DRIVING RANGE (miles)	400	Average
SEATING	7	
LENGTH (inches)	189.9	Average
HEAD/LEG ROOM (in.)	39.4/39.9	Cramped
INTERIOR SPACE (cu. ft.)		
CARGO SPACE (cu. ft.)	126	Large

Specifications may vary.

Prices

Model	Retail	Mkup
Villager GS Cargo Van	19,385	10%
Villager GS	19,940	10%
Villager LS	24,300	11%
Villager Nautica	26,390	11%

Competition

	POOR → GOOD	Pg.
Mercury Villager	(no rating)	181
Chevy Lumina Mnvn	poor side	120
Ford Aerostar	below average	134
Pontiac Trans Sport	below average	204
Toyota Previa	below average	219

*Due to the importance of crash tests, cars with no results as of publication date cannot be given an overall rating.

Mitsubishi Diamante

For 1996, the Diamante is left with only one trim level, the ES, after dropping the other two, the LS and Wagon. A new Diamante, interestingly to be built in Australia, will debut next year. Dual airbags are standard and ABS is optional

The Diamante uses a less-powerful version of the 3000GT's 3-liter V6; with dual cams, you will get plenty of power. The Diamante comes with very few options. The ride is smooth, but handling is just average. Rear seat room is surprisingly stingy for a car this size. The sleek look helps make this a favorite among luxury car buyers. Now that the ES model is the only one offered and has a lower price than the other two offered last year, more people will be looking Diamante's way. This car competes nicely with the other luxury cars of its size.

The Ratings

	POOR	GOOD
COMPARATIVE RATING	■	
CRASH TEST		■
SAFETY FEATURES		■
FUEL ECONOMY		■
PM COST	■	
REPAIR COST	■	
WARRANTY		■
COMPLAINTS		■
INSURANCE COST		■

Safety

CRASH TEST	Good
AIRBAGS	Dual
ABS	4-wheel (optional)
SIDE CRASH PROTECT.	Weak
BELT ADJUSTORS	Standard
BUILT-IN CHILD SEAT	None
OCCUPANT INJURY	Average

General Information

WHERE MADE	Japan
YEAR OF PRODUCTION	Fifth
PARKING INDEX	Average
BUMPERS	Weak
THEFT RATING	Poor
TWINS	
DRIVE	Front

Specifications

FUEL ECONOMY (cty/hwy)	18/24	Poor
DRIVING RANGE (miles)	399	Average
SEATING	5	
LENGTH (inches)	190.2	Average
HEAD/LEG ROOM (in.)	38.6/43.9	Roomy
INTERIOR SPACE (cu. ft.)	94	Average
CARGO SPACE (cu. ft.)	14	Average

Specifications may vary.

Prices**

Model	Retail	Mkup
Diamante LS	35,250	25%
Diamante LS w/Traction Ctrl.	35,950	25%

Competition

	POOR	GOOD	Pg.
Mitsu. Diamante	■		**182**
Cadillac Seville		■	113
Chrysler LHS/NY'er		■	124
Infiniti J30		■	155
Saab 9000		■	206

** 1996 prices not available at press time. Prices based on 1995 data.

Mitsubishi Eclipse

As a twin of the Eagle Talon, a sedan brother of the Mitsubishi Galant, and the coupe cousin of the Chrysler Sebring and Dodge Avenger, the Mitsubishi Eclipse tries to stand on its own. It enters 1996 with no major additions from its recent redesign in 1995. Dual airbags are standard, but you'll still have to pay extra for ABS.

The RS is the stripped-down base model and the GS has a few more bells and whistles, some of which are optional. Both of those models get the standard 2-liter engine, which may not be powerful enough for sports enthusiasts. The up-level GS-T and GSX both get a turbo version that pumps out 50% more power, and the GSX comes with all-wheel drive. The Eclipse does have a back seat, but it's not really meant for adults. With all this extra power, expect high insurance bills.

The Ratings

	POOR GOOD
COMPARATIVE RATING	
CRASH TEST	
SAFETY FEATURES	
FUEL ECONOMY	
PM COST	
REPAIR COST	
WARRANTY	
COMPLAINTS	
INSURANCE COST	

Safety

CRASH TEST	Good
AIRBAGS	Dual
ABS	4-wheel (optional)
SIDE CRASH PROTECT.	Strong
BELT ADJUSTORS	Standard
BUILT-IN CHILD SEAT	None
OCCUPANT INJURY	Very Poor

General Information

WHERE MADE	U.S./Japan
YEAR OF PRODUCTION	Second
PARKING INDEX	Easy
BUMPERS	Weak
THEFT RATING	
TWINS	Eagle Talon
DRIVE	Front/All

Specifications

FUEL ECONOMY (cty/hwy)	23/31	Average
DRIVING RANGE (miles)	439	Long
SEATING	4	
LENGTH (inches)	172.2	Very Short
HEAD/LEG ROOM (in.)	37.9/43.3	Average
INTERIOR SPACE (cu. ft.)	79	Vry. Cramped
CARGO SPACE (cu. ft.)	15	Average

Specifications may vary.

Prices

Model	Retail	Mkup
Eclipse RS man.	14,970	15%
Eclipse RS auto.	15,670	15%
Eclipse 2.0-liter man.	17,330	15%
Eclipse GS-T man.	20,940	15%
Eclipse GSX man.	23,910	16%

Competition

	POOR GOOD	Pg.
Mitsubishi Eclipse		183
Acura Integra		98
Ford Mustang		139
Ford Probe		140
Honda Prelude		150

Mitsubishi Galant

The Galant, redesigned last in 1994, enters 1996 with very few changes. It is competing in a crowded size class against the likes of the Honda Accord and Toyota Camry. Dual airbags are standard and help make this a safer car. ABS will still cost you extra.

The base S, mid-level ES, and up-level LS all come with the same 2.4-liter 4-cylinder engine; power is good, but fuel economy is average. You can choose the 2.5-liter V6 engine and gain more power, but will sacrifice even more fuel efficiency. The Galant's ride is on the firm side. Handling is OK, typical of mid-size Japanese sedans. The Galant's rear seat is somewhat uncomfortable, and the front seat's head and leg room is excellent. The price of the Galant helps it to hold its ground against the more popular competition.

The Ratings

	POOR → GOOD
COMPARATIVE RATING *	(no rating)
CRASH TEST	(no rating)
SAFETY FEATURES	▮ (high)
FUEL ECONOMY	▮ (mid)
PM COST	▮ (low)
REPAIR COST	▮ (low-mid)
WARRANTY	▮ (mid)
COMPLAINTS	▮ (low)
INSURANCE COST	▮ (mid)

Safety

CRASH TEST	No government results
AIRBAGS	Dual
ABS	4-wheel (optional)
SIDE CRASH PROTECT.	Strong
BELT ADJUSTORS	Standard
BUILT-IN CHILD SEAT	None
OCCUPANT INJURY	Average

General Information

WHERE MADE	U.S./Japan
YEAR OF PRODUCTION	Third
PARKING INDEX	Easy
BUMPERS	Weak
THEFT RATING	Average
TWINS	Sebring, Avenger
DRIVE	Front

Specifications

FUEL ECONOMY (cty/hwy)	23/30	Average
DRIVING RANGE (miles)	439	Long
SEATING	5	
LENGTH (inches)	187.0	Average
HEAD/LEG ROOM (in.)	39.4/43.3	Vry. Roomy
INTERIOR SPACE (cu. ft.)	96	Average
CARGO SPACE (cu. ft.)	12	Small

Specifications may vary.

Prices

Model	Retail	Mkup
Galant S man.	14,920	12%
Galant S auto.	15,810	12%
Galant ES auto.	19,790	17%
Galant LS auto	22,860	17%

Competition

	POOR → GOOD	Pg.
Mitsubishi Galant	(no rating)	**184**
Honda Accord	▮ (low-mid)	146
Mazda 626	▮ (low-mid)	166
Oldsmobile Ciera	▮ (high)	195
Toyota Camry	▮ (low-mid)	215

*Due to the importance of crash tests, cars with no results as of publication date cannot be given an overall rating.

Mitsubishi Mirage

The Mirage, which was the cousin of the no-longer-available Dodge and Plymouth Colt, gets no major additions for 1996. If you are looking for anything other than a coupe, you are out of luck because sedans are only being sold to large fleet buyers. Coupes are offered in two trim levels, S and LS. All Mirages have dual airbags, but ABS is not available.

The 1.5-liter 4-cylinder engine that comes with the Mirage S is not very powerful, though you'll be pleased with its fuel economy. The 1.8-liter engine on the LS is much more powerful, but gas mileage suffers dramatically. The Mirage handles crisply, and the interior is fairly comfortable for four people. Ride is decent. Many things you would think are standard are not, such as the day/night rearview mirror, so shop wisely. The Mirage's attractive styling is unchanged, and it still remains competitive in its size class.

The Ratings

	POOR GOOD
COMPARATIVE RATING	▪
CRASH TEST	■
SAFETY FEATURES	■
FUEL ECONOMY	■
PM COST	■
REPAIR COST	■
WARRANTY	■
COMPLAINTS	■
INSURANCE COST	■

Safety

CRASH TEST	Good
AIRBAGS	Dual
ABS	None
SIDE CRASH PROTECT.	Weak
BELT ADJUSTORS	Standard
BUILT-IN CHILD SEAT	None
OCCUPANT INJURY	

General Information

WHERE MADE	Japan
YEAR OF PRODUCTION	Fourth
PARKING INDEX	Very Easy
BUMPERS	Weak
THEFT RATING	Good
TWINS	Eagle Summit
DRIVE	Front

Specifications

FUEL ECONOMY (cty/hwy)	32/39	Very Good
DRIVING RANGE (miles)	462	Long
SEATING	5	
LENGTH (inches)	171.1	Very Short
HEAD/LEG ROOM (in.)	38.6/42.9	Roomy
INTERIOR SPACE (cu. ft.)	87	Cramped
CARGO SPACE (cu. ft.)	11	Small

Specifications may vary.

Prices

Model	Retail	Mkup
Mirage S man.	10,440	9%
Mirage S auto.	10,980	9%
Mirage LS man.	13,290	11%
Mirage LS auto.	13,950	11%

Competition

	POOR GOOD	Pg.
Mitsubishi Mirage	■	**185**
Chevrolet Cavalier	■	118
Eagle Summit	■	130
Ford Escort	■	138
Toyota Corolla	■	217

Nissan 240SX

The 240SX, all-new in 1995, receives few changes for 1996, the only notable one being a new grill. The 240SX is less of a sports car than a luxury vehicle and it looks more like a Lexus than a Camaro. Dual airbags are standard, but you'll have to pay extra for ABS.

The 2.4-liter 4-cylinder engine is adequate, but won't please performance-seekers; unfortunately, you do not have another engine choice. The 240 comes in two trim levels, base or SE. With its re-design last year, the 240 gained much needed interior room, making it a very comfortable car to ride in. However, adults in the rear seats will still not be comfortable. The ride is smooth and the handling is good due to the wide stance the car has. If you choose the SE, you will get a firmer "sport-tuned" suspension, but will probably be just as happy in the base coupe.

The Ratings

	POOR — GOOD
COMPARATIVE RATING	
CRASH TEST	
SAFETY FEATURES	
FUEL ECONOMY	
PM COST	
REPAIR COST	
WARRANTY	
COMPLAINTS	
INSURANCE COST	

Safety

CRASH TEST	Average
AIRBAGS	Dual
ABS	4-wheel (optional)
SIDE CRASH PROTECT.	Strong
BELT ADJUSTORS	None
BUILT-IN CHILD SEAT	None
OCCUPANT INJURY	

General Information

WHERE MADE	U.S./Japan
YEAR OF PRODUCTION	Second
PARKING INDEX	Very Easy
BUMPERS	Weak
THEFT RATING	
TWINS	
DRIVE	Front

Specifications

FUEL ECONOMY (cty/hwy)	21/26	Average
DRIVING RANGE (miles)	304	Very Short
SEATING	4	
LENGTH (inches)	170.1	Very Short
HEAD/LEG ROOM (in.)	39.1/42.3	Average
INTERIOR SPACE (cu. ft.)	71	Vry. Cramped
CARGO SPACE (cu. ft.)	9	Very Small

Specifications may vary.

Prices

Model	Retail	Mkup
240SX Standard	18,359	13%
240SX SE	22,249	13%

Competition

	POOR — GOOD	Pg.
Nissan 240SX		186
Ford Mustang		139
Honda Prelude		150
Mazda MX-6		172
Pontiac Firebird		200

Nissan Altima

The Altima enters its fourth year with no notable changes. A year after receiving some cosmetic changes to the grill and taillights, the Altima hopes to gain more attention in the crowded intermediate market. The Altima's styling mimics the Infiniti J30, though it comes with a much smaller price tag. Dual airbags are standard, but you'll have to pay extra for ABS. Unfortunately, on the base XE and mid-level GXE, you'll have to buy expensive option packages before you can order ABS.

The 2.4-liter 4-cylinder engine is powerful enough, though you'll by no means feel like you're in a performance car. Fuel economy is pretty good. Handling is average and the ride is a bit on the rough side. Gauges and controls are easy to use. You have your pick of four trim levels (XE, GXE, SE and GLE) and options are plentiful, so shop carefully. The Altima continues to be a strong contender in the mid-sized sedan class.

The Ratings

	POOR — GOOD
COMPARATIVE RATING	
CRASH TEST	
SAFETY FEATURES	
FUEL ECONOMY	
PM COST	
REPAIR COST	
WARRANTY	
COMPLAINTS	
INSURANCE COST	

Safety

CRASH TEST	Average
AIRBAGS	Dual
ABS	4-wheel (optional)
SIDE CRASH PROTECT.	Weak
BELT ADJUSTORS	Standard
BUILT-IN CHILD SEAT	None
OCCUPANT INJURY	Poor

General Information

WHERE MADE	U.S./Japan
YEAR OF PRODUCTION	Fourth
PARKING INDEX	Average
BUMPERS	Weak
THEFT RATING	Average
TWINS	
DRIVE	Front

Specifications

FUEL ECONOMY (cty/hwy)	24/30	Average
DRIVING RANGE (miles)	413	Average
SEATING	5	
LENGTH (inches)	180.5	Short
HEAD/LEG ROOM (in.)	39.3/42.6	Roomy
INTERIOR SPACE (cu. ft.)	94	Average
CARGO SPACE (cu. ft.)	14	Average

Specifications may vary.

Prices

Model	Retail	Mkup
Altima XE man.	15,649	12%
Altima XE auto.	16,479	12%
Altima GXE man.	16,999	14%
Altima SE man.	19,299	14%
Altima GLE auto.	20,999	14%

Competition

	POOR — GOOD	Pg.
Nissan Altima		**187**
Honda Accord		146
Mazda 626		166
Olds Cut. Supreme		196
Toyota Camry		215

As the 1996 Maxima shows up in showrooms hardly changed from last year, Nissan must be thinking: why change a good thing? And who can blame them. Dual airbags are standard. You'll have to pay extra for ABS, and it's not available on the manual transmission GXE.

The 3-liter V6 is very powerful and quite fuel efficient. The GXE and GLE trim levels come standard with an automatic transmission, while the SE comes with a five speed manual. The large wheelbase increases interior room, making the front seats quite comfortable, and improves the ride, but handling is mediocre. The rear seats will be adequate for smaller adults. You'll have the typical Nissan variety of trim levels and many options and packages to choose from, so shop carefully. With improved styling, power and comfort, the Maxima is a good alternative to more expensive sports sedans.

The Ratings

	POOR → GOOD
COMPARATIVE RATING	▉ (middle)
CRASH TEST	▉ (right of middle)
SAFETY FEATURES	▉ (good side)
FUEL ECONOMY	▉ (middle)
PM COST	▉ (right of middle)
REPAIR COST	▉ (right of middle)
WARRANTY	▉ (poor side)
COMPLAINTS	(blank)
INSURANCE COST	▉ (middle)

Safety

CRASH TEST	Average
AIRBAGS	Dual
ABS	4-wheel (optional)
SIDE CRASH PROTECT.	Strong
BELT ADJUSTORS	Standard
BUILT-IN CHILD SEAT	None
OCCUPANT INJURY	Average

General Information

WHERE MADE	Japan
YEAR OF PRODUCTION	Second
PARKING INDEX	Easy
BUMPERS	Weak
THEFT RATING	
TWINS	Infiniti I30
DRIVE	Front

Specifications

FUEL ECONOMY (cty/hwy)	21/28	Average
DRIVING RANGE (miles)	426	Long
SEATING	5	
LENGTH (inches)	187.7	Average
HEAD/LEG ROOM (in.)	40.1/43.9	Vry. Roomy
INTERIOR SPACE (cu. ft.)	100	Roomy
CARGO SPACE (cu. ft.)	15	Average

Specifications may vary.

Prices

Model	Retail	Mkup
Maxima GXE man.	20,999	12%
Maxima GXE auto.	22,679	14%
Maxima SE man.	22,679	14%
Maxima SE auto.	23,679	14%
Maxima GLE auto.	26,279	14%

Competition

	POOR → GOOD	Pg.
Nissan Maxima	▉ (middle)	**188**
Dodge Intrepid	▉ (left of middle)	128
Honda Accord	▉ (poor side)	146
Toyota Camry	▉ (poor side)	215
Volkswagen Passat	▉ (good side)	222

With the Quest and its look-alike twin the Villager, Nissan and Mercury have tried to catch up with Chrysler's successful minivans. They've been successful on many fronts and with several new changes for 1996, they move one step closer. New for '96 are updated grilles, bumpers and tail-lamps, and most importantly, dual airbags. ABS is optional.

The only available engine is a 3-liter V6, but acceleration and power are good. Fuel economy is poor. Ride and handling are good by minivan standards. On the interior, seating is comfortable though leg room may be cramped, and now the Quest comes with integrated child safety seats. There is plenty of cargo space. With these new additions, the Quest is sure to attract more attention. The Chrysler minivans are all-new this year, however, so the Quest may still be left behind.

The Ratings

	POOR — GOOD
COMPARATIVE RATING *	(blank)
CRASH TEST	(blank)
SAFETY FEATURES	▉
FUEL ECONOMY	▉
PM COST	▉
REPAIR COST	▉
WARRANTY	▉
COMPLAINTS	▉
INSURANCE COST	▉

Safety

CRASH TEST	No government results
AIRBAGS	Dual
ABS	4-wheel (optional)
SIDE CRASH PROTECT.	Weak
BELT ADJUSTORS	Standard
BUILT-IN CHILD SEAT	Optional
OCCUPANT INJURY	Good

General Information

WHERE MADE	U.S./Japan
YEAR OF PRODUCTION	Fourth
PARKING INDEX	Hard
BUMPERS	Weak
THEFT RATING	Very Good
TWINS	Mercury Villager
DRIVE	Front

Specifications

FUEL ECONOMY (cty/hwy)	17/23	Poor
DRIVING RANGE (miles)	400	Average
SEATING	7	
LENGTH (inches)	189.9	Average
HEAD/LEG ROOM (in.)	39.5/39.9	Cramped
INTERIOR SPACE (cu. ft.)		
CARGO SPACE (cu. ft.)	125	Large

Specifications may vary.

Prices

Model	Retail	Mkup
Quest XE	20,899	14%
Quest GXE	25,699	14%

Competition

	POOR — GOOD	Pg.
Nissan Quest	(blank)	**189**
Ford Windstar	▉	143
Honda Odyssey	▉	149
Pontiac Trans Sport	▉	204
Toyota Previa	▉	219

*Due to the importance of crash tests, cars with no results as of publication date cannot be given an overall rating.

Nissan Sentra

Nissan introduced an all-new, slightly enlarged Sentra late in '95 and has made only minor changes to the '96. The styling of the Sentra will be slightly more rounded and contemporary than in past years. Nissan has dropped the two-door version from the Sentra name-plate to compete solely with the sedan versions of the Honda Civic, Toyota Tercel, Saturn and Neon. The two-door version is called the 200SX. The Sentra has dual airbags and optional ABS.

The 1.6-liter 4-cylinder engine is only adequate, but gets good gas mileage. There are no other engine choices, only your choice of a manual or automatic transmission. The Sentra handles and rides better than its predecessors and is good, basic transportation. With dual airbags and contemporary looks, the Sentra competes well in the crowded subcompact market.

The Ratings

	POOR → GOOD
COMPARATIVE RATING *	Good side
CRASH TEST	Good side
SAFETY FEATURES	Good side
FUEL ECONOMY	Good side
PM COST	Middle
REPAIR COST	Good side
WARRANTY	Poor side
COMPLAINTS	(none marked)
INSURANCE COST	Poor (far left)

Safety

CRASH TEST	Good
AIRBAGS	Dual
ABS	4-wheel (optional)
SIDE CRASH PROTECT.	Strong
BELT ADJUSTORS	Standard
BUILT-IN CHILD SEAT	None
OCCUPANT INJURY	Very Poor

General Information

WHERE MADE	U.S./Japan
YEAR OF PRODUCTION	Second
PARKING INDEX	Very Easy
BUMPERS	Weak
THEFT RATING	
TWINS	
DRIVE	Front

Specifications

FUEL ECONOMY (cty/hwy)	30/40	Good
DRIVING RANGE (miles)	436	Long
SEATING	5	
LENGTH (inches)	170.1	Very Short
HEAD/LEG ROOM (in.)	39.1/42.3	Average
INTERIOR SPACE (cu. ft.)	87	Cramped
CARGO SPACE (cu. ft.)	10	Small

Specifications may vary.

Prices

Model	Retail	Mkup
Sentra Base	11,499	6%
Sentra XE man.	13,529	8%
Sentra XE auto.	14,329	8%
Sentra GXE man.	14,459	12%
Sentra GLE man.	15,229	12%

Competition

	POOR → GOOD	Pg.
Nissan Sentra	Good side	190
Chevrolet Cavalier	Middle-left	118
Eagle Summit	Poor (far left)	130
Ford Escort	Middle	138
Mitsubishi Mirage	Poor (far left)	185

*Due to the importance of crash tests, cars with no results as of publication date cannot be given an overall rating.

The Eighty Eight enters 1996 with many changes. This twin of the Buick LeSabre and Pontiac Bonneville is Oldsmobile's entry into the plush mid-sized car market. The 88 used to come in three trim levels, but now only two (base and LS), as the LSS trim level becomes its own line. But don't be fooled, it's still based on the 88.

The 88's 3.8-liter V6, connected to an automatic overdrive, delivers plenty of smooth power. You no longer have another engine choice as in years past, but this one should do well. The 88's suspension favors a too-soft ride at the expense of handling. However, the optional touring suspension and speed-sensitive steering renders good handling and a comfortable ride. There's room for five and trunk space is generous. The LSS is slightly smaller and aimed at the import car buyer. It is a good choice if you're not quite ready for the biggest of American sedans.

The Ratings

	POOR — GOOD
COMPARATIVE RATING	▮ (mid-high)
CRASH TEST	▮ (mid-high)
SAFETY FEATURES	▮ (mid-high)
FUEL ECONOMY	▮ (low-mid)
PM COST	▮ (mid-high)
REPAIR COST	▮ (high)
WARRANTY	▮ (low)
COMPLAINTS	▮ (mid-high)
INSURANCE COST	▮ (highest)

Safety

CRASH TEST	Good
AIRBAGS	Dual
ABS	4-wheel
SIDE CRASH PROTECT.	Weak
BELT ADJUSTORS	Standard
BUILT-IN CHILD SEAT	None
OCCUPANT INJURY	Very Good

General Information

WHERE MADE	U.S.
YEAR OF PRODUCTION	Fifth
PARKING INDEX	Hard
BUMPERS	Strong
THEFT RATING	Very Good
TWINS	LeSabre, Bonneville
DRIVE	Front

Specifications

FUEL ECONOMY (cty/hwy)	18/27	Poor
DRIVING RANGE (miles)	378	Short
SEATING	5/6	
LENGTH (inches)	201.6	Long
HEAD/LEG ROOM (in.)	38.7/42.5	Average
INTERIOR SPACE (cu. ft.)	100	Roomy
CARGO SPACE (cu. ft.)	16	Average

Specifications may vary.

Prices

Model	Retail	Mkup
88	20,405	5%
88 LS	22,810	7%
88LSS	26,010	7%

Competition

	POOR — GOOD	Pg.
Oldsmobile 88	▮ (mid-high)	**191**
Buick LeSabre	▮ (mid-high)	104
Chrysler LHS/NY'er	▮ (low-mid)	124
Eagle Vision	▮ (mid)	133
Ford Crown Victoria	▮ (mid-high)	137

This year, the 98 is being marketed between the lower-priced 88 and the higher-priced Aurora. Olds will try to entice buyers to the 98 with a more powerful engine. Only one trim level, the Regency Elite, is being offered, though you'll still have plenty of options to choose from, including traction control. Standard safety features include dual airbags and 4-wheel ABS.

The standard 3.8-liter V6 engine is powerful enough and, unlike past years, it's the only engine offered. Like most big American cars, the 98 favors a mushy ride over good handling. Room and comfort are good for up to six, and trunk space is ample. Olds is trying to simplify the previously-complicated options list, but shop carefully nevertheless. Name recognition is no problem for the 98; it's name has been around since 1941 and will help it compete in a difficult market.

The Ratings

	POOR				GOOD
COMPARATIVE RATING *					
CRASH TEST					
SAFETY FEATURES			■		
FUEL ECONOMY		■			
PM COST			■		
REPAIR COST			■		
WARRANTY	■				
COMPLAINTS				■	
INSURANCE COST					■

Safety

CRASH TEST	No government results
AIRBAGS	Dual
ABS	4-wheel
SIDE CRASH PROTECT.	Weak
BELT ADJUSTORS	Standard
BUILT-IN CHILD SEAT	None
OCCUPANT INJURY	Very Good

General Information

WHERE MADE	U.S.
YEAR OF PRODUCTION	Sixth
PARKING INDEX	Hard
BUMPERS	Strong
THEFT RATING	Very Good
TWINS	Buick Park Avenue
DRIVE	Front

Specifications

FUEL ECONOMY (cty/hwy)	19/29	Average
DRIVING RANGE (miles)	414	Average
SEATING	6	
LENGTH (inches)	205.7	Very Long
HEAD/LEG ROOM (in.)	38.8/42.7	Roomy
INTERIOR SPACE (cu. ft.)	108	Roomy
CARGO SPACE (cu. ft.)	20	Large

Specifications may vary.

Prices

Model	Retail	Mkup
98 I	28,405	7%
98 II	29,260	7%

Competition

	POOR			GOOD	Pg.
Oldsmobile 98					192
Buick Roadmaster	■				108
Chrysler LHS/NY'er		■			124
Merc. Gr. Marquis			■		177
Mitsu. Diamante	■				182

*Due to the importance of crash tests, cars with no results as of publication date cannot be given an overall rating.

Oldsmobile Achieva

The smallest Oldsmobile is styled much more conservatively than its twins, the Buick Skylark and Pontiac Grand Am, but there are big changes for '96. The exterior has stayed much the same, but an all-new interior, which includes dual airbags, is sure to attract much attention. Because of the addition of dual airbags, the dreaded door mounted belts have disappeared!

The Achieva is nearly as large as some mid-size cars, but you'll find its back seat cramped for adults. The new standard 2.4-liter 4-cylinder engine is adequate, and the optional 3.1-liter V6 only gives you five more horsepower; at least you don't lose much in fuel economy. Speed-sensitive steering is standard, and the suspension has been firmed up since last year. Considering the cost of a well-equipped Achieva, you should explore several cars that may offer the same value, such as a Mazda 626 or Nissan Altima.

The Ratings

	POOR ... GOOD
COMPARATIVE RATING *	
CRASH TEST	
SAFETY FEATURES	▮
FUEL ECONOMY	▮
PM COST	▮
REPAIR COST	▮
WARRANTY	▮
COMPLAINTS	▮
INSURANCE COST	▮

Safety

CRASH TEST	No government results
AIRBAGS	Dual
ABS	4-wheel
SIDE CRASH PROTECT.	Weak
BELT ADJUSTORS	Optional
BUILT-IN CHILD SEAT	None
OCCUPANT INJURY	

General Information

WHERE MADE	U.S.
YEAR OF PRODUCTION	Fifth
PARKING INDEX	Easy
BUMPERS	Strong
THEFT RATING	Very Good
TWINS	Skylark, Grand Am
DRIVE	Front

Specifications

FUEL ECONOMY (cty/hwy)	23/33	Average
DRIVING RANGE (miles)	395	Average
SEATING	5	
LENGTH (inches)	187.9	Average
HEAD/LEG ROOM (in.)	37.8/43.1	Average
INTERIOR SPACE (cu. ft.)	88	Cramped
CARGO SPACE (cu. ft.)	14	Average

Specifications may vary.

Prices

Model	Retail	Mkup
Achieva SC Coupe I	13,495	5%
Achieva SC Coupe II	14,495	7%
Achieva SL Sedan II	14,495	7%
Achieva SC Coupe III	16,495	7%
Achieva SL Sedan III	16,495	7%

Competition

	POOR ... GOOD	Pg.
Olds Achieva		**193**
Honda Accord	▮	146
Mazda 626	▮	166
Oldsmobile Ciera	▮	195
Toyota Camry	▮	215

*Due to the importance of crash tests, cars with no results as of publication date cannot be given an overall rating.

Olds is counting on the Aurora to bring it into the 21st century, and so far, so good. They are distancing themselves from the past by calling this the Aurora by Oldsmobile instead of the Oldsmobile Aurora. Whatever they call it, it's a big, heavy, powerful machine. Dual airbags, ABS, traction control, speed-variable power steering, and a host of other items are standard.

The Aurora benefits greatly from a very rigid structure and rides well for a car its size. However, the car wallows in turns like all large cars. The 4-liter V8 is more powerful than most any of its competitors, and its fuel economy, though not notable by any means, holds its own with the competition. Room for five is more than spacious, though not quite as generous as some of the larger domestic cars, and it's priced lower than the smaller imports it targets.

The Ratings

	POOR — GOOD
COMPARATIVE RATING	▮ (6)
CRASH TEST	▮ (4)
SAFETY FEATURES	▮ (7)
FUEL ECONOMY	▮ (3)
PM COST	▮ (6)
REPAIR COST	▮ (6)
WARRANTY	▮ (6)
COMPLAINTS	
INSURANCE COST	▮ (4)

Safety

CRASH TEST	Average
AIRBAGS	Dual
ABS	4-wheel
SIDE CRASH PROTECT.	Weak
BELT ADJUSTORS	None
BUILT-IN CHILD SEAT	None
OCCUPANT INJURY	

General Information

WHERE MADE	U.S.
YEAR OF PRODUCTION	Second
PARKING INDEX	Hard
BUMPERS	Strong
THEFT RATING	
TWINS	Buick Riviera
DRIVE	Front

Specifications

FUEL ECONOMY (cty/hwy)	17/26	Poor
DRIVING RANGE (miles)	400	Average
SEATING	5/6	
LENGTH (inches)	205.4	Very Long
HEAD/LEG ROOM (in.)	38.4/42.6	Average
INTERIOR SPACE (cu. ft.)	102	Roomy
CARGO SPACE (cu. ft.)	16	Average

Specifications may vary.

Prices

Model	Retail	Mkup
Aurora	34,360	8%

Competition

	POOR — GOOD	Pg.
Olds Aurora	▮	**194**
Chrylser LHS/NY'er	▮	124
Merc. Gr. Marquis	▮	177
Saab 9000	▮	206
Volvo 850	▮	223

Virtually little has changed since its introduction in 1982 except for the name. What used to be known as the Cutlass Ciera is now simply the Ciera; but, unlike its new name, the car is showing its age. ABS and a driver's airbag are standard, but front seat occupants get dreadful door-mounted belts instead of a passenger airbag. The lack of dual airbags and these door-mounted belts keeps the Ciera from being one of our "Best Bets."

Like the Century, the Ciera offers a smooth ride on the highway, but unresponsive handling. The 4-cylinder engine, which is standard on the sedan, has inadequate power; the V6, which is standard on the wagon and optional on the sedan, is more powerful, but less economical, especially in the city. Room inside and comfort for four are average. The dashboard and controls are a real throwback to the early eighties. Options are few and far between. You may do better to look at the competition.

The Ratings

	POOR — GOOD
COMPARATIVE RATING	■ near good
CRASH TEST	■ good side
SAFETY FEATURES	■ poor side
FUEL ECONOMY	■ middle
PM COST	■ good side
REPAIR COST	■ good
WARRANTY	■ poor
COMPLAINTS	■ good side
INSURANCE COST	■ good

Safety

CRASH TEST	Good
AIRBAGS	Driver
ABS	4-wheel
SIDE CRASH PROTECT.	Weak
BELT ADJUSTORS	None
BUILT-IN CHILD SEAT	None
OCCUPANT INJURY	Good

General Information

WHERE MADE	U.S.
YEAR OF PRODUCTION	Fifteenth
PARKING INDEX	Average
BUMPERS	Strong
THEFT RATING	Avg. (Wgn.=Very Good)
TWINS	Buick Century
DRIVE	Front

Specifications

FUEL ECONOMY (cty/hwy)	24/31	Average
DRIVING RANGE (miles)	446	Long
SEATING	5	
LENGTH (inches)	193.2	Long
HEAD/LEG ROOM (in.)	38.6/42.1	Average
INTERIOR SPACE (cu. ft.)	97	Average
CARGO SPACE (cu. ft.)	16	Average

Specifications may vary.

Prices

Model	Retail	Mkup
Ciera SL Sedan I	14,455	5%
Ciera SL Sedan II	16,455	7%
Ciera SL Wagon	17,455	7%

Competition

	POOR — GOOD	Pg.
Oldsmobile Ciera	■	195
Chrysler Concorde	■	123
Mercury Mystique	■	178
VW Golf/Jetta	■	221
VW Passat	■	222

The Cutlass Supreme joins cars that previously outclassed it by finally offering standard dual airbags and manual seat belts. An added benefit of the dual airbags is the recently redesigned instrument panel. Speed-sensitive steering and ABS are standard, and all Cutlass Supremes meet the 1997 side impact standard.

The sedan models do not handle well and have a ride best-suited to smooth roads. The convertible is no longer being offered this year, so the firmer suspension is no longer an option. All Cutlass Supremes have an automatic overdrive trans-mission, which helps both acceleration and gas mileage. The 3.1-liter V6 is adequate, but the 3.4-liter V6 is much more powerful, if you don't mind sacrificing a few mpg. The Cutlass Supreme has been rated as just an average car in the past, but with dual airbags, it's a step above.

The Ratings

	POOR — GOOD
COMPARATIVE RATING	▮ (right of center)
CRASH TEST	▮ (center-left)
SAFETY FEATURES	▮ (right)
FUEL ECONOMY	▮ (center)
PM COST	▮ (right of center)
REPAIR COST	▮ (left of center)
WARRANTY	▮ (left)
COMPLAINTS	(blank)
INSURANCE COST	▮ (far right)

Safety

CRASH TEST	Average
AIRBAGS	Dual
ABS	4-wheel
SIDE CRASH PROTECT.	Strong
BELT ADJUSTORS	Std. (sdn. only)
BUILT-IN CHILD SEAT	None
OCCUPANT INJURY	Very Good

General Information

WHERE MADE	U.S.
YEAR OF PRODUCTION	Ninth
PARKING INDEX	Average
BUMPERS	Strong
THEFT RATING	Very Good (2-dr.=Good)
TWINS	Buick Regal, Pont. Gr. Prix
DRIVE	Front

Specifications

FUEL ECONOMY (cty/hwy)	20/29	Average
DRIVING RANGE (miles)	393	Average
SEATING	5	
LENGTH (inches)	193.7	Long
HEAD/LEG ROOM (in.)	38.7/42.4	Average
INTERIOR SPACE (cu. ft.)	100	Roomy
CARGO SPACE (cu. ft.)	16	Average

Specifications may vary.

Prices

Model	Retail	Mkup
Cutlass Supreme I	17,455	5%
Cutlass Supreme II	18,455	7%
Cutlass Supreme III	18,960	7%
Cutlass Supreme IV	21,160	7%

Competition

	POOR — GOOD	Pg.
Olds Cut. Supreme	▮ (right of center)	**196**
Dodge Intrepid	▮ (center)	128
Honda Accord	▮ (left)	146
Nissan Maxima	▮ (center)	188
Toyota Camry	▮ (left)	215

The Oldsmobile Silhouette and its twins, the Pontiac Trans Sport and the Chevy Lumina Minivan, have been good competition for the Chrysler minivans. Although the Silhouette performs well in the government's frontal impact crash test, a second airbag is sorely missed in this family vehicle. It is scheduled to be all-new in '97.

There is only one engine choice this year - a powerful 3.4-liter V6 which out-performs the past engines Olds has offered. You have your choice of one or two built-in child restraints, an excellent option. Ride is competent on good roads, but handling is unresponsive at highway speeds. The optional touring suspension and traction control, which you have to buy together, improve handling. You'll need some time to get used to the driving position and visibility. The Silhouette will have a tough time competing with the new Chrysler minivan, especially with only one airbag.

The Ratings

	POOR	GOOD
COMPARATIVE RATING		
CRASH TEST		
SAFETY FEATURES		
FUEL ECONOMY		
PM COST		
REPAIR COST		
WARRANTY		
COMPLAINTS		
INSURANCE COST		

Safety

CRASH TEST	Good
AIRBAGS	Driver
ABS	4-wheel
SIDE CRASH PROTECT.	Weak
BELT ADJUSTORS	None
BUILT-IN CHILD SEAT	Optional (two)
OCCUPANT INJURY	

General Information

WHERE MADE	U.S.
YEAR OF PRODUCTION	Seventh
PARKING INDEX	Hard
BUMPERS	Weak
THEFT RATING	Average
TWINS	Lumina Mnvn, Tr. Sport
DRIVE	Front

Specifications

FUEL ECONOMY (cty/hwy)	19/26	Poor
DRIVING RANGE (miles)	420	Average
SEATING	7	
LENGTH (inches)	194.7	Long
HEAD/LEG ROOM (in.)	39.2/40.0	Cramped
INTERIOR SPACE (cu. ft.)		
CARGO SPACE (cu. ft.)	113	Large

Specifications may vary.

Prices

Model	Retail	Mkup
Silhouette Series I	21,355	11%
Silhouette Series II	22,655	11%

Competition

	POOR	GOOD	Pg.
Olds Silhouette			**197**
Chevy Lumina Mnvn			120
Ford Windstar			143
Honda Odyssey			149
Toyota Previa			219

The Voyager, along with the other Chrysler minivans, is totally redesigned for 1996. These industry leaders carry on with standard dual airbags and a structure that meets 1997 government side impact standards for passenger cars. ABS is now standard. This new look should help keep the Voyager ahead of its competition.

You get to choose between four engines: an inadequate 2.5-liter 4-cylinder, an adequate 3-liter V6, or the more powerful 3.3-liter or 3.8-liter V6s. All except the 3.8-liter are equally efficient. Since Grand Voyagers have a longer wheelbase and a body with more room, the 3.3-liter is worth the extra money. Handling improves with the heavy duty suspension, and the ride remains good. The built-in child restraints are an excellent option. The new Voyager should serve many needs while still being fun to drive.

The Ratings

	POOR GOOD
COMPARATIVE RATING *	
CRASH TEST	
SAFETY FEATURES	
FUEL ECONOMY	
PM COST	
REPAIR COST	
WARRANTY	
COMPLAINTS	
INSURANCE COST	

Safety

CRASH TEST	No government results
AIRBAGS	Dual
ABS	4-wheel
SIDE CRASH PROTECT.	Strong
BELT ADJUSTORS	Standard
BUILT-IN CHILD SEAT	Optional (two)
OCCUPANT INJURY	Good

General Information

WHERE MADE	U.S./Canada
YEAR OF PRODUCTION	First
PARKING INDEX	Average
BUMPERS	Strong
THEFT RATING	
TWINS	Caravan, T & C
DRIVE	Front

Specifications

FUEL ECONOMY (cty/hwy)	20/26	Average
DRIVING RANGE (miles)	440	Long
SEATING	7	
LENGTH (inches)	186.3	Average
HEAD/LEG ROOM (in.)	39.8/41.2	Average
INTERIOR SPACE (cu. ft.)		
CARGO SPACE (cu. ft.)	146	Very Large

Specifications may vary.

Prices

Model	Retail	Mkup
Voyager Base	16,160	10%
Voyager SE	18,855	10%
Grand Voyager Base	17,410	10%
Grand Voyager SE	19,595	10%

Competition

	POOR GOOD	Pg.
Plymouth Voyager		**198**
Chevy Lumina Mnvn		120
Ford Windstar		143
Olds Silhouette		197
Toyota Previa		219

*Due to the importance of crash tests, cars with no results as of publication date cannot be given an overall rating.

Pontiac Bonneville

The Bonneville, GM's sportiest large sedan, brings with it a dizzying array of option groups into 1996. The base model is the SE, and the SSE is the up-level version. The SLE is a sporty package available on the SE. Traction control is available on the SSE, and a supercharged engine is available on both the SE and SSE. Dual airbags and ABS are standard on all models, and daytime running lamps are a new safety feature this year.

You can easily spend over $25,000 for a Bonneville, so shop wisely. Stick to the base SE with the performance and handling package and 16-inch wheels. The base 3.8-liter V6 is powerful enough; the optional supercharged V6 only adds a little more power and more repair complexity. Room for four or five is ample, as is trunk space; driver's visibility could be better. The Bonneville provides good domestic competition to the Japanese luxury sports sedans.

The Ratings

	POOR — GOOD
COMPARATIVE RATING	■ (near good)
CRASH TEST	■ (mid)
SAFETY FEATURES	■ (mid)
FUEL ECONOMY	■ (mid)
PM COST	■ (mid-high)
REPAIR COST	■ (mid-high)
WARRANTY	■ (low)
COMPLAINTS	■ (high)
INSURANCE COST	■ (good)

Safety

CRASH TEST	Good
AIRBAGS	Dual
ABS	4-wheel
SIDE CRASH PROTECT.	Weak
BELT ADJUSTORS	Standard
BUILT-IN CHILD SEAT	None
OCCUPANT INJURY	Very Good

General Information

WHERE MADE	U.S.
YEAR OF PRODUCTION	Fifth
PARKING INDEX	Hard
BUMPERS	Strong
THEFT RATING	Very Good
TWINS	LeSabre, Eighty Eight
DRIVE	Front

Specifications

FUEL ECONOMY (cty/hwy)	19/30	Average
DRIVING RANGE (miles)	414	Average
SEATING	5/6	
LENGTH (inches)	201.2	Long
HEAD/LEG ROOM (in.)	39.2/42.6	Roomy
INTERIOR SPACE (cu. ft.)	110	Vry. Roomy
CARGO SPACE (cu. ft.)	18	Large

Specifications may vary.

Prices

Model	Retail	Mkup
Bonneville SE	21,589	10%
Bonneville SSE	26,559	10%

Competition

	POOR — GOOD	Pg.
Pontiac Bonneville	■	**199**
Chevrolet Lumina	■	119
Eagle Vision	■	133
Saab 900	■	205
Volvo 850	■	223

Like its twin the Camaro, the Firebird also enters 1996 with minor changes. The Firebird has always been a strong performer in the crash tests, and is even safer now by meeting the 1997 standard for side impact a year early. Also standard on the '96 Firebird are dual airbags and 4-wheel ABS.

New under the hood this year is a 3.8-liter V6 that comes with more power than the one offered last year. Pontiac has added a new trim level, the RS, to complement the coupe, convertible and Trans Am versions. The Trans Am comes standard with a 5.7-Liter V8 that is more powerful and only slightly less economical than the standard 3.8-liter engine. The ride is firm and the handling is good. Room inside is good for the driver and front seat passenger, but the back seat will be cramped, even for small children. With its high crash rating and numerous safety features, the Firebird is a good choice.

The Ratings

	POOR ⟶ GOOD
COMPARATIVE RATING	▮ (2nd)
CRASH TEST	▮ (10th)
SAFETY FEATURES	▮ (7th)
FUEL ECONOMY	▮ (5th)
PM COST	▮ (8th)
REPAIR COST	▮ (7th)
WARRANTY	▮ (3rd)
COMPLAINTS	▮ (2nd)
INSURANCE COST	▮ (1st)

Safety

CRASH TEST	Very Good
AIRBAGS	Dual
ABS	4-wheel
SIDE CRASH PROTECT.	Strong (cpe. only)
BELT ADJUSTORS	None
BUILT-IN CHILD SEAT	None
OCCUPANT INJURY	Average

General Information

WHERE MADE	U.S.
YEAR OF PRODUCTION	Fourth
PARKING INDEX	Average
BUMPERS	Strong
THEFT RATING	Average
TWINS	Chevrolet Camaro
DRIVE	Rear

Specifications

FUEL ECONOMY (cty/hwy)	19/30	Average
DRIVING RANGE (miles)	357	Short
SEATING	4	
LENGTH (inches)	193.2	Long
HEAD/LEG ROOM (in.)	37.2/43.0	Cramped
INTERIOR SPACE (cu. ft.)	82	Vry. Cramped
CARGO SPACE (cu. ft.)	13	Average

Specifications may vary.

Prices

Model	Retail	Mkup
Firebird	15,614	9%
Firebird Trans Am	21,414	9%

Competition

	POOR ⟶ GOOD	Pg.
Pontiac Firebird	▮	200
Chevrolet Camaro	▮	116
Ford Mustang	▮	139
Mazda MX-6	▮	172
Nissan 240SX	▮	186

Pontiac's best-selling ace gets a facelift for 1996 with new interior and exterior designs, including new headlamps, a new hood, new fenders, and a redesigned instrument panel. More importantly, they now come with dual airbags and daytime running lamps; more good news includes the disappearance of the door-mounted seat belts. Instead, you can find adjustable safety belts. ABS is standard.

A new 2.4-liter Twin Cam engine is now standard with all Grand Am's, adding slightly more power, but the fuel economy is still low. Seating is tight when you have large adults in the back seat. The trunk is average for a car of this size. Ride is good and the Grand Am handles well. There are many options so shop carefully. With the redesign, the Grand Am becomes a better car and as economical as some of its competitors, such as the Nissan Altima.

The Ratings

	POOR — GOOD
COMPARATIVE RATING *	(no rating)
CRASH TEST	(no rating)
SAFETY FEATURES	▉
FUEL ECONOMY	▉
PM COST	▉
REPAIR COST	▉
WARRANTY	▉
COMPLAINTS	▉
INSURANCE COST	▉

Safety

CRASH TEST	No government results
AIRBAGS	Dual
ABS	4-wheel
SIDE CRASH PROTECT.	Weak
BELT ADJUSTORS	Standard
BUILT-IN CHILD SEAT	None
OCCUPANT INJURY	Average

General Information

WHERE MADE	U.S.
YEAR OF PRODUCTION	Fifth
PARKING INDEX	Easy
BUMPERS	Strong
THEFT RATING	Very Good
TWINS	Skylark, Achieva
DRIVE	Front

Specifications

FUEL ECONOMY (cty/hwy)	23/33	Average
DRIVING RANGE (miles)	395	Average
SEATING	5	
LENGTH (inches)	186.9	Average
HEAD/LEG ROOM (in.)	37.8/43.1	Average
INTERIOR SPACE (cu. ft.)	101	Roomy
CARGO SPACE (cu. ft.)	13	Average

Specifications may vary.

Prices

Model	Retail	Mkup
Grand Am SE Coupe	13,499	9%
Grand Am SE Sedan	13,499	9%
Grand Am GT Coupe	15,499	9%
Grand Am GT Sedan	15,499	9%

Competition

	POOR — GOOD	Pg.
Pontiac Grand Am	(no rating)	201
Chrysler Sebring	▉	125
Honda Accord	▉	146
Mazda 626	▉	166
Oldsmobile Ciera	▉	195

*Due to the importance of crash tests, cars with no results as of publication date cannot be given an overall rating.

The Grand Prix shares its body and chassis with the Buick Regal and Oldsmobile Cutlass Supreme. The Chevrolet Lumina used to be a twin as well, but it got an overhaul last year, leaving its twins behind. The Grand Prix appeals to people who enjoy driving. Though the Grand Prix has dual airbags for the third year, the coupe still has awful door-mounted belts; you can avoid them by getting the sedan, which has motorized belts. You'll have to pay extra for ABS.

The base SE rides OK, but the GT package (GTP for the coupe) adds a sportier feel and firmer suspension. Pontiac is touting the Grand Prix's damage-resistant bumpers, which will protect the car in collisions up to 5 mph. Room and comfort is OK for four, and trunk space is generous for a car this size. With safety features like dual airbags and ABS, the Grand Prix is a good choice.

The Ratings

	POOR				GOOD
COMPARATIVE RATING				■	
CRASH TEST				■	
SAFETY FEATURES					■
FUEL ECONOMY			■		
PM COST				■	
REPAIR COST			■		
WARRANTY	■				
COMPLAINTS				■	
INSURANCE COST					■

Safety

CRASH TEST	Average
AIRBAGS	Dual
ABS	4-wheel (optional)
SIDE CRASH PROTECT.	Strong
BELT ADJUSTORS	Std. (sdn. only)
BUILT-IN CHILD SEAT	None
OCCUPANT INJURY	Very Good (2-dr.=Gd.)

General Information

WHERE MADE	U.S.
YEAR OF PRODUCTION	Ninth
PARKING INDEX	Average
BUMPERS	Strong
THEFT RATING	Average
TWINS	Cutlass Supreme, Regal
DRIVE	Front

Specifications

FUEL ECONOMY (cty/hwy)	20/29	Average
DRIVING RANGE (miles)	393	Average
SEATING	5	
LENGTH (inches)	194.8	Long
HEAD/LEG ROOM (in.)	37.8/42.3	Cramped
INTERIOR SPACE (cu. ft.)	95	Average
CARGO SPACE (cu. ft.)	15	Average

Specifications may vary.

Prices

Model	Retail	Mkup
Grand Prix SE Coupe	18,359	9%
Grand Prix SE Sedan	17,089	9%
Grand Prix GTP Coupe	19,994	9%
Grand Prix GT Sedan	20,851	9%

Competition

	POOR			GOOD	Pg.
Pontiac Gr. Prix			■		202
Honda Accord		■			146
Hyundai Sonata			■		153
Mercury Mystique				■	178
Toyota Camry		■			215

The Sunfire, brand-new in 1995 like its sibling the Chevy Cavalier, is longer and wider than the 14-year-old Sunbird it replaces. The Sunfire's design is certainly a break from its heritage and strikingly like the Saturns from the front wheels forward. The coupes, and especially the convertibles, have borrowed heavily from the Firebird's design, and this helps in catering to young drivers looking for an affordable, sporty car. Dual airbags and ABS are standard; for 1996, standard daytime running lamps and optional traction control are new.

The SE coupe, sedan and convertible come standard with a 2.2-liter engine that is only adequate. The GT coupe has a 2.4-liter dual cam engine with 25% more power. Attractive styling, adequate performance and generous front seat room make the Sunfire a strong choice among inexpensive sports cars.

The Ratings

	POOR → GOOD
COMPARATIVE RATING	▮ (center)
CRASH TEST	▮ (center)
SAFETY FEATURES	▮ (center-right)
FUEL ECONOMY	▮ (center-right)
PM COST	▮ (center)
REPAIR COST	▮ (center-right)
WARRANTY	▮ (poor)
COMPLAINTS	(blank)
INSURANCE COST	▮ (left-center)

Safety

CRASH TEST	Average
AIRBAGS	Dual
ABS	4-wheel
SIDE CRASH PROTECT.	Weak
BELT ADJUSTORS	Standard
BUILT-IN CHILD SEAT	None
OCCUPANT INJURY	

General Information

WHERE MADE	U.S.
YEAR OF PRODUCTION	Second
PARKING INDEX	Average
BUMPERS	Strong
THEFT RATING	
TWINS	Chevrolet Cavalier
DRIVE	Front

Specifications

FUEL ECONOMY (cty/hwy)	25/37	Good
DRIVING RANGE (miles)	441	Long
SEATING	5	
LENGTH (inches)	182.0	Short
HEAD/LEG ROOM (in.)	37.6/42.4	Cramped
INTERIOR SPACE (cu. ft.)	88	Cramped
CARGO SPACE (cu. ft.)	12	Small

Specifications may vary.

Prices

Model	Retail	Mkup
Sunfire SE Coupe	11,504	8%
Sunfire SE Sedan	11,674	8%
Sunfire SE Convertible	17,734	8%
Sunfire GT Coupe	13,214	8%

Competition

	POOR → GOOD	Pg.
Pontiac Sunfire	▮ (center-right)	203
Chevrolet Cavalier	▮ (center)	118
Eagle Summit	▮ (poor)	130
Ford Escort	▮ (center)	138
Toyota Corolla	▮ (center-right)	217

The Trans Sport receives only minor changes as it prepares to be totally redesigned in 1997. Like its twins, the Chevrolet Lumina and Oldsmobile Silhouette, the Trans Sport offers reliable family transportation. Traction control is now optional, and a driver's airbag and ABS remain standard.

The only engine offered is a more powerful 3.4-liter V6 with automatic overdrive. It provides plenty of power and even gets better gas mileage than the old engines Pontiac offered. You have the choice of one or two fold-out child safety restraints, which is an excellent option. Ride is generally smooth, but handling is sluggish on the open road. The windshield posts are distracting. The Trans Sport has much less cargo space than other minivans. One fancy option is the new power sliding door, designed to overcome the traditional difficulties with heavy minivan side doors.

The Ratings

	POOR	GOOD
COMPARATIVE RATING		
CRASH TEST		
SAFETY FEATURES		
FUEL ECONOMY		
PM COST		
REPAIR COST		
WARRANTY		
COMPLAINTS		
INSURANCE COST		

Safety

CRASH TEST	Good
AIRBAGS	Driver
ABS	4-wheel
SIDE CRASH PROTECT.	Weak
BELT ADJUSTORS	None
BUILT-IN CHILD SEAT	Optional (two)
OCCUPANT INJURY	Very Good

General Information

WHERE MADE	U.S.
YEAR OF PRODUCTION	Seventh
PARKING INDEX	Hard
BUMPERS	Strong
THEFT RATING	Average
TWINS	Lumina Mnvn, Silhouette
DRIVE	Front

Specifications

FUEL ECONOMY (cty/hwy)	19/26	Poor
DRIVING RANGE (miles)	420	Average
SEATING	7	
LENGTH (inches)	192.2	Long
HEAD/LEG ROOM (in.)	39.2/40.0	Cramped
INTERIOR SPACE (cu. ft.)		
CARGO SPACE (cu. ft.)	113	Large

Specifications may vary.

Prices **

Model	Retail	Mkup
Trans Sport SE	17,889	11%

Competition

	POOR	GOOD	Pg.
Pontiac Tr. Sport			**204**
Ford Aerostar			134
Ford Windstar			143
Honda Odyssey			149
Toyota Previa			219

** 1996 prices not available at press time. Prices based on 1995 data.

The Saab 900 enters 1996 with only minor changes after a relatively successful 1995. This new generation 900 has more contemporary styling, forsaking the curved back end that made it famous. Dual airbags and ABS are standard, as are daytime running lights.

The 900 S comes with an adequate 2.3-liter 4-cylinder engine, but the SE sedan and convertible come with a more powerful 2.5-liter V6. For even more power, choose the turbocharged version of the 4-cylinder available on the SE coupe and convertible. The 900 has room for four, plus plenty of luggage, though large adults will be cramped in the rear of the convertible. Handling is responsive, and controls are designed well and easy to use. A dealer-installed integrated child safety seat is an excellent option.

The Ratings

	POOR ... GOOD
COMPARATIVE RATING	Good side
CRASH TEST	Good side
SAFETY FEATURES	Good
FUEL ECONOMY	Middle
PM COST	Good side
REPAIR COST	Poor side
WARRANTY	Good side
COMPLAINTS	Poor
INSURANCE COST	Poor side

Safety

CRASH TEST	Good
AIRBAGS	Dual
ABS	4-wheel
SIDE CRASH PROTECT.	Strong
BELT ADJUSTORS	Standard
BUILT-IN CHILD SEAT	Optional
OCCUPANT INJURY	Good

General Information

WHERE MADE	Germany/Sweden
YEAR OF PRODUCTION	Third
PARKING INDEX	Easy
BUMPERS	Strong
THEFT RATING	Poor
TWINS	
DRIVE	Front

Specifications

FUEL ECONOMY (cty/hwy)	19/27	Average
DRIVING RANGE (miles)	414	Average
SEATING	5	
LENGTH (inches)	182.6	Short
HEAD/LEG ROOM (in.)	39.3/42.3	Roomy
INTERIOR SPACE (cu. ft.)	114	Vry. Roomy
CARGO SPACE (cu. ft.)	24	Very Large

Specifications may vary.

Prices

Model	Retail	Mkup
900 Base	23,995	13%

Competition

	POOR ... GOOD	Pg.
Saab 900	good side	**205**
BMW 3-Series	poor side	102
Infiniti J30	good side	155
Nissan Maxima	middle	188
Volvo 850	good side	223

Saab 9000

The Saab 9000 does not change much for 1996, although it does drop the 4-door sedan model. While most Americans shy away from hatchbacks, the Saab is one auto maker that continues to have success with the 5-door model. The 9000, which has been a strong performer in the government crash test program since its second year, has standard dual airbags and ABS.

The 9000 comes in only two trim levels, the CS and CSE, both of which are hatchbacks. With three engine choices, you are sure to find the right amount of power, although the 2.4-liter base engine does quite well. The interior is spacious and comfortable. The 9000 also comes with daytime running lights, which help make it even safer. Luggage space is generous, and controls and instruments are easy to use. With its strong safety rating and standard safety features, the Saab 9000 is an excellent choice.

The Ratings

	POOR — GOOD
COMPARATIVE RATING	▮ (good end)
CRASH TEST	▮
SAFETY FEATURES	▮
FUEL ECONOMY	▮
PM COST	▮
REPAIR COST	▮
WARRANTY	▮
COMPLAINTS	▮
INSURANCE COST	▮

Safety

CRASH TEST	Good
AIRBAGS	Dual
ABS	4-wheel
SIDE CRASH PROTECT.	Strong
BELT ADJUSTORS	Standard
BUILT-IN CHILD SEAT	None
OCCUPANT INJURY	Very Good

General Information

WHERE MADE	Germany/Sweden
YEAR OF PRODUCTION	Eleventh
PARKING INDEX	Easy
BUMPERS	Strong
THEFT RATING	Average
TWINS	
DRIVE	Front

Specifications

FUEL ECONOMY (cty/hwy)	20/28	Average
DRIVING RANGE (miles)	418	Average
SEATING	5	
LENGTH (inches)	187.4	Average
HEAD/LEG ROOM (in.)	38.6/41.7	Cramped
INTERIOR SPACE (cu. ft.)	123	Vry. Roomy
CARGO SPACE (cu. ft.)	24	Very Large

Specifications may vary.

Prices

Model	Retail	Mkup
9000 Base	29,995	11%

Competition

	POOR — GOOD	Pg.
Saab 9000	▮	**206**
BMW 3-Series	▮	102
Mazda Millenia	▮	169
Merc.-Benz C-Class	▮	174
Volvo 850	▮	223

The SC, which has been around since 1991, is scheduled for a redesign in 1997. However, in 1996, there are a few changes to this coupe. You can pick either the basic SC1 or the sportier SC2. The styling of the SC will be very distinct from the SL (sedan) and SW (wagon), at least until '97. The SC comes with dual airbags, while both ABS is standard and traction control is optional.

The twin-cam engine on the SC2 is quicker than the base 4-cylinder on the SC1, yet almost as economical. The 5-speed is more pleasant than the automatic and a better match with the base engine. Handling is generally very good. Front seat comfort is okay, but the back is cramped and uncomfortable for adults. This good selling car will benefit from a make over in '97, though it still beats the competition in '96.

The Ratings

	POOR — GOOD
COMPARATIVE RATING	██████████▉
CRASH TEST	████████▉
SAFETY FEATURES	██████▉
FUEL ECONOMY	███████▉
PM COST	██▉
REPAIR COST	█████████▉
WARRANTY	███▉
COMPLAINTS	████████▉
INSURANCE COST	▉

Safety

CRASH TEST	Very Good
AIRBAGS	Dual
ABS	4-wheel
SIDE CRASH PROTECT.	Weak
BELT ADJUSTORS	None
BUILT-IN CHILD SEAT	None
OCCUPANT INJURY	Average

General Information

WHERE MADE	U.S.
YEAR OF PRODUCTION	Sixth
PARKING INDEX	Easy
BUMPERS	Strong
THEFT RATING	Very Good
TWINS	
DRIVE	Front

Specifications

FUEL ECONOMY (cty/hwy)	25/35	Good
DRIVING RANGE (miles)	371	Short
SEATING	4	
LENGTH (inches)	173.2	Short
HEAD/LEG ROOM (in.)	37.5/42.6	Cramped
INTERIOR SPACE (cu. ft.)	77	Vry. Cramped
CARGO SPACE (cu. ft.)	11	Small

Specifications may vary.

Prices

Model	Retail	Mkup
SC1 Coupe man.	12,195	15%
SC1 Coupe auto.	13,025	15%
SC2 Coupe man.	13,295	15%
SC2 Coupe auto.	14,125	15%

Competition

	POOR — GOOD	Pg.
Saturn SC	██████████▉	**207**
Chevrolet Cavalier	████▉	118
Eagle Summit	▉	130
Ford Escort	████▉	138
Toyota Corolla	███████▉	217

Both the SL (sedan) and the SW (wagon) are new for 1996, leaving behind the SC (coupe), which is scheduled for a redesign in '97. The new design has brought a higher roofline and new safety features like standard daytime running lamps. The SL and SW also come with standard airbags and optional ABS and it meets the 1997 standard for side impact protection.

The dual over-head cam engine available on the SL and the SW is more powerful than the base 4-cylinder model, and only reduces fuel efficiency slightly. With the raised roofline comes added headroom which will make the sedan and wagon more comfortable, although the back seat is still tight for adults. Ride is good on smooth roads. These new '96 models should compete nicely with the Neon and the Cavalier.

The Ratings

	POOR → GOOD
COMPARATIVE RATING *	(blank)
CRASH TEST	(blank)
SAFETY FEATURES	■ (9th)
FUEL ECONOMY	■ (7th)
PM COST	■ (3rd)
REPAIR COST	■ (10th)
WARRANTY	■ (4th)
COMPLAINTS	(blank)
INSURANCE COST	■ (6th)

Safety

CRASH TEST	No government results
AIRBAGS	Dual
ABS	4-wheel (optional)
SIDE CRASH PROTECT.	Strong
BELT ADJUSTORS	Standard
BUILT-IN CHILD SEAT	None
OCCUPANT INJURY	Average

General Information

WHERE MADE	U.S.
YEAR OF PRODUCTION	First
PARKING INDEX	Easy
BUMPERS	Strong
THEFT RATING	
TWINS	
DRIVE	Front

Specifications

FUEL ECONOMY (cty/hwy)	25/35	Good
DRIVING RANGE (miles)	371	Short
SEATING	5	
LENGTH (inches)	176.8	Short
HEAD/LEG ROOM (in.)	39.3/42.5	Roomy
INTERIOR SPACE (cu. ft.)	89	Cramped
CARGO SPACE (cu. ft.)	12	Small

Specifications may vary.

Prices

Model	Retail	Mkup
SL Sedan man.	10,495	15%
SL1 Sedan man.	11,395	15%
SL2 Sedan man.	12,295	15%
SW1 Wagon man.	11,995	15%
SW2 Wagon man.	12,895	15%

Competition

	POOR → GOOD	Pg.
Saturn SL/SW	(blank)	**208**
Chevrolet Cavalier	■ (4th)	118
Eagle Summit	■ (1st)	130
Geo Prizm	■ (3rd)	145
Toyota Corolla	■ (8th)	217

*Due to the importance of crash tests, cars with no results as of publication date cannot be given an overall rating.

The Impreza, which replaced the Loyale in 1995, enters 1996 with few changes, but still offers a dizzying array of choices. The sedan and coupe come in base, L or LX, and the wagon comes in L, LX or Outback. Standard on the Impreza are dual airbags; ABS is optional.

Base models are front-wheel drive, while LX models are all-wheel drive, and L and Outback models can be either. As with the trim levels, there are plenty of engine choices. The base model's engine is a 1.8-liter 4-cylinder, though a more powerful 2.2-liter 4-cylinder is standard on the LX and optional on the L and Outback. Other choices include full-time all-wheel drive or front-wheel drive. The best choice is the LX—with its rear stabilizer bar, it out handles the cheaper models, and it has ABS. Front seats are comfortable; the back seat is the typical subcompact squeeze, and trunk space is small.

The Ratings

Rating	POOR ... GOOD
COMPARATIVE RATING *	(no rating)
CRASH TEST	(no rating)
SAFETY FEATURES	Good
FUEL ECONOMY	Below average
PM COST	Very Good
REPAIR COST	Good
WARRANTY	Poor
COMPLAINTS	Good
INSURANCE COST	Average

Safety

CRASH TEST	No government results
AIRBAGS	Dual
ABS	4-wheel (optional)
SIDE CRASH PROTECT.	Strong
BELT ADJUSTORS	Std. (sdn/wgn only)
BUILT-IN CHILD SEAT	None
OCCUPANT INJURY	Very Poor

General Information

WHERE MADE	Japan
YEAR OF PRODUCTION	Fourth
PARKING INDEX	Very Easy
BUMPERS	Strong
THEFT RATING	Very Good
TWINS	
DRIVE	Front/All

Specifications

FUEL ECONOMY (cty/hwy)	25/31	Average
DRIVING RANGE (miles)	356	Short
SEATING	5	
LENGTH (inches)	172.2	Very Short
HEAD/LEG ROOM (in.)	39.2/43.1	Roomy
INTERIOR SPACE (cu. ft.)	84	Cramped
CARGO SPACE (cu. ft.)	11	Small

Specifications may vary.

Prices

Model	Retail	Mkup
Impreza L Coupe	13,495	8%
Impreza LX Coupe	17,295	10%
Impreza L Sedan	15,595	10%
Impreza LX Sedan	17,795	10%
Impreza Outback	17,595	10%

Competition

	POOR ... GOOD	Pg.
Subaru Impreza	(no rating)	209
Chevrolet Cavalier		118
Eagle Summit		130
Mercury Tracer		180
Mitsubishi Mirage		185

*Due to the importance of crash tests, cars with no results as of publication date cannot be given an overall rating.

The Legacy, all-new in '95, has no exterior changes, but a new option under the hood for 1996. The fresh styling the Legacy received last year helped make this car a good seller and it should continue that way for a number of years. ABS is optional and dual airbags are standard across the board. It also meets the 1997 standards for side impact protection.

Unlike last year, you now have two engines to choose from: a 2.2-liter 4-cylinder or a 2.5-liter 4-cylinder with 20 more horses. Both engines will deliver decent gas mileage. The base model is front-wheel drive, while the LS and LSi models are all-wheel drive; the L model comes in either. Traction control is available for the front-wheel drive vehicles. New for this year, the Legacy wagon will come in an Outback version that is meant to appeal to sport utility buyers. It comes with larger wheels, a roof rack and a 12-volt outlet for camping.

The Ratings

	POOR ... GOOD
COMPARATIVE RATING	
CRASH TEST	
SAFETY FEATURES	
FUEL ECONOMY	
PM COST	
REPAIR COST	
WARRANTY	
COMPLAINTS	
INSURANCE COST	

Safety

CRASH TEST	Very Good
AIRBAGS	Dual
ABS	4-wheel (optional)
SIDE CRASH PROTECT.	Strong
BELT ADJUSTORS	Standard
BUILT-IN CHILD SEAT	None
OCCUPANT INJURY	Average (Wg.=Good)

General Information

WHERE MADE	U.S.
YEAR OF PRODUCTION	Second
PARKING INDEX	Easy
BUMPERS	Strong
THEFT RATING	
TWINS	
DRIVE	Front/All

Specifications

FUEL ECONOMY (cty/hwy)	24/33	Average
DRIVING RANGE (miles)	429	Long
SEATING	5	
LENGTH (inches)	180.9	Short
HEAD/LEG ROOM (in.)	38.9/43.3	Roomy
INTERIOR SPACE (cu. ft.)	97	Average
CARGO SPACE (cu. ft.)	13	Average

Specifications may vary.

Prices

Model	Retail	Mkup
Legacy L (FWD)	17,690	
Legacy L AWD	19,390	
Legacy GT AWD	22,790	
Legacy Wagon L (FWD)	18,390	
Legacy Wagon Outback AWD	22,490	

Competition

	POOR ... GOOD	Pg.
Subaru Legacy		**210**
Honda Accord		146
Mazda 626		166
Olds Cut. Supreme		196
Toyota Camry		215

Subaru SVX

The SVX, the sportiest and most expensive Subaru, changes little in 1996. Its styling is noted by an unusual stripe along the windows, as it tries to be both a luxury and a sport coupe all in one. Dual airbags are standard, although you'll have to pay extra for ABS on the front-wheel-drive L.

The SVX is powered by a 3.3-liter 6-cylinder engine linked to an automatic transmission, resulting in adequate power and poor fuel economy. The base L comes in front- or all-wheel drive, or choose the up-level LS in FWD or LSi in AWD. If you want a plusher AWD vehicle than the base L, the LSi gives you leather interior, heated outside mirrors and a CD player, along with speed-sensitive steering and an anti-theft system. The rear seat is not too useful and only part of the strange side windows roll down.

The Ratings

	POOR	GOOD
COMPARATIVE RATING *		
CRASH TEST		
SAFETY FEATURES		
FUEL ECONOMY		
PM COST		
REPAIR COST		
WARRANTY		
COMPLAINTS		
INSURANCE COST		

Safety

CRASH TEST	No government results
AIRBAGS	Dual
ABS	4-wheel (optional)
SIDE CRASH PROTECT.	Strong
BELT ADJUSTORS	Standard
BUILT-IN CHILD SEAT	None
OCCUPANT INJURY	Good

General Information

WHERE MADE	Japan
YEAR OF PRODUCTION	Fifth
PARKING INDEX	Easy
BUMPERS	Strong
THEFT RATING	Average
TWINS	
DRIVE	Front/All

Specifications

FUEL ECONOMY (cty/hwy)	17/24	Poor
DRIVING RANGE (miles)	370	Short
SEATING	4	
LENGTH (inches)	182.1	Short
HEAD/LEG ROOM (in.)	38.0/43.5	Roomy
INTERIOR SPACE (cu. ft.)	85	Cramped
CARGO SPACE (cu. ft.)	8	Very Small

Specifications may vary.

Prices **

Model	Retail	Mkup
SVX L FWD	27,250	10%
SVX L 4WD	28,750	10%
SVX LSi	34,800	10%

Competition

	POOR	GOOD	Pg.
Subaru SVX			**211**
Chevrolet Camaro			116
Ford Mustang			139
Honda Prelude			150
Nissan 240SX			186

** 1996 prices not available at press time. Prices based on 1995 data.

211

Making its debut this year, the Esteem is the largest car Suzuki has ever tried to sell in the U.S. Suzuki is entering the compact-sedan market, a very difficult and crowded market to break into. It comes standard with dual airbags and ABS is optional. The low price tag should attract consumers.

You can choose between the base model or the upgrade GLX, though both come with the same engine. The standard 1.6-liter 4-cylinder engine offers poor power and little excitement. The interior promises to be tight as the car is nearly 20 inches shorter than the already small Ford Contour; trunk space will not be any better. Suzuki has taken a big step forward into a new market, but it will have to do more to entice buyers away from the Esteem's well-equipped competitors such as the Ford Escort and the Toyota Corolla.

The Ratings

	POOR — GOOD
COMPARATIVE RATING *	
CRASH TEST	
SAFETY FEATURES	
FUEL ECONOMY	
PM COST	
REPAIR COST	
WARRANTY	
COMPLAINTS	
INSURANCE COST	

Safety

CRASH TEST	No government results
AIRBAGS	Dual
ABS	4-wheel (optional)
SIDE CRASH PROTECT.	Strong
BELT ADJUSTORS	Standard
BUILT-IN CHILD SEAT	None
OCCUPANT INJURY	

General Information

WHERE MADE	Japan
YEAR OF PRODUCTION	First
PARKING INDEX	Very Easy
BUMPERS	Weak
THEFT RATING	
TWINS	
DRIVE	Front

Specifications

FUEL ECONOMY (cty/hwy)	31/37	Good
DRIVING RANGE (miles)	446	Long
SEATING	4	
LENGTH (inches)	165.2	Very Short
HEAD/LEG ROOM (in.)	39.1/42.3	Average
INTERIOR SPACE (cu. ft.)	86	Cramped
CARGO SPACE (cu. ft.)	12	Small

Specifications may vary.

Prices

Model	Retail	Mkup
Prices unavailable at press time.		
Expected range: $11-14,500		

Competition

	POOR — GOOD	Pg.
Suzuki Esteem		**212**
Eagle Summit		130
Ford Escort		138
Geo Prizm		145
Toyota Corolla		217

*Due to the importance of crash tests, cars with no results as of publication date cannot be given an overall rating.

Suzuki Swift

The Swift, along with its twin the Geo Metro, got a much-needed overhaul in 1995 and receives few changes for '96. The increase in size from the 1994 model offers much needed headroom and interior room for passengers. All Swifts meet 1997 government side impact standards. Dual airbags are now standard, and those awful door-mounted belts are gone. ABS is optional.

The Swift offers the same 1.3-liter 4-cylinder engine as before and comes only in a hatchback. Fuel economy is great when compared to larger cars; however, efficiency suffers dramatically at the hands of the optional automatic transmission, so stick to the standard 5-speed. Room for two is tight; the rear seat is really for kids only. Handling is quick and precise, but crosswinds and large trucks can pose a problem. This is true basic transportation.

The Ratings

	POOR GOOD
COMPARATIVE RATING	▪ (low)
CRASH TEST	▪ (high)
SAFETY FEATURES	▪ (high)
FUEL ECONOMY	▪ (high)
PM COST	▪ (mid)
REPAIR COST	▪ (low)
WARRANTY	▪ (low)
COMPLAINTS	(none)
INSURANCE COST	▪ (low)

Safety

CRASH TEST	Good
AIRBAGS	Dual
ABS	4-wheel (optional)
SIDE CRASH PROTECT.	Strong
BELT ADJUSTORS	None
BUILT-IN CHILD SEAT	None
OCCUPANT INJURY	

General Information

WHERE MADE	Canada
YEAR OF PRODUCTION	Second
PARKING INDEX	Very Easy
BUMPERS	Weak
THEFT RATING	
TWINS	Geo Metro
DRIVE	Front

Specifications

FUEL ECONOMY (cty/hwy)	39/43	Very Good
DRIVING RANGE (miles)	435	Long
SEATING	4	
LENGTH (inches)	149.4	Very Short
HEAD/LEG ROOM (in.)	39.1/42.5	Roomy
INTERIOR SPACE (cu. ft.)	89	Cramped
CARGO SPACE (cu. ft.)	10	Small

Specifications may vary.

Prices**

Model	Retail	Mkup
Swift Base	8,699	9%

Competition

	POOR GOOD	Pg.
Suzuki Swift	▪ (low)	**213**
Chevy Cavalier	▪ (mid)	118
Eagle Summit	▪ (low)	130
Ford Aspire	▪ (low)	135
Mercury Tracer	▪ (low)	180

** 1996 prices not available at press time. Prices based on 1995 data.

The Toyota Avalon, a model built exclusively in Kentucky, is basically a stretched version of the successful Camry. With more interior room and a higher price tag than the Camry, the Avalon moves a bit upscale to compete with cars like the Mercury Sable. Dual airbags are standard, but ABS will cost extra on the XL.

The Avalon is longer than the Camry, making the ride a bit smoother, but it does not weighmuch more, so handling is just as responsive. The Avalon comes in two trim levels, base XL and deluxe XLS, both with the same powerful 3-liter V6 and automatic transmission. Fuel economy is average for a car this size. Although the Avalon is a foot longer than the Dodge Intrepid, interior space on the two vehicles is comparable. Five adults will be comfortable, but don't count on fitting three adults comfortably on the front bench seat.

The Ratings

	POOR — GOOD
COMPARATIVE RATING *	▪ (poor side)
CRASH TEST	▪ (good side)
SAFETY FEATURES	▪ (good side)
FUEL ECONOMY	▪ (middle)
PM COST	▪ (middle)
REPAIR COST	▪ (middle)
WARRANTY	▪ (poor side)
COMPLAINTS	(blank)
INSURANCE COST	▪ (middle)

Safety

CRASH TEST	Very Good
AIRBAGS	Dual
ABS	4-wheel (optional)
SIDE CRASH PROTECT.	Strong
BELT ADJUSTORS	Standard
BUILT-IN CHILD SEAT	None
OCCUPANT INJURY	

General Information

WHERE MADE	U.S./Canada/Japan
YEAR OF PRODUCTION	Second
PARKING INDEX	Average
BUMPERS	Weak
THEFT RATING	
TWINS	
DRIVE	Front

Specifications

FUEL ECONOMY (cty/hwy)	20/29	Average
DRIVING RANGE (miles)	426	Long
SEATING	5/6	
LENGTH (inches)	190.2	Average
HEAD/LEG ROOM (in.)	39.1/44.1	Vry. Roomy
INTERIOR SPACE (cu. ft.)	106	Roomy
CARGO SPACE (cu. ft.)	15	Average

Specifications may vary.

Prices

Model	Retail	Mkup
Avalon XL Bucket Seat	23,418	
Avalon XL Bench Seat	24,228	
Avalon XLS Bucket Seat	27,448	
Avalon XLS Bench Seat	27,448	

Competition

	POOR — GOOD	Pg.
Toyota Avalon	▪ (poor side)	**214**
Infiniti J30	▪ (good side)	155
Merc.-Benz C-Class	▪ (good side)	174
Mitsu. Diamante	▪ (poor end)	182
Nissan Maxima	▪ (middle)	188

*Due to the importance of crash tests, cars with no results as of publication date cannot be given an overall rating.

Options are everywhere for the Camry as buyers have 12 different models to choose from in 1996. There are three body styles: coupe, sedan and wagon, and 4 trim levels: DX, LE, XLE, and SE. Dual airbags are standard. ABS is standard on deluxe XLE models and optional on all others.

To satisfy a wide range of prospective mid-sized car buyers, Toyota offers two engines (a 2.2-liter 4-cylinder and a 3-liter V6), and two transmissions (manual or automatic, though manual is not available with the V6). The Camry rides smoother with the V6, but handles better and is more economical with the 4-cylinder engine. If you buy the wagon, the V6 will haul the added weight better. The interior is spacious and comfortable for four, and the trunk is nicely shaped. Options, packages and other choices abound, so shop carefully.

The Ratings

	POOR	GOOD
COMPARATIVE RATING	■	
CRASH TEST **		■
SAFETY FEATURES		■
FUEL ECONOMY		■
PM COST	■	
REPAIR COST	■	
WARRANTY	■	
COMPLAINTS		■
INSURANCE COST	■	

Safety

CRASH TEST	Very Good
AIRBAGS	Dual
ABS	4-wheel (optional)
SIDE CRASH PROTECT.	Strong (sdn/wgn only)
BELT ADJUSTORS	Std. (sdn/wgn only)
BUILT-IN CHILD SEAT	None
OCCUPANT INJURY	Very Good

General Information

WHERE MADE	U.S./Canada/Japan
YEAR OF PRODUCTION	Fifth
PARKING INDEX	Easy
BUMPERS	Weak
THEFT RATING	Average (Wgn.=Good)
TWINS	Lexus ES300
DRIVE	Front

Specifications

FUEL ECONOMY (cty/hwy)	23/31	Average
DRIVING RANGE (miles)	481	Very Long
SEATING	5	
LENGTH (inches)	187.8	Average
HEAD/LEG ROOM (in.)	38.4/43.5	Roomy
INTERIOR SPACE (cu. ft.)	97	Average
CARGO SPACE (cu. ft.)	15	Average

Specifications may vary.

Prices

Model	Retail	Mkup
Camry DX Sdn 4-cylinder man.	16,758	18%
Camry LE Sdn V6	22,448	18%
Camry DX Cpe 4-cylinder man.	16,468	18%
Camry LE Cpe V6	22,158	18%
Camry LE Wgn 4-cylinder	21,608	6%

Competition

	POOR	GOOD	Pg.
Toyota Camry	■		**215**
Dodge Intrepid		■	128
Honda Accord		■	146
Mazda 626		■	166
Nissan Maxima		■	188

**Data given for 2 dr. model. See Safety Chapter for difference in crash test results. Overall rating for 4 dr. model is Very Poor (1).

The Celica receives new front and rear fascias as it enters 1996 and begins to pick up the lost sales from the discontinued MR2. You can choose between a liftback, a coupe or a convertible. Dual airbags are standard and four-wheel ABS is optional.

The base model ST gets a 1.8-liter 4-cylinder engine that's meek for a supposed performance car, although fuel economy is pretty good. The up-level GT coupe and convertible get a slightly more powerful 2.2-liter 4-cylinder engine that's not quite as economical. The manual and automatic are both good performers. The standard suspension handles well, but the sport suspension available on the GT is even better. Ride is decent. The dashboard is functional and intelligently laid out. The interior has room for two; the rear seat seems to be an afterthought.

The Ratings

	POOR — GOOD
COMPARATIVE RATING *	(no rating)
CRASH TEST	(no rating)
SAFETY FEATURES	Good
FUEL ECONOMY	Good
PM COST	Poor
REPAIR COST	Very Good
WARRANTY	Poor
COMPLAINTS	Good
INSURANCE COST	Very Poor

Safety

CRASH TEST	No government results
AIRBAGS	Dual
ABS	4-wheel (optional)
SIDE CRASH PROTECT.	Strong
BELT ADJUSTORS	None
BUILT-IN CHILD SEAT	None
OCCUPANT INJURY	Average

General Information

WHERE MADE	Japan
YEAR OF PRODUCTION	Third
PARKING INDEX	Average
BUMPERS	Weak
THEFT RATING	Good
TWINS	
DRIVE	Front

Specifications

FUEL ECONOMY (cty/hwy)	29/34	Good
DRIVING RANGE (miles)	493	Very Long
SEATING	4	
LENGTH (inches)	174.2	Short
HEAD/LEG ROOM (in.)	38.4/44.2	Vry. Roomy
INTERIOR SPACE (cu. ft.)	78	Vry. Cramped
CARGO SPACE (cu. ft.)	10	Small

Specifications may vary.

Prices

Model	Retail	Mkup
Celica ST Coupe man.	16,958	17%
Celica GT Coupe man.	19,468	18%
Celica ST 3-door Liftback man.	17,318	17%
Celica GT 3-door Liftback man.	19,978	18%
Celica GT Convertible man.	24,178	18%

Competition

	POOR — GOOD	Pg.
Toyota Celica	(no rating)	216
Acura Integra	Poor	98
Eagle Talon	Poor	132
Ford Probe	Very Poor	140
Honda Prelude	Poor	150

*Due to the importance of crash tests, cars with no results as of publication date cannot be given an overall rating.

Toyota Corolla

The Corolla can cost up to two thousand dollars more than its twin, the Geo Prizm, but three times as many people buy it because of Toyota's reputation for quality (despite the fact that the two cars roll off the same assembly line in California). Unlike Prizms, Corollas come in wagons as well as sedans. Dual airbags are standard, and ABS is optional.

The major change for 1996 is the 1.6-liter base engine is not quite as powerful, in order to meet emissions requirements. The optional 1.8-liter 4-cylinder adds a touch more power with only a slight loss in fuel efficiency. The Corolla can transport four people in moderate comfort with room for luggage. Handling and ride are good, and the controls are logical and easy to use. This is a solid choice, but a bit overpriced. Be sure to look at the Prizm before purchasing the Corolla.

The Ratings

	POOR ... GOOD
COMPARATIVE RATING	▮ (7th)
CRASH TEST	▮ (8th)
SAFETY FEATURES	▮ (8th)
FUEL ECONOMY	▮ (8th)
PM COST	▮ (3rd)
REPAIR COST	▮ (4th)
WARRANTY	▮ (2nd)
COMPLAINTS	▮ (8th)
INSURANCE COST	▮ (1st)

Safety

CRASH TEST	Good
AIRBAGS	Dual
ABS	4-wheel (optional)
SIDE CRASH PROTECT.	Weak
BELT ADJUSTORS	Standard
BUILT-IN CHILD SEAT	Optional
OCCUPANT INJURY	Very Poor (Wgn.=Avg.)

General Information

WHERE MADE	U.S./Canada/Japan
YEAR OF PRODUCTION	Fourth
PARKING INDEX	Very Easy
BUMPERS	Weak
THEFT RATING	Average (Wgn.=Good)
TWINS	Geo Prizm
DRIVE	Front

Specifications

FUEL ECONOMY (cty/hwy)	31/35	Good
DRIVING RANGE (miles)	422	Average
SEATING	5	
LENGTH (inches)	172.0	Very Short
HEAD/LEG ROOM (in.)	38.8/42.4	Average
INTERIOR SPACE (cu. ft.)	89	Cramped
CARGO SPACE (cu. ft.)	16	Average

Specifications may vary.

Prices

Model	Retail	Mkup
Corolla STD man.	12,728	12%
Corolla STD auto.	13,228	12%
Corolla DX man.	13,908	16%
Corolla DX auto.	14,708	16%
Corolla DX Wagon man.	15,058	16%

Competition

	POOR ... GOOD	Pg.
Toyota Corolla	▮	**217**
Ford Escort	▮	138
Geo Prizm	▮	145
Chevrolet Cavalier	▮	118
Mitsubishi Mirage	▮	185

The Paseo receives major revisions for 1996. As in the past, the Paseo shares a platform with the Tercel that was redesigned last year. Paseo continues as Toyota's least expensive sports car. It now comes standard with dual airbags and ABS is optional. It also meets the '97 side impact standards.

The new 1.5-liter 4-cylinder engine cranks out slightly less power than the previous year (done to meet emissions requirements) and both the standard manual and optional automatic transmissions are fairly fuel efficient. If you're tall, you probably won't fit inside comfortably. Forget the rear seat and the trunk is very small. The ride is smooth on good roads, but handling doesn't match up with the sporty looks. Sound insulation is skimpy. Controls and gauges are easy to use. This car does not compete well with the Neon or Escort.

The Ratings

	POOR — GOOD
COMPARATIVE RATING *	(no rating)
CRASH TEST	(no rating)
SAFETY FEATURES	███
FUEL ECONOMY	███
PM COST	██
REPAIR COST	██
WARRANTY	█
COMPLAINTS	███
INSURANCE COST	█

Safety

CRASH TEST	No government results
AIRBAGS	Dual
ABS	4-wheel (optional)
SIDE CRASH PROTECT.	Strong
BELT ADJUSTORS	None
BUILT-IN CHILD SEAT	None
OCCUPANT INJURY	Very Poor

General Information

WHERE MADE	Japan
YEAR OF PRODUCTION	Fifth
PARKING INDEX	Very Easy
BUMPERS	Weak
THEFT RATING	Average
TWINS	
DRIVE	Front

Specifications

FUEL ECONOMY (cty/hwy)	30/35	Good
DRIVING RANGE (miles)	381	Short
SEATING	4	
LENGTH (inches)	163.6	Very Short
HEAD/LEG ROOM (in.)	37.8/41.1	Vry. Cramped
INTERIOR SPACE (cu. ft.)	74	Vry. Cramped
CARGO SPACE (cu. ft.)	8	Very Small

Specifications may vary.

Prices

Model	Retail	Mkup
Paseo man.	13,038	15%
Paseo auto.	13,838	15%

Competition

	POOR — GOOD	Pg.
Toyota Paseo	(no rating)	**218**
Chevrolet Cavalier	██	118
Eagle Summit	█	130
Ford Escort	██	138
Mercury Tracer	██	180

*Due to the importance of crash tests, cars with no results as of publication date cannot be given an overall rating.

The Previa enters '96 with no exterior changes, but does improve under the hood. It comes in two trim levels, DX or LE. Dual airbags are standard, and ABS is optional on all models. It also meets the 1997 standard for side crash protection.

The Previa is offered in rear- or four-wheel drive. They all seat seven people. Automatic overdrive is standard except on the rear-drive DX. The standard, and only engine, is a 2.4-liter supercharged engine which was optional last year, and is much more adept at carrying this big vehicle. Handling and ride are about the best you can get in a minivan, especially if you buy an All-Trac version. The interior is comfortable and cargo space is even greater than in the Chrysler "Grand" models. However, the Previa may have a difficult time keeping up with the all-new Chrysler minivans.

The Ratings

	POOR	GOOD
COMPARATIVE RATING		
CRASH TEST		
SAFETY FEATURES		
FUEL ECONOMY		
PM COST		
REPAIR COST		
WARRANTY		
COMPLAINTS		
INSURANCE COST		

Safety

CRASH TEST	Average
AIRBAGS	Dual
ABS	4-wheel (optional)
SIDE CRASH PROTECT.	Strong
BELT ADJUSTORS	Standard
BUILT-IN CHILD SEAT	None
OCCUPANT INJURY	Avg. (4WD=Vry. Gd.)

General Information

WHERE MADE	Japan
YEAR OF PRODUCTION	Sixth
PARKING INDEX	Average
BUMPERS	Weak
THEFT RATING	Average
TWINS	
DRIVE	Rear/All

Specifications

FUEL ECONOMY (cty/hwy)	18/22	Poor
DRIVING RANGE (miles)	376	Short
SEATING	7	
LENGTH (inches)	187.0	Average
HEAD/LEG ROOM (in.)	39.4/40.1	Cramped
INTERIOR SPACE (cu. ft.)		
CARGO SPACE (cu. ft.)	152	Very Large

Specifications may vary.

Prices

Model	Retail	Mkup
Previa DX (2WD)	24,318	17%
Previa DX (All-Trac)	27,858	17%
Previa LE (2WD)	28,858	18%
Previa LE (All-Trac)	32,198	18%

Competition

	POOR	GOOD	Pg.
Toyota Previa			**219**
Ford Aerostar			134
Ford Windstar			143
Honda Odyssey			149
Pontiac Trans Sport			204

The Tercel, all-new for 1995, has few changes in 1996. Cloth interior is now standard, as Toyota did away with the vinyl. Dual airbags are standard on the Tercel, though you'll still have to pay extra for ABS. The Tercel meets the 1997 standard for side crash protection.

The 1.5-liter 4-cylinder engine does a decent job at powering the vehicle, but it only offers 93 horse-power. What you lose in power, you gain in fuel efficiency, though you will lose some of this if you choose the automatic transmission. You can choose standard or DX trim levels in two- or four-door models. Base prices are low, but options and pack-ages can add up. Interior room is not as large as other vehicles in its size class and it is rather noisy inside during hard accelerations. Not a sporty choice, but a sound, economical option.

The Ratings

	POOR GOOD
COMPARATIVE RATING	■
CRASH TEST	■
SAFETY FEATURES	■
FUEL ECONOMY	■
PM COST	■
REPAIR COST	■
WARRANTY	■
COMPLAINTS	
INSURANCE COST	■

Safety

CRASH TEST	Average
AIRBAGS	Dual
ABS	4-wheel (optional)
SIDE CRASH PROTECT.	Strong
BELT ADJUSTORS	Std. (sdn. only)
BUILT-IN CHILD SEAT	None
OCCUPANT INJURY	Very Poor

General Information

WHERE MADE	Japan
YEAR OF PRODUCTION	Second
PARKING INDEX	Very Easy
BUMPERS	Weak
THEFT RATING	
TWINS	
DRIVE	Front

Specifications

FUEL ECONOMY (cty/hwy)	30/39	Very Good
DRIVING RANGE (miles)	405	Average
SEATING	5	
LENGTH (inches)	161.8	Very Short
HEAD/LEG ROOM (in.)	38.6/41.2	Cramped
INTERIOR SPACE (cu. ft.)	80	Vry. Cramped
CARGO SPACE (cu. ft.)	9	Very Small

Specifications may vary.

Prices

Model	Retail	Mkup
Tercel STD Coupe man.	10,348	
Tercel STD Coupe auto.	11,048	
Tercel DX Coupe man.	11,598	
Tercel DX Sedan man.	11,908	
Tercel DX Sedan auto.	12,618	

Competition

	POOR GOOD	Pg.
Toyota Tercel	■	220
Chevrolet Cavalier	■	118
Eagle Summit	■	130
Ford Escort	■	138
Saturn SC	■	207

VW makes several cars on the Golf/Jetta platform. There is the Golf, the sportier Golf Sport, the GTI VR6, the Jetta GL, the mid-level Jetta GLS, the up-level Jetta GLX, and the convertible Cabrio. Though each of these cars has its own character, they all have the same basic specifications and components, and change little in '96. Dual airbags are standard, all models meet 1997 government side impact standards, and ABS is available.

The Golf and Jetta offer a 2-liter 4-cylinder engine or a 2.8-liter V6, though the Cabrio comes only with the more fuel-efficient 3-cylinder, and the GTI gets a peppier V6. All models come with 5-speed manual or automatic overdrive, and a 10-year/100,000 mile power train warranty. Handling is responsive, and the seats are comfortable. Interior room is cramped for large adults; the trunk is large for a compact car.

The Ratings

	POOR — GOOD
COMPARATIVE RATING	▮ (good side)
CRASH TEST	▮ (middle)
SAFETY FEATURES	▮ (good side)
FUEL ECONOMY	▮ (middle-poor)
PM COST	▮ (good side)
REPAIR COST	▮ (middle)
WARRANTY	▮ (good)
COMPLAINTS	▮ (poor)
INSURANCE COST	▮ (poor-middle)

Safety

CRASH TEST	Average
AIRBAGS	Dual
ABS	4-wheel (optional)
SIDE CRASH PROTECT.	Strong
BELT ADJUSTORS	Standard
BUILT-IN CHILD SEAT	None
OCCUPANT INJURY	Very Poor

General Information

WHERE MADE	Mexico
YEAR OF PRODUCTION	Third
PARKING INDEX	Very Easy
BUMPERS	Weak
THEFT RATING	Good
TWINS	
DRIVE	Front

Specifications

FUEL ECONOMY (cty/hwy)	22/28	Average
DRIVING RANGE (miles)	363	Short
SEATING	5	
LENGTH (inches)	160.5	Very Short
HEAD/LEG ROOM (in.)	39.2/42.3	Roomy
INTERIOR SPACE (cu. ft.)	88	Cramped
CARGO SPACE (cu. ft.)	17	Large

Specifications may vary.

Prices

Model	Retail	Mkup
Golf 4-door	13,150	10%
Jetta 4-door	14,250	10%
Jetta GLS	16,300	10%
Jetta GLX	20,610	10%

Competition

	POOR — GOOD	Pg.
VW Golf/Jetta	▮ (good side)	221
Ford Escort	▮ (middle-poor)	138
Hyundai Sonata	▮ (poor)	153
Mercury Tracer	▮ (poor)	180
Toyota Corolla	▮ (middle)	217

Volkswagen Passat

The Passat, VW's plushest model, has received few changes after a restyling last year. One new change is the addition of the TDI (Turbo Direct Injection) trim level. Dual airbags are standard, as is traction control and ABS. All Passats meet 1997 government side impact standards.

The Passat has the same potent 2.8-liter V6 as the GTI, with 5-speed manual or automatic transmission, and a 10-year/100,000 mile power train warranty. The new TDI comes with a 2-liter turbocharged diesel engine. Acceleration is impressive. The Passat is rigid, and handling is responsive with a firm, sometimes uncomfortable, ride. From the outside, the car looks about the size of the Camry, but its interior room resembles a larger car as seats are roomy enough for four and well designed for long trips.

The Ratings

Scale: POOR to GOOD

COMPARATIVE RATING	Good
CRASH TEST	Above average
SAFETY FEATURES	Good
FUEL ECONOMY	Below average
PM COST	Poor
REPAIR COST	Below average
WARRANTY	Good
COMPLAINTS	Below average
INSURANCE COST	Poor

Safety

CRASH TEST	Good
AIRBAGS	Dual
ABS	4-wheel
SIDE CRASH PROTECT.	Strong
BELT ADJUSTORS	Standard
BUILT-IN CHILD SEAT	None
OCCUPANT INJURY	Average

General Information

WHERE MADE	Germany
YEAR OF PRODUCTION	Seventh
PARKING INDEX	Average
BUMPERS	Weak
THEFT RATING	Poor
TWINS	
DRIVE	Front

Specifications

FUEL ECONOMY (cty/hwy)	20/27	Average
DRIVING RANGE (miles)	426	Long
SEATING	5	
LENGTH (inches)	181.5	Short
HEAD/LEG ROOM (in.)	39.3/45.1	Vry. Roomy
INTERIOR SPACE (cu. ft.)	99	Roomy
CARGO SPACE (cu. ft.)	14	Average

Specifications may vary.

Prices

Model	Retail	Mkup
Passat Sedan	18,490	11%
Passat Wagon	19,860	11%

Competition

Scale: POOR to GOOD

	Rating	Pg.
VW Passat	Good	**222**
Honda Accord	Poor	146
Mazda 626	Poor	166
Olds Cut. Supreme	Above average	196
Toyota Camry	Poor	215

There are no major changes to the Volvo 850 for 1996. One important option is a side impact airbag, which inflates from the side of the seat. These driver and passenger side airbags are standard on Turbo sedans and wagons, and a $500 option on base and GLT sedans and wagons. 850s also meet 1997 government side impact standards and have standard dual airbags, daytime running lights and ABS.

This is the first front-wheel drive vehicle Volvo sold in the U.S. The 5-cylinder engine is powerful, but not extremely smooth; the turbo is probably unnecessary. The 850 is biased more toward cornering ability than comfort in ride. Inside, the 850 accommodates four people comfortably, though five is a squeeze. A fold-out booster seat for children is standard on wagons and optional on sedans. Traction control is available. Cargo and trunk space are generous.

The Ratings

Rating	POOR ———— GOOD
COMPARATIVE RATING	████████░░ (Good)
CRASH TEST	███████░░░
SAFETY FEATURES	█████████░
FUEL ECONOMY	████░░░░░░
PM COST	█░░░░░░░░░
REPAIR COST	██████░░░░
WARRANTY	████████░░
COMPLAINTS	██░░░░░░░░
INSURANCE COST	██████████

Safety

CRASH TEST	Good
AIRBAGS	Dual
ABS	4-wheel
SIDE CRASH PROTECT.	Strong
BELT ADJUSTORS	Standard
BUILT-IN CHILD SEAT	Optional (wgn.=std.)
OCCUPANT INJURY	Very Good

General Information

WHERE MADE	Belgium
YEAR OF PRODUCTION	Fourth
PARKING INDEX	Easy
BUMPERS	Weak
THEFT RATING	Good
TWINS	
DRIVE	Front

Specifications

FUEL ECONOMY (cty/hwy)	20/29	Average
DRIVING RANGE (miles)	444	Long
SEATING	5	
LENGTH (inches)	183.5	Average
HEAD/LEG ROOM (in.)	39.1/41.4	Average
INTERIOR SPACE (cu. ft.)	98	Average
CARGO SPACE (cu. ft.)	14	Average

Specifications may vary.

Prices

Model	Retail	Mkup
854 O	26,125	
854 GTO	27,150	
854 Turbo	32,650	
855 O	27,425	
855 Turbo	33,950	

Competition

	POOR ———— GOOD	Pg.
Volvo 850	████████░░	**223**
BMW 3-Series	███░░░░░░░	102
Mazda Millenia	██░░░░░░░░	169
Merc.-Benz C-Class	████████░░	174
Saab 9000	█████████░	206

Volvo 900 Series

For 1996, Volvo has decided to discontinue the 940 series. So, only the 960 series will be available, in sedan and station wagon models. The 960, Volvo's top-level model, is relatively unchanged for 1996. Daytime running lamps, dual airbags and ABS are standard. New for 1996, side-impact airbags are now standard—a first in the industry. With 1997 side impact standards met a year early, the 940 is one of the safest cars on the road today.

Independent rear suspension on the 940 provides an excellent ride and above average steering, though the smaller 850 is more maneuverable. The 940's fuel efficiency is disappointingly low. Comfort and room for four is OK, but leg room can get a bit cramped. The rear center seat should be saved for children—you'll find a fold-out child booster seat, standard in wagons and optional in sedans. The 940 is a strong choice among its competitors, the Saab 9000 and the Mazda Millenia.

The Ratings

	POOR	GOOD
COMPARATIVE RATING*		
CRASH TEST		
SAFETY FEATURES		
FUEL ECONOMY		
PM COST		
REPAIR COST		
WARRANTY		
COMPLAINTS		
INSURANCE COST		

Safety

CRASH TEST	No government results
AIRBAGS	Dual
ABS	4-wheel
SIDE CRASH PROTECT.	Strong
BELT ADJUSTORS	Standard
BUILT-IN CHILD SEAT	Optional (wgn.=std.)
OCCUPANT INJURY	Good (Wgn.=Vry. Gd.)

General Information

WHERE MADE	Canada/Sweden
YEAR OF PRODUCTION	Sixth
PARKING INDEX	Very Easy
BUMPERS	Weak
THEFT RATING	Average (Wgn.=Good)
TWINS	
DRIVE	Rear

Specifications

FUEL ECONOMY (cty/hwy)	18/26	Poor
DRIVING RANGE (miles)	437	Long
SEATING	5	
LENGTH (inches)	191.8	Long
HEAD/LEG ROOM (in.)	37.4/41.0	Vry. Cramped
INTERIOR SPACE (cu. ft.)	91	Average
CARGO SPACE (cu. ft.)	16	Average

Specifications may vary.

Prices

Model	Retail	Mkup
964	33,960	
965	35,260	

Competition

	POOR GOOD	Pg.
Volvo 900 Series		**224**
Chrysler LHS/NY'er		124
Mazda Millenia		169
Mitsu. Diamante		182
Saab 9000		206

*Due to the importance of crash tests, cars with no results as of publication date cannot be given an overall rating.